"Tabbia also has an extraordinary ability and generosity to share with the reader an intimate experience in which he unravels the mysteries of mental life and its states. The text does not stop at the mere transmission of theoretical concepts, which in itself would already be valuable, but Tabbia, with mastery and creativity, advances not only in levels of understanding of the concepts, but also updates them, they emerge as living concepts".

María Eugenia Cid, *Clinical Psychologist, Psychoanalytic Psychotherapist, and a Psychoanalyst Member of the Madrid Psychoanalytic Association (IPA), and currently the President of the European Federation for Psychoanalytic Psychotherapy*

The Clinical Comprehension of Meaning

In *The Clinical Comprehension of Meaning*, Carlos Tabbia addresses fundamental questions of psychoanalytic theory and technique, unfolding them for the reader in an elegant, passionate, and poetic style.

This book illustrates three pillars of a psychoanalytic clinic: the structure of the personality, the development of thought, and the ability to foster close relationships with patients. These three pillars show the conditions for the creation of meanings and the difficulties that can be manifested in fanatical functioning, psychosomatic disorders and dreaming, as well as isolation and boredom in adolescents. Using clinical vignettes throughout, Tabbia also analyses the issues surrounding the establishment of an intimate relationship, as well as the issues psychoanalysts must face within themselves. Throughout the volume, Tabbia looks to the work of Bion, Meltzer, Freud, and Klein as well as philosophers such as Plato, Wittgenstein, Russell, Max Scheler, and Levinas, and others such as poets and painters.

Including a prologue by Alberto Hahn and translated into English for the first time, this seminal text will be of interest to psychoanalysts and psychotherapists, as well as students and candidates undertaking psychoanalytic training.

Carlos Tabbia is a Psychoanalyst and Psychologist who specialises in Clinical Psychology. He is a founding member of the Barcelona Psychoanalytic Group, and fellow of the Argentine Society of Psychoanalysis (SAP), and lecturer of the European Federation for Psychoanalytic Psychotherapy (EFPP). He carries out teaching and supervision work in several psychoanalytic training institutions in Barcelona and other Spanish cities, as well as Italy, Argentina, Mexico, and Chile.

The Clinical Comprehension of Meaning

The Bion/Meltzer Vertex

Carlos Tabbia

Routledge
Taylor & Francis Group

LONDON AND NEW YORK

First published in English 2023
by Routledge
4 Park Square, Milton Park, Abingdon, Oxon OX14 4RN

and by Routledge
605 Third Avenue, New York, NY 10158

Routledge is an imprint of the Taylor & Francis Group, an informa business

© 2023 Carlos Tabbia

Translated by Sherry Lupinacci Vigilio and Guy Rimmer

Book published for the first time by the publisher of the Argentine
Psychoanalytic Association

British Library Cataloguing-in-Publication Data
A catalogue record for this book is available from the British Library

Library of Congress Cataloging-in-Publication Data
Names: Tabbia, Carlos, author.
Title: The clinical comprehension of meaning : the Bion/Meltzer
vertex / Carlos Tabbia.
Other titles: Clínica del significado. English
Description: Abingdon, Oxon ; New York, NY : Routledge, 2023. |
Includes bibliographical references and index. |
Identifiers: LCCN 2022061455 (print) | LCCN 2022061456
(ebook) | ISBN 9781032388571 (hardback) | ISBN 9781032373942
(paperback) | ISBN 9781003347156 (ebook)
Subjects: LCSH: Meaning (Psychology) | Psychoanalysis.
Classification: LCC BF463.M4 T33 2023 (print) | LCC BF463.M4
(ebook) | DDC 121/.68—dc23/eng/20230415
LC record available at https://lccn.loc.gov/2022061455
LC ebook record available at https://lccn.loc.gov/2022061456

ISBN: 978-1-032-38857-1 (hbk)
ISBN: 978-1-032-37394-2 (pbk)
ISBN: 978-1-003-34715-6 (ebk)

DOI: 10.4324/9781003347156

Typeset in Times New Roman
by codeMantra

Contents

About the Author   xi
Prologue   xiii

Introduction   1

1 The Conceptual Framework   7
1.1 Psychic Reality 9
1.2 Values 15
    1.2.1 Philosophical Vertex 15
    1.2.2 The Psychoanalytic Vertex 19
        1.2.2.1 Sigmund Freud 20
        1.2.2.2 Melanie Klein 23
        1.2.2.3 Wilfred R. Bion 24
        1.2.2.4 Donald Meltzer 25
    1.2.3 The Function of the Parental Object 27
    1.2.4 The Combined Object as an Ethics Ideal 28
    1.2.5 Ausiàs, the Combined Object 31
    1.2.6 Respect-Responsibility 33

2 Elements of a Post-Kleinian Nosology   39
2.1 Framework for the Observation of the Personality 49
2.2 Dimensions for Diagnosis 59

3 The Tripod of Psychoanalytic Practice   63
3.1 The Structure of Personality 65
    3.1.1 Denial of Psychic Reality 66
        3.1.1.1 An Inaccessible Psychic Reality 66
        3.1.1.2 Opposition to the Analytic Situation 69
        3.1.1.3 Getting Rid of Psychic Reality 71
        3.1.1.4 Synthesis: The Possibility of Thinking 72

3.1.2 Dissociation and Intrusive Identification 74
    3.1.2.1 Opposing Intrusiveness 74
    3.1.2.2 Fear of Introjection and Madness 77
    3.1.2.3 The Danger of Unreality 80
    3.1.2.4 Anal Grandiosity 82
    3.1.2.5 Manipulating with Passivity 85
    3.1.2.6 Synthesis: On Intrusive and "Aspirated" Identification 88
3.1.3 Immaturity and Struggle Against the Combined Object 91
    3.1.3.1 An Immature State of Mind 91
    3.1.3.2 In the Belief of Being a Combined Object 92
    3.1.3.3 Obsessiveness 94
    3.1.3.4 On the Threshold of the Depressive Position 98
    3.1.3.5 Synthesis: The Fate of Preconception 101
3.1.4 The Organisation of the Self and the Analyst's Interest 102
3.1.5 Living in Intrusive Identification 105
    3.1.5.1 Clinical Material 111
    3.1.5.2 Conclusion 114
3.2 Thinking 119
3.2.1 Observation and Description in the Genesis of Meaning 120
    3.2.1.1 Language 121
    3.2.1.2 Meaning 125
    3.2.1.3 Observation 127
    3.2.1.4 Description 133
    3.2.1.5 Interpretation Is a Description 137
3.2.2 Fanaticism, Identity, and Thinking 139
    3.2.2.1 The Context of Fanaticism 140
    3.2.2.2 The Group 146
    3.2.2.3 Imagination 148
    3.2.2.4 Abstraction 150
    3.2.2.5 Identity 153
3.2.3 Difficulties in Dreaming 155
    3.2.3.1 The Models 157
    3.2.3.2 Difficulties in Dreaming 159
    3.2.3.3 Other Difficulties in Dream Symbolisation 162

3.2.4 *The Boredom of the Adolescent and the Analyst 167*
    3.2.4.1 The Adolescent and Boredom 169
    3.2.4.2 Language and Groups in the Life of an
             Adolescent 170
    3.2.4.3 The Analyst's Boredom 175
    3.2.4.4 Some Answers from the Analyst 175
    3.2.4.5 Your Boredom Bores Me 179
    3.2.4.6 Boredom Created by a Lack of Contact 181
    3.2.4.7 Approaches to Boredom 182
3.2.5 *Writing with the Body 185*
    3.2.5.1 Alterations to the Organism 189
    3.2.5.2 Hypochondria 191
    3.2.5.3 Psychosomatics 195
    3.2.5.4 Arnoldo's Vicissitudes 199
    3.2.5.5 A Session with Arnoldo 202
    3.2.5.6 Interpretations of the Material 206
3.3 Intimacy 223
3.3.1 *The Concept of Intimacy in Meltzer's Thinking 224*
    3.3.1.1 Distance 226
    3.3.1.2 Emotions 230
    3.3.1.3 Trust 232
    3.3.1.4 Intimacy in Infantile, Perverse, and Adult
             States of Mind 234
    3.3.1.5 Julio's Dream 237
3.3.2 *Passionate Kindness 240*
    3.3.2.1 Intimate Relationships 244
    3.3.2.2 On Love 248
    3.3.2.3 The Effects of Love 251
    3.3.2.4 The Clinical Relationship 253
    3.3.2.5 Notes from a Session 255
    3.3.2.6 The Strong Woman Model 257
3.3.3 *Placental Model of Intimacy 257*
3.3.4 *Intimacy in Analytic Work 262*
3.3.5 *The Isolated Adolescent 268*
    3.3.5.1 The Shift from Latency to
             Adolescence 268
    3.3.5.2 Gerard 273
    3.3.5.3 Alejandro 274
    3.3.5.4 Héctor 275
    3.3.5.5 Conclusion 276

4   The Analyst's Task   285

   4.1 The Analyst Faced with Protomental Functioning 287

   4.2 The Analyst's Mental Availability 293

   4.3 Psychoanalytic Attitude, Faith, Belief, and Intuition 301

      4.3.1 Observing with "Faith"? 302

      4.3.2 Beliefs 306

      4.3.3 A Beam of Tremulous Light... 309

Index   321

About the Author

Carlos Tabbia is a psychoanalyst and psychologist who specialises in clinical psychology. He holds a doctoral degree in psychology (University of Barcelona) with undergraduate degrees in philosophy and psychology from Argentinean universities.

A resident in Barcelona since 1975, Tabbia worked for 25 years in community assistance programmes for severe mentally disordered patients, the subject of his doctoral thesis. His clinical perspective was transformed by his involvement with Dr. Donald Meltzer, from 1986 to 2004, in seminars and supervisions in Barcelona and Oxford. His knowledge of Bion's thought has also been enriched through seminars with R. Bassols (Barcelona), L. Grinberg and D. Sor (Buenos Aires), as well as J. Thomas and A. Hahn (London).

Carlos Tabbia is a founding member of the Grupo Psicoanalítico de Barcelona, and fellow of the Sociedad Argentina de Psicoanálisis (SAP), of the Asociación Madrileña y Catalana de Psicoterapia Psicoanalítica, and is a training member at the European Federation for Psychoanalytic Psychotherapy (EFPP). He is a teacher and supervisor at various psychoanalytic training institutions in Barcelona and other cities in Spain, Italy, Argentina, Chile, and Mexico. He engages in full-time clinical work in Barcelona.

He was co-editor, with L. Jachevasky, of *Adolescentes* by Donald Meltzer and Martha Harris (Spatia, Buenos Aires, 1998); co-author with Meltzer, the Grupo Psicoanalítico de Barcelona, and C. Mack Smith of *Psychoanalytic Work with Children and Adults: Meltzer in Barcelona* (London, Karnac, 2002); co-author with Meltzer, Castella and Farré of *Supervisions with Donald Meltzer* (London, Karnac, 2003); co-author of *De un taller psicoanalítico a partir de Donald Meltzer* (Barcelona, Grafein, 2007); and co-author with F. Spadaro of *Il Fanatismo. Dalle origini psichiche al sociale* (Rome, Armando editore, 2007). Additionally, he has published numerous scholarly papers in various specialised journals.

Prologue

In this book, the emphasis has been placed on creating a mood conducive to mental development along the vertex of post-Kleinian nosology, which was created basically from the theoretical and clinical contributions of W. Bion and D. Meltzer. Observation, thinking, and interpretative intervention are central to this project. It is also an invitation to observe the author working tirelessly to understand and think about the contributions of these authors while paying attention to their state of permanent curiosity. The latter ultimately translates into a display of clinical creativity and ideas that successfully provide us with an emotional experience of knowledge and acknowledgement. It is an experience that enhances our work tools: attention and perception, the value of countertransference and intuition, the central role of dream life, and so many other contributions that create a cornucopia whose contents would be difficult to enumerate.

The process of learning provides the mould of our personal experience and consists of being able to achieve intimate knowledge of our masters' ideas in order to apply this knowledge to analytic practice. Many clinical cases found in this book, described in exhaustive detail, are drawn from the author's personal experience in both his clinical practice and his supervisory role.

We can think of this book as a homage to what Tabbia calls "the four horsemen of the discovery of mental life": Freud, M. Klein, Bion, and D. Meltzer. It is not, nonetheless, merely a homage to their wisdom but rather to the personal analytic attributes belonging to each and every one of these pioneers who knew that the analyst's mind is an organising centre of understanding of the complete analytic process. Thus, the author conducts a minute examination of projective identification, whether in early relationships, latency, adolescence, or adulthood, that requires a gifted analyst who can comprehend not only alterations in language and thinking but also the states of mind that arise from changes in the identity and perception of objects. In this text, there are numerous examples of how the ability to find meaning works, and the reader finds themselves involved in an activity that oscillates between being an apprentice of "new" concepts or the critic of the complexities that arise in the task of observation, and description or interpretation. Venturing an interpretation of our reading of the patient's unconscious phantasies often creates a sense, both in the analyst and in the patient, of insecurity since it is not possible to foresee whether we are creating a potentially catastrophic internal environment or creating an opportunity for the integration of split parts of the personality. I believe this insecurity is frequently responsible for the resistance that appears as a defence in the transference situation. The importance of this subject is reflected in the richness of Section 3.2.1.

The same could be said about the complex meaning of language. The philosophical analysis of language lends an interesting nuance to comprehending the difficulties inherent in communicating sincerity, affection, and envy, or clarifying misunderstandings. This was a theme that always held a great deal of interest for Dr. Meltzer in his attempts to clarify states of mind through verbal communication, where words have limitations, as does our tendency to feel we are capable of saying what we think directly and convincingly. In addition to words, we are challenged by other forms of communication that are related to the precursors of verbal development—"song-and-dance"—or the creation of dream images that may be suggestive or turbulent. On the one hand, communication through projective identification generally has an emotional charge that requires the analyst's personal sensitivity to pick up on the ineffable messages in intimate relationships, often through silence. On the other hand, confusion or boredom can be detected by their manifestations in unconscious phantasies. This type of language would further demonstrate how our visceral response commits us to analyse the message communicated by that medium.

The author, who shares with us the source of his creativity, offers us not only the opportunity to learn but also provides a model that allows us to emulate and, through identification, stimulate our ability to read.

Reading encompasses not only what is heard or seen but also the projective systems that, in their effusiveness, can transmit states of mind of great conflict and pain. This is a situation that requires a total, intuitive response.

The rich bibliography quoted in this book adds different artistic, philosophical, and epistemological nuances, germinating new ideas in the reader. Ultimately, we have an opportunity to learn how to think with the model that the author generously offers us.

The other area where this book provides a seminal contribution is in the discussion regarding the body and its relation to the mind and vice versa. Bion's influence here is the intrigue and creativity of his ability to stimulate curiosity about bodily intervention in states of mind and the mind in cases of physical alterations. The most immediate tragic example was the description of studies related to the current pandemic and the ravages of the Covid-19 virus. Its virulent presence, which brings about a breakdown in thinking and attacks the future, points to an invisible malignancy that creates an urgent search for relief, both in the areas of physiopathology and in human relationships. This is the response to terror in the face of the possibility of not surviving this catastrophic change and the contemplation of the end of life in an intolerable context of "negative capability".

The careful Meltzerian reading of "intimacy" is another good example of learning through research and identification. The author navigates the literature with the enviable ease of one who feels comfortable with a familiar subject, both known and acknowledged in his relationships with his patients. Intimacy is an inspiring theme, not only because it is "our daily bread" but also because it is a state that permanently lends itself to observation and scrutiny; we feel stimulated by a tropism, an attraction to participate more actively in the invitation to reciprocity that intimacy generates, either as a point of urgency in the analytical journey or as a problem. In the discussion on Dr. Meltzer's quotes, Tabbia transmits intimacy and affection for a master who has made an exceptional contribution to understanding object relations in all developmental stages. The baby, the adolescent, and the adult are all heard, observed, and understood through the analyst's personal response. The analyst can conceptualise the complex needs that arise in the transference relationship from their own unconscious mind.

This not only stimulates the development of the evolution of the transference but also involves the commitment of the countertransference, a sensitive mental mechanism that picks up information about the patient and is also capable of attributing meaning to the unconscious phantasies generated in the bond between analyst and patient. This self-analytic task points to an intervention of "complementarity", where interpretation is capable of contact with the neediest infantile parts of the patient.

It is a great pleasure to witness, through my reading of this book, the functioning of analytic activity in the mind of a colleague who passionately covers such a broad spectrum of knowledge. On the one hand, it generates a sincere response of gratitude for enriching our sensitivity in relation to clinical activity while, on the other hand, demonstrating how it is possible to learn, creatively, from our masters and other inspiring figures, such as the pioneers of the psychoanalytic movement. Obviously, creative seriousness and the enthusiasm of the descriptions highlight the importance of devotion to our discipline in the encounters with our patients.

Dr Alberto Hahn
London
28 August 2020

Introduction

Only the reader can give full meaning to the pages of this book. The container generates meaning and creates the book. The container is the relationship between text and reader. When I first felt the urge to write this book, I had no idea what harbour would welcome me, how far I would get, or even if it all made any sense. The path before me was long and intertwined with the fears mentioned by Kavafis (1863–1933) in the poem *Ithaka*. The seas to be sailed, realm of choleric Poseidon, will not prevent us from reaching unexplored territories if we face them with high ideals and courage. In his poetry, Kavafis gives a name to those fears that nest in the inner world of every seafarer and any writer: those anthropophagous giants, the Laestrygones, who would devour the whole culture without leaving as much as a scrap, albeit with the short-sightedness of the Cyclopes, whose single eye renders them incapable of protecting their territories. However, my urge did not bring me to a standstill before Poseidon's deep waters… My only solace was that these beasts hid in my internal world, and I thought I could trust the company of the thinkers who dared to navigate oceanic territories. I distance myself from those authors who believe their writings to be original creations. To quote my predecessors is my way of feeling accompanied during the journey and recognising the container of my contributions.

The reference to Poseidon and the oceans also comes about from the comparison that Money-Kyrle (1969) established between sanity and madness, recognising the unconscious to be far bigger than the habitable ego islands or the thoughts and metaphors that one can write. Accompanied by the four horsemen of the discovery of mental life (Freud, Klein, Bion, and Meltzer), who were able to think and symbolise not only war, famine, death, glory, love, and passion, but all of the emotions, I dared to walk to Ithaka—accompanied by them, and recognising the reality of each one of them. Along these lines, Bloom's warning (1994, p. 20)—the very same Bloom who considered Shakespeare to be the insurmountable creator—resonates in me:

> Coming after Shakespeare, who wrote both the best prose and the best poetry in the Western tradition, is a complex destiny, since originality becomes peculiarly difficult in everything that matters most: representation of human beings, the

DOI: 10.4324/9781003347156-1

role of memory in cognition, the range of metaphor in suggesting new possibilities for language. These are Shakespeare's particular excellences, and no one has matched him as psychologist, thinker, or rhetorician.

Neither coming after nor surpassing, but merely learning and providing meaning. I once heard Meltzer say that, as adults, we spend our time questioning what happened to us in adolescence. The question is not only limited to the period of adolescent turbulence. Perhaps it will seem an exaggeration to say that the questioning lasts a lifetime: we question our past, our present, and our future. The search for meaning is permanent. At this time, we are the only living creatures that question the meaning of life and the meaning of our actions. This is what the crossing to Ithaka consists of, after that enigmatic O that Bion formulated. The search for meaning is the essence of what is nowadays called the post-Kleinian position. Meltzer (1997, p. 82) expressed it in the following manner: "We as analysts are in pursuit of the meaning of things, and we are not medical men seeking to prolong life, to diminish pain, to rescue, and so on". It is not about pain or joy, but the meaning of these experiences.

Meaning is not a product easy to come by, nor is its vehicle, language. It is but a simple phenomenon. Valdés Villanueva (1991, p. 9) is correct when he says:

One of the phenomena most present in our daily experience is, without a doubt, language. Almost all of our activities are full of things like talking, listening to someone who talks, reading, writing, etc. The main characteristic of all of these events, and what makes them language is that we say that all of them have meaning. Thus being, it seems that linguistic meaning is something that we encounter very often. It is something we are more familiar with than anything else.

Meaning is what makes us subjects. However, speaking does not necessarily or immediately convey meanings. Meaning is learned and created. It is social and idiosyncratic. It is public and private. It is not always accessible. The confusing mixture of sounds, the noise present in communications, and the penumbra of associations all impede our grasp of meanings. Languages or terminologies cannot be understood all of the time, nor is it even possible to change them "every time a meaning requires refinement" (Meltzer, 1967, p. 101). Nor is the meaning of a term discovered by reducing it to its implicit elements. Thus, Wittgenstein proposes identifying meaning by how it is used in context. Simplification is not good company when it is about languages or meanings, and above all, in a world hard put to recognise affects as containers for meaning. Faced with this complexity, languages (musical, gestural, lexical) become essential instruments to construct meaning[1] "in a world which does not have a meaning in itself" (Verschueren, 1999, p. 8).

The issue of meaning becomes increasingly more complex when speaking about meaning in psychoanalysis because psychoanalysis demands a transferential context capable of facilitating the "emotional experience" where meaning is born. In order for this experience to become meaning, analytical work must be based on non-parasitic cooperation between container and contained, similar to a couple in an intimate relationship. There is an even more intimate requisite: it consists of tolerating the relinquishment of the pre-eminence of consciousness for the generation of meanings, as happens in dream life. That is why the character BION[2] from *A Memoir of the Future* (1991, p. 95) cries out that "It's quite bad enough going to sleep and being driven off the stage of conscious, waking, real life by dreams". But it would be more alarming to remain adhered to the concrete data of consciousness. Intimacy with oneself and with this other transferential someone are the containers for generating meanings. Relationships threatened with being reduced to "an activity which is only a more or less ingenious manipulation of symbols" (Bion, 1991, p. 92). This strong warning from the character SHERLOCK is not meaningless because the threat of reducing psychoanalysis to a boring and devitalising jargon persists.

Thus formulated the complex network of the generation of meanings, I believe that psychoanalytic work can be considered to be the *work of meanings not always achieved*, that generally manifest in misunderstandings, failed symbolisation, personality disorders, and symptoms... "Give sorrow words. The grief that does not speak whispers the o'er-fraught heart and bids it break" (Shakespeare: *Macbeth*, Act IV, Scene III). The manifestations of *unachieved meanings* are each a new language awaiting a new reading able to discover their meanings. Beta elements await their opportunity; rather than lacking meaning, they have not yet found a transforming container.

The post-Kleinian model sinks its roots into Freud's metapsychology, Klein's discoveries about the child's mind, and the successive contributions of Bion and Meltzer. "Kleinian developments" became insufficient. Nowadays, we speak of Bionian and Meltzerian developments. Thought seeks new thinkers to accommodate it.

Starting with his work with groups, his epistemological concerns (that enveloped the world of Cambridge and Oxford), and his roots in Hinduism, Bion studied the group dimension of the personality that, in dialogue with the other, pursues a truth that eludes him, but that makes him a subject. Quest and truth both constitute the subject. The subject depends on the group for the construction of the internal world but, at the same time, must fight it to break free of the non-mental functioning of the group. The pack does not encourage thinking, and fears thought.

Another element constituting a post-Kleinian metapsychology was the contribution made by Esther Bick. Her observation of the child in its family group, mainly with the mother, provided knowledge that had an impact on Meltzer's developments, to the extent that he came to consider psychoanalysis as a method close to that of the upbringing of a child, according to the childcare model. This led to lessening interest in psychopathology—following Klein's trail—a decreased concern about eliminating weeds (the psychopathology), and more of an interest in the emerging green shoots (new developments in the area of personality).

The emotional turbulence developed and observed in the mother-infant relationship led to a greater consideration of the emotions that can develop in the clinical relationship, producing a profound modification in the psychoanalytic method. Within the carefully curated psychoanalytic framework that has been kept free of interferences ("Without memory, desire, or understanding"), the vitality of the infantile parts, as well as those parts that oppose all development—the non-mental and psychotic parts of the personality—can express themselves. The interplay between container and contained and that of the Ps↔D dynamic make development a possibility, albeit not always unhindered. The outcome is uncertain.

Both inspired and supported by the masters that accompanied me on the voyage I have ventured upon, recognising, as Antonio Machado does, that we do not know "where the path will lead", I have travelled this path as can be seen in the following chapters, many of which have already been published[3] in specialised journals; that is why some repetitions will be found, that, far from being distracting, facilitate comprehension. I have had generous analysts and good masters to guide me on my path, who[4] have been very present, most of the time through their work; my hat off to them! Amongst the learning experiences, the most moving and surely the richest were the clinical seminars and supervisions with Donald Meltzer (in Barcelona and Oxford) and the meetings with my colleagues of the Psychoanalytic Group of Barcelona. However, there is one colleague, whom I am honoured to have as a friend, who helps me not to drown in Poseidon's kingdom: Dr. Alberto Hahn (London); his seminars, his supervisions, his attentive readings of this book, and his generous contributions constitute priceless help. An indispensable collaboration in navigating these and other oceans has been provided by my wife, María Elena Sammartino Rovirosa, who, as a psychoanalyst and philologist, has read and made rich contributions to the book; without her company, it would have been impossible to endure this voyage. Dr. Hahn and my wife have worked on this task as a good combined object. My patients and supervisees have made me grow as a psychoanalyst; and my children, as a father. To all of them: thank you.

Notes

1 I think it is necessary to establish a differentiation between "building meaning" and "generating meaning". Construction, as a "construct", refers to a more conscious and active participation in the production of the meaning of language. Generation or emergence of meaning takes into account more "the language user's active contribution to the processes under discussion and for their more spontaneous activation beyond the direct control of a language user's intentionality" (Verschueren, 1999, p. 8). And continuing with the differentiations, it should be noted that "the problem of meaning has been widened from a view that placed it as a fact of external reality which had to be *apprehended*, to a more internal position as something to be *generated* and deployed" (Meltzer, 1984, p. 26).

2 W. R. Bion (1991) in his book *A Memoir of the Future* presents characters that may trouble the reader who is unfamiliar with his work; as examples of these characters, I will name P.A. BION, ROSEMARY, ALICE, PRIEST, GHOST, SHERLOCK, SOMITE, etc. These characters will appear with upper case letters.

3 At the foot of each text the references of journals where they have been published will appear, and for which I have kindly been given the authorisation to include in this book. My gratitude to all of them.

4 I use as mine the words of Parthenope Bion Talamo (2011, p. ix) who said:

> It is true that with regard to the history of science it is important to be able to attribute correctly to their authors the paternity of the concepts used, but it is also true that thinking dies if it is not re-fertilised and subsequently developed in the generation and the mind of each thinker.

Bibliography

Bion, W. R. (1991): "The dream", *A Memoir of the Future*, London, Karnac Books.

Bion Talamo, P. (2011): "Some notes on the theories of structure and mental functioning underlying A Memoir of the Future by W. R. Bion (1993): festschrift for Francesco Corrao", in W. R. Bion (1993), *Maps for Psychoanalytic Exploration*, edited by Chris Mawson, London, Karnac Books, 2015, pp. 103–116

Bloom, H. (1994): *The Western Canon*, New York, Harcourt Brace & Company.

Kavafis, K. (1911): "Ithaka", in *C.P. Cavafy: Collected Poems*, Translated by Edmund Keeley and Philip Sherrard, London, Chatto & Windus, 1978, p. 29

Klein, M. (1932): *The Psycho-Analysis of Children*. New York, W W Norton & Co.

Meltzer, D. (1967): *The Psycho-Analytical Process*, London, William Heinemann Medical Books Limited.

Meltzer, D. (1984): *Dream-Life: A Re-Examination of the Psychoanalytic Theory and Technique*, London, Karnac Books, 2009.

Meltzer, D. (1997): *Meltzer In São Paulo*, London, Karnac, 2017.

Money-Kyrle, R. (1969) "On the fear of insanity", in *The Collected Papers of Roger Money-Kyrle*, edited by Donald Meltzer, Strathclyde, Clunie Press, 1978, pp. 434–441.

Valdés Villanueva, L. (1991): *La búsqueda del significado*, Madrid, Ed. Tecnos, S. A.

Verschueren, J. (1999): *Understanding Pragmatics*, London, Edward Arnold.

Chapter 1

The Conceptual Framework

The upper Palaeolithic cave paintings of the Grotte de Niaux (France), the urbanisation of Machu Pichu (Peru), the reflections of the once contemporaries—Confucius and Plato—Dvořák's New World Symphony or those of Mahler, Shakespeare's dramas, the stories in the Pentateuch, etc. are milestones of humanity seen questioning itself. Buber asked "what is man?", a question with no resolution and open to all possible answers. It is a question as immense as solving the mystery of the Holy Trinity, according to the anecdote related by St. Augustine: it would be as impossible to fathom that mystery as it would be to pour the whole ocean into a hole in the sand on a beach. Notwithstanding the magnetism and the magnitude of the question, one could remain silent. Another option would be to pretend to answer it omnipotently. Yet another would be to narrow it down and try to delve deeply into some area.

Psychoanalysis is a vertex that questions humans and itself as an ideology. It has its limits as it has its assumptions. Although it can be fascinating because it illuminates the many inscrutable recesses of a person's mind, it holds no ultimate truth. It possesses one truth; its own, whether one or many. The first of these is the conviction that psychic reality is determinant and that transference is pure psychic reality. The second is that values derive from psychic reality. These will be the topics that we will discuss in upcoming pages.

DOI: 10.4324/9781003347156-2

1.1

Psychic Reality

If a fundamental and controversial concept exists in psychoanalysis, it is that of psychic reality. It is fundamental in that it is the object of study, research, and the work of psychoanalysts. It is fundamental because the development of people and cultures derives from psychic reality. It is controversial because there is not one sole way of describing, conceptualising, and explaining what it is, nor how it can be destroyed. In this brief introductory section, I will mention topics that will be developed in subsequent chapters.

I believe one way to approach the comprehension of psychic reality is shown by an artist, who focuses on an object and reflects on how it may be seen. The artist's regard describes contents that unfold inside the observer, in the face of the observed.

The avant-garde Catalan painter Antoni Tapies (1923–2012) wrote an exquisite and brief text in 1967 which illustrates the way to approximate psychic reality. He called it "The Game of KnowinG How To LooK":

How can we look cleanly, without wanting to find in things what we have been told is there but rather what is simply there? This is the innocent game I propose we play.

Whenever we look, we tend to see only what is given around us: stuff, normally quite humble, barely glimpsed in the middle of the infinite. Take a look at the simplest of objects. Let's take, for example, an old chair. It seems like nothing. But think of the universe comprised within it: the sweaty hands cutting the wood that used to be a robust tree, full of energy, in the middle of a luxuriant forest by some high mountains. The loving work that built it, the joyful anticipation of the one who bought it, the tired bodies it has helped, the pains and the joys it must have endured, whether in fancy halls or in a humble dining room in your neighbourhood. Everything, everything shares life and has its importance! Even the most worn down of chairs carries inside the initial force of the sap climbing from the earth, out there in the forest, and will still be useful the day when, broken into kindling, it burns in some fireplace.

Look, look deep! Let yourselves be guided fully by what resounds within you in response to what our gaze grasps, as one who attends a concert in a new suit

DOI: 10.4324/9781003347156-3

and an open heart looking forward to listening, to hearing in all its purity without demanding that the sounds of the piano or the orchestra represent a certain landscape, or the portrait of a general, or a scene from history. […] It is a game. But to play does not mean to do things 'just because.' And as in all children's games, artists do not do things 'just because.' […] Playing… playing, we make our spirit grow, we widen the field of our vision, of our knowledge. Playing… playing, we say things and we listen, we awaken those who fell asleep, and we help those who do not know or those whose eyes have been covered to see. When you look you must not think that painting—like all things in this world— 'has to be', you must not think of it what many want it to be exclusively. […] I invite you to play, to look attentively…

I invite you to think.

Only an artist can say so much, with so few words, and so beautifully!

Tapies' invitation is not so innocent. It responds to the need to rid ourselves of prejudices that condition our perspective and, occasionally, push us into giving a quick and superficial glance at something… because we are pressed for time, or because it scares us, or because we already know it and it seems trivial and inconsequential, or because it is not in fashion. However, if we know how to play, the field of our vision, as well as that of our internal world, broadens, freed from the pressure of what must be done, wished for, or omitted… Tapies ends by inviting us to play and to look attentively, with the outcome essentially coming down to his inviting us to think. This invitation would seem to be a poetic version of Freud's *Formulations on the Two Principles of Mental Functioning*, taken up again by Bion as seen in The Grid through the use of attention, inquiry, register, and thought, and by Meltzer through poetry; an event, a coming ever closer to the symbol, to poetry, to art, to thought.

Psychic reality is a stable *organisation* that allows us to recognise ourselves and observe the reality that surpasses us. It is a reality built upon slowly, from primordial times when we danced in the amniotic ocean to our last introjections. This psychic reality that allows us to see, without excessive prejudice, if we are fortunate enough to be able to see without wearing envious blinkers that make us, not infrequently, believe that it is only a chair, a mere chair. Or is it the impoverishment of the observer who is unable to grasp the stories embedded in that simple object? Are there simple objects? Or is simplification employed to allow us to tolerate the impact of an overwhelming world? Do we believe that we can know everything or that we only know the little we can know? Bion used to say that there is not enough time in a lifetime to know everything or even enough time to know everything that should be known about one sole thing (Caper, 1998). What do we know about that poor chair or about the reality of a child of ours? Perhaps this is why the question "Who do you think you are?" formulated by Bion (1961) can offend. If it were well tolerated, the answer could possibly be: it is the individual who feels curiosity about who they are and what things are. And to humanise themself, the meaning of the different realities must be grasped with the help of their senses that inform them about both the wide world, and that of the symbolic one—the world of meanings. In the face of such yearning, the offensiveness can come from the absence of the necessary internal and external allies; maybe their ego, like platonic horses, is easily frightened and prefers to close its eyes, or destroy them like Oedipus, thus decreeing what reality is. Omniscience and suicide are effective and brutal anaesthetics against curiosity, but if we have good internal allies—those psychic objects—we will be able to tolerate conflicts and anxieties to benefit the development of our psychic reality.

Tapies said that "Playing…playing, we make our spirit grow, we widen the field of our vision", to which we might add: our psychic reality; an essential and specifically human reality that will have to process stimuli coming from the internal and external world, transforming them into a narrative that is communicable to oneself and to the community.

Psychic reality is an *efficient organisation* (it makes us do things) more or less *structured* (there are areas in different stages of development that remain dissociated from one another, while at the same time attached through both positive and negative bonds which are in conflict) and only partially *known* (comparable to an iceberg where the essential part is hidden from sight; hence Bion called it O). If this reality is seen without the liberty expressed in the game suggested by Tapies, then psychic reality can be reduced to behaviour or to conscious actions. That is to say, the surface, and probably only a measurable and quantifiable wooden chair, will be seen. If, however, you play seriously, you will have to recognise that reason is not enough to unravel the multiple meanings that nest in that simple chair, and without noticing that the simpler the object, the more complex its nature. Similarly, the more simplistic a subject, the more psychic reality is denied, the subject stubbornly reaffirming that it is only a chair.

Tapies' proposal would seem to invite us to fantasise freely based on what that object inspires to discover stories embedded in its wood and function… but it is fantasising through thought; that is why it invites you to think… as if proposing an active discovery initiative. This carries with it, however, the danger of finding what is not being sought out. In this sense, the *negative capacity* proposed by Bion bids us to open our mental diaphragm to the utmost to be impacted by the stimuli coming from the object. This availability assumes that the subject is minimally organised to record the impact, and that they have the ability to look at what they have registered in order to intuit meanings. An opposing attitude to this would be found in the neurotic or the psychotic individual who dumps their internal life into external reality. In this case, you would see a diabolical chair, or a dirty chair, or no chair at all.

Between the only quantifiable consideration of the chair at one extreme and the hypertrophied consideration of meaning at the other, a territory exists for the encounter between internal world and external world. The model for the Paranoid-schizoid Position↔Depressive Position is suitable for granting it a place in psychic reality. Two worlds that clash, oppose each other, become confused, discriminate, articulate and symbolise. From this generative alternation, a psychic reality emerges,

> ...a reality which is individual, fantastic, thought, desired, subjective, unreal, hallucinated, unknowable and internal to the psychic apparatus construed by each psyche, and is therefore opposed to the reality which is common, general, social, true, material, imposed, objective, realistic, knowable and external, the latter being generalisable and even universal.
>
> (Puget, 1994, p. 89)

Complementing this formulation, Berenstein (1994, p. 19) would say:

> Psychic reality is considered a set of experiences, emotions and unconscious representations, personified as objects, which the ego feels to be internal and real. It is related to, and differentiated from, another reality, called external in relation to the ego, which the latter feels outside itself and inhabited by people as well as institutions, cultural norms, laws, etc.

This is the difference between a simple chair and my chair. It is this *my* that defines psychic reality. The psychic reality that unfolds before the eyes of the psychoanalyst and remains within their reach. It is a *my* that retains its emotionality expressed in the transference, such as that of Anna O that frightened Breuer or the intensity of Dora that puzzled Freud.

When Freud stopped believing in hysterias and recognised the value of phantasies, this opened the door to a recognition of psychic reality, as opposed to material, external reality, which is concrete-measurable, as he said in *The Development of the Symptoms* (Freud, 1916–1917, pp. 321–321):

> ...It is a fact that the patient is able to create such phantasies for himself, and this is of scarcely less importance for his neurosis than if he had really undergone the experience which he imagines. These phantasies possess psychological reality in contrast to physical reality, and so we gradually come to understand that in the realm of neuroses the psychological reality is the determining factor.

This statement is not circumscribed to the world of neuroses but rather comprehends all subjects independently of their degree of mental health. Psychic reality is decisive because it generates and exports meaning, and because it is a knowledge engendered by the same patient and, in clinical practice, with the help of the analyst's countertransference.

Another fundamental step in the recognition of psychic reality is the step taken by Klein when she developed the theory of internal objects; this produced "...a revolutionary addition to the model-of-the-mind, namely that we do not live in one world, but in two—that we also live in an internal world which is as real a place of life as the outside world" (Meltzer, 1981, p. 178). It is an internal world created by contact with the external world. *We live in both, although it is in the internal world where the meaning that is exported to the external world is generated. In turn, this—mainly through the decoder function of the first object—will have the task of modulating and polishing those internal constructions, often contaminated with omnipotence.*

The interaction between projection and introjection—components of the internal world—is as dependent on the instinctual load of the subject as on the object's attitude. An infant can come into the world with intrauterine experiences that condition its contact with external reality, or be overwhelmed by parents with no respect for their child.

If psychic reality is decisive both for mental health as well as for mental illness, "how can we look cleanly, without wanting to find in things what we have been told is there but rather what is simply there?" (Tapies). The word "simply" makes us shudder once again when thinking about it in relation to psychic reality. We are moved because the psychoanalyst is not in search of reality or the chair, but rather the different representations achieved up to the present. The state of mind of the patient who consults us today is not what it was in the child. This is why I am in agreement with Grinberg (1995, p. 272) when he states that

> The analyst's interpretative work does not consist of 'correcting' the patient's distortion, bringing it nearer to the 'correct' reality, but rather analytic work is using analytic instruments to aid the analysand in becoming conscious of their internal and subjective reality, to show the analysand discrepancies between different psychic realities within themselves, or showing the rigid nature of the patient's internal reality that deprives them of making choices or developing.

Individuals who consult a psychotherapist or psychoanalyst may think their problem "seems like nothing" (Tapies) because they believe they are only dealing with a chair. The experienced analyst begins to detect that "Everything, everything shares life and has its importance!" (ibid.) and stands amazed before the mystery of the consultee, questioning whether they dispose of enough tools to discover the multiple meanings of the patient who had only considered the chair. Looking closely, however, accepting the invitation to play, and confident that "Playing…playing, we make our spirit grow, we widen the field of our vision, of our knowledge" (ibid.), the analyst can throw themselves into the task of discovery … until, after a time of hard work together,[1] the patient discovers a new perspective of themselves and external reality, because this external reality shed the scales that prevented things being seen that were not just a chair ….

Note

1 With "hard work together", I'm referring to the complex experience of playing; it is complex because playing is not always pleasurable because, as with dreams, dreaded, primitive areas of the patient's personality are approached. Focusing on "the work we share" during the clinical encounter, I say that it is work and it is shared because it

requires effort to observe, within the context of the transference to name what is unconscious and allow the emergence of alpha elements that lead to the discovery and naming
of the multiple meanings of the chair, of a dream, or a game. A shared effort also because
emotional turbulence is not limited to the patient's personality, but rather compromises
the analyst's. For that reason, the analysis of the countertransference becomes a necessary task to protect both the patient as well as the observer.

Bibliography

Berenstein, I. (1994): "Realidad psíquica y técnica clínica"; Buenos Aires, en *Revista de
Psicoanálisis*, editada por la Asociación Psicoanalítica Argentina. Tomo LI, N° 3, 1994.

Bion, W. R. (1961): "The conception of man", in *The Complete Works of W. R. Bion*, edited
by Chris Mawson, London, Karnac, 2014, vol. xv, pp. 9–30.

Caper, R. (1998): "The clinical thinking of Wilfred Bion. By Joan and Neville Symington",
International Journal of Psychoanalysis, 79, pp. 417–420.

Freud, S. (1916–1917): "XXIII. The development of the symptoms", in *A General Introduction to Psychoanalysis*, translated by G. Stanley Hall, New York, Boni and Liveright,
1920, pp. 311–327.

Grinberg, L. (1995): "Realidad psíquica y el rol de la intuición en la práctica psicoanalítica",
in *El Psicoanálisis es cosa de dos*, Valencia, Editorial Promolibro, 265–287.

Meltzer, D. (1981): "The Kleinian expansion of Freudian Metapsychology", *International
Journal of Psychoanalysis*, 62, pp. 177–185.

Puget, J. (1994): "La realidad psíquica o varias realidades", *Revista de Psicoanálisis*, APA,
LI, 3, pp. 87–95.

Tapies, A. (1967): "The game of knowing how to look", in *Antoni Tàpies, Collected Essays*
(Complete Writings, Volume ii), Bloomington & Indianapolis, Indiana University Press,
2011. https://fundaciotapies.org/wp-content/uploads/2020/03/Fitxes-ANG.pdf

Values[1]

"Values" necessarily refers to "psychic reality"; they are interdependent.

Values and anti-values express not only emotional states and mental organisations, but also moments of community. Values have changed throughout history but not their meaning. In the same way that variations exist of the scale of values in the different moments of each individual, and although some are fundamental and permanent, throughout history they have varied, albeit not always progressively. Just as it was possible to amend the values of slavery, virginity, or racial superiority, that does not prevent the persistence of groups where nostalgia for these anti-values prevails. The values that justify the objectification of people reduced to the status of useful objects should be reviewed. When groups are governed by the simplifying law of supply and demand, which is not based on respect for fundamental values but rather on market and auction values governed by the quantifiable, a perversion of human relations and a lack of care for nature loom on the cultural horizon. That is a lack of *respect*. I highlight this lack because I believe that respect implies recognising the uniqueness and specialness of the other person who has a value in their own right.

The inquiry regarding the origin of values and their different scales, whether individual or collective, is present in the history of thought, especially when considering that values are in an intimate relationship with the social nature of the human being. There are no values without a group in the same way that there is no person or internal group without an external or social group.

Before entering the specific field of psychoanalysis, it would be wise to look to philosophy for the meaning of the term *value* and to refer to *value systems*.

1.2.1 Philosophical Vertex

Values as a theme has always been present in the history of philosophy and has required laborious discriminations that have not always concluded in transcendent syntheses. In contemporary thought, the theory of values oscillates between relativist and absolutist positions. For some, values depend on the observer; whereas for others, they are intrinsic to the valued object. While integration has yet to be achieved, extreme positions have been smoothed out. It is therefore recognised that value cannot be contingent on subjective arbitrariness and, on the other hand, that

DOI: 10.4324/9781003347156-4

value is meaningless if it is not referred to a person who holds it in high esteem (Ferrater Mora, 1966).

Although it sounds tautological, the reality of value lies in what it is worth. Picasso's painting of Guernica has an aesthetic, documentary, and pictorial value in itself, although some do not recognise this, or do but reject it. Its value is objective (absolutist position), that is, it does not depend on individual preferences, but remains beyond all personal appreciation and estimation of value. The high significance, at the same time, that it has for Spanish republicans and the history of art, nevertheless, fundaments its value.

The significance of an object changes as soon as it is given a value. Values cannot be confused with *goods* because values name valuable things, that is to say, things plus value. Nor must value be confused with *price*. The meaning of an object varies as soon as a value is incorporated into it. It is also advisable to differentiate between a "value" and "the idea of something's value", for instance, beauty and the idea of beauty. Beauty is neither a "real object", nor is it an "ideal entity". Real objects are determined by spatiality, temporality, and causality. Ideal entities (mathematical and logical entities) are timeless. The "idea of beauty" participates in the timelessness of "ideal entities" but is an abstraction of "real objects". These different realities demand different modes of apprehension: ideal entities are intellectually grasped, whereas values are emotionally understood. Values affect us.

The ability to provoke is characteristic of values: they do not admit indifference.

> Our reaction, and the corresponding value—says Frondizi (1999, p. 20)—will be positive or negative, of approximation or rejection. There is no work of art that is neutral, no person who remains indifferent when listening to a symphony, reading a poem or looking at a painting.

This statement bears full meaning when the subject is in a position to connect with reality, because in states of autistic withdrawal, for example, reality is stubbornly ignored, while the subject takes refuge in maximum indifference.

The ability to provoke, that is to say, to call out to us, to summon us, is associated with the bipolar character of values. These values present themselves as polarised, or

> ... unfolding into a positive value and the corresponding negative value. Thus, beauty is opposed by ugliness; the bad, to the good; the unjust, to the just, and so on. Do not believe that the devaluation, or negative value, implies the mere absence of the positive value: the negative value exists by itself and not by consequence of the positive value. 'Ugliness' has as much effective presence as 'beauty'; we meet it all the time. The same can be said of other negative values such as injustice, disgustingness, disloyalty, etc.
>
> (ibid., pp. 19–20)

Another characteristic of values is their hierarchy. Values are present in different classes and each one of them in a fixed order—superior or inferior—in relation to other classes. Fixed does not mean immutable, universal, or absolute, because the scales of values reflect the interplay between subjects, objects, and concrete cultural situations. In the history of thought and religions, there have been many systematisations of values or commandments. Here, only as an exemplification of a hierarchy of values that organises and articulates values acceptable to a culture, I will present the table proposed by Max Scheler (1874–1928). For this German philosopher, the table was something a priori (unalterable by experience), that is, immutable and absolute. I do not think contemporary liquid society (Bauman) agrees with Scheler's ideas. Neither immutable nor liquid, nor dogmatic, nor without categories; every community requires norms based on values to prevent impulsivity from harming coexistence. Scheler organised the values into four ranks:

- *Base rank*: values of agreeable and disagreeable.
- *Second rank*: vital values of the noble, the vulgar, the healthy, and the unhealthy.
- *Third rank*: spiritual (psychic) values that comprise:

  - Aesthetic values: the beautiful and the ugly.
  - Juridical values: the fair and the unfair.
  - Values of pure knowledge: the true and the false.

- *Supreme rank*: religious values: the sacred and the profane.

The consideration of values in terms of ranks implies intentionality and indicates a direction to follow that—in Max Scheler's proposal—would be to transition from the world of hedonistic sensuality towards religious values. In Scheler's cultural world, these religious values would be fundamentally those of Christianity, with everlasting life being the overall goal. In Judeo-Christian religious mythology, there is a longing for a return to the house of the Father-God, according to Catholicism, and a transition towards Heaven, recognising, in the post-mortem ritual, being the mother's child, according to the Jews. These mythologies spill over with nostalgia and are based on the universal experience of helplessness.

In the face of threats and suffering, contemporary humanity has overvalued knowledge and technology, to the point that love of truth has eclipsed, to some extent, love of neighbour. Lévinas (1982, p. 74), the Lithuanian thinker who integrates the Bible, Greek thinkers, and contemporary phenomenologists into his thinking, questions the sufficiency of modern humanity who

> ...persists in its sovereign being, concerned only with securing *the powers of its sovereignty*. Everything that is possible is allowed [...] The marvel of modern Western freedom that does not disturb any memory or regrets, and that welcomes a 'radiant future' where everything is rectifiable. Only death is unfathomable. The obstacle of death will be unbearable, fundamentally incomprehensible, inexorable... The sphere of the irreparable.

In the face of the collapse of technological human sufficiency, which may not respect the object/Nature, death[2] presents itself as an obstacle and also as the possibility of a new inquiry. This new inquiry will not focus on an ontological question about being; it will be an ethical inquiry centring around the responsibility towards this Other that constitutes us as subjects. I am not because I think, in the Cartesian style, but rather I am because before me there was an object willing to take me in and name me, before whom I feel responsible. Far from self-sufficiency, there is vulnerability and fear of harming those others who constitute and claim me; those others that Lévinas calls the astonished and suffering faces of widows, widowers, orphans, foreigners, and the dispossessed, that is, those who have suffered loss, and feel their nakedness. Before them—is there anyone who is always clothed?—there is only responsibility.[3] It becomes the knot of subjectivity. The subject is responsible for the other in the disposition to become a being-for-the-other. This generosity would find an ethical model in gestation, where the woman is prepared to welcome within herself a new life with the risks that this entails.

If it is good to take responsibility for the other, the absence of moral values in the intentional gradation of Scheler's table is surprising. Aranguren (1978, p. 97) attributes it

> to the fact that moral values—that is, good and bad—do not have their own 'matter', but instead their reality consists in the realization of other values according to the just order of preference and 'resolution'. Good and evil consist of deciding on the realization of the value that—rightly or wrongly—has been recognised as preferable or adjournable.

Aranguren raises here the moral dilemma that oscillates between responsibility and moral emptiness. It is a dilemma of all times, not only of contemporary or technological humanity. In this sense, I agree with Paciuk (1995, p. 116) when he says that

> every moment of the human life process involves values, referring in particular to that centre of gravity that is the interhuman relationship. It is an ethic that can be understood as being built concomitantly with the process of edifying the subject through the path of experience. It will then follow that ethics is not something that should be inculcated, or that the subject should apprehend, or something innate. Central to this process is the relationship with the other, an 'other' that goes from being taken as an *object* to being unveiled as *otherness*.

We arrive, again, at the alternative proposed above: that of considering-objectifying the other as a useful or valuable object according to my prejudiced[4] scale of values, or considering them a subject of rights, an object to be discovered and responsibly respected.[5] Feelings of gratitude, derived from the ability to love (Klein, 1957), are no strangers to the latter way of bonding; a capacity that would be sustained from the beginning of each subject in "an innate aptitude in the child for *love* or *gratitude*, which is reinforced by good maternal functioning" (Kristeva, 2000, p. 150).

Although Scheler's gradation can be questioned, depending on ideologies and alternative values, I believe that his table preserves elements that acquire other meanings when contemplated from the psychoanalytic perspective.

1.2.2 The Psychoanalytic Vertex

Restricting Scheler's goal-oriented final version, based on helplessness, to Judeo-Christian culture would be unfair because it is typical of religions to place hope in some idealised figure (human or not).

The architectural structure of religious temples, whether in the East or the West, has caught my eye; in general, when the faithful go there, they usually pray or make an offering (e.g. the smoking incense sticks in Buddhist temples in China, and candles in Catholic temples) as an expression of gratitude and/or expectations of something—solace? Temples represent, for me, a container that is always available. If an intentional look at the architectural plan of a temple is allowed, it seems that it is organised so as to represent an interior space—genital and uterine—of the mother with her entrance (the *introitus*); further on, in a prominent place, there is a spot for a venerated object to reside, as if that distribution were an evocation of that former resident that we all once were, or of a hope: that of a return to a sheltered, maternal interior (see Section 3.1.5). To prevent regressive yearnings, a statue of Buddha, the Torah, or a bishop has been installed in an eye-catching place in the temple; that is to say, the statue of a third other to prevent just such a return. Cultures will vary, but in every one, there are those idealised/sacred ever-available spaces to generate the illusion of being taken into a welcoming bosom that drives away the pain of helplessness; initiation rituals and burial practices are examples of the fantasy of being within a container.

The experience of the helplessness of, for example, mammals helps the young to grow, for an extended period of time, in close proximity to their parents, like planets orbiting the sun. Starting with the sensation of absolute dependence, religions are created in which a divine figure who provides organisation, protection, and orientation must always exist. The religious values proposed by Scheler as being of a "superior rank" and that function as the ultimate goal reveal themselves, in my opinion, as a "primary", basic foundation for the development of the subject. It is a foundation built in the repeated experience of the relationship with the parents who are present, above all in difficult moments. This object, capable of sustaining pain and sharing joy, can become a model for adult functioning. The re-bonding with objects present in infancy can lead to an identification with parental functions and the basis of religious ideas or ideologies.[6] The possibility of becoming an internal object that functions as a guide, a lookout, and a support system, almost always exists. Freud called that internal object a superego, and Meltzer referred to the superego as our internal gods around which mental life develops. Every subject can, using their original clay, build an internal object that carries a variety of meanings, capable of performing organising, regulatory, and inspirational functions. When difficulties in building internal and polyfunctional objects exist, the ground is laid for psychopathology.

Just as religions emerge from imitation and transformation of the family planetary model, the children fluttering around their parents—those omnipotent gods—the mental apparatus becomes organised through the recreation of the parental couple that organise the life of the mind. The parental function consists in guaranteeing the survival and development of the babies and of life in general. The biological and emotional dimensions of this aspiration are possible when a family has been internalised and a parental couple with the capacity to preside over it has been built. If to the contrary, the family is presided over by devitalised and/or destructive objects, this will encourage the physical and/or mental death of the progeny, the outcome being that a future, and therefore even life itself, will not be guaranteed.

When referring to an internal family presided over by a couple, I manifest the supposition that the mind and the personality are organised like a group. It was Freud's merit to describe—above all in the structural model of the mind—the components of this structure.

As the children of a parental group, raised in a family-community group, we dispose of an internal group developed through identifications; an object-seeker. Another significant discovery is that we live in different worlds: in the internal world, in the external world, in the internal meaning of objects (external and internal), and it is even possible to get lost in the delusional space. Values arise in the interrelationships between different members of these internal and external groups-families.

I will now present contributions made by Freud, Klein, Bion, and Meltzer, that account for mental principles and organisations that give rise to different, complementary, and/or antithetical values.

1.2.2.1 Sigmund Freud

Freud had an ambivalent relationship with groups. He was suspicious of the masses and the tyrannies of dominant groups. Painful experiences with intolerant governments, World War I, and the rise of fascism did not prevent his curiosity about the phenomenon of groups from being stimulated. In Freud's initial writings (*The Project* and *Studies on Hysteria*), the group appears as a model to conceptualise the structuring and functioning of the mental apparatus. His first representation of the unconscious was of a dissociated psychic group.

Freud proposed three models of grouping to give "an account of the formations and processes of psychic reality brought into play in the quantitative passage from the individual to the series, and from the series to the organised intersubjective set" (Kaës, 2000, p. 26). These models appeared in three emblematic works. In *Totem and Taboo* (1912), he proposes the passage from the paternal horde to social organisations and the beginning of human morality based on guilt, responsibility, and the need for atonement.[7] In *Group Psychology and The Analysis of the Ego* (1921), one can see the role of identifications and ideals in the links between various individuals and in the constitution of the ego. In *Civilization and Its Discontents* (1929), he states that love and culture are based on the renunciation of impulsive ends.

The norms of social relations, elaborated by the cultural superego, are included in the concept of ethics.

Freud never abandoned the model of psychoanalysis as a social psychology or the group model of the psyche in which the ego relates to and negotiates with three masters.

The second aspect I would be interested in pointing out is that the psyche, organised as an internal group, is governed by principles. In 1911, Freud formulated the two principles that determine mental functioning: the pleasure principle and the reality principle. The reality principle would also never be abandoned by Freud throughout his entire research. The pleasure principle is characterised by a concern for the present. It is a principle that pertains only to the present and has no ability to anticipate anything. This explains why Freud initially called it the displeasure principle, for he was motivated by the displeasure of the moment and not the possible pleasure of a future time. The pleasure principle almost entirely governs people who have no capacity for the postponement of pleasure, and who demand satisfaction as soon as desire arises. This type of functioning, which is infantile, can be related to the autoerotism implicit in behaviours which are determined by "agreeable and disagreeable" on Max Scheler's scale of values. The purified-pleasure ego governed by the pleasure principle recognises agreeable/pleasurable as its own, while assuming everything disagreeable as foreign and irrelevant, and rejecting it. The most distant to this purified-pleasure ego is the idea of death and the passing of time, which leads it to behave as if it were immortal, or to deny the existence of time. This timeless functioning is observed, for example, in adolescents when they complain that their parents are always thinking about the future, while they "are busy with other things". I recall an adolescent who prepared for his university exams by devoting himself to a mere three hours of study, and was later surprised not to have passed. This way of functioning was far from the "attentive interest in oneself, or from what would allow us to know what is best for us", according to Meltzer's description of the reality principle (1998, p. 69). The reality principle manifests in an attitude of curious interest in reality in the convenience of registering experiences that may be able to resolve future necessities. Without motivation, memory does not develop. It is, nevertheless, an interest that focuses on oneself.

Behaviour based on the pleasure principle can be observed in the narcissistic functioning present, for example, in two different situations. One refers to a denial of death. Freud (1914, p. 91) in *On Narcissism:An Introduction* says:

The child shall have a better time than his parents; [...] The child shall fulfil those wishful dreams of the parents which they never carried out ... At the most touchy point in the narcissistic system, the immortality of the ego, which is so hard pressed by reality, security is achieved by taking refuge in the child. Parental love, which is so moving and at bottom so childish, is nothing but the parents' narcissism born again, which, transformed into object-love, unmistakably reveals its former nature.

This reminds me of the case of a man who was organising a complex group situation for the purpose of perpetuating himself by having a biological child, without any consideration for the place given to the child, nor for the physical and emotional consequences for the carrier of the fertilised egg, nor even for the consequences in the relationship with his current infertile partner. His denial of death did not only manifest in his anxiety to perpetuate himself through the birth of a child, but also in his denial of the possibility of becoming ill. He was far from being capable of recognising his own mortality—a recognition that would allow him to escape from his narcissistic system; as Vorchheimer (1997, p. 218) says, it would be

> the recognition of one's own finitude that would make the child emerge as transcendent descendance, because recognition of the passage of time and of finitude imposes upon the psyche the strong demand for renunciation in the face of narcissistic pleasure, to donate it or give it to the children, entering and continuing the chain of filiation.

The other type of functioning based on the pleasure principle manifests itself in the avoidance of work. This can be observed, for example, in the clinical situation where the patient leaves all analytic work to the analyst, hoping to reap the fruit of the work without having participated in the sowing. When this parasitic attitude is stirred up, patients, bewildered, complain and become suspicious of the analyst who deprives them of pleasure. It will take a lot of work before comradeship emerges in the analytical task.

The internal group, governed by the pleasure principle, does not know the concept of responsibility; on the contrary, whatever is ruled by the reality principle will consider it an honour to work so that life (for instance, of the species, of culture) can continue. Honour based on identification with post-oedipal parents who become the ego ideal. This ideal, in addition to the supervisory function of the superego, constitutes the integrated set of personality values. The quality of both members of this group (superego and ego ideal) will depend equally on the quality of the parents built through the interaction between introjection-projection, as well as on the quality of the real parents.

The severe patriarchal shadow that colours the Freudian view of the superego can, at certain times, stimulate the desire for a new parricide (in the style of *Totem and Taboo*) to free the children from the dreaded tutelage. The consequences of this desire are not very promising, as frequently observed nowadays in clinical practice with young people. Lacking criteria, they surrender themselves to pure sensual satisfaction, replacing that tyranny with more deadly ones represented by pride, addiction, pseudo-maturity, and anomie, quite unable to sustain an autonomous life. When internal persecution becomes intolerable, suicide arises with force as an option to kill the persecutory object, since internal persecution is inescapable. Alternatively, psychopathic-paranoid acting-out can appear.

1.2.2.2 Melanie Klein

The observation of her own children's play, as well as that of her child patients, permitted Klein to intuit the internal world, which she perceived as a theatrical stage on which different characters interacted. Shortly after, she began introducing the name of the assembly or community of internal objects in constant interplay. Freud's "internal group" became broader with Klein's concept of "geography of phantasy". In Kleinian geography, the self occupies

> ...two worlds, internal and external, with which it carried on a continual commerce in meaning through processes of introjection and projection, gradually integrating itself and its objects from an earlier state, characterized by splitting and persecution, by the agency of good experiences and a depressive orientation.
>
> (Meltzer, 1978b, p. 367)

The continuous and oscillating interaction between the internal and external worlds modifies the qualities of internal objects. In the internal world, emotionality and the emotional meaning of experiences that allow us to build a vision of the external world in terms of meanings and values are distilled.

The process of integration (PS$\leftrightarrow$D) of the object and the self is full of consequences, and above all, in the case of the internal object called the superego.

Within schizoid-paranoid functioning, no temporal dimension exists, and everything is reduced, according to the displeasure-pleasure principle to considering the object that is present as good, and conversely, the absent one as bad. When integration advances, it becomes possible to discover that the absent object and the present one are both, in fact, the same object, and temporality emerges as the alternating of the object between being present and absent. With object integration, the superego emerges as a relationship with more complete parents, and can be felt to be the source of not only feelings of guilt but also protection. When trust in the objects increases, a new process begins: a concern for oneself gives way to an interest in our loved ones. The process puts a new system of values in place. This system comes from the internal parents and

> ...they are the origin of our system of values, and we constitute our ethical aspirations through identifications with them. They influence our way of life in that our choices in the world must take into account the well-being of the object. This means that we must shift the centre of our concerns from anxieties regarding the self to the examination of our motivations as a way of life.
>
> (Nemas, 2000, pp. 31/32)

The need to examine our motivations resides in the permanent, intrinsically human struggle between selfishness, unlimited ambition, mercilessness with the adversary or competitor, and, alternatively, altruism, concern for the other, being capable of renunciation and sacrifice, and respect for the object's privacy and mystique.

The psychopathology of psychotic, borderline, narcissistic, and obsessive states amply illustrates the ravages of a way of functioning based on the schizoid-paranoid model of relating. In the play *Endgame* (see Section 3.1.5) by Samuel Beckett (1957), the consequences for the self and objects of relationships determined by schizoid (splitting and intrusive identification) and obsessive (omnipotent control and separation of objects) mechanisms are masterfully elucidated; thus, it is that in this play the parents appear mutilated, separated, and closed up in rubbish bins, while the son remains paralysed and blind, functioning like a pathetic, terrified dictator.

1.2.2.3 Wilfred R. Bion

Bion's pre-psychoanalytic experience working with groups always accompanied him and enriched his psychoanalytic postulates. Bion recuperated the tribal dimension of the mind that served Freud to fundament the origin of morality in papers such as *Totem and Taboo*.

Freud's "internal group" was enlarged upon by Klein in the model of the mind as a theatre in which internal objects generate meaning. Bion takes it still further. In Bion's view, humans are gregarious animals, and their more primitive mentality is overwhelmingly concerned with belonging to groups. Whereas for Freud and Klein, this concern springs from the family, for Bion, it derives from non-mental, phylogenetic groups that predate family life, although without ruling out or excluding participation in both groups. The relationships in groups and in the family are radically different, and this implies ethical consequences while also demanding different mental apparatuses, as Meltzer (1978b, p. 280) states:

> man's primitive heritage makes it necessary for him to be a member of a group and that he has mental equipment for doing this of two different sorts, making possible his participation in two contrasting groupings: the basic assumption group and the work group.

In the basic assumption group, relationships are determined by tropism, and the individualities are subsumed to the needs of the group. That is why the emergence of any thinking is very poorly tolerated because it betrays the uniqueness of the messenger, and the group feels threatened. The basic assumption group is characterised by a search for satisfaction, denying the need to count on reality and putting in the effort of work. Its law is the avoidance of suffering; in this sense, it would function in accordance with the displeasure-pleasure principle. Trapped in omnipotent, magical thinking, comfort is found in the "group illusion" that Anzieu (1978) described. The denial of temporality is part of its trappings. Irresponsibility is the natural corollary, as in *Fuenteovejuna* by Lope de Vega (1562–1635). And paranoia lurks behind the denial of time and reality. It encourages passivity, laziness, parasitism, sensualism, or vandalism, as can be seen in some alternative groups.

The work group relates to reality, with temporality, and develops by learning from experience. Individuality emerges from the work group's experience and from the functioning of family life in a similar way to this group. Intimate relationships promote the development of personality. For that very reason, they are so different from relationships based on conditioning which favour the development of an exoskeleton (Bion) apt for adaptation. The family can function by fostering intimate relationships or deteriorate and function in accordance with the basic assumptions. In the latter case, it would then function like a non-family that coerces its members to a silent, delinquent loyalty or operate like a gang looting in the community. When the family functions as a container for the emotional needs of its members, symbolic development is promoted. Conversely, if deprived of intimate bonds and the experience of containment, the development of thought disorders, as observed in clinical practice with some groups suffering emotional and/or economic deprivation, is fostered.

So, whereas in Freud, *good* was pleasant, and in Klein, it was the object present, in Bion, good was, at the beginning, what made pain disappear. That is to say; food was good because it made the persecutory sensation of hunger disappear. Later on, in Bion's epistemological period, good became the object that contains pain and transforms impressions into alpha elements, apt for the development of thinking. *Bad* would be the object that strips something of meaning or sows lies.

Incorporating the model of the three links, Bion broadened the confrontation between mental/non-mental (work group/basic assumption group) to the fight between emotionality and anti-emotionality as the generator of symbolic development or of hypocrisy, passiveness, and anti-thinking derived from anti-emotionality.

The differentiation made by Max Scheler within "spiritual values" is not sustained by Bion because he considers the values of aesthetics and pure knowledge to be inseparable: falsehoods are as ugly as truth is beautiful.

1.2.2.4 Donald Meltzer

Meltzer takes up the heritage passed down by Freud, Klein, and Bion and goes a step further in value systems. For him, the gods no longer dwell in the temples but inside each of us. The object of contemplation and veneration will be a parental couple—that combined object composed of whole objects (male and female) that take care of each other, tolerate painful turmoil, and work with enjoyment, without denying the effort involved, in the development of children, and of thought and culture. The psyche is modelled after the family, with all of the emotionality and anti-emotionality of primary groups. Paternal-filial differentiations and separations will stir up conflict while promoting conundrums that will stimulate the development of the offspring. Because they need to recover from the fatigue brought on by their work, these parents periodically retire to their private space, where they restore one another through dialogue, play, and amorous encounters. Faced with the parents' private space, antagonistic possibilities appear: to imagine or invade. If they opt for imagination, they will be able to intuit and generate meanings and, in this way, discover amorous life; on the other hand, if they opt for invasion, the consequences will be harmful both for the object as well as for the invaders who will end up feeling omniscient. Conversely, if the children tolerate the privacy of the paternal couple well, they will feel reverential fear and jealousy at the door to their parent's room. Nevertheless, they will recognise and preserve their intimacy and conform to exercising their imagination to intuit the inscrutable nature of that encounter. On the other hand, if jealousy and resentment are too intense, the children will try to invade their parents' private space, in which case what they see will be transformed into pornography, leaving them confused and disoriented, unable to comprehend what they perceive.

When the pain that the object's mystery awakens is poorly tolerated, the subject can search for alternatives to avoid it. For instance, the work of learning can be avoided, or the subject can attempt to appropriate the admired qualities or want the ruin of the admired object and, in that vein, seek to belittle it. Whether the object is intrusively invaded, or hated parts of the subject are projected into it, the outcome is that the subject is left mutilated in its capacity to observe the external and internal worlds.

Meltzer considers truth to be the only thing that can free human beings from more primitive models of mental functioning that affect their judgement and guide their actions. The rectification of these models implies a transformation of values, because truth not only frees people from persecutory anxieties but necessarily imposes a love for both the inner and outer world with the consequent feeling of responsibility for the treatment given to objects (cf. Meltzer, 1978, pp. VIII–IX).

Responsibility for the world implies a concern for the state of not only one's own objects but also that of others. In this manner, if introjective identification predominates with parental functions, the adult will be concerned that the objects do not become damaged by the invasion of lies constructed to elude pain. The adult, despite trusting in the ancestral foundation of the internal objects gathered together in their heritage, fears not being capable enough to sustain the continuity of life; nevertheless, despite feeling moderately insecure, the adult is overall confident that the wisdom inherited and reconstructed will guide them well. Their concern arises from a fear of remaining very involved with the stimuli of external reality and that this prevents them from perceiving the inspiration proceeding from their internal objects.

From the concept of the *Aesthetic conflict* formulated by Meltzer (Meltzer and Harris Williams, 1988), suggestive ethical consequences are derived, and these intertwine with different spiritual values formulated by Max Scheler in his value system. The desire to understand the enigma of an object (mysteriously beautiful in the person of the mother-goddess) entails the desire to not alter it with lies or to degrade it with possession. With good objects, the same thing occurs as with temples: there is always the possibility that they can be desecrated. When a respectful attitude predominates, something akin to veneration, there is a desire to preserve the object's privacy, which makes it possible to curb the imperious and violent character of the most primitive desires. Additionally, when the desire to not invade the object prevails, the desire to recover what had become embedded in it arises. Then, acting in this way, and at the same time that the object is released or restored, there is a movement towards the reintegration of the self. Re-integrating what had been expelled both to liberate the object and to recover its own aspects, relieves the work of the internal objects in their task of mutual repair, a task that only they can perform. Recovering what had previously been projected and depositing it in a metabolising, internal container will allow for the clearing away of lies and truths, leading to a needed enrichment of the self. Therefore, according to this model, *good* is not only the object that is present, or the pleasant or the pleasing, but also and fundamentally that object-function that allows one to continue thinking. The much celebrated "know thyself" is again resignified within the psychic economy and, in this way, becomes a basic value. The development of the capacity to think and to self-analyse will not occur as much through rational development as through introjective identification with a combined object functioning as a work group in the service of metabolising emotional experiences. To avoid pain, perhaps defensive lies will be used to provide momentary numbness, but it is a ruinous business, as shown by the people trapped in schizoid types of functioning, or yet again, the omniscient know-it-alls. Although painful, the truth about oneself is more profitable than alternative paradises.

1.2.3 The Function of the Parental Object

An understanding of the stimulating capacity of the values became increasingly more complex and enriching with the contributions made by psychoanalysis. It is a journey that goes from the pure aspiration of pleasure to the feeling of responsibility. Thus, it becomes the territory of moral values, as Aranguren (1978) pointed out, where what is significant is the choice and realisation of other values.

Freud said that the ego becomes reasonable when it is capable of the postponement of pleasure and instead obeys the reality principle, which

> ...at bottom seeks to obtain pleasure, but pleasure which is assured through taking account of reality, even though it is pleasure that is postponed and diminished. The transition from the pleasure principle to the reality principle is one of the most important steps forward in the ego's development.
>
> (Freud, 1916, p. 356)

For the infant to be able to take on such a transition, they *need to feel supported by an object* that is capable of tolerating ambivalence. As Klein (1958, p. 5) says:

> There is an inherent need in the young child—and, I assume, even in the very young infant—to be protected as well as to be submitted to certain prohibitions, which amounts to a control of destructive impulses. I have recently suggested in my book *Envy and Gratitude*, that the infantile wish for an ever-present, inexhaustible breast includes the desire that the breast should do away with or control the infant's destructive impulses and in this way protect his good object as well as safeguard him against persecutory anxieties.

As I showed earlier, the object accrued increasingly new functions throughout the development of psychoanalytic thinking. The object that was present that gratified and controlled destructive impulses became, in Bionian thinking, the object that contains pain, thus making access to thinking a possibility. Meltzer (1999) added that the stimulus to development in children arises from the attractiveness of the parental couple. The couple's attractive and even fascinating character emerges from the mystery that originates in the relationship between two people, capable of generating projects. That is to say, imagining in the absence of the concrete/immediate, sustaining them—calibrating possibilities and tolerating difficulties—producing changes and not collapsing when faced with pain, but only searching for meaning. Along with admiration of the parental couple, rejection also exists because of jealousy that generates feelings of pettiness that can be felt when competition intensifies. Despite all of the ambivalence, this couple constitutes the greatest focus of attraction and interest in the subject's life and is the source of great suffering when not achieved in adulthood.

When facing the value of the internal couple, the narcissistic personality organisation that tries to seduce infantile parts and captain the immature ones, struggles against the construction of a family in the internal world, with serious repercussions to personality development and the development of thinking and values, these are topics that will be taken up in the following pages.

1.2.4 The Combined Object as an Ethics Ideal

Various different types of combined objects exist. These objects can either describe a monstrous object (cf. Klein) or a good model (cf. Meltzer). The representation is monstrous when the combination between objects (part or whole) is at the service of the parents' autoerotic, narcissistic, and exhibitionist satisfactions, with the aim of projecting envy, frustration, and neediness into offspring. This monstrous object can either be built on the basis of the stimuli provided by immature or troubled parents, fundamentally exhibitionist and/or abusers, or on the intolerance of insatiable children.

The combined object can be an ethical ideal in the service of life when it is constituted as a work group. In the latter, pleasure is associated with the task, the construction, and games, including sexual games, both genital and pregenital. Also, the encounter with the other is characterised by respect for the freedom of both parties and implies as much separation as it excludes domination, tyranny, slavery, degradation or other forms of violence.

The model that underlies this way of understanding the combined object is that of the relationship between container and contained (Bion, 1970), in which both members of the relationship function as a container for the other, in which both come out winning, enriched with new qualities and truths felt to be the best nutrient for their development. The combined object functions as an ethical ideal when there is mutual availability to become the container of the other member of the couple.

For this combined object to be constructed and introjected as an ethical ideal, many roads must be traversed without knowing about the opposition that comes from the infantile parts that usually organise themselves in a guerrilla war against the object. It is not strange that the beauty of the object be felt to be something so dazzling that it becomes overwhelming to the point where, in order to tolerate the encounter, some kind of protection is required; this protection must be differentiated from the opposition or resistance that comes from the infantile parts of the personality that refuse to abandon the pleasure principle.

Below I present some examples of this resistance of the infantile parts to assuming the model of the combined object as a working group (Bion).

In every fight, the most vulnerable flank of the adversary is usually targeted; in this case, the weakest point of a couple may be the *bond* between the two, which is why we try to split it. The metaphor of the insidious serpent sowing doubt abounds in the literature of jealousy and family struggles.

To continue with this somewhat bellicose vocabulary, the first weapon to take up against bonds is *dissociation*, as seen in the *separation between words and their emotional content*. Once achieved, words can be used without any emotional or ethical repercussions. At that point, the intention becomes the negotiation of everything, to the point that wars can only be valued based on the number of dead that one is willing to tolerate. In this war, only quantities and statistics are relevant. With this split, it is easy to construct logically organised discourses that become verbal attacks that make thinking difficult and can easily cause confusion. Whatever is easy increases in value.

Resentful infantile parts have a decidedly political vocation. For that reason, they become devoted to making propaganda to obtain votes and impose trickery based on quantity, as if this could become the basis for thought. That dedication to propaganda is based on the insecurity and arrogance of the childish parts that feel prodded to hide behind numbers as if they were truths. The problem is compounded when they form pressure groups because they can take over the media to spread their biased truths by creating opinion and anti-thought through propaganda.

Another dissociation manifests itself in the separation between a *sensation and the experience of satisfaction*, as can be observed in the case of eating disorders, where the experience of assimilating is not perceived. This dissociation can lead to a passive and hedonistic sensualism that ensnares more than a few adolescents. If this splitting is combined with an unreachable ideal, it can all lead to living a pseudo-infancy as prolonged in time as can be found in some adults who embrace a hairless aesthetic and dress as if they were children. For these infantile adults, value is what they feel to be pleasant, and their irritation is intense when they become frustrated. Anchored in the pleasure principle, they try to live on the margins of time. When they perceive their peers to have experiences that seem impossible to them, such as having children and taking care of them, they isolate themselves and take refuge in specular groups that hide reality from them. The grotesque lurks in their use of fashion and their adolescent interests.

When the family is made up of pseudo-adults, an alteration can be observed in the task of the combined object. If the specific task, carried out in privacy, is to care for and develop children—whether babies or works of art—the infantile parts may consider *the task as an exhibition*. It would be easier to understand through the resentful complaint,[8] that was not baseless, of a patient who said: "My father took care of us when he wanted to show us off, to photograph us and be seen as the head of the family" (see Section 3.1.2.3). Functioning to the exclusive benefit of oneself is characteristic of infantile parts of the personality, as in the case of the man who wanted to perpetuate himself. The use of the object is closer to mercantile values rather than a true ethical attitude towards one's children. For example, the same can be found in the world of architecture, where some architects are more concerned with creating an object to be admired than to be lived in, as if they were proposing buildings to be photographed. There would be no concern in creating a container capable of accommodating contents in its interior. This type of corruption is based on exhibition values whose intention is to bewitch and dominate. The natural corollary of the dilemma between the care and use of the object is the feeling of abandonment, as experienced in large families where access to the mother is a chimaera similar to sharing time with parents.

One way of devaluing the combined object as an ethical ideal is to *deny differences*. In the name of equality and democracy, an attempt is made to eliminate the differences between the adult and the child, between masculine and feminine, good and bad, healthy and ill, etc. Differences are considered to be harmful without notice taken of how much more devastating confusion can be. The need for some of these revindications arises from the existing confusion between collaboration and dominance; not infrequently, domestic violence is confused with gender-based violence. Bernarda Alba's (García Lorca) violence was not very different from Medea's (Euripides) or Pinochet's. Violence is violence independently of the executioner's hand and the degree of cruelty involved. Violence is exercised in a home when dependent children are abandoned, tyrannised, ignored, or used to the benefit of the adults ("Mother Courage" in Brecht), or when confused children tyrannise, exploit, and subjugate their parents. Violence manifests itself in multiple ways. A subtle but appalling way is to standardise all the members of the family group, making them colleagues, friends, or flatmates. If everyone is the same, specific functions of the family will not be fulfilled, above all if there are children. The family can deteriorate and behave more like an antisocial gang where the children will suffer the consequences.

Yet another form of violence becomes evident when a person is used as a prosthesis for a personal deficit. This can be seen, for example, in the interplay of functions and roles that develop in the family group. In any couple, one of the two can colonise and use the other to the benefit of a fault in the personality organisation of one of its members. It is not odd that immature types of functioning take root in a confusing environment. Whether due to an intolerance of the filial position vis-à-vis the parental couple, or to a manic need to create it when absent, children are often trapped in types of functioning that make their development difficult. A consequence of these alternatives can be observed when a child manages to penetrate into the parental couple and ends up lost in a manic pseudo-existence, as occurred with Ausiàs, who, in his 30s, came to see me.

1.2.5 Ausiàs, the Combined Object

In our first meeting, Ausiàs told me that he was bisexual but could not manage to establish himself in a stable relationship because he became anguished. He had many different girlfriends and a boyfriend with whom he had lived, without being able to commit. He expressed how in his relationships, he seemed to evaporate, to disappear. His ability to express himself was as rich as it was impossible to connect with him. "I give of myself, but nobody can reach me", he said.

> I have a way with words. I'm in public relations in a multinational, and I speak various languages fluently. My parents wanted to give the image of a conventional family, where there was a man and a woman, but reversed. My mother worked and supported the family, and my father took care of me, woke me up, bathed me, and took me to school; he used to sleep naked with me.

This was a conventional family but reversed, that is to say, an absent mother that left the child to a sensually aroused father who was also probably confused about his identity.

Ausiàs had a frenetic work life, always rushing around and intent on balancing his earnings with his expenses. Paying for a session that he had lost was something that irritated him to no end and awakened persecutory anxieties of being abused.

His agitation was neither a good ally for introspection nor for thinking. There was no time to lose. That is why he always looked out for signs that immediately acquired meaning. Therefore, when he wanted to distinguish between his homo- or heterosexual identity, he looked for signs of excitation both in other men, for example, at the gym, or in himself. If he became aroused with another man, this indicated that he was homosexual. The meaning of things was *obvious* and did not require any investigation.

From a position of anxious omniscience, he rejected my interpretations because he already had a reply to everything. In this respect, Meltzer underlined in supervision the

> simple vision of the world that he had, his childish way of thinking. It is a world of excitation or of the lack of excitation that is indicated by the presence or absence of his erections in his penis and his nipple.

In his binary functioning, emotions and their meanings were replaced by the presence or absence of excitation. His frenetic functioning was motivated by his need to maintain his balance—a balance that could be upset by any unexpected event. He needed an obsessive balance, far from the mature person who considers different vertices.

When treatment began, he established a relationship with a woman whom he idealised and whose domestic expenses he financed. This led him to make a greater effort to "balance his economy". In this way, he fled from the resolution of his obsessive pseudo-maturity, moving towards a repetition of the pseudo-family in which he felt himself to be the centre of gravity. Ausiàs functioned like a juggler who maintains the balance with his partner in the same way that as a child, he had to feel like the articulator of family life, the object that combined everything.

A dream contributed to disentangling his phantasy of being a combined object in the middle of the family stage. In his dream, "a young man was on the stage, and suddenly unbuttoned his shirt to show a pair of breasts". This dream acquires more meaning in the light of children's stories, such as the following: he slept between his parents in such a manner that his father spooned him from behind, and the patient, in turn, spooned around his mother from behind. Meltzer's comment was that Ausiàs was

> …on the verge of discovering the combined object, but he doesn't succeed because he's so convinced that his dad is a homosexual that wants to anally penetrate the child and that he's not at all interested in mummy to form a combined object […] He's is the young man who unbuttons his shirt to reveal that he's got a pair of breasts. He's bisexual. There's no combined object because he combines everything. That's why when you try to clarify things for him … you run into his denial of psychic reality. He cannot think because to think is to be accompanied by an object, the more combined, the better, but he being the combined object, produces words in spurts, thinking in terms of quantities, not meanings. The value system here is that of an accountant's balance.

Here Meltzer takes up again the proud opinion of the patient about having a way with words and the precision with which he expressed himself and polemicised. That is why he said that Ausiàs

> …doesn't manage to make the change from thinking in quantities to thinking in qualities […] It's important to see the element of grandiosity that lies behind this concept of black and white, and of precision, the quantitative arithmetic. Nowadays, when this grandiosity is clothed in the language of computers and physical sciences, etc., it is difficult to reduce it; we live in a culture of quantities, of balancing the economy.

The value system based on balancing black and white in which everything is reduced to quantitative considerations is pure *vulgarity*, with all of the *cynicism* that this entails. Vulgarity and cynicism are two terms that are almost synonyms. Vulgarity means something that lacks novelty and importance, truth or foundation, so the term "vulgo" refers to all people who know nothing but the surface of each matter. This is not dissimilar to the meaning of *cynic*, that in Oscar Wilde's opinion (1854–1900), is someone who knows the price of everything but gives value to nothing. For this reason, Meltzer said that Ausiàs was "a vulgar character who doesn't think, who has a way with words and who believes that his tongue is the testicles of the world". Far from being an ethical model. A precise description of cynicism is found in the effects of the anti-links (-L, -H, -K) (cf. Meltzer, 2004). When puritanism predominates (-L) with its rejection of intimate relationships, hypocrisy (-H) and its essential pretence, and philistinism (-K) with the systematic rejection of new ideas, there is no alternative but vulgarity, superficiality, and quantity.

The term cynic has, in addition, other connotations; it names not only vulgar people but also those that do not trust others, that live their lives scorning and/or doubting human nature or the goodness or sincerity of others. In this sense, Ausiàs did not trust my analytic dedication and thought my interest lay in "buying myself a car with the money I took from him" as if mechanically repeating the phantasy that he put in the mother what he had taken from the father. In a world not based on amorous exchange but rather on the bartering of part objects, there is no place for emotions, responsibility, or meaning. Everything is reduced to quantities, like the accounted excitations.

Ausiàs felt unstable in the pseudo-position of functioning as an omniscient combined object (my thinking was passed on to his girlfriend) because, by his unconscious strategy, he should be possessed and dominated by the analyst/father. His life was spent between scepticism about relationships in general and entrapment in a statistical world that prevented him from accessing the emotional world in which values are born.

Ausiàs' way of functioning, based on the quantitative, the factual, the concrete, and the immediate, is characteristic of the opposition to knowledge. Opposition is present at all times, although it seems to characterise the current culture of liquid values.

1.2.6 Respect-Responsibility

If the subject of values in psychoanalysis is expanded by the model of relationship Ps↔D formulated by Klein, it is Bion who, by introducing O as an unachievable goal, broadened the margins for a theory of values based on a quest. It is a quest without knowing "where the path will lead".[9] Adults will recognise that the only path consists of continuing to walk under the inspiration of the internal objects in continual remodelling, development, or deterioration. On the contrary, the childish parts will insistently want to find shortcuts to reaching a goal by avoiding pain, without losing possessions that have already been achieved, and following already travelled paths in a clearly conservative attitude.

The concept of "Aesthetic conflict" (Cf. Meltzer and Harris Williams) shows that the encounter with the (bright/opaque, beautiful/ugly, alive/dead) object, always complex and mysterious, can only count on the company and inspiration of the internal objects. Whereas previously it was thought that the absent object gave rise to anxiety, and there were attempts to set that in stone; nowadays it is pointed out that anxiety is caused by the object that is present—always similar in its outer appearance, but whose states of mind will always be unknown. Each encounter raises a question regarding the reality of the object: the state it is in, its motivations, and its intentions. There are no longer certainties in the path that must be walked every day. Experience weaves a mesh that guides the reading of the object's signs. Faced with so many challenges, defensive strategies arise, such as the attempt to decompose the complexity and simplify the object even if the apparatus of consciousness has to be dismantled, and the poor result of slogans, clichés, and superficiality, which last as fleetingly as a sigh. Ausiàs tried to quantify, control, possess, purchase, and count to elude the challenge of understanding his complex family and mental organisation. The relationship with his heterosexual partner appeared to be more in the service of fleeing from a history of abandonment than a desire to discover the mystique of women, of his girlfriend, as a separate person. Ausiàs was far-off from the passionate falling in love that he was seeking. Trachtenberg (2005) says that "passion, related to the hidden interior of the aesthetic object invites us to make love, to explore the possible". Making love is, however, the opposite of possessing one's love object, in the same way that discovery is the antithesis of possession. To have.... the price of everything but not understand value... To have or be/being: this is an ethical alternative.

The possession of knowledge can bring with it a placid sensation, typical of bourgeois latency, while assuming the task of sustaining the object's interrogation dislodges it from the safe position and beckons discovery and risk. A simplified, possessed object is an object without respect. On the contrary, an ethical attitude based on the consideration of the object implies assuming the limitation (castration) of only having approximations of reality; that is why I agree with Trachtenberg (2005) when he says that

> ... the aesthetic conflict, in its dimension of mystery, carries the notion of respect with an ethical-aesthetic connotation that distances it from its habitual impregnations for morality. Bion (1974/1975) says that mystery is defined by the capacity to feel respect for the unknown, the capacity to not become so frightened of what we do not know.

On the other hand, when Nemas (2005) states that "responsibility is the central category of ethics", I believe that he is picking up the Kleinian and Lévinasian legacy; while agreeing with this, I propose another essential element for a *combined object of ethics*: admiring consideration, capable of forming the team of *respect and responsibility*. A team that is capable of becoming inspired by the recognised values and which does not ignore the silent but ubiquitous alternative of anti-link solvents (-H, -K, -L).

To look at reality from the "respect-responsibility" pair means looking at it considering its complexity and mystery, without infantile simplification, obsessive possession, perverse mutilation, or dementalising dismantling. Just as the amazement of the pre-Socratics was the origin of philosophy, the greater or lesser tolerance to the complexity of the world opens up possibilities for values and disvalues to germinate.

Notes

1 This chapter comprises a paper entitled *Los sistemas de valores de la realidad psíquica*, published in *Intercambios. Papeles de psicoanálisis*, N° 14, June 2005, Barcelona, pp. 51–61, along with another paper entitled *Grupo familiar (externo-interno) y ética*, published in *Psicopatología y salud mental*, Sant Boi, Barcelona, 2011, 17, pp. 83–92.
2 Not just death, but rather *my* death that triggers the horror of dying alone, with no assistance as recently occurred with victims of the Coronavirus pandemic. In the face of total helplessness, the solidary presence of the other becomes more urgent.
3 "Responsibility that is not the deprivation of knowledge of understanding and apprehension, but the excellence of ethical proximity in its sociality, in its love without concupiscence" (Lévinas, op. cit., p. 106).
4 Irreflexive, non-mental.
5 Respect even the very same fictional characters, as MYSELF, a character from *A Memoir of the Future* demands: "I indicate without definition, that the opinions expressed by me, even if fiction, are worthy of being treated with respect" (Bion, 1991, p. 95).
6 The identification can also be structured on the rejection of the experienced models.
7 "Society was now based on complicity in the common crime; religion was based on the sense of guilt and the remorse attaching to it; while morality was based partly on the exigencies of this society and partly on the penance demanded by the sense of guilt" (Freud, 1912, p. 170).
8 In this complaint, it is important to differentiate between frustration based on real experiences and frustration based on the struggle of the narcissistic parts against object dependence (Cf. Meltzer, 1967, p. 79).
9 *Yo voy soñando caminos*, poem by Antonio Machado (1875–1939).

Bibliography

Anzieu, D. (1978): *El grupo y el inconsciente*, Madrid, Biblioteca Nueva.
Aranguren, J. L. (1978): Ética, Madrid, Revista de Occidente.
Beckett, S. (1957): *Fin de Partie*. Paris, Les Éditions de Minuit. 1993. Translated from the original French by the author, *Endgame*, London-Boston, MA, Faber and Faber Limited, 1988.
Bion, W. R. (1991): "The dream", in *A Memoir of the Future*, London, Karnac Books.
Ducach, P. & Tabbia, C. (2003): "Los sistemas de valores del sado-masoquismo: la fascinación por el poder, la Ley del Talión y la supervivencia", in *Más allá del Principio del Placer. Sobre masoquismo, el desinvestimiento y la destructividad*, Barcelona, Gradiva, pp. 54–61.
Ferrater Mora, J. (1966): *Diccionario de filosofía*, Buenos Aires, Ed. Sudamericana.

Freud, S. (1895): "Project for a scientific psychology", in *The Origins of Psycho-Analysis*, edited by Marie Bonaparte, Anna Freud and Ernst Kris, London, Imago Publishing Co, pp. 347–445, 1954.

Freud, S. (1911): "Formulations on the two principles of mental functioning", in The Standard Edition of the Complete Psychological Works of Sigmund Freud, edited by J. Strachey, London, Hogarth Press, 1966, Vol XII, pp. 218–226.*The*

Freud, S. (1912): *Totem and Taboo*, London, Routledge, 1950.

Freud, S. (1914): *On Narcissism: An Introduction*, London, Karnac, 1991.

Freud, S. (1916): "Introductory lectures on psycho-analysis", in The Standard Edition of the Complete Psychological Works of Sigmund Freud, edited by J. Strachey, London, Hogarth Press, 1966, Vol XVI, pp. 1–463.

Freud, S. (1921): *Group Psychology and the Analysis of the Ego*, London, The Hogarth Press, 1949.Freud, S. (1929): *Civilization and Its Discontents*, London, Penguin Books, 2004.

Freud, S. & Breuer, J. (1895): "Studies on hysteria", in The Standard Edition of the Complete Psychological Works of Sigmund Freud, edited by J. Strachey, London, Hogarth Press, 1966, Vol II, pp. 1–306.

Frondizi, R. (1958): ¿Qué son los valores?, México, FCE, XV ed. 1999.

Kaës, R. (1999): *Las teorías psicoanalíticas del grupo*, Buenos Aires, Amorrortu ed. 2000.

Klein, M. (1957): *Envy and Gratitude and Other Works 1946–1963*, edited by M. Masud R. Khan New York, The Free Press, A Division of Simon & Schuster, 1975.

Klein, M. (1958): "On the development of mental functioning", *International Journal of Psychoanalysis*, 39, 84–90.

Kristeva, J. (2000): *Female Genius. Melanie Klein*, New York, Columbia University Press, 2001.

Lévinas, E. (1982): "Ética como Filosofía Primera", A Parte Rei. Revista de Filosofía, 43, Enero 2006, pp. 67–108. Palabras Preliminares: Oscar Lorca Gómez, http://serbal.pntic. mec.es/AParteRei/

Meltzer, D. (1967): *The Psycho-Analytical Process*, London, William Heinemann Medical Books Limited.

Meltzer, D. (1978a): *The Collected Paper of Roger Money-Kyrle*, Scotland, Clunie Press.

Meltzer, D. (1978b): *The Kleinian Development*, London, Karnac, 2008.

Meltzer, D. (1992): *The Claustrum. An Investigation of Claustrophobic Phenomena*, Strath-Clyde, The Clunie Press.

Meltzer, D. (1999): *Clinical Seminars in the Psychoanalytic Group of Barcelona* (unpublished).

Meltzer, D. (2004): *Transfert, Adolescenza, Disturbi del pensiero. Mutamenti nel metodo psicoanalitico*, a cura del Gruppo di Studio Racker di Venezia, Roma, Armando editore, 2004, pp. 19–23.

Meltzer, D. & Harris, M. (1998): *Adolescentes*, edited by L. Jachevasky & C. Tabbia, Buenos Aires, ed. Spatia.

Meltzer, D. & Harris Williams, M (1988): *The Apprehension of Beauty: The Role of Aesthetic Conflict in Development, Art, and Violence*, London, Karnac, 2008.

Nemas, Cl. (2000): "Development is beauty, growth is ethics", in *Exploring the Work of Donald Meltzer*, edited by M. Cohen and A. Hahn, London, Karnac Books, pp. 27–42.

Nemas, Cl. (2005). El conflicto estético en el área de los valores, www.grupopsicoanaliti-cobarcelona.org

Paciuk, S. (1995): "De los valores en la cura", en Ética y psicoterapia, M. Lucrecia Rovaletti (Editora), Buenos Aires, Ed. Biblos, pp. 105–117.

Tabbia, C. (2003): "Los valores en la clínica", *Intercambios, Papeles de psicoanálisis*, Barcelona, Junio, pp. 53–65.

Trachtenberg, R. (2005): "De la pasión por el psicoanálisis al psicoanálisis de la pasión", *Revista Chilena de Psicoanálisis*, 22(2), pp. 185–193.

Vorchheimer, M. (1997): "Pensando con Freud acerca del Ideal del Yo", Buenos Aires, *Rev. de la Asoc. Escuela de Psicoterapia para Graduados*, 23, pp. 213–232.

Chapter 2

Elements of a Post-Kleinian Nosology

When Freud (1937) stated that the objectives of psychoanalysis consisted of freeing people from their neurotic symptoms, inhibitions, and character anomalies, he had not only constructed the bases of psychoanalysis and indicated its areas of intervention and methods but had also opened the gates to an "interminable" exploration of the unconscious. Abraham, Ferenczi, Klein, and Bion, to only name some of the great psychoanalysts that contributed to this task of freeing not only people but also the very same psychoanalysis from its limitations as a new discipline. Each one of these contributors fertilised it (Parthenope Bion, 2011) and offered a vision of psychoanalysis. It was not only them who attempted to define an object of study; one could say, with no qualms, that each and every psychoanalyst, consciously or unconsciously, defines their psychoanalysis, their aim (cure? foster personality development?), their field of application, their methods and allies: medicine, psychiatry, philosophy, and education. For example, Meltzer (1967, p. xiv) delimited the field of psychoanalysis and even claimed new diagnostic categories when he said: "Embracing an area somewhere in the triangle between psychological medicine, education and child-rearing, it seems ready to develop a nosology, prognostic system, and method of evaluation of progress separate from the clinical descriptive method used by psychiatry". By framing this triangle, he aimed to create a nosology and a method of purely psychoanalytic prognosis, far from an ontological psychiatry[1] of an organic basis. The psychoanalytic model of personality thinks about ill patients rather than illness, as Foucault (1958, p. 7) put it when he said "illness was seen as an intrinsic alteration of the personality, an internal disorganization of its structures, a gradual deviation of its development; It had reality and meaning only within a structured personality". For that reason, a psychoanalytic nosology[2] is not a simple nomenclature of technical voices, nor can it be reduced to a classification of illnesses, instead, it describes the present and active elements in a state of mind. Just as nosology[3] names the theoretical knowledge of a disease or the internal disorganisation of the structures of a personality, nosology classifies them (Lázaro, 2013).

In order to move ahead to the description of the elements needed to understand a person, I will begin by referring to the concept of personality structure to go on later to talking about the states of mind. Without a model of mental structure, it is

DOI: 10.4324/9781003347156-5

difficult to grasp one's own state of mind as well as someone else's, and above all, when this state of mind is disturbed or disorganised. Not only do various different models of mental structure exist, but everyone has also their own model, whether noticed or unnoticed.

The differentiation of mind/brain and the conception of the mind as a structure were discoveries that were fundamental to understanding psychic functioning in general and the alterations of the personality and the disorganisation of internal structures in an ill person. Segal (2001) underlines the great merit of Freud's discovery of the mind in the first topic, as a three-strata structure (conscious, preconscious, and unconscious) as well as for the second topic, incorporating the superego, the ego, and the id (ibid., p. 157), and says: "the psychic world, like the physical world, can be studied in terms of elements, or parts, combining into a structure. This can become a subject of detailed study of the different parts and their interactions". This allowed for the Freudian model of mental structure to become more comprehensive when Klein introduced internal objects, their qualities, and relationships, in accordance with the model of positions, giving rise to a representation of mental structure as an assembly or population of internal objects. It becomes still more wide-reaching with Bion's considerations of the mind seen in his masterful presentation of the same in *A Memoir of the Future*:

> ...a big stage on which is performed not the drama of six characters in search of an author, but of the author grappling with a crowd of mental parts, each of which rises to become a character in its own right, in fact allows a glimpse of a conceptualisation of the mental structure that is much more chaotic than the Freudian one. The mental elements, at least when they have the status of α-elements, seem to enjoy a notable mobility, moving between conscious and unconscious—Bion had, however, eliminated the preconscious from his own theoretical baggage, considering it superfluous—and the ego or superego functions seem to be subdivided among different agencies of the personality— Myself, Bion, Psychoanalyst and Priest, to indicate only a few. Perhaps it might be argued that the dinosaurs Albert Stegosaurus and Adolf Tyrannosaurus also express aspects of the id.
>
> (Parthenope Bion, 2011, p. 110)

Meg Harris Williams (1983) aptly used the term "internal voices" for those mental elements that claim a place in the present, always polarised between a saurian and prenatal past and an unnamed future; voices that were not always in harmony with one another, capable of converging on thought as well as detaching themselves in alternative and antagonistic worlds. In the same way that the different voices of a choir contribute to artistic creation, the elements of the personality can articulate themselves for the development of the personality depending on the interplay of the positive and negative links (L, H, K). The originality and the quality of the creation do not depend only on the materials but more so on what they were transformed into. When intolerance to mental pain seriously hinders normal development, these pathological structures that are created are so out of tune that harmonic polyphony is no longer possible; these structures are anchored in immovable fixation points (Freud), or mired in the impossibility of accessing depressive functions (Klein), or of being transformed from beta elements by the alpha function (Bion).

Observing the elements of the personality in their mutual relationship not only allows for a nosological consideration (that from the present observes the past) but also opens the doors to considering the possible change (from the present towards the future) of the structure. Freud did not only discover—says Segal (op. cit. pp. 83–84)—that structures

> ...are the result of dynamic conflicting forces; not only forces in the past, defining a structure once and for all; he also saw it as something happening in the present, that is, that the same forces which were responsible for setting up the structure continue to maintain it. The implication of this is that if the interplay of those forces changes, there is a possibility of a change in the structure, and this, of course, is essential from the point of view of therapeutic possibilities.

This would be the space for *prognosis*, demanded by Meltzer.

The suggestion that we approach the patient without memory, desire, or a zealous search to understand aims at preparing us to be surprised by their *states of mind*. Morales (2004) says that it may happen that if we go looking for Oedipus "often it will be Narcissus who opens the door, and Narcissus, instead of being an arrogant and unpleasant individual who complicates poor Oedipus' life, will be a tormented beggar who has had no luck in life".

Hence, the need for that negative capacity (Bion) that allows us to find without searching. Find the state of mind that remains behind the manifest data. In this regard, Bion's warning (1970, p. 57), when he said that, although it can

> ...be precisely stated that the patient is married and has four children it is not easily stated that his state of mind is that of a married man with four children because there is no such state of mind. Furthermore, such a 'memory', and the remembrancer that such a note would provide, would greatly obscure observation of the patient's state of mind suppose it were to be more nearly what one might expect of a bachelor.

For instance, Laius was far from being a father; his state of mind was much closer to being a confused, terrified, self-centred man.

With the term *state of mind*, the emotional condition is mentioned, the way that this person feels at this time, and how that may change when elements of their personality vary. The characterisation of "state" is opposed to "being like this", which would be more characteristic of an essentialist conception of symptoms and of illness. Referring to "states" correlates with "personality structures" and this, with "the relationship between his elements"; for example, a grandiose state of mind can correlate with intrusive identification in an idealised internal object.

One characteristic of states of mind is their transience and dynamism, except in chronic states; but even in severe mental disorders, transient states can manifest as long as there are parts of the personality that are not completely committed to the disorder and can function based on non-psychotic identifications. The transience of states of mind allows the differentiation with *psychic reality*, as Cecilia Muñoz expresses it (2011, p. 41):

> States of mind will be the direct consequences of the configuration of the internal space, of characters, of the relationship between them and with the self, but they would differ from psychic reality in that more than a world and a stage with actors and actions, they are momentary ways of looking at the world and assuming and expressing values, reacting emotionally through transitory states of mind, that are expressed verbally or through gestures.

States of mind express psychic reality.

The differentiation between states of mind[4] contributes to the creation of a psychoanalytic nosology because they express the type of relationship (projective, introjective) maintained with parental objects, which is the basis of the personality. I believe, like Klein[5] (1960), that one of the elements of the well-integrated personality is *emotional maturity*, and that mature states of mind or their alternative, which includes psychopathological states, account for the degrees of personality integration to which I will refer in the following pages.

Immaturity is not explained with a tautological definition: lacking maturity. It is also not circumscribed to a minor, like a child. As a state of mind, it names a person split and caught in the struggle between adult and child parts to achieve control of the organ of consciousness. The value of this organ is that it allows access to motility. The infantile parts governed by the pleasure principle and trapped in paranoid-schizoid ways of functioning, distant from the feeling of responsibility, fight against these others that are capable of functioning according to the reality principle; for these adult parts, access to motility entails a feeling of responsibility. Not infrequently, one observes people who are capable of functioning in parallel worlds—responsible in the professional sphere of their lives and profoundly infantile in their emotional relationships.

Unlike *immaturity*, *maturity* struggles for the integration of emotions and anti-emotions, for the working through of primitive and neurotic anxieties in favour of a minimally dissociated personality. The mature person is guided by goals and prioritises thinking above immediate gratification. The mature person does not fear depending on other people because the mature individual does not feel omnipotent or omniscient and is not frightened of merging with the other or being host to a parasitic other. In this sense, it would be appropriate to mention the differentiation that Fairbairn (1952, p. 145) made between infantile dependence characterised by "a one-sided attitude of incorporation" and a yearning for emotional identification with the feeding object and mature dependence that is "characterized by a capacity on the part of a differentiated individual for co-operative relationships with differentiated objects". Differentiating immaturity from maturity does not mean that they are mutually or totally exclusive.

> Some measure of infantile dependence—says Fairbairn (ibid, p. 281)— may be revealed in the case of the most 'normal' individual. The truth is that emotional maturity is never absolute but always a matter of degree. Infantile dependence is equally a matter of degree, never being entirely absent, but being subject to an infinite degree of variation from individual to individual.

As said elsewhere (Tabbia et al., 1973):

> Mature dependence is characterised by the full differentiation of the ego and the object (overcoming primary identification) and, therefore, for the capacity to value the object for itself, and to give as well as to receive. This is expressed physically in the ability to maintain truly genital relationships that represent mutual cooperation and the act of giving in a couple whose two members are equal. Thus, the adult is not mature because they are genital, but rather because they are capable of maintaining proper genital relationships because they are mature.

Meltzer formulated a similar construction of emotional maturity when he relates introjective identification with differentiated parents and functioning as a "work team" (Bion) capable of dedicating themselves to the development of children and culture. From that identification, a search continues for objects that merit admiration to be introjected, broadening the aspirational field of internal objects functioning as an ego ideal. The dependence on these internal objects, far from humiliating them, protects them and stimulates them towards responsible autonomy.

The path to maturity, ever in reconstruction, has its conditions that Meltzer (1967, p. 22) summarises in *The Psycho-analytical process* when he refers to the resolution of geographical confusions or of the subject-object differentiation:

> ...the resolution of this configuration of object relation stands as the border between mental illness (psychosis) and mental health, just as the resolution of the obstacles to the dependent introjective relation to the breast traverses the border between mental instability and mental stability, and as the passing of the Oedipus complex leads from immaturity to maturity.

Maturity is therefore based on the differentiation of parental objects and the recognition of their private relationship. Introjective identification with the combined object will allow access to fully genital relationships.

Formulated in this way, the mature state of mind is something under permanent conquest. It becomes an oscillating state, like the tides, that depends on the state of the internal objects and their mutual relationship. Thus, a mature state of mind is considered a model of mental health. It would be worthwhile to question oneself regarding the limits between health and illness. When facing mental suffering and conflicts, defensive mechanisms—or lies, as Bion called them—are available to regulate or deny them. Meltzer spoke of modulating anxiety. The more massive and far-reaching the defence, the more we penetrate into the terrain of pathological structures.

There are three pathological personality organisations that I will now present because of their resemblance in how they manifest and for sharing a feeling of inexistence or fraudulence: the *false self* (Winnicott), *pseudo-maturity* (Meltzer), and the *exoskeleton* (Bion).

Winnicott (1967) states that those who have felt helplessness, traumatism, and wounds have had to build unconscious defences such as:

> ...organize a false-self front to cope with the world, this false front being a de-
> fence designed to protect the true self. (The true self has been traumatized and it
> must never be found and wounded again.) Society is easily taken in by the false-
> self organisation, and has to pay heavily for this. The false self, from our point
> of view here, though a successful defence, is not an aspect of health. It merges
> into the Kleinian concept of a manic defence.

The false self as a defence arises from projective identification into an object capable of functioning, allowing for feeling a certain degree of capability. Because it is the result of this omnipotent phantasy (projective identification), and therefore without mourning, it creates a feeling of fraudulence, of appearing to be real but finally experimenting a sensation of inauthenticity and of not being known by anybody. It is an inefficient defence in moments of need, as the very same Winnicott (1960, p. 142) says in another of his texts:

> ...the False Self sets up as real and it is this that observers tend to think is the
> real person. In living relationships, work relationships, and friendships, how-
> ever, the False Self begins to fail. In situations in which what is expected is a
> whole person the False Self has some essential lacking. At this extreme the True
> Self is hidden.

The person who defends themselves with a false self pays the high price of being excluded from intimate relationships and emotional development, although this person can overcompensate with intellectual development.

Given the difficulties to establish mature dependence, and in the face of longing for infantile dependence, as indicated by Fairbairn, the alternative arises of confounding oneself with the object. This narcissistic defence finds new expression in the omnipotent phantasy of penetrating into the internal object. If Klein (1946) formulated the phantasy of projective identification in the external object, Meltzer (1965) extends it, through projective identification, to the internal object from which the subject relates to the external world. Intrusive identification into the internal object, specifically in its different compartments, numbs the subject to the anxiety of separation from the admired/envied object and will elude the working through of the oedipal problem, but the outcome will be a *pseudo-mature* state of mind that in children generates, "…a pre-oedipal (ages 2–3) crystallisation of character manifest by docility, helpfulness, preference for adult companionship, aloofness or bossiness with other children, intolerance of criticism, and high verbal capacity" (Meltzer, 1965, p. 16). In adults, it generates

> The feeling of fraudulence as an adult person, the sexual impotence or pseudo-potency (excited by secret perverse fantasies), the inner loneliness and the basic confusion between good and bad, all create a life of tension and lack of satisfaction, bolstered, or rather compensated, only by the smugness and snobbery which are an inevitable accompaniment of the massive projective identification.
>
> (ibid.)

The confusion of identity derived from intrusive identification not only alters the perception of identity and time but also entails the painful experience of losing vital time (see Section 3.1.5).

The pseudo-mature person lives in a pseudo-reality, without becoming fully delusional, as "seen in so many cases of borderline psycho-pathology" (Meltzer, 1967, p. 40).

Just as the false self affords protection to the true self from possible wounds, the pseudo-maturity defends against all those differentiations that expose it to frustrations, an exoskeleton[6] (Bion) safeguards against new ideas or uninvited curiosity towards our internal world. When the subject feels fragile and without solidity based on the introjective identification with parental functions, it covers itself with a structure or artificial shell in the style of animals that have no shell and depend entirely for their very subsistence on the hardness that covers them; hardness that can be seen in fanatical ways of functioning (see Section 3.2.2) that defend against the danger of breakdown. As with all defences, the exoskeleton entails disadvantages[7] similar to the state of mind that derives from living in intrusive identification—that of a pseudo-existence far removed from emotionality, and therefore from development. As Meltzer (1989) pointed out,

> the exoskeleton of the personality is only capable of maintaining casual or contractual relationships and not intimate relationships. It operates primarily in the mode of a computer, by mimicry and not by emotionality and thinking, and its social relationships are essentially precarious and completely insincere.

These people, because they live inwardly, in a world almost entirely lacking stimuli, have been forbidden access to curiosity in the style of those "post-natals unable to learn because they are unable to be curious, having lost their sense of smell—the only really effective mode of exercising curiosity as any animal knows, except these domesticated, educated, cultivated creatures that have 'forgotten'" (Bion, 1991, p. 448). When the sense of smell is directed towards an object, in search of support and clarification, different outcomes can occur from those that arise when focusing on the odours that emanate from one's own body. The greater the opposition to mature dependence on the feeding object, the closer it approaches the world of psychopathology.

In "Interview with Freud" (1930), George Sylvester Viereck dialogues with Dr. Sigmund Freud. At one point, they speak about the appreciation that Freud had for dogs, and Freud says,

> They do not suffer from a divided personality, from the disintegration of the ego, that arises from man's attempt to adapt himself to standards of civilisation too high for his intellectual and psychic mechanism. The savage, like the beast, is cruel, but he lacks the meanness of the civilised man. Meanness is man's revenge upon society for the restraints it imposes. This vengefulness animates the professional reformer and the busybody. The savage may chop off your head, he may eat you, he may torture you, but he will spare you the continuous little pinpricks which make life in a civilised community at times almost intolerable. Man's most disagreeable habits and idiosyncrasies, his deceit, his cowardice, his lack of reverence, are engendered by his incomplete adjustment to a complicated civilisation. It is the result of the conflict between our instincts and our culture. How much more pleasant are the simple, straightforward, intense emotions of a dog...

Here Freud expressed the reasons that human beings become ill: the struggle between instincts and the limitations that society imposes, while at the same time that he pointed out that the demands defeat man's intellectual and mental capacity. This image of fragility acquires another dimension upon comparing it to the expression of violence that Freud himself experienced towards his ideas. His exile illustrates the fanatical functioning that, in response to a few ideas, can give free rein to all of the violence that only humankind is capable of. When violence cannot be acted out nor symbolised, it finds expression through psychopathology. The ego does not always have the resources to negotiate with the demands of the external world, the superego, and the id, and may break.

If, for Freud, humanity's task is to negotiate with various masters, then for Klein, it consists of sustaining the constant struggle between love and hate with a divided mind. Mental health will depend on the presence and identification with a good internal object capable of buttressing the ego from the threats emanating from destructive forces. Without the good internal object and without the tolerance for the admiration/envy that is awakened, projection and introjection, and therefore also growth and development, will be impeded.

For Bion, mental disorders arise due to the proliferation of lies and confusion that poisons the mind.[8] If the collaboration of a container (external and later internal) produces alpha elements capable of building approximate representations of reality and the truth of that reality, a possibility exists for the mind to develop. On the contrary, if the alpha function is reversed or denaturalised and, instead of producing alpha elements capable of articulating themselves, it creates beta elements suitable only for agglutination and confusion, the development of the mind will be made impossible. When the apparatus for thinking thoughts does not receive enough supplies, an internal intoxication will drive the expulsion of toxic/beta elements, broadening the field so that psychopathology germinates (thought disorders and/or psychosomatic disorders, hallucinations, and non-mental functioning). The beta elements, incapable of sustaining bonds with internal objects, can agglomerate in an alternative world that is delusional and typical of schizophrenias.

The complexity of the states of mind mentioned so far demands an examination capable of discriminating between constituent elements.

Notes

1 Pinel's psychiatric ontology, inspired by Linnaeus' naturalistic classifications (Duero, D. and Shapoff, V., 2009), considered diseases as autonomous entities.
2 Such as that called for by Meltzer (1967), gathering the contributions and efforts of other analysts such as Glover.
3 Formerly, the hospitals in Spain where the sick were treated and where diseases and health problems were investigated were called "*nosocomios*".
4 In the Harris model, Harris and Meltzer (1976, p. 436) differentiate between the following states of mind: "the adult, the bi-sexual, masculine, feminine, masculine-delinquent, feminine-delinquent, and inverted (or perverted)".
5 "A well-integrated personality is the foundation for mental health. I shall begin by enumerating a few elements of an integrated personality: emotional maturity, strength of character, capacity to deal with conflicting emotions, a balance between internal life and adaptation to reality, and a successful welding into a whole of the different parts of the personality" (Klein, 1960, p. 268).
6 In *A Memoir of the Future* (Bion, 1991c, p. 3), the character P. A. thinks about the advantage of science over religion because one can detach oneself from the former; so he goes on to state: "I have no more difficulty with a scientific theory than an insect has with the form it bursts out of. Some of us, I admit, have ideas like exo-skeletons" that drown all thinking and turn psychoanalysis into dogma.
7 "What I discovered gradually, as I became more successful at helping patients escape from that state of mind, was the realisation that while patients are living in projective identification you *do not know them*. Not only is the world that they are living in different from the world that you, as a sane person, are living in, but the personality of such patients is different, is adapted to that grotesque world of projective identification, and when they emerge from that state of mind, they emerge as from a chrysalis of some sore, and they throw off what Bion calls their *'exoskeleton'*" (Meltzer, 2000, p. 3; my italics).
8 Poison is made with confusion and lies. This is the thanatotic alternative, in the language of drives, that fights against the discovery of "the truth of the meaning and the significance of emotional experiences and of any new idea that may be inherent. This is the food of the mind, essential to Its growth and development" (Harris & Meltzer, 1976, p. 404). Lies are the result of a parasitic relationship that destroys the container and the contained. "The envy, jealousy, and possessiveness aroused are the mental counterparts of toxic elements in physical parasitism", Bion says (1970, p. 104). Hatred of the truth hinders contact the subject could have with the object, by offering lies as seductive alternatives.

Bibliography

Bion Talamo, P. (2011): "Some notes on the theories of structure and mental functioning underlying A Memoir of the Future by W. R. Bion (1993)", in *Maps for Psychoanalytic Exploration,* edited by Chris Mawson, London, Karnac, 2015, pp. 103–116

Bion, W. R. (1970): *Attention and Interpretation*, London, Karnac.

Bion, W. R. (1991): "The dawn of oblivion", in *A Memoir of the Future*, London, Karnac Books, pp. 427–578

Duero, D. & Shapoff, V. (2009): "El conflicto nosológico en psicopatología: notas críticas sobre el diagnóstico psiquiátrico", *Revista CES Psicología*, 2(2), pp. 20–48.

Fairbairn, R. D. (1952): *Psychoanalytic Studies of the Personality*, New York, Routledge, 2001.

Foucault, M. (1958): "Maladie mentale et personnalité", *Revue Philosophique de la France et de l'Etranger*, 148, pp. 279–280. *Mental Illness and Psychology*, translated by A. Sheridan, Berkeley, University of California Press, 1987

Freud, S. (1937): "Analysis terminable and interminable", *International Journal of Psychoanalysis*, 18, pp. 373–405.

Harris, M. & Meltzer, D. (1976): "A psychoanalytic model of the child-in-the-family-in-the-community", in *Sincerity and Other Works*, edited by Alberto Hahn, London, Karnac, 1994, pp. 387–454.

Harris Williams, M. (1983): "'Underlying pattern' in Bion's memoir of the future", *International Review of Psycho-Analysis*, 10, pp. 75–86.

Klein, M. (1946): "Notes on some schizoid mechanisms", *International Journal of Psychoanalysis*, 27, pp. 99–110.

Klein, M. (1960): "On mental health", in *Envy and Gratitude and Other Works 1946–1963*, edited by M. Masud R. Khan, The Free Press, A Division of Simon & Schuster, 1975, pp. 267–274.

Lázaro, J. (2013): "Dilemas contemporáneos de la nosología psiquiátrica: El caso de las neurosis", *Revista de Neuro-Psiquiatría*, 76(2), pp. 85–94.

Meltzer, D. (1965): "The Relation of Anal Masturbation to Projective Identification", *International Journal of Psychoanalysis,* 47, pp. 335–342.

Meltzer, D. (1967): *The Psycho-Analytical Process*, London, William Heinemann Medical Books Limited.

Meltzer, D. (1989): Clinical seminars in the Psychoanalytic Group of Barcelona: Felipe (unpublished).

Meltzer, D. (2000): "A review of my writings", in *Exploring the Work of Donald Meltzer. A Festschrift*, edited by Margaret Cohen and Alberto Hahn, London, Karnac, pp. 1–11.

Morales Paiva, P. (2004): "Entre Narciso & Edipo. Propuestas desde la Psicoterapia Analítica a propósito de las patologías actuales", in *IX Jornada Interna,* del Centro de Psicoterapia Psicoanalítica de Lima (Perú).

Muñoz Vila, C. (2011): *Reflexiones Psicoanalíticas,* Bogotá, Editorial Pontificia Universidad Javeriana.

Segal, H. (2001): "Psychic structure and psychic change – changing models of the mind"", in *Yesterday, Today and Tomorrow*, edited by Nicola Abel-Hirsch, London, Routledge, 2007, pp. 83–91 Tabbia, C., Cosimi, A., Guida, H., & Sánchez, A. (1973): "W. R. Fairbairn: Aproximación a su concepto de salud y enfermedad" (unpublished), Facultad de Psicología, Univ de Mar del Plata, Argentina .

Winnicott, D. (1960): "Ego distortion in terms of true and false self", in *Studies in the Theory of Emotional Development*, London, Karnac Books Ltd, 1965.

Winnicott, D. (1967): "The concept of a healthy individual", A Talk Given to the Royal Medico-Psychological Association, Psychotherapy and Social Psychiatry Section, 8 March 1967, in *Home is Where We Start From: Essays by a Psychoanalyst*, edited by Clare Winnicott, Ray Shepherd and Madeleine Davis, New York, W.W.Norton & Company, 2014

Framework for the Observation of the Personality

Understanding present-day states of mind demands a description of the level of development that has been achieved, "both in terms of self and of objects" (Meltzer, 1992, p. 62). With that purpose in mind, I would think it appropriate to employ the six items named by Meltzer in the first seminar that he gave in Barcelona in 1986. I think these are elements that permit a metapsychological view of the patient. Each item will appear in italics to differentiate it from other contributions made. Therefore, to understand states of mind, it would be appropriate to observe:

1 *"How the infantile parts endure in the patient's personality as a whole"*
   In this statement, we find the concept of lack of mental unity, inherited from Klein, and the coexistence (with a distinct degree of integration/disintegration) between parts that are infantile, adult, idealised, resentful, incapable of tolerating the "aesthetic conflict", etc. To characterise infantile states of mind, it would be wise to mention that:

   > ...The most central concept related to infantile states that differentiates them from the adult state of mind is their very close relation to the body with its sensations and urges or Impulses. Sensuality and action are therefore their most characteristic modes of experience and participation in the world; whereas observation, emotionality, and thought, all of which require some degree of inhibition of action for their full experience, enter secondarily, usually either by training or by identification.
   >
   > (Harris and Meltzer, 1976, p. 438)

   Both their relationship to the body and their dependence on the external world to satisfy needs makes them vulnerable; a vulnerability that also characterises the infantile state. I would like to add another trait to those mentioned above: the longing for the perpetuity of pleasure, as Meltzer (1987, p. 32) said in another seminar (case H):

   > ...the inborn tendency in the child to be conservative, to think that if something is good, it has to go on repeating itself infinitely, again and again.

DOI: 10.4324/9781003347156-6

Mrs Klein always insisted on the need for an optimum level of mental pain for development to take place. Development, which is driven forward by anxieties, always takes place during the search for something that has been lost, and it is therefore of a deeply conservative nature: in a way, it's rather like the quest for paradise lost. This is characteristic of the infantile parts of the personality: to be in perpetual search of a past state of happiness.

The perpetuation of infantile parts is not only manifest during infancy. In some cases, presented in the following pages (see Section 3.3.5, Héctor), the persistent yearning for sexual functioning can be observed.

2   *"... What are the qualities of internal objects and their mutual relationships"*
Here it is about characterising the quality of the objects: whether they are whole and/or part, broken and dismantled, potent and weak, joyful and depressed, non-mental, immature, immoral, etc., along with a degree of relationship between them: in harmony, in freedom, with respect for each other, in collusion, in submission, bound by perverse pacts, with secrecy, humiliating babies, etc. The quality of these objects and the type of relationship will determine the states of mind referred to (maturity, immaturity, pseudo-maturity, psychopathology). By way of examples, we can point to a depression derived from identification with a destroyed/perforated object, or the lack of symbolic development in children who are identified with parents who are non-mental (practical, operative/unaware of emotional and psychic reality), etc.

Whatever object accesses control of the organ of consciousness, the gateway to action, has particular significance. Considering that the infantile parts have particular difficulty moderating the tendency to act and reflect, whoever takes control will determine the state of mind.

3   *"...To what degree the adult part of the personality has arisen from the introjection and the identification with internal objects, or to what degree this adult part of the personality has been substituted for a pseudo-mature part that has arisen through projective identification with internal objects"*
The development of the adult part of the personality arises from mourning and introjective identification with whole objects capable of relationships of respect and collaboration. The pseudo-mature alternative rises in rebellion against loss and opts for projective identification, generating identity confusion. In the case of H mentioned above, Meltzer characterised the adult part of the personality as the type of functioning that is inspired by internal objects, unlike infantile types of functioning motivated by sensuality:

The adult part of the personality functions according to an entirely different value system. It is sufficiently detached from what is corporal and sensual as to become bored with repetition. Furthermore, the development of the adult part of the personality is not driven forward by anxiety, but rather by aspirations and admiration towards the parental figures. This defines what Bion calls 'learning from experience' and would also represent a kind of spirit of adventure, of trying to face up to new experiences and learn from them. The paradox is that, as the adult part of the personality develops as a result of having new experiences, a parallel development of internal objects also takes place, so that these always come before reality. [...] the adult parts pursue a lineal end, infinite, in a forward direction...

Just as the infantile parts are moved by sensual pleasure and immediate gratification, the adult parts of the personality capable of integrating polymorphism and sexual differentiation seek an intimate encounter with the other (see Section 3.3). A related issue is that of the frigidity of pseudo-mature states. These states were explored by Meltzer (1965) in his pioneering paper "The Relation of Anal Masturbation to Projective Identification", where he established a causal relationship between intrusion and pseudo-maturity.

Another item to describe the structure of the personality consists of watching to see if the envious and jealous infantile parts of parental objects have created...

4 *"... a delinquent type of gang organisation that corresponds to the infantile narcissistic part of the personality to attack internal Objects"*

Here Meltzer takes up again the developments of Herbert Rosenfeld (1987, p. 109) on the "destructive narcissistic organization" idealising falsehoods that, like a mafia gang, exercises

> ...a powerful destructive influence; they are directed against life and destroy the links between objects and the self by attacking or killing parts of the self, but they are also destructive to any good objects by trying to devalue and eliminate them as important.

This destructive part of the self silently works to build alternative worlds, claiming that pandemonium[1] is more stimulating than family life. It attempts to seduce the infantile parts to remove them from the gravitational pull of the parental objects. One of the manifestations of this narcissistic organisation is the negativism present in the origin of perversions. Cultural relativism can also nourish itself from such an organisation.

Another aspect to consider is:

5 *"...if parts of the personality that seem to be constantly living inside an internal object and, in this sense, in a psychotic state, exist"*

This element requires some clarifications: the differentiation between different types of splitting. We can differentiate structuring dissociations, which are capable of organising categories (sweet-bitter, awake-asleep, good-bad, etc.) from those rigid dissociations that, upon fragmenting the self in an aberrant way (minuscule splits, splits that do not respect structures) and invading the object, produce confusion, bizarre objects, and psychotic states.

"Psychotic state" names a condition of "constantly living inside an internal object"; this means intolerance to the subject/object differentiation, splitting of the self, appropriating confusion of aspects of the object from which the external world is valued, and alteration of perception and the sense of reality. The quality of "constant" differentiates between momentary states of confusion and the stable, rigid ones typical of psychotic functioning.

Psychotic functioning occurs within the sphere of relationships with objects. If Meltzer's model of the mind is planetary, where children flutter and revolve around parental objects, psychotic functioning fights against dependence on objects and tries to invade them to appropriate their qualities. However, the schizophrenic organisation lives in another world, aloof from the gravitational attraction to internal objects. This organisation can share the personality with a non-schizophrenic functioning capable of maintaining different relationships (of respect, admiration, invasion, etc.) with objects. Meltzer (1987, p. 8) gave an example of this consideration when he spoke about the patient Casimiro. "Diagnostically speaking, he is suffering from a schizophrenic illness and the non-schizophrenic part of his personality is suffering from a psychotic illness: a geographical psychotic illness living in projective identification". Living constantly in a psychotic state did not prevent him from perceiving that his schizophrenic self was like something foreign to him and besieged him ("It's a little animal that self-generates, and since it feeds on me, it doesn't die and I need some sort of medicine that will kill it off so I can defecate it"; ibid., p. 4). From his non-schizophrenic part, he perceived the threat and the loneliness of the delusional system.

Occasionally, Meltzer employs the diagnostic "borderline psychotic" which refers to the defensive rigidity that seeks to nullify or neutralise the recognition of damage to the object and usually appears on the threshold of the depressive position (Hahn, 2010). To differentiate between borderline psychosis and incipient psychosis, see Section 3.1.1.3.

Lastly, he said that

6   *"...we have to attempt to identify areas of the personality that function in a non-mental way, in the sense of lacking mental activity"*

This last item is a consequence of the previous items because thinking depends on the internalisation of a combined object (of whole objects) with the capacity to observe and abstract, generalise, and conceptualise. While this internalisation does not come about, an external object is relied upon to help with thinking; another possibility is that of living conditioned by fashion, prejudices, slogans, etc. One of the first consequences of non-mental functioning is *the denial of psychic reality*. Faced with the universal need to find meaning in one's own history and everyday life, denying psychic reality seriously undermines the structure of the personality, threatens the stability of the ego, and generates boredom. Because of its significance, I wish to mention the denial of psychic reality in infantile, adolescent, and borderline states of mind, independently of the chronological age, therefore alternative states to the adult state.

The dependence of the infantile parts on the satisfaction of needs and their primitive emotionality that does not admit delay, unlike adult functioning capable of symbolisation, produces a calculating relationship that adapts to reality, but where there is no place for psychic reality, imagination, or sensitivity towards the feelings of others; superficiality and materialism complete their characterisation (Meltzer, 1971). Just as infantile states are so dependent on material comfort, pubertal-adolescent states depend greatly on the opinion of other adolescents. So, in this community, sexual experiences, more than personal satisfaction or an amorous experience, take on the meaning of "what other people think you have experienced" (Meltzer and Harris, 1998, p. 326). Identity depends both on the opinion of the group and on belonging to a group (see Section 3.3.5). The emotional significance of adolescent experiences emerges towards the end of this stage, when they begin to fall in love and to feel concern for the other. This is not the attitude of borderline personalities. Their difficulty in letting go of the concrete and venturing on to independence of what is real detains symbolic development when it does not fragment it. A delusional system is not necessarily created, but in a healthy part of the self, they are not able to grasp the meaning of the experiences. This is why these personalities are usually very much trapped in the immediate, in the concrete, in what one is supposed to do. For them—as Meltzer (1998) said in the case of a woman that was out of contact with psychic reality—

> things are what they appear to be: she's a married woman with an adequate sex life, with a well-decorated house, who takes care of her husband, and dresses elegantly enough so that her husband won't be ashamed to go out with her and she's very much adapted to his insignificant, meaningless world.

An exemplary expression of the concreteness of realities and the denial of meaning can be found in fanatical functioning (see Section 3.2.2).

I think that within these adapted and concrete ways of functioning, we could include those patients that Joyce McDougall called "normopaths". They would be those normal people who have created for themselves a suit of armour that protects against all awakening of their neurotic and psychotic conflicts. She points out that:

> ...such a person respects the ideas that have been handed down to him as he respects the rules of society; there is no apparent conflict, for the wish to transgress these rules of thought and behaviour does not appear, even in imagination. The nostalgic fragrance of Marcel Proust's *madeleine* awakens no remembrance of things past, and he will waste no time in searching for *les temps perdus*. Yet he too has lost something precious. In the construction of his solid wall of normality, the richness of fantasy seems to be lacking; or perhaps it would be nearer the truth to say that this restraining wall keeps the subject out of contact with himself and his imaginative life.
>
> (McDougall, 1972, pp. 481–482)

If only the *madeleine* were a cake, a simple cake, Proust would not have been able to reminisce about stories and find meanings in them. To such an end, the presence of a person, of a mind, was necessary.

Within *non-mental functioning*, in the sense of lacking mental activity or in the sense of opposition to thinking and discovering, different ways of functioning can be differentiated, to which I will refer below.

Initially, I will refer to ways of functioning based on basic assumptions (Bion, 1961). Unlike individual mentality, these types of functioning are characterised by the absence and even the opposition to observation, to thinking, and therefore to judgement. The basic assumptions are based on the gregarious nature of the human being who, moving through valencies, adapts to ways of avoiding work (T), and thinking. Bion (1961, p. 116) contrasts "valency" with "cooperation" and differentiates between them by proposing to reserve:

> ...the word 'cooperation' for conscious or unconscious working with the rest of the group in work, whereas for the capacity for spontaneous instinctive cooperation in the basic assumptions [...] I shall use the word 'valency'. I mean to indicate, by its use, the individual's readiness to enter into combination with the group in making and acting on the basic assumptions [...] I wish also to use it to indicate a readiness to combine on levels that can hardly be called mental at all but are characterized by behaviour in the human being that is more analogous to tropism in plants than to purposive behaviour...

To function in accordance with the assumptions, it is not necessary that you keep in mind the nuances of emotional experiences but instead the degree or the quantity of excitation (Meltzer and Harris Williams, 1988). The primitive way of functioning by tropism is counterposed to function with thinking.

A way of understanding this primitive, unidimensional state[2] is to consider it as a type of magnetic functioning capable of producing actions remotely, such as mutual attractions and repulsions. These movements can be observed in autistic children who move away if the therapist gets too close to them, or, inversely, the child can become attracted to the therapist, and they become stuck to one another (Meltzer et al., 1975, chap. IX; Meltzer & Psychoanalytic Group of Barcelona, 1995, p. 153).

A kind of functioning based on the basic assumptions is manifest in the non-families or groups of subjects for whom the parental function of modulating mental pain, sustaining hope, and stimulating thinking was absent. In these cases, the family is substituted by a gang that hates thinking.

Other types of non-mental functioning manifest through thought disorders, hallucinations, lies, and confabulations that attempt to rid the subject of emotional experiences when they cannot be contained and symbolised. Faced with an overwhelming profusion of words that often lack all meaning, and derived from severe thought disorders, as happens with many patients, exceptional tolerance and expertise is required of the analyst to become container and decoder of the tragedy. To unravel the meanings of the fragments, the analyst needs to differentiate the primitive and wild beta elements from those beta elements with remnants of self and superego that survived the explosion of phantasies and emotional experiences.

Non-mental ways of functioning find expression in psychosomatic disorders. This disorder manifests itself when the body must sustain the text that the mind cannot express (see Section 3.2.5). The body is asked to experience emotions and affects, and struggles against desire and the conditionings of culture… but with little symbolising ability. Although this type of patient reflects non-mentality, they are not "boring because their psychosomatic symptoms indicate some kind of emotional turmoil that has still been unable to penetrate into the mind" (Meltzer, 1991). It does not mean that this type of patient is not a challenge in psychoanalytic practice.

Can schizophrenic functioning be included among non-mental functioning? In that seminar, Meltzer did not refer to this; I believe his silence was a response to the fact that schizophrenic functioning does not participate in the world of relationships. Schizophrenic-delusional functioning creates a world apart; it is the world of delusion. In a case like that, a human in-the-middle-of-nowhere wilderness has been chosen/found where part and mutilated objects have built an inhabitable cabin that is offered up as a luxurious suite to capture guests capable of sharing their absolute loneliness. In reality, more than non-mentality, we should speak of anti-mentality capable of anthropomorphising everything through an overdetermination built with bizarre elements. This anti-mental world always works in parallel with symbolic developments that allow for some contact with reality. It guides the therapeutic approach taken with a person who inhabits different worlds and demands a constant struggle on the part of the patient and a continuous evaluation by the therapist to recognise whom the therapist is speaking with at that moment. A text by Meltzer (1980) from a conference in Uruguay brings together many of these concepts and metaphorises them following a spatial model:

> We can think about schizophrenia as a process that develops in a similar way to the escape mechanism in a spaceship. It spins and spins until reaching the escape speed required to be launched into space. In much the same way, once a part of the personality penetrates a delusional system, it is perhaps impossible to recover. Seen in this way, the psychoanalysis or psychotherapy of a schizophrenic patient is, essentially, the psychoanalysis of the non-schizophrenic part of the personality. It seems to me that it is possible to build a model for schizophrenia based on this special concept that can later be introduced to the concept of bizarre objects and their origin. In this way, growth of the personality will be conceived of as a constant struggle, on the one hand, between good objects that use truth and Bion's grid to think, while on the other, the destructive part of the personality that employs lies and the negative grid, both in rivalry for the attention and the loyalty of infantile parts of the personality.

In summary, even though the part of the personality that is trapped in the delusional system keeps itself out of human life—in infinite space—and therefore is non-mental, this does not prevent there being other patients who have some possibility of developing symbolic development associated with an introjective identification with some part or whole object. The non-schizophrenic parts are the fulcrum that sustains the hope that the lost parts in the delusional world can be rescued.

In that first seminar, when Meltzer finished enumerating the previous items, he said that

> this is the complexity of Kleinian theory with which nowadays we attempt to see the patient. We try to study his adult structure, his narcissistic organisation, his psychotic trends and the non-mental areas of his personality. This takes a long time.

Here we recall Klein's response to a colleague that alleged that Kleinian theory was very complicated. Klein replied by saying that it was not the theory that was complicated, but rather the person, the mind....

Notes

1   "Pandemonium" is the name of an alternative world to Paradise (Milton) and is based on lies and confusion, made from the negative grid (Bion).
2   This oscillating and polarised state stimulated Meltzer (1995, p. 127) into remembering what occurs when one tries to feed squirrels:

> If it is at a certain distance and it is frightened, the squirrel will go away; however, if it is right here eating and it becomes frightened, what it will do is bite. When this occurs with autistic children, they get stuck. Individuality disappears, and what happens is that 'one swallows the other up'. This is related to extremely primitive anxieties that can be observed in very small children, especially in the bath, when they are terribly frightened of being sucked down the drain.

Bibliography

Bion, W. R. (1961): *Experiences in Groups and Other Papers*, New York, Tavistock Publications Limited.

Hahn, A. (2010): "Seminar on The Claustrum – an investigation of claustrophobic phenomena" (unpublished), Barcelona.

Harris, M. & Meltzer, D. (1976): "A psychoanalytic model of the child-in-the-family-in-the-community", in *Sincerity and Other Works*, edited by Alberto Hahn, London, Karnac 1994, pp. 387–454.

McDougall, J. (1972): *Plea for a Measure of Abnormality*, New York, Brunner/Mazel, 1992.

Meltzer, D. (1965): "The relation of anal masturbation to projective identification", *International Journal of Psychoanalysis,* 47, pp. 335–342.

Meltzer, D. (1971): "Sincerity: A study in the atmosphere of human relations", in *Sincerity and Other Works*, edited by Alberto Hahn, London, Karnac, 1994, pp. 184–284

Meltzer, D. (1980): "El desarrollo kleiniano", *Rev. Uruguaya de Psicoanálisis*, N 60, ISSN 1688-7247.

Meltzer, D. (1987): "Clinical seminars in the Psychoanalytic Group of Barcelona: Victor", in *Psychanalytic Work with Children and Adults - Meltzer in Barcelona*, edited by Donald Meltzer and The Psychoanalytic Group of Barcelona, Karnac, 2002, pp. 21–43.

Meltzer, D. (1991): Clinical seminars in the Psychoanalytic Group of Barcelona: Alicia (unpublished).

Meltzer, D. (1992): *The Claustrum. An Investigation of Claustrophobic Phenomena*, Strath-Clyde, The Clunie Press.

Meltzer, D. (1998): Clinical seminars in the Psychoanalytic Group of Barcelona: Quetty (unpublished).

Meltzer, D. & Harris, M. (1998): *Adolescentes*, edited by L. Jachevasky & C. Tabbia, Buenos Aires, Spatia ed.

Meltzer, D. & Harris Williams, M. (1988): *The Apprehension of Beauty: The Role of Aesthetic Conflict in Development, Art, and Violence*, London, Karnac, 2008.

Meltzer, D., Psychoanalytic Group of Barcelona & McSmith, C. (1995): *Psychanalytic Work with Children and Adults – Meltzer in Barcelona*, London, Karnac, 2002.

Meltzer, D. et al. (1975): *Explorations in autism a psycho-analytical study*, Strath-Clyde, Clunie Press.

Rosenfeld, H. (1987): "Destructive Narcissism and the Death Instinct. Impasse and Interpretation: Therapeutic and anti-therapeutic factors in the psychoanalytic treatment of psychotic, borderline, and neurotic patients", *New Library of Psychoanalysis*, 1, pp. 105–132.

Dimensions for Diagnosis

The complexity of Kleinian theory, enriched with Bion's collaborations, stimulates us to search for paths that allow us to diagnose and orient clinical practice without getting lost in the denseness of the human forest. Hope lies in that

> The further the analysis progresses—says Bion, 1970, p. 59—the more the psychoanalyst and the analysand achieve a state in which both contemplate the irreducible minimum that is the patient. (This irreducible minimum is incurable because what is seen is that without which the patient would not be the patient.)

In this sense, it is no longer possible for diagnosis and psychiatric nosology to

> ... account for the complexity and richness of mental functioning. In this sense, psychoanalytic diagnosis constitutes a reference that, although it has sacrificed its initial precision, is broader and more flexible to guide treatment, a process that by its very nature is an individual design, in accordance with the characteristics of each subject.
>
> (Leiberman de Bleichmar and Bleichmar, 2001, p. 301)

In order to not get lost in the complexity and the richness of the subject, I think it is appropriate to mention another encounter with Meltzer in June of 1996, where three dimensions arose to describe a patient rather than to guide treatment. For him, the only guidance was based on loyalty to the psychoanalytic method, and the transference and countertransference, because the objectives were clouded by memory and desire. In that opportunity, Meltzer had supervised material from Inés (see Section 3.1.1.2), a patient with a borderline and manic-depressive personality in whom we see a tenacious denial of psychic reality, and who was particularly difficult to understand. For Inés, it was all external reality, and therefore everything was material; everything consisted of winning (being manic) or losing (being depressed). At the end of the supervision, Meltzer said:

> ...when speaking with colleagues about patients, the most important thing is to try to describe the type of structure that the patient has, visualise in your mind

DOI: 10.4324/9781003347156-7

the type of personality you are busy with. There aren't that many types of structures to make it difficult to define the description. It is, indeed, quite a simple thing to do.

Then he said:

1   There are some structures that are characterised by the denial of psychic reality; structures that are defined by splitting processes;
structures that are defined in terms of projective identification;
        structures that are characterised by uncontrolled emotionality and without objects; and there are personality
        structures that are characterised by delusional systems, although this is typical of schizophrenia, and, in this case, I don't know if it can properly be called a personality.
2   When describing the personality, I think that the second dimension after structure is to define the degree to which the person lives in relationships with other people, or lives in groups[…].
3   After all this, we are entering the dimension of thinking and thought disorders. A patient (Inés) like the one we have just seen is a person describing her borderline mental illness that makes thinking impossible for her. She can't think. The only thing available to her are strategies that she can use to win.

I think that all of this, basically, would cover what could be said about the personality and what differentiates each person from the other:

-   in first place, structural differences,
-   in second place, the differences that happen depending on whether or not you devote yourself to groups or to intimate relationships and the family, and
-   in third place, it has to do with the capacity to use methods of thinking with the aim of treating relationships.

When I reconsidered (see Section 3.3.1) these three dimensions, I proposed that the second could be the foundation and condition of the other two. Therein, I proposed that intimacy hinges on three pillars. The first is the need for "optimal distance, adequate proximity, geographical contiguity, names that show us the conditions for the development of intimacy". The second was that, to have true relationships, "the possibility of emotionality being either fully experienced or accepted" (Meltzer, 1971, p. 245). The third mentioned the base that sustains the search for an object and aspiring to intimacy, that in the words of Klein, is named the unconscious oneness, "based on the unconscious of the mother and of the child being in close relation to each other. The infant's resultant feeling of being understood underlies the first and fundamental relation in his life" (Klein, 1959, p. 247). She later said that

the adult part of the personality arises from the introjective identification with good objects and, therefore it is natural that the greatest degree of adult intimacy manifests in the relationships where dialogue predominates, made up of words and silences, generosity, respect, non-violence, freedom, the ability to share suffering and joy, interests and curiosities, and where loss is tolerated.

Understanding intimacy and its conditions in this way, I consider the patient's ability for intimacy to be a sufficiently all-encompassing criterion to evaluate their state of mind, although this does not exclude the meaning of the other dimensions, in that they mutually enrich each other for a metapsychological understanding of the patient.

Bibliography

Bion, W. R. (1970): *Attention and Interpretation*, London, Karnac.

Klein, M. (1959): "Our adult world and its roots in infancy", in *Envy and Gratitude and Other Works 1946–1963*, edited by M. Masud R. Khan, New York, The Free Press, A Division of Simon & Schuster, 1975, pp. 246–262

Leiberman de Bleichmar, C. & Bleichmar, N. (2001): *Las perspectivas del psicoanálisis*, Paidós, México.

Meltzer, D. (1971): "Sincerity: A study in the atmosphere of human relations", in *Sincerity and Other Works*, edited by Alberto Hahn, London, Karnac, 1994, pp. 185–284.

Meltzer, D. (1996): Clinical seminars in the Psychoanalytic Group of Barcelona: Inés (unpublished).

Chapter 3

The Tripod of Psychoanalytic Practice

The tripod on which psychoanalysts support themselves to understand mental functioning is composed of the following points of support: personality structure, developments in thinking, and the capacity to establish intimate relationships. From there, the elements that, amongst others, contribute to the development or hinder it can be observed.

Despite the contents of this chapter, as well as the whole of the book carrying the traces of my own experience, I do not want to assume more merit than what would be my due, and that is why I do not want to repeat the playful irony that Bion (1991) writes about in *A Memoir of the Future*: "I bet the fellow who succeeds in getting his name on the cover of this book thinks it is his". In my case, I can affirm that it comforts me to quote those authors from whom I have learned and enjoyed. Chapter 3 was organised on the basis of an intervention by Meltzer (1996) that functioned as an articulating *selected fact* from a series of supervisions and works of mine published in different specialised books and magazines; the words that suggested the structure of this book were:

> I believe that the therapeutic method that we use that studies transference and countertransference influences three dimensions with a movement in the direction of psychic reality, the other in the direction of intimate relationships and the last in the direction of thinking and communication. In reality, planning the therapy is not what one must do, but rather, simply follow the method and try to understand what's happening. Fortunately, these three dimensions can also produce an unlimited variation between individuals in such a way that two therapies will never be similar. Many possibilities exist to see different types of problems, the variations being practically infinite.

The variations are infinite… as varied as the situations to which I was summoned when presenting the 12 clinical materials. Section 3.1 presents some of the organisations of the self, analysed in the clinical seminars and private or group supervisions conducted by Donald Meltzer. Participating in the meetings with Meltzer and sharing them with my colleagues of the *Psychoanalytic Group of Barcelona*, both in Barcelona and in Oxford, was undoubtedly one of my richest professional

DOI: 10.4324/9781003347156-8

experiences. This book is my way of expressing my gratitude. The way in which I grouped the materials in this section participates in the arbitrariness of diagnoses. In that sense, I agree with Anne Alvarez (2012, p. 136) when she said that "human beings refuse to allow themselves to be neatly framed in these schematic categories, which I only use for the purposes of discussion". Meltzer would ratify this opinion because he considered that these categories only serve to dialogue with colleagues. Although the Procrustean bed haunts this organisation, my warning remains: reality surpasses description. In order to understand the complexity, some categories are required to guide exploration and dialogue. In this section, I have chosen three major categories characterised by the denial of psychic reality, the predominance of splitting and intrusive identification, and a third group of people who were negotiating the oedipal conflict.

Section 3.2 is about thinking and not thinking. Bion (1961) used to say that "thinking is the attribute that characterises man, and the central problem calling for scientific investigation", but the paradox is that it must be done with the same tool that is the subject of investigation. Here we will deal with symbolisation as well as with the problems of symbolisation suffered by patients and the difficulties that the analysts themself may have in cooperating in the transforming task; it is undeniable that meaning is the challenge for psychoanalytic clinical practice.

Section 3.3 addresses the subject of intimacy, an essential condition for the development of the personality; despite its meaning, it is not an experience within reach of many people, as Bauman (2003) or Marie-France Hirigoyen (2007) shows. It is not uncommon for the therapeutic relationship to occasionally become one of the few intimate experiences for both the patient and the analyst, surely because both participants in the clinical encounter are willing to expose themselves to the mystery of self and others that emerges from their respective unconscious minds. Without intimacy, there is no transformation, either in private life or in the clinical relationship.

Chapter 3 closes with a synthesis of the material presented, and it is associated with the analyst's task. Lastly, the meaning of the omnipotent phantasy of "living in intrusive identification" will be explored.

Bibliography

Alvarez, A. (2012): *Un cuore che pensa*, Roma, Astrolabio.

Bauman, Z. (2003): *Liquid Love: On the Frailty of Human Bonds*, Cambridge, Polity Press.

Bion, W. R. (1961): "The conception of man", in *The Complete Works of W. R. Bion*, edited by Cris Mawson, London, Karnac, 2014, Vol. xv, pp. 9–30.

Bion, W. R. (1991): *A Memoir of the Future,* London, Karnac Books.

Hirigoyen, Marie-France (2007): *Las nuevas soledades. El reto de las relaciones personales en el mundo de hoy,* Buenos Aires, Paidós contextos, 2015.

Meltzer, D. (1996): Clinical seminars in the Psychoanalytic Group of Barcelona: Inés (unpublished).

The Structure of Personality

As opposed to Freud's structural model (ego, superego, and id), Klein opted for terms such as subject, ego, or self interchangeably to account for the structure of the personality and the internal mobility derived from the relationship with objects. Klein's world is presented as a stage of relationships where

> the 'citizens' of the inner world, the 'assembly' of objects (part or whole) maintain the most varied and multiple relationships with the subject. They love and hate, complain, command, forbid, betray, plot against each other, give support, provide protection, etc. The ego responds to all these actions of the internal objects with reactions that also belong to the register of the interindividual relationship.
>
> (Baranger, 1971, p. 400)

In this internal assembly, the objects and the subject, the ego, interact and affect each other mutually and incessantly because even while sleeping (Meltzer, 1984), they can be engaged in the production of meanings.

Personally, the term "subject" seems to provide more clarity when I am comparing it or relating it to the "object"; In this case, I am accentuating the relationship between the two. It has the disadvantage of suggesting an almost conscious relationship or can be derived towards a subjective-objective opposition. However, as Hinshelwood (1989) well expresses it, this would be "a simplistic dichotomy when dealing with human science" because the nature of the psychic object is subjective and, to quote Heimann, demands an objective attitude when dealing with the abovementioned phenomenon. That is why, faced with the possible subject/object counter-position, the term self has the advantage of naming not only the relationship with external objects, but also the intrapsychic relationship between different internal objects and instances. For example, the superego as an internal object. The self gives a name to the whole of the personality. To differentiate between these complex terms with so many meanings, it would be opportune to turn to the contributions of León and Rebeca Grinberg (1971, pp. 44–45), where they say that the self

> includes the ego and the no-ego. It is the whole of the person, including the body with all of its parts, the psychic structure with all of its parts, the relationship

DOI: 10.4324/9781003347156-9

with external and internal objects, and the subject as opposed to the world of objects.

Having now made these precisions, I will use personality and self indistinctly.

I will begin the presentation of supervised clinical material with the cases where the denial of psychic reality was particularly evident.

3.1.1 Denial of Psychic Reality

The denial of psychic reality is a product derived from the lack of imagination (caused by the absence of introjective identification with the combined object). It leads to a mental restriction that promotes the belief that reality remains circumscribed to a known, concrete, and immediate sphere. If the restriction is accompanied by a belief in language as something concrete, then the exact combination is created for the "evacuation of emotional experiences and in this way prevent them coming to form a part of the mental experience" (Meltzer and Harris, 1998, p. 324).

3.1.1.1 An Inaccessible Psychic Reality

Ferrán was a young, immature patient, polymorphous and occasionally addicted to multiple substances, who lived with an expansive and mentally fragile woman. He admired her capacity to express herself. From the first interviews onwards, the profile of a weak and dependent personality appeared and confirmed itself throughout the treatment. In this sense, after the first meeting, he said: "it's okay here", and after the second meeting, he said that to set up times for his treatment, he would have to consult with his boss, whom he was dependent on. It became increasingly possible to observe a little boy who was mentally an orphan and organised his life in *triangular scenes, of part objects,* in whom he lodged himself. The first scene became present when he introduced his boss into our relationship: he would have to negotiate the times of our meetings with him. Another scene that completed this organisation could be seen when he related our meeting to a friend; then he said: "We were at home one night with Felipe, who's gay, and my wife, having a good time together; Felipe and I caressed one another and he had sexual intercourse with Ada, my wife, while I looked on". The way he regarded life reflected fragility at the same time that he idealised his partner. "She is very communicative, but when I'm with her, I feel very different from her", Ferrán said; in reality, he felt small, and he protected himself by idealising her. However, he felt that "walking on the street, I have the feeling that my image doesn't command respect, and I'm frightened that some low-life [petty thief, delinquent] will pick a fight with me". His fear of indistinctly attracting homosexuals, delinquents, or low-lifes who would assault him, rob him, or evacuate into him all that was denigrated, completed the representation of a very primitive, infantile, triangular scene. This scene evoked another where a mother held him in her arms and communicated with him, like a baby sucking on an idealised nipple, but at the same time, he was not calm because his backside was exposed to an anal attack as if he had felt that he was lacking paternal protection. If good communication came from the front (with Ada/idealised mother), from behind Ferrán/baby came everything that had been rejected in an uncontainable evacuation/projection and would return still more irritated. Ferrán believed that "he transmitted bad vibes" and that people could see that, which obliged him to watch over distances and encounters carefully.

In his triangular scenes, his wife satisfied various functions. One was to transport one man's genital to another man to confer identity (cf. Ferrán watching Ada's intercourse). Another primitive function was to organise chaos and to connect him to the world: Ferrán's social world was Ada's. There was, however, yet another function attributed to his wife: the function of differentiating front from back because this provides relief from overexcitation. On that subject, on one occasion, the patient said that the previous night he had gone to bed with his wife, both very tired, and they fell asleep after caressing each other a bit. He woke up excited, left the room, and masturbated, feeling very ashamed. He went back to bed and dreamt that "he and his wife were in the bathroom, and he had uncontrollable diarrhoea twice", and then woke up. Ferrán related the dream with masturbation and the need to expel everything, returning to things that had been dealt with in previous sessions. In supervision, Meltzer coincided in that masturbation represented both the homosexual excitation and the evacuation of what he felt in his anus. Here we see the primitive front/back differentiation: when with his wife (front), he can evacuate (behind) the bad penis, which makes it possible to be with her in an idealised relationship ("she's capable of expressing herself"). In this scene, a difficult situation for the baby is represented in a different way: that of having in the front Mummy's big breasts, while in the back, he has Daddy's big genitals. It is a difficult situation because it excites him and imprisons him in sensualism (see Section 3.1.3.2).

His almost absolute dependence on his external objects (Ada, his boss, me in the therapeutic relationship, etc.) and his difficulty in being introspective of his emotional states, together with a susceptibility towards the external world, are the elements that impede him in his investigation of his psychic reality. Meaning had to be suggested by his external objects. Not infrequently, I was led to think that he suffered from a thinking disorder because he was incapable of observing and referring to singular events at the same time that his speech was ambiguous and full of generalisations. This caused me to ask him about the events he was speaking about because to the contrary, it was difficult to understand what he was referring to or wanted to talk about. Occasionally, I would feel as if I were looking at a misty scene. Meltzer related Ferrán's difficulty communicating with his concern for himself, essentially with the image of himself he gave others, preventing him from observing another reality and communicating it. In this manner, Ferrán said: "I don't manage to become close to other people. Maybe I'm running away from frequent contact; I wouldn't know what to think. I'm afraid they will think that I'm not likeable…". His concern for himself prevented him from becoming interested in something not him; in this emotional state, psychic reality was the victim because

> when concerned with one's own appearance, with how others see you—Meltzer said—this doesn't produce an emotional experience. Everything remains in the realm of phantasy, ruminations, etc. In this material, the unconscious can't operate in a constructive way. When thinking is not based on real, actual events, it can't be transformed into nocturnal dreams. Everything remains at the level of diurnal phantasy.

Without observing external or internal reality and eluding all contact—given his susceptibility and intolerance to pain—the alpha function cannot transform data without meaning, and rather than develop a *contact barrier* that would allow him to discriminate external reality from psychic reality, the conditions are created to produce pseudo-thoughts, hallucinations, or psychosomatic disorders. Ferrán not infrequently suffered intestinal disorders (diarrhoea).

His immature dependence on Ada correlated with his difficulty building and conserving a creative parental couple. This caused primitive anxieties to emerge when he separated from his wife or the analyst, such as the anxieties of becoming diluted. When faced with this threat, Ferrán defended himself by constructing appearances (building up muscle in the gym or theorising on justice) albeit with the superficiality proper of a bidimensional personality. This kind of functioning has consequences for the clinical relationship because when unable to observe or to refer to what happens in your interior, the relationship becomes impeded, possibility awakening countertransferential irritation. When faced with material of this kind, Meltzer thought that with these patients it was

> …useless to try to investigate his life outside of analysis, because they never express it directly. The only thing they tell you are fantasies about what might happen or what has already happened. We must concentrate on the transference, investigate the transference. Although as usually happens with patients of this type, they resist a lot because they have a noticeable fear of intimacy in the transference. […] With these patients, interpretative work is very important. You have to create concepts, differentiations, and resolve confusion. With this type of patient, one gets the impression that it is the relationship itself that can bring about therapeutic benefits. You have to really be the father and the mother. The adequate attitude guides you to establish a very strong bond" That's why "in this type of therapy the most important thing is not the contents of the interpretations, but rather the analytic ambience and the fact that you are a strong figure that can help…

giving very descriptive interpretations, connections, and associations. "It will take a long time—he continued—for the patient to present observations regarding his mental life. At the moment, he only produces ruminations that may reflect his state of mind". A state full of fear that cornered Ferrán, and so he felt that "I don't ever get intimate…".

3.1.1.2 *Opposition to the Analytic Situation*

Manic-depressive oscillation characterised Inés' personality. Her emotional instability, manifested from childhood, was connected to incompetent competition with
her older sister. The incompetence was also expressed in the area of her studies and
her relationships with men. In the supervision of Inés' material, Meltzer wondered
if the essence of the manic-depressive state might not consist of a fluctuating struggle between winning and losing. Inés conceived of her life as a game of chess.
When she won, she felt triumphant, and when, in the vicissitudes of everyday life,
she lost, she felt depressed. This drove her to flee from any situation that made her
feel pain. Suffering meant failure.

> Everyone—according to how Meltzer described the patient's state of mind—is
> winning the game except for her, who doesn't understand the cause, and that's
> why she's completely furious. She's driven to orient herself simply towards
> knocking over all of the pieces on the chessboard. That's her idea of suicide:
> 'the end of the game'. It's got nothing to do with some idea that she might have
> regarding life or death, but rather it's just about being the 'end of the game',
> and she tries to look for another game where she might be a more skilful player.
> That's why it seems very natural to her to go from one game to another, although
> what happens is that she always realises that she's not a good player in any kind
> of game. Even when she follows the rules and regulations of the game, she lacks
> the necessary skill to be able to continue playing and sometimes win. For her,
> winning a game means that the others feel envious, and she feels triumphant.
> This seems to be the only reason for the game, even though, in reality, the ob-
> jective of most games is to win. In fact, it's not about winning but rather about
> making the others lose. For this reason, she never plays well because she's al-
> ways playing so others will lose. I assume she plays the analytic game with you
> in the same manner, not so much as to win but to make you lose. Every time
> you leave, and she finds herself in danger of losing, she develops some type of
> strategy to avoid losing, coming up with all of these plans for the weekend. As
> such, when someone says to her "I know that you're not well", she adopts an-
> other strategy to manage to invert the situation, and she begins to ask about their
> weight, or them being overweight … this is how she turns the tables around.

In her frenetic and wrathful competition, she not only failed but also created another victim: psychic reality. When life is reduced to winning or losing, life lacks
meaning. Triumph consists of stripping human experiences of meaning. The success for manic-depressive patients consists of their techniques to not think: "turning the tables around". Part of the technique consists of reducing everything to
external reality. Triumph would materialise in success in business, ascending the
social ladder or sexual promiscuity. Speed and secrecy are admired resources. The
faster and more impersonal she can be, the safer her escape from pain will be. A
well-developed resource in Inés was her verbal skill and quickness, whether turning things around or mentioning things that had never been talked about before,

considering them to have been already explained. This obliged me to run after her words, increasing my sensation that she led me, just as in the external world she wants to lead her acquaintances, her children, her partners, or her work colleagues. Conceptual impoverishment lies behind this skilfulness. This is how Meltzer himself expressed it:

> It seems inevitable that we will find a tremendous conceptual impoverishment in manic-depressive patients. Concepts are extremely infantile, like those of winning and losing. There's a great difficulty in establishing differentiations between things, for example, differentiating between 'being in debt' and 'gratitude'. Gratitude is experienced as being in debt to someone. Not all of these differentiations have been established. It's not only about trying to move them from the paranoid-schizoid position to the depressive position, but rather we must make efforts to show them how completely ignorant they are of the existence of the depressive position and what it consists of. This means describing to them in detail the conceptual defect they suffer from in relation to depressive values, their values being strictly materialist, and aesthetic values are ignored. It's not only about their voracity, but also about the futility of acquiring things constantly, etc. They must be shown all of these values in the depressive position because they keep themselves completely unaware of them. In adolescence, these states can be found in some teenagers who have the idea that they're going to get rich as soon as possible in order to be able to retire at 30. When asked what they will do then, they answer with: 'Whatever I want to', and if you persist, they answer: 'Well, …you know, …well…'. Here is precisely where the teaching function of the analyst comes in, because these patients are really very ignorant about the world of values. They'd never thought about them before.
>
> (see Section 1.2)

The continuous task of discriminating between concepts and emotions can be so exhausting that it is not hard to act out the countertransference, punishing with silence or getting annoyed; that is why

> …it's not about playing the game with her, but rather describing the movements that she's making. As if it were about a chess game, when she moves a piece, you're not supposed to respond by moving your bishop or your knight, but to tell her: 'Now you're waiting for me to move my bishop so that afterwards you can move this and that and checkmate me.' You concentrate then on the position of describing to her all of her movements in the transference, in her acting-out in the transference: 'Now you're playing this game trying to make me fall in the trap, you try to teach me, to drive this analysis telling me what I have to do playing the suicide card', etc. […] She constantly takes you away from the transference talking about Julio, about Alberto, her mother, her sister, or about Nùria, etc. and to return her to the analytic situation you have to make her see that: 'This is exactly what you are doing with me'. Basically, what must be

done, as also occurs with patients in the *Claustrum*, is to establish the analytic situation. This turns out to be very difficult with these patients, and it can take years, as with the *Claustrum* patient, although the problem is different in this type of manic-depressive patient. I think that this theory about roles in a game, about winning and losing as a value system, is something that can be used to place oneself in a very powerful interpretative position. From experience, what eventually can be found, in the measure that actings-out in the transference decrease, is the subject of love in the transference, that gradually emerges despite the tremendous resistance put up.

A lot of patience will be needed before feelings of love and pain come together in these patients because their hypersensitivity to pain makes them quickly distrust the experience of love.

3.1.1.3 *Getting Rid of Psychic Reality*

The circumstances surrounding Florencia's early infancy were complex enough to feel helped very little. Her father had to emigrate, and her mother was overwhelmed by her oldest son's illness. Florencia was sent to a relative's house. This relative had no particular interest in children. This unfortunate arrival in the world seated the bases for a resentful person at war with the world. Florencia was particularly beautiful, but her beauty was used to oppress her partners, who would end up fleeing. This increased her hatred even more and ended in explosions (throwing objects, compulsively eating or masturbating). Behaving capriciously was her law. Introspection was not her most outstanding quality nor her main interest. She was capable of action, and her main victim was psychic reality. She looked for help because of her violence. A serious family situation scared her to such a point that, advised by a friend, she began analysis.

At the beginning of analysis, she longed for us to be lovers; in her dream life, however, she produced dreams in which she embraced her mother, wary, nevertheless, that her mother might claw her or bite her. At that point, it became evident that there was sadism and excitation in her objects. She could not know what her mother had inside her: hatred or love? It was as if within the maternal breast, there could only be rage (her father's emigration, her son's illness). This would justify her hostile attitude towards the world. And in her world, the objects of her wrath were the analyst in each session and her husband in everyday life. We were both monitored and punished if we moved with freedom of thought. It reminded me of the girl from the film *The Exorcist*. Denying the fear it generated in me, I felt that the patient aroused my interest, but anything I said to her was used against me. To introject was to feel vulnerable; therefore, meanings were examined to discover toxicities and were generally discarded. It was a nightmare.

The problem was how to approach treatment. In this sense, Meltzer thought that for this quite psychopathic woman, it was necessary to understand the therapeutic method described in the gospel, which consists of expelling the patient's bad spirit, and placing it in pigs that would subsequently be thrown off a cliff. This entailed that the patient's destructive and voracious irritability, her madness, had to be projected into her husband and later into me, in the transference, so that she could later get rid of us. She tried this on various occasions. Despite the turbulence present in my office, Meltzer pointed out the tedious character of this material, trapped in vindication, excitement, and discharge. It is important not to lose sight of the fact that the patient's attacks were aimed at destroying the individuality of the analyst, not so much as a transferential object, but rather as a concept of father or mother. By attacking the formation of concepts, she would manage to avoid the emotional impact of finding herself with the analyst's maternal and paternal functions. The strategy to avoid or prevent symbolic formation was eroticisation and acting-in. The patient could get up brusquely from the couch, jumping up without any preamble, or wear clothes that made it easier to see her breasts or buttocks. At the time, she acted out her aggression. By the end of the analysis, she could also feel and be concerned about this violence.

At the time of the supervision, she was considered an incipient psychotic. This diagnosis allowed a differentiation to be established between *borderline psychosis*, and *incipient psychosis*. The difference lies in that the borderline psychotic has a damaged relationship with reality due to the use of intrusive identification, while the incipient psychotic is bounding down the slope of madness and tries to save themself by exporting their psychosis to their surroundings. This was Florencia's self-therapy method; exploiting her irresistible beauty. When these types of patients are trapped in the acting-out of the expulsion of their psychosis, they are incapable of observing their psychic reality. In the immediacy of the transference, it is the analyst's task to observe the danger of falling down the ravine that besieges both patient and analyst. In that respect, it would be good to remember—as Meltzer said—that "psychoanalysis is the science of observation, and not of explanation. When you begin to offer explanations to patients, you are really going backwards".

When faced with a patient like Florencia, who invites you to establish an alternating sadomasochistic relationship, Meltzer has shown that the analyst's task is

> that of preserving hope when you are faced with helplessness when there is nothing you can do. The only thing you can do is to listen and think. In that way, by listening and thinking, you are showing your therapeutic qualities in the hope that the patient will come to identify with you. In these circumstances, the main quality required of the analyst is perseverance. Eventually, the evidence of the patient's identification with this kind of object [watching and thinking] will be the appearance of sincerity in their communications; it will be to mean what you say, not just to say something, but to say it sincerely.

3.1.1.4 Synthesis: The Possibility of Thinking

A possibility; because in these three patients with such a poor capacity for observation, thinking was only a possibility.

Ferrán had an ambiguous way of speaking, and his speech was full of generalisations that made one presume he had some thought disorder, a disorder that arose
from his persistent preoccupation with the image he gave off, and that prevented
him from having emotional experiences. Everything was reduced to daytime fantasies and ruminations. The alpha function had serious difficulties creating elements
apt for building nocturnal dreams. His difficulty did not prevent him from being attentive to what was said to him. The proof of this was that his partner stopped being
only a transference figure to become a person, although with deficits. Ferrán, however, continued to be dependent on the presence of the object for its breast-alpha
function that helps babies think. Being alone awakened his own fear of babies who,
in the loneliness of the night, go to their parents' room out of loneliness, and the
fear of dreams that appear while asleep. It will be a long time until he can observe
his own mental life, a necessary condition for developing thought and recognising
psychic reality.

In her current manic-depressive condition, *Inés* had developed techniques to
avoid thinking and remove all meaning from her experiences, except winning and
feeling manic or losing and being depressed. Among her difficulties in thinking,
there were no confabulations that would have made thinking unnecessary. Faced
with contact with an object, the basis of thinking, she eluded the experience by
turning her attention quickly to a circumstantial element. If she had confabulated,
she would not only have despised the objects but would have created them.

Florencia often found herself trapped in arguments that were caused by misunderstandings. Emotions could not be thought but instead were quickly transformed
into vindications. Far from functioning as bridges towards reality, the communicative function of emotions was denied. Not infrequently, she felt powerful when her
own functioning was governed by anti-links (-L, -H, -K): she was authoritarian,
fanatical, cynical, and cold, although other times she looked like an abandoned
child that clamoured for and/or demanded to be held in her carer's arms. She lacked
the capacity to modulate the violence of her emotions. For example, her love (L)
demanded a sexual encounter. Her mental problem became complicated when the
anti-links were added to her symbolic equations derived from zonal confusions.
This combination naturally prevented the observation of each object or situation,
thereby reinforcing her feeling of injustice.

What these three people hold in common is their inability to observe and investigate psychic reality in order to think and to develop intimate relationships.
There were, however, also differences. Whereas in Inés and Florencia, the rejection
and expulsion of psychic reality predominated, in Ferrán, due to his superficiality,
contact could not be made with his psychic reality. Another difference is that Inés
did not tolerate the analytic relationship, and it did not take her long to break it off,
whereas Florencia and Ferrán sustained it, with positive results.

Patients like these put the analyst's ability to become impassioned to the test.
When facing patients who are incapable of observing psychic reality, or who become excited with the destruction of reality and the rejection of meaning, then
all that is left is to trust in one's own psychic reality to be able to tolerate these

encounters. But can we use the term "encounter" for these overwhelming moments of anti-links manifestations? "The clinical situation of overwhelming affects—says Murillo (2010, p. 313)—from an excess of L, H, or K can provoke a difficulty in thinking in the therapist, too concerned with simple survival or of keeping their place", exactly as happened to me with Florencia's explosions, Inés' contempt, or Ferrán's emptiness… Whether overwhelming due to excess or defect … it awakened my hatred (H) for not being able to communicate with them. A warm, not cynical hatred. Passion not only surges with the convergence of links, but also in the presence of some anti-links, as long as neither dissociation nor the predominance of the thanatical triumph. It is easy to love those who love you, or to investigate with those who are willing to know. Passion demands the presence of the three links but without ruling out a certain negotiation with the anti-links. In this sense, I agree partially with Grotstein (2007, p. 312) when he says:

> L, H, and K are the components of passion. Passion must be shared in order to qualify as passion. Passion conveys the emotion of suffering as well as that of warmth. It is the *sine qua non* of the analyst's capacity to contain. […] I believe that L, H, and K function inseparably, but at any given moment, one of them can become prominent as the others seem to recede. Fundamentally, we can only K an object by knowing how we feel (L ↔ H) about it. Bion often stated that we cannot love without hating and cannot hate without loving. Bion scholars and others more often mention K, but it is my opinion that there can be no K without L and H, only attempts at the pretence of their absence.

In their sincerity with themself, the analyst negotiates the combination of emotions and the quality of their state of mind to sustain the task at hand. Pretending can be an expression of the analyst's insincerity to elude a situation that overpowers them, but that, far from bringing relief, increments suffering. The difficulty in recognising hatred (H) when faced with the tenacious opposition from non-mental parts of patients can move the analyst in the direction of the negative grid or the reversal of the alpha function, stripping experiences of their possible meanings. Collusion was a possibility with Ferrán, Inés, and Florencia.

3.1.2 Dissociation and Intrusive Identification

In the same way that the representation of the world develops through structuring dissociations capable of organising categories, psychopathology feeds poorly off of aberrant dissociations or excessive dissociations along with the use of intrusive identifications.

3.1.2.1 Opposing Intrusiveness

Young *Jana* came to our first meeting with all of the characteristics typical of people who pay attention to fashion, with the pleasantness that is typical of an expert in social and business relationships, at the same time that she generated a distance that transformed her in a cold and enigmatic person. She had acquired the social skills typical of people brought up in big families, from siblings to servants, but where affects were but an occasional experience. She was incapable of establishing inti-mate relationships. This characteristic made itself present from the initial moments of our relationship. I perceived a sensation similar to the two of us being separated by a screen, as if something were in between us, preventing close communication. Sincere communication was only a longing. She could speak about her sex life, her masturbation, or her perverse practices without inhibitions. There were, however, inaccessible, unpassable areas. She justified her reservations by saying that our relationship was not real because she could not ask me about my private life or have intimate physical contact with me. With Jana, a contractual relationship was understood: a bartering relationship between parties (be it information, comments, or interpretations) but where emotions are forbidden, excluded ... except when she bursts out crying or in anger, as occurred on occasions. At that moment, the char-acterological armour cracked. Then, an orphan appeared, although always ready to guard her cave, her perimeter, and attack if someone tried to approach beyond the red lines she had drawn. She only felt safe and somewhat triumphant if she ruled the relationship and disciplined me. She seemed like an animal tamer alert to the slightest gestures of independence from the animals. The loneliness, characteristic of her emotional state, was more bearable than the painful muscle contractions resulting from her permanent state of tension.

The absence of any desire to have children caught my attention. She lived with her partner like *"vintage"* youth, fashionable, with no perception of the passing of time. Temporality was only present in the fact that she was preparing to fill the position of the future family heir. This was in response to the following social phe-nomenon. Jane lived in a house where various generations lived. In this big family, where women functioned like managers, there was only one woman who func-tioned as the mother/manager of all. The grandmother held this function for years. Her mother is exercising this function at present, and she is waiting for her turn; her desire and expectations do not respect the natural order that the eldest daughter substitutes the mother/manager because Jana is not one of the eldest children.

Her managerial vocation comes from her confusion of identities with her mother. In Jana, it is possible to observe behaviour derived from relationships based on in-trusive identification. Identified like this with her mother/grandmother/manager, she is capable of organising work efficiently in the company where she works. Her efficiency comes from her intelligence, the merit of being capable, and the need to arouse admiration to confirm her worth. In this way, she can get rid of the admira-tion/envy that she felt for other women who were less trapped in pseudo-maturity than herself. At the same time, however, that she triumphed (manically) for having seized the idealised characteristics of the admired object, for example, efficiency, she paid the price of the muscular contractions that imprisoned her.[1] The feeling of fraudulence was another price she paid to function intrusively because she is not living from her own personality but from the object she penetrated.

The invitation to carry out a pseudo-analysis is always present in patients like Jana. She came to my office to get information or techniques to later manage them on her own at home in her house (cave), doing as she liked. Establishing the analytic situation and finding tools to relate with these patients is a real challenge. Of all the contributions made by Meltzer during the supervision of Jana on technique, I will only mention two: the need to interpret actings-out within the transference, and the need to observe what the patient does with interpretations.

Starting from the premise that each patient will receive interpretations in their own time, Meltzer established the following distinctions between different types of patients and moments:

> In the case of adult patients, the analyst hopes to have sufficiently rich mate-
> rial to analyse its content. They also hope to not always have to look for and
> investigate the acting out or acting in the transference. In cases where the pa-
> tient appears with symptoms but not disturbances of character, it is generally
> very easy and faster to enter into this type of content within the material. With
> patients that arrive with character disturbance, what must be investigated and
> interpreted are the actings in and out of the transference, and a couple of years
> approximately are required for patients to begin to cooperate with the analyst.
> On the other hand, in the case where there is symptomology, the patient will
> collaborate sooner. The problem of interpreting acting-ins is that it is very easy
> to embarrass or humiliate the patient when showing them at the moment, when
> it happens, how they are behaving. […] In order to diminish feelings of humili-
> ation, offence and anger that this type of interpretation can cause, it is recom-
> mended to try to explain to the patient what is being done when interpreting
> in this way. It comes down to asking permission of the patient and in that way
> obtaining their cooperation.

Exquisite treatment of the patient's feelings requires being attentive to the meaning of the actings-in because

> …it's designed for the patient to awaken in the analyst the reaction that they
> want, and thus be able to control it. In the acting-in, what patients do is employ
> techniques that they've developed and elaborated earlier in their lives and that
> have proven successful. As to how they've been elaborated during the patient's
> life and the way they develop is something hard to perceive for the analyst
> because they appear easily and speedily, without "squeaking". It's only after
> they've happened many times that the analyst is able to see what it's all about
> and is usually surprised, because they aren't prepared for this situation.

In this respect, I remember how the patient placed many objects (cigarettes, sun-glasses, a book or magazine, wallet, tissues) around her, which suggested a wall from which I was observed, treated with informality, repeating compartments that she had already established in the places she frequented.

The other element that characterised her defensive functioning was how she treated my clarifications and interpretations. Often, she agreed with what I said, but she only received it intellectually, with the added danger of turning them into other tools for defensive usage. If I interpreted something in relation to her mother or her confusion with her, she reverted the perspective and listened as if I were interpreting or talking to her mother. It did not take her long to lose all interest, which manifested in her loud yawns.

Her paternalist attitude, her rejection of the emotionality present in the relationship, and the severity of her character disorder made the patient opt for body techniques. The premature interruption of her treatment prevented her psychic reality from being explored or developed.

3.1.2.2 Fear of Introjection and Madness

Rocío, like Jana, had difficulties in introjecting. The possibility of something entering her was not considered. She lives in distrust. That is why she does not communicate sincerely either. Not even with her psychiatrist, "to whom she didn't tell everything". Here, just like Jana built a wall around herself and did not tolerate trespassers who crossed the red line, Rocío had, from early infancy, her own fantasy. This consisted of sitting in the backseat of the family car and looking out the window, with a knife splitting all of the people the car drove past into two. This was her way of protecting herself, by deciding who could enter her territory at each moment.

Taking into account the presence of zonal confusion and jealousy with respect to her mother, it was difficult to tell if the desired object which she had allowed to come into her territory was a nipple or a penis. This became an alternative object when she believed that her mother did not love her. The guest, however, had no way of imagining that participating in the feast organised by Rocío was just a lure to be trapped/controlled.

During our initial meetings, she told me about the following dream:

I opened my belly horizontally with a knife. This was how I punished someone. There were people around me. Dark men wearing hats. There were also women. I saw pink flesh and red blood. I felt no pain. It was a triumphant situation. I said to myself: now you can finish. So I emptied myself out, and was left like a shell, the hollow of my eyes black. It was like a betrayal. It was as if I were on the side of those men. I bought myself a coat and dark glasses There was a child somewhere. Later I saw myself walking with an aunt of mine in a park. I was wearing my coat and glasses. I thought: 'they don't know how I am'.

Before it was all about being "inside" a car, and now it's about expelling what's "inside" of her. Here we see a state of mind anchored in confusion and a violent desire to differentiate herself from everyone who is not herself. At that same time, she watches who occupies her internal space and does not doubt to remove them—emptying herself out. She closely watches who is around her to split them down the middle.

Although Rocío was borderline, possessive of her space, and controlling, this dream permitted establishing a needed differentiation between a *psychotic depressive reaction* and a *neurotic depressive reaction*. In the psychotic depressive reaction, Meltzer said that "there is an identification with the lifeless, empty object, while in the neurotic depressive reaction there's emptiness because the subject is unable to introject". The psychotic patient is identified with a mutilated object, and the neurotic patient suffers from an empty self because they cannot introject. This was Rocío's problem: she was empty because she could not introject because she distrusted the object's intentions. She was far from being able to have an intimate relationship with the analyst because an erotic paternal transference, along with the fear of betraying her mother, predominated. This caused her so much distrust that she was afraid of being tricked and invited into a deceptive, erotic relationship. At that time, this coincided with a change of psychiatrist and an improvement in how she was feeling. This well-being generated the fantasy of having been invited to take part in a sexual relationship with this partner (composed of her psychiatrist and me), which in her fantasy was the equivalent of a parental couple. The corollary of this fantasy was that after being seduced, she would be rejected and thrown into madness.

Fear of madness was always present for Rocío. This could be observed in another dream:

> There was a group of people and we had to take some tests. We had to get naked; we stripped and felt no shame. One of the tests was that we had to take a pathway that led somewhere, in the centre of the earth, hell. We walked down stairs that had been carved out of the stone in a tube that became increasingly more narrow. It was like an inverted cone. At the end there was a kind of trap and we couldn't get out. We were going to die. In that space there was poo—she mentioned here that for days she'd been having various dreams in which there was poo all over the place, and she hadn't said anything about it yet, continuing to tell me her dream—Everything was a hoax. I tried to fix it but because we were naked, we had nothing on us. Maybe we could dig a tunnel to the surface …

Here, another element of her struggle against the occupants of the space appeared: her infidelity. She could leave and go to a different space of analysis—her recent change of psychiatrist and her hiding things were present. She was afraid of being expelled. Not infrequently, she had manifested her fear of me or that I would not like her. During the encounter, Meltzer interpreted this dream as the entrance into the *Claustrum*, with the rectal compartment.

> I would interpret this dream—he said—as a dream about her fingers that she's putting in her anus. When naked fingers enter her rectum, at the start this produces a very exciting sensation, but once the naked finger touches faeces, she realizes it's a deception, a trap. She thinks these fingers have been invited to have

a sexual relationship inside the object, but when she touches the excrement, she realizes that, in reality, she hasn't been invited to this relationship, but rather to a trap with faeces... and forever.

Naked, she could be taken anywhere, for example, to an idealised relationship with her parents (in the session: the psychiatrist and the analyst). Here, the *aspirated*[2] *projective identification* (her invited) is complemented by her *intrusive identification* (her wanting to enter into the couple), with the result of her being locked in the rectal compartment with only one way out: schizophrenia (poo = madness).

After pointing out this maddening way out, Meltzer made another contribution:

> She gives the impression that, in addition to all of this concern for especially pregenital sexuality, there is another part of the personality that she's developing that's capable of learning and working. What occurs is that in psychotherapy, it's very difficult to enter into contact with this part. She only shows us the sick little girl part, but there is another one that brings her here, takes her to work and makes her learn and function in the external world. It is important to realise that there's an infantile part that's living in projective identification and completely conceals the differences between the infantile and adult parts. This happens because the identifying part [of the projective identification] gives this little girl the sensation of being an adult, and this is where we see her pseudo-maturity. You must not only illustrate for her that the adult part exists, but you must show her the pseudo-maturity that she manifests through her grandiosity that grows from these identificatory aspects.

Without establishing an alliance with the mature part, it is difficult to approach the pseudo-maturity and rescue the infantile parts trapped in this pseudo-existence. This is reminiscent of what Winnicott used to say about the false self taking care of the real self while waiting for someone to arrive and rescue it.

Grandiosity usually manifests as omniscience and with the feeling of certainty that was so evident in Jana. While Rocío showed more of her claustrophobic, suffering aspect and concealed her ability, Jana was just the opposite: she showed her wisdom (based on omniscience) to govern everyone but did not tolerate recognising her claustrophobic anxiety that was somatised through muscular contractions. The greater awareness of suffering helped Rocío tolerate the psychoanalytic help that Jana, with her character difficulties, resisted so greatly. Thus, in the same way that Jana wanted my tools to be able to give herself therapy, Rocío, in her desire to control everything, could not permit her thinking or her mind to function free of conscious control. Meltzer expressed it like this:

> She's so worried about thinking things consciously that she cannot allow her mind to absorb things and come to think them unconsciously. She does not allow her internal objects to think, and she intends for the self to do everything. Patients who deny psychic reality have the feeling that they've got nothing inside them that can help them to think.

This is Rocío's drama and the predicament of all patients who live in projective identification: because they live employing this mechanism, they become emptied out and simultaneously fear that those around them want to colonise, invade, and occupy them in the same way that they themselves control their surroundings. They also want to control their interior with the pretension of ruling over the course of their thinking. That is why they become anxious when they dream; at the same time, however, their healthy part is joyous because some of their functioning escapes their conscious control. This control can lead to insomnia because they continuously watch what moves about in their mind.

The phantasy of penetrating and descending the tube towards the anus-hell-madness in the dream we have seen may contribute to some technical suggestions about the kind of therapeutic distance that Rocío and other patients with the same structure require. Using intrusive identification preferentially (invading the object to the fullest), paranoid anxieties of being invaded and controlled increase. That is why "temperature and distance" (Meltzer, 1976) must be watched with them, avoiding being neither too warm nor very cold, neither very hard nor obedient because their distrust is always present. Therefore, work consists of, among other resources, waiting to establish the maternal transference that allows the little girl to find her analyst/mother and, in this way, begin slowly to like the words that come from the analytic nipple.

3.1.2.3 The Danger of Unreality[3]

Jordi was an excellent professional who emerged from an undifferentiated family group. This group was presided over by a powerful and distant father-leader who supported himself with a fascinated and obedient wife who always wanted to please him. This self-satisfied couple contributed to their multiple children remaining anonymous and in the care of servants or sent to prestigious boarding schools far from home or abroad. The representation that arose of this group was very similar to that of a pyramidal organisation, in the cusp of which lives a powerful loved/hated leader and at the base a bunch of desperate children struggling to get a place in the structure at constant risk of falling apart.

Jordi's successful career alternated with a feeling of emptiness and loneliness that he numbed with a secret sexual life. The centre of his fantasies was occupied by the big penis of a black man that Jordi looked at on his tablet, enraptured, while masturbating. His voyeurism did not calm him down for long. Once he had left the companies where he was admired and applauded, he felt empty and went looking for that penis that sustained him. Jordi believed that, through his gaze, he could enter another person's private world and acquire their qualities. This is reminiscent of Fabian's fantasy in the novel by Julien Green (1947) with similar results: idealisation is only a fleeting illusion. The emptiness returned with the added fear of being discovered in his inconsistency and reported to the police. He was frightened that the glow would fade and that they would stop looking at him. Not being looked at or being left alone was tantamount to being cast out into nothingness or madness.

This fear compelled him to be bright and helpful. The problem arose when he was not rewarded or recognised. This led him to explode with jealousy if, in a triangular situation, the woman left with another man, not so much out of jealousy but because she took the penis (always idealised from the other men), kept it for herself and did not pass it on to him.[4] This personality organisation refers to his resentment against the mother who did not look at him, blinded by her fascination with her fantastic husband, who also kept the great stallion's penis to himself, throwing him into the anonymous, infantile world. Without an introjective identification with a mother (capable of containing him and offering him alpha elements), Jordi struggled against a feeling of unreality: thus, while he was in the company of people, he felt like he was someone, and vice versa. That is why when he separated from the analyst at weekends, he deflated, and the analyst disappeared. Something happened to him that was similar to what another patient recently told me: "When I return to the session, you reappear". Not only does the patient reappear, but the analyst himself, as if periods of reality alternated with unreality. For this reason, Jordi not only found it difficult to give continuity to his own psychic reality but also could not conceive that the analyst had internal objects capable of orienting him in his relationship with the world. For Jordi, the analyst was an interpreter. This same occurred with Rocío for whom I was a representative of a "psychotherapy" institution and not a person. At the base of these conceptions resides the inability to tolerate the individuality of parents or recognise the parental couple.

It was particularly difficult for Jordi to recognise a cooperative relationship between his parents. This difficulty was at the origin of his pathological splittings, similar to the splittings underlying sexual perversions. For him, the combined object penis/testicle was intolerable because the generative function of the testicles stimulated envy, jealousy, and competition in him. Separating the penis from the generative function of the testicles managed to reduce it to a part object, a triumphant fetish that he incorporated through his eyes. Through masturbation, he was able to feel as powerful as his idealised object. Another consequence of this splittings was that the experience could be reduced to a purely sensual and innocent level by denying his envy, jealousy, and feelings of competition. The elimination of meaning opens the door to the absence of limits, to polymorphism or promiscuity. At this moment in the supervision with Meltzer, it could be said that Jordi had a secret religion where he worshipped the great penis while sending his mother and women to hell—useful objects to serve as admirers. In this state of mind, it was not strange that adult sexuality had an obscure place in his emotional life in the same way that the illusion of being a father[5] was almost inexistent, coinciding with Jana. I say almost because not his whole self was trapped in the object. His healthier or more adult self encouraged him to be analysed.

Jordi was between two worlds: the adult capable of paying attention to reality, and the adult who used magical resources to put denial of reality before all else. Like this, a father could become a no-father through the sole use of the resource of placing denial ahead of everything and finding an idealised vacation destination consisted simply of denying unpleasant or frustrating elements. The possibility of sliding into unreality was very conspicuous in this patient, as it is in patients from the *Claustrum*. However, Jordi did not reside in the *Claustrum* because he would go in and out of projective identification. Diagnostically, he was borderline because he was between the external world of values and meanings versus a world where concrete behaviours predominated, devoid of meaning, valued only quantitatively: the size of the black penis and the number of female followers, for example. Meltzer deemed his state of mind to be borderline because of the "ease with which he could slide into perverse, sadomasochistic processes with loss of contact with reality".

When meaning is not taken into consideration, it is easy to slip into or reside in a bidimensional world. This accounts for the extreme dependence in these patients on the external object for their existence. Jordi, who was a slave to looks and applause, had sufficient intelligence to talk, analyse, or joke with the people he held in high esteem. He had skilfully surrounded himself with people who were capable of compensating for his deficits: on one hand, a new partner freed him of any task (shopping, managing the agenda, taking him places), and on the other, an analyst who decoded meanings and kept him from finally falling into unreality. These palliative resources would be the expression of the triumph of the projective identification of his adult qualities deposited in external support systems and functioning as an eternal exoskeleton.

3.1.2.4 Anal Grandiosity[6]

Eduardo's anal grandiosity was inversely proportional to his capacity to recognise the fecundity of his parents. His parents had created a family together composed of several sons and daughters, all generally responsible professionals who cared for their own children. Belonging to a well-to-do social class, however, seemed to colour relationships with a certain snobbery. Not infrequently, comments could be heard that suggested that in this group, price indicated value. At the time of the supervision of this material, Eduardo still lived with his parents. His inability to leave the paternal home resided in his internal world which was governed by part and devitalised objects, lending him a state of mind that he attempted to conceal through boastfulness. Good looks and an abundance of money concealed a little boy still trapped in the anal phase. This reminds me of the dream of another patient who, seated in the centre of a room, was surrounded by women dancing and applauding. Not infrequently, I have come to feel that Eduardo used me in a similar fashion: to applaud his creations....

In the two sessions that, at the time, I took to Oxford to supervise, a distortion of dependence and fierce opposition to take in interpretations could be observed. If he had approached the dependent relationship in earlier sessions, he was now in an opposing position. The first session that I presented began in the following manner:

> I had a strange dream: 'A worm was rising up' (reminiscent of a dildo—said Eduardo—I read some publicity about it; there were different sizes like a cobra rising). It was an upright worm stuck to the floor with a suction cup.' I felt anxious.

After a brief pause, he continued, saying that some girls wanted to seduce him and that an industrialist proposed that he represent him.... Following this, he referred to his father as being bored and jealous. "In my opinion, it's good to accumulate experience from my father". The material finished here. The problem was figuring out where he accumulated the experience, because he seemed more disposed to accumulate it in his anus than in his mind. For Eduardo, learning meant accumulating. Meltzer (2003, p. 92/93) pointed out that

> ...according to the dream he sees himself as a long faecal filament coming out of his father's bottom; one part of it stays stuck to his father's anus, but the rest of that filament has quite a lot of freedom to act, to go riding his motorbike, to go out with girls, to buy an apartment. The question is if the truth of the psychic reality is precisely the opposite of that: that he sees his father rather as the faecal filament coming out of his own anus, an important father, with a good name, and being able to defecate a father like that gives him a position, a standing in the world. The image is of a small child still in the period of sphincter control, sitting on the toilet, passing a motion, and the mum, sisters, all the women are saying: How marvellous! What a good shape! [...] It is a distortion of dependence, where instead of recognizing that you depend on your objects, you are generous and you give them something, you allow them, for example, to fight over the TV remote control inside your bottom. It will end in financial, economic, and psychic ruin.

The danger of insanity announces itself like this. The reference to the TV remote control refers to a domestic dispute between the parents for the remote control and him treating them like children having a spat. Completing this inversion of dependence, Meltzer (ibid., p. 94) points out what occurs with people with difficulties assimilating and introjecting.

> Anorexics suffer from this too, particularly the ones who suffer from the bulimic variety where they eat and take emetics and laxatives. They are so preoccupied with seeing what comes out of them that they can't see that nothing is going in.

This opposition to taking in/learning was observed when the father wanted to teach him something about the company, and Eduardo seemed incompetent. Meltzer referred to it as *negativist stupidity*. Stupidity compensated by verbosity and the accumulation of objects, something equivalent to boasting of great culture because of a big library, even though half of the books are unread. The possessiveness with objects, and pride are the antithesis of a sincere recognition of his father's teachings, and his mother's disposition towards him. That is why "...the only way he can go through life is as an extension of his parents, in projective identification with part-objects, most probably his father's penis and also almost certainly his mother's bottom" (ibid.).

Eduardo's state of mind was governed by geographic and zonal confusions. As a result, he had serious learning difficulties, and that drove him to seduce homosexuals who penetrated him and sometimes robbed him. Far from getting depressed, he always emerged from the experience boasting that, in this way, he could understand the world of women—those beings who were incomprehensible to him—putting himself in their place, obviously, and confusing anus with vagina and mouth. The anus was the place for assimilating. For him, through his anus, he could receive and accumulate books, penises, sports cars, flats, etc., because according to him, "everything leaves something, a mark", without realising that the mark that is left is not one of development of internal objects, but rather ruin. I often felt concerned that he would contract a serious infection.

In the other session presented at the supervision, it could be seen how the patient thought he organised his parents' lives (he said that he would buy them something or other, or that he would take them to such-and-such a place without his parents finding out or giving their opinions beforehand). This repeated itself in the transference when he tried to control my mind. In the session, he told me angrily about a meeting of the community of flat owners in the building where he lives with his parents. At that meeting, the other owners confronted his grandiosity and his father's arrogance, opposing a decision that his father had one-sidedly made without consulting the community. At least at that moment, the figure of the law, although repudiated, appeared: someone can denounce that limits exist. In the face of the irritation limits caused him, he reacted in multiple ways, for example, by arguing confusingly, fallaciously, or threateningly. It was particularly difficult to argument something with him. As Meltzer pointed out, it was "difficult to establish real communication with him; he goes a different way and answers your comments with negatives" (ibid., p. 99). At this moment in the supervision, I referred to the language that had been most successful in getting him to listen: talking to him as if talking to a small child.

> Most probably that mummy-and-daddy language—said Meltzer, ibid, p. 99— suits this boy who is still in the phase of sphincter control, terribly interested in what comes out of his bottom or what goes in through his bottom. It is true he is a great confusion creator, and it is difficult to understand what he is talking about[…] it is important to force him to be specific about what he is saying, describe it better. Because once you make him describe exactly what he is narrating, then with factual knowledge you can say: 'How stupid, that is a lie!' […] What he is telling you is nonsense, rubbish; a lot of rubbish comes out of his mouth, and you can take that and tell him clearly: 'you are undifferentiated, confused'.

The creation of confusion was not only a reflection of being trapped in his anality but also part of the fight against dependence on parental objects. In the transference, with his confusion and verbosity, he was attempting to control me, or buy or sell me whatever, in order to feel that he was repeating with me what he believed his parents had done with him. While he felt so powerful, we may suppose his parents felt desperate about having such a confused son.

His family might have been well-to-do, but Eduardo was basically poor. From the dream of the suction cup, it could be inferred that he would be thrilled if I liked it as much as he did, stuck to the chair five times each week, while he masturbated. Eduardo would want me not to reject it. He would want me to like it, and feel pleasure in it. He wanted the two of us to transform it together and conceive of it as a great aesthetic experience. That same experience that he could not tolerate because of his mother's beauty. Unable to experience the emotions of the aesthetic conflict, he split off himself, and through projective identifications, he built that pseudo-maturity anchored in anality. Meltzer (ibid., p. 101/102) went on to state that

> Unless you stick very close to the transference, you get lost in this labyrinth. You have to say to him: "being used as a piece of faecal mass in your bottom is not a great aesthetic experience for me" Of course, this kind of interpretation implies a threat; it is saying, "you are not going to use me in that way indefinitely", but I can't see a way of avoiding a threat in an interpretation of this kind. [...] At the beginning it can be interesting to see this configuration, but as the time goes by and you see no progress you stop being interested.

The irritation at the intervention made by the community of property owners awakens hope that one can intervene and introduce a law to unravel this grandiosity, as long as one has enough patience and perseverance to tolerate the indolence and insolence of an arrogant little boy. If one does not manage to do this, the danger of insanity and economic ruin appears on the horizon.

3.1.2.5 Manipulating with Passivity

On another occasion, I presented Meltzer with the initial diagnostic interviews of a patient named *Ismael*, a young man of 23 in the middle of a psychotic breakdown. The father, a former political militant who had been taken prisoner in his country and who knew me through a third party, asked me to see his son, who had taken refuge in a city close to Barcelona because he felt persecuted. After talking briefly by telephone with Ismael, he agreed to come to my office. His father remained in the waiting room. Ismael presented a confused state of mind with delusional interpretations of persecution. It was difficult to discriminate between the different elements present in this situation. Circumstances converged that were typical of this moment in life (the end of university and plans to move away from home to another city, thus leaving home), he had taken drugs, and his parents were momentarily separated. The family culture was characterised by the absence of intimacy because "between us, there's nothing to hide", his father told me. Meanwhile, on the outside, there were great enemies (Reagan, for example). Ismael's family was presided over by a father who controlled everyone's life. Ismael's ambivalence with respect to the paternal figure manifested, during his breakdown, through two fantasies: In the first, his father was hit by a car and run over in the street. The other consisted of Ismael throwing himself into the sea to rid himself of microphones that had been implanted under his skin.

Other scenes developed before me, forming an image that allowed me to understand his confusional state. In the two interviews that I took to Meltzer, Ismael could not tolerate spending much time alone with me, and he called his father and asked him to come and be with us. But not only present—he tried to get me and his father to talk to one another while he listened or slept. On the one hand, we could think that he was fearful of a relationship with me, but on the other, it seemed that he was trying to organise the scene and my task.

An element that oriented my understanding of this moment was the reference to having been compulsively watching the film *The Matrix*, in which the need arises to inject life through the nape of one's neck; besides, in this film, there is a messianic character who would change the order of things. This reference to someone who injects something, along with the belief that his father and I were revolutionaries who would transform the world, suggested a confusional state that originated in projective identification: in this state, all activity would come from the revolutionary leaders (his father and me) while he would remain passive—he insistently asked me to put him to sleep—while awaiting the transformation. This longing for passivity, however, was not sustainable due to the push derived from the possibility of finalising his degree (he only had to present his final paper), and the hatred of these very same leaders was visible in the following acting-out that occurred in the second interview:

> (...) Patient: "Give me something to sleep. Put me to sleep"!
>
> Therapist: If you fall asleep we won' t be able to talk and that's why you've come.
>
> P.: "Call my father", he orders
>
> T.: "You yourself can do it".
>
> P.: "Call him!" He gets up, opens the door, and calls out, "Dad!". Ismael's father comes in. Ismael stretches, puts his head at the end of the couch, where the feet go, he remains in silence, and then says: "The two of you can talk!"
> His father says: "You talk to him".
>
> "I want to sleep", says Ismael.
>
> T: Maybe you're afraid, and that's why you move your head away from me, and you want your father and me to talk.
>
> P: "I want to sleep. My head hurts".
>
> T: You have many thoughts that cause you pain.
>
> P: He jumps up and sits on the couch; he snorts, closes his arms around himself and clenches his fists, gets up, looks all around, goes towards the back of my office where a degree hangs on the wall;[7] he grabs my doctoral degree in psychology off of the wall and moves quickly towards me, furious, carrying it as though it were a tray (I thought he was going to break it over my head), but he stopped and rested it on the floor at my feet, slightly tilted and began to read it. He said: "It seems you're intelligent". Immediately, and in a loud, menacing voice, he added: "I'm not

going to break it, don't worry". He picked it up, walked away towards the back of my office again, and put it on a piece of furniture. From there, angrily, he threatened to break it and put the broken glass in my anus. Meanwhile, he talked about the military men "that wanted to kill you…"

In this story, an impulse to grab at and destroy a phantasy derived from the presence of the internal persecutors (the military men who wanted to make his parents and me disappear, according to his story) and his desire to free himself from the revolutionary leaders who oppressed him, when he pulled off the microphones. Faced with the admiration for a degree that I already had and that he was not sure he ever would, his reaction could be understood as an envious act. At all times, I perceived that, psychopathically, he was making me feel his terror of internal persecutors and paternal control over his life. The father/Ismael relationship suggested a collusive pact derived from the projective identification of Ismael's capacity and potency in the father, and the aspirated projective identification[8] of the father on Ismael. The result of such a pact was Ismael's passive attitude and longing for a saviour (Matrix). The mother had little authority to interdict this type of relationship, although she served a modulating function. Therefore, I believe that the mother's absence precipitated the breakdown. Meltzer thought Ismael's adolescent confusional state was complicated by drugs and political activities—issues that there was no time to explore.

Ismael had been admitted to a psychiatric hospital. The context of the moment became complicated. The psychiatrists did not agree to any dialogue with me or allow me to meet with Ismael. Psychiatrist friends of Ismael's parents gave their opinions about the best method to help Ismael. His parents were ambivalent or even resistant … When Ismael was released, we had a meeting, and I presented that meeting in the supervision. Meltzer then pointed out that:

You can't fight against all of those people. The parents are divided. The psychiatrists are divided in their opinions, and the patient is very passive. You have to wait. You don't know what's going to happen. It appears that he expects you to be that messiah. He's imprisoned in this state of projective identification. He uses everybody, setting you all against each other. He's playing with you. It's important that you don't let yourself be led to this situation which is so similar to the film Matrix, where there are two realities. You should explain to him why you won't be accepting the video. Tell him why you won't watch the film. Surely, he'll continue with ups and downs for quite a long time. I don't believe that he's taking drugs regularly. A film can be addictive, but it's not the same as a drug. His father will want to remove him from his therapy. I don't think the psychiatrist will protect the therapeutic relationship. It depends on him; it's time he stops being passive and abandons the pleasure he gets from setting you against each other. It's a question of patience and waiting. If he continues to take LSD, he'll have a very bad trip, and it'll be hard for him to get out of it. His passivity is a reason for great concern.

Because of his passivity and longing for someone to assume his potency, Meltzer suggested interpreting:

> ...how he's turning you into his saviour and crucifying you by making it impossible for you to do anything. While he's going up and down, there's no real danger, except the danger of him having a bad trip and not being able to get out of it because, even though he's in a manic state, he's on a road that could lead to schizophrenia. This film Matrix seems very schizophrenic. When you interpret to him, it's important that you emphasise your inability to do anything [...] It's very difficult to recover from those multiple illnesses because many things come together at the same time: politics, divisions between parents, drugs, comradeship with friends, and uncertainty regarding his education and professional future. The only thing that you can do is to establish a position of inability from which to contain, and resist taking action of one kind or another; and that he obliges you to be very worried.

How can Ismael's psychosis, this Ismael capable of warm contact at the same time as manic, be contained? Meltzer's suggestion was to be willing to feel powerless, i.e. "vulnerable to his projections and undefended against them", by trying to discover their meaning.

3.1.2.6 Synthesis: On Intrusive and "Aspirated" Identification

Because she denies all types of emotionality in relationships, *Jana* often has a feeling of loneliness that she tries to compensate for through intrusive identification with the admired-envied object: women-managers. It gratifies her to feel admired. She consequentially employs all of her resources to that end. She believes herself to be the admired object. She pays a high price, though: isolation, loneliness, a sensation of fraudulence, and in addition, being closed up in her muscular armour. Her difficulties in establishing an analytic relationship were expressed, for instance, in her paternal attitude towards the therapist whom she forgave, educated, and instructed.

Trapped in pseudo-maturity, *Rocío* was wary of all relationships. It was difficult for her to differentiate between a relationship based on a confusing invitation derived from aspirated projective identification, or from an invasion by the object, from another type of relationship based on respect. While she was trapped in an intrusive type of functioning, she felt omnipotent (she could rid herself of everything that was not her, like in the dream), and she believed herself capable of controlling her surroundings. Because she functioned intrusively, she distrusted relationships, as if they followed the principle of "an eye for an eye". Loneliness and fear of betrayal and madness were always present in her.

Jordi, a brilliant polemist, had developed a pseudo-identity based on his loquacity. He tried to compensate for his fragility with voyeurism (penetrating the internal world of the object and controlling it) or exhibitionism (cultural) in the continuous in-and-out oscillation of projective identification. When he felt important (for instance, that he was being convincing and winning votes) that momentarily erased his loneliness. His grandiosity, reinforced by his success in politics, freed him of feelings of unreality, but when he failed to succeed, he could become violent.

Eduardo's fragile structure was sustained by part and devitalised objects, an emotional situation that he tried to conceal by flaunting his wealth and erotism. His personality organisation was supported by a grandiose fantasy: he believed himself to be able to defecate a famous father and, thus, walk around awakening admiration in others. This infantile position stimulated his belief that he organised the family's life and the analysis while making him incapable of learning, becoming independent, and having intimate relationships. Although he was far from being what he thought he was, he belonged to a well-to-do family of certain fame and permitted himself to treat others with contempt.

Ismael had split off his own capacity and projected it into the paternal figure who had sucked him in. The result of this ruinous encounter was that he became trapped in a passive state of mind and, at the same time, triumphant because he controlled everyone.

In cases such as these, one can observe how the narcissistic defence of avoiding differentiation between subject and object impedes personality development. Whether it be through splitting off and identifying projectively with the qualities of another object, or invading it to dispossess it and acquire a false identity, the consequences amount to the deterioration of the subject and a lack of respect for the object. Jana, Jordi Pi, and Eduardo felt admirable, Rocío and Ismael felt powerful, and all of their different states of mind derived from confusion. But they all have similar results: deterioration, ruin, loneliness, and madness.

In this material, mental functioning derived from the omnipotent phantasy of intrusive identification can be clearly observed. The richness of this term was accompanied by another concept that is intended to be a clarification. In a clinical seminar with Meltzer, he used the term *aspirated projective identification* to describe situations where the child or patient was made to become a part of the pathology of the adult; as if by being swallowed by the object. I am not sure if this term is enough of an entity for it to be called a personality organisation or to demarcate a relationship, and I wonder if it can cause more confusion than clarity. I will not detain myself in describing the meaning of the term "intrusive identification" because I covered that subject in a paper reproduced in Section 3.1.5. In that study, I focused on the material of Jordi Pi, but I could have used Jana's, as both of them, forcing entry into an object, would acquire its qualities. One of the "benefits" of intrusive functioning is the sensation of grandiosity; a sensation that will have characteristics in accordance with the meaning attributed to the compartment of the internal object that was invaded (Tabbia, 2000). The "price paid" has already been described: fraudulence, etc.

As explained in note 2, the expression "aspirated projective identification" is confusing. The term "aspiration" refers to the stimulating function of internal objects as well as to possessive and tyrannical longing over people.

In the first meaning, stimulating refers to promoting the identification with the functions of the internal objects promoting development. Meltzer (1976, p. 10) expresses the type of relationship typical of one that inspires:

> the direct relation of the adult structure is to the internal objects with whom it is identified in an aspirational sense, as to teachers or mentors. This relation may be externalised in the form of an adult transference, as in religious belief, or to inspirational figures in the outside world, current or historic.

This intrapsychic relationship finds its equivalent in the interpersonal relationship, for example, when parents stimulate their child to develop certain types of learning or initiatives; it is something equivalent to the very same pedagogic function of psychoanalysis that stimulates the recognition and assessment of psychic reality. Stimulate, however, means to suggest, invite, and offer. Correlative to these proposals are acceptance and rejection. This characterises a scene where an interchange is possible. However, if, for example, the son has to study the degree that the family decided on, under penalty of being disinherited, then respect has been abandoned. The possibility of a reaction demands a personal capacity that is not always available, for example, in the case of immature people or rigid personalities or because they are in a relationship of dependence, etc.

Aspiration becomes imposition when a transference figure (a boss, a psychoanalyst, whether masculine or feminine) directed more by their own needs and motivations, finds a son, employee, or patient without sufficient personal organisation, so as to discuss the situation, and leads, guides, or conforms it according to a personal model. This would be the place where the expression "aspirated projective identification" would find some meaning. This could be observed in the case of Ismael. His father was so confused by his son that when he introduced him to me in the initial interviews, he referred to himself and Ismael saying "we are the disappeared", a term used for those who had been kidnapped during the Argentine dictatorship, but without that being the case of Ismael. The father's control over the family's life[9] and the therapy, to the point of breaking it off, suggested that throwing himself into the sea to remove the microphones could be a way that Ismael expressed his rebellion towards the paternal aspiration. I think, though, that there was a complementary mechanism to paternal aspiration, the mechanism that the very same Ismael exerted over his father and the rest of the family, as he manifested before me. In both directions, there was no respect or freedom. I think that the scant place that Ismael's mother had in the family dynamics was proportional to the mutual idealisation and confusion between father and son. Not infrequently, I experienced his attempt to include me in the idealisation of revolutionaries. The sealed arrangement of this relationship, so typical of a *folie-à-deux*, placed me in such a peripheral position that I could only aspire to join the confusion.

I was able to observe a similar situation to being excluded from a confused relationship between Ismael and his father, when another patient, an adult, was excluded from a *folie-à-deux* composed of his wife and their son. Both the mother and the son were united in fostering a parasitic and contemptuous attitude towards the father. Both members of this dyad swallowed or sucked each other up: the mother protected the parasitism of the son, and the son protected the mother in her resentment. This relationship caused their son to have severe difficulties in establishing a therapeutic relationship because being in treatment meant, among other things, betraying his mother. In Ismael's case, allowing his treatment entailed renouncing the shared *folie*. Paradoxically, a third person is usually sought after to break the therapeutic relationship and thus perpetuate the pathology. The psychiatrist friends of Ismael's father were the ones who opposed his continuing therapy.

Does it make sense to keep the formulation *aspirated projective identification*? Insofar as it is confusing with the inspirational function of internal objects capable of stimulating the development of the personality, and that with intrusive identification names can account for the phenomena of identity confusion and lack of respect for privacy, I think it is better not to use it unless its meaning can be explained.

3.1.3 Immaturity and Struggle Against the Combined Object

3.1.3.1 An Immature State of Mind

With *Marcela*, we approach yet another state of mind. In previous cases (Rocío, Jordi Pi, Eduardo), we found ourselves in the territory of geographical confusion and intrusive identification, a space where boundaries are abused and rejected. This was the territory where a fierce battle was fought against dependence on the combined object—the battlefield of more or less confused functioning and manic defences.

With Marcela, we entered into a territory of immaturity, oscillation, and mobility between states of mind. When "the person is very dissociated—said Meltzer (1996)—and their infantile parts alternate with adult parts in an attempt to control behaviour, one can speak about immaturity, immature states of mind"; this is the description that comes the closest to Marcela's state of mind. She was a nurse not only capable of the utmost dedication to her patients, but she could also live in isolation and fear, longing for someone to hold her in their arms—the hugs that were missing when she was little and were found far from the paternal home. Year after year, there was another event or birth that demanded her mother's dedication. What was surprising about Marcela was the contrast between a responsible adult type of functioning, in which she was capable of travelling far to handle situations that demanded courage, and her infantile, little-girl attitude, holed up in a corner awaiting a tender look from someone. Not infrequently, she sat on the divan, huddled up, to look at me, longing for a smile from me. Her look held enough softness and adhesiveness to suggest her longing to stick to me. It could be said that remnants of adhesive functioning alternated with structuring introjective identifications. This alternating provoked a particular fascination in the observer since a dialogue could be established both with an adult, and with an abandoned kitten. This coy attitude concealed various types of functioning. On the one hand, she managed her encounters with others to receive affection and be looked at. How important being looked at was for her! If occasionally we had to have the session on the telephone, she suffered because she could not look at me/touch me. On the other hand, she could be totally insensitive to the feelings of others. Occasionally she seemed cold and hard when facing the pain of people close to her. Her infantile selfishness alternated with solidarity that seemed reactive. Probably the problem resided in knowing who needed whom. When she was the nurse who stood in solidarity with abandoned children in refugee camps, the pain belonged to the children. This repeated itself in the transference. Not infrequently, it was necessary to be attentive to the reversing of demand. She longed for an exclusive relationship and, above all excluding all others. That is to say; she did not want the analyst to have other patients or even family. She sought a tranquil situation governed by stability, so she avoided relationships with objects that could upset her. She feared someone wanted to enter her internal world, as revealed in a dream where something dark wanted to enter her bedroom. We could observe that this dark part object represented a nipple/penis part object that offered her something. She felt incapable of accepting it because the initiative had been made by the object and not by herself. Aesthetic conflict was a serious threat to Marcela. She shared Rocío's fear of the object's initiative.

An outstanding infantile characteristic of Marcela was her sensitivity to odours; at times she reminded me of Jean-Baptista Grenouille, the character in the novel *The Perfume* (P. Süskind). Marcela had managed to create a kind of greenhouse where she grew aromatic plants, and she was an expert at using them for cooking exquisite dishes. Her marmalades had acquired fame in the area. Perhaps, the similarity with Grenouille was that both had been born in painful circumstances. The difference was that Marcela could partially symbolise her frustrations and devote herself to making cakes and marmalades and taking care of children while sustaining a cruel harshness in her relationship with her partner, who was another abandoned and dependent child.

3.1.3.2 In the Belief of Being a Combined Object[10]

Ausiàs was an intelligent and loquacious man in his 30s and an expert in human relationships. He spent his life looking for balance in order to avoid catastrophes. His life lacked stability in two fundamental areas that he was unable to conquer: the area of intimate relationships and that of thinking. While he had suffered significant losses (his father became seriously ill when he was young, and a very close family friend, and great personal mentor, died suddenly), I think the catastrophe he also feared facing when he came to see me was that of giving up his manic defences and accepting dependence on parental objects. Proximity to the threshold of the depressive position was a possibility for development and a threat to pseudo-maturity. Like a good obsessive, he believed that his stability depended on him suppressing his emotions. He lacked sufficient interest to investigate the meaning of his experiences; he only wanted solutions.

The zonal confusions were very active in his state of mind, so, for example, if an oral need could not be immediately satisfied, the anus appeared as an available alternative. His anus, or his partner's anus, functioned like an available resource for emergencies. Even though this zonal confusion was not yet symbolised, it was never sodomised.

His parents organised family life in such a way that the mother, a successful businesswoman, brought home the money, whereas his father took care of their off-spring; his father, however, was a man confused about his sexual identity, as could be inferred from the fact that he encouraged his son to share the marriage marital bed with him, both naked and in the absence of the mother. This was complemented with games where the little boy slept with his parents, pressing his bottom against his father's genitals while pressing his own genitals against his mother's bottom. This created the phantasy that the child was the transmitter of the father's sexuality towards the mother: he received it from the father and gave it to the mother. The organisation of the oedipal scene was thus disturbed.

Ausiàs not only considered himself bisexual but also sustained the fantasy about manic agitation in which he believed that he could do everything. According to this fantasy, the parents were not needed parents because he was the "combined object, the object that combines everything", as Meltzer said. Ausìas was not excluded from copulation; instead, he was the mediator of the primary scene. He was at the centre of the scene. In this manner, he managed to deny his jealousy, and if some-one had to suffer jealousy, it should be the mother who vacated the marital bed or, in the transference, the analyst who should run after Ausìas' verbosity to exercise his parental function.

A triumphant Ausiàs was alertly watching that his representation of the world not change. He lived watching how relationships around him developed. How-ever, instead of observing behaviours and the emotions in the people near him, he watched excitations. In his infantile functioning, he thought that taking into account only a part of an object was sufficient to control the situation. The part object he chose was the penis. This caused him to live with an eye on the penises of the men around him. As an alternative to penises (his own and those of other men), nipples became equivalents, and accordingly, he counted any sign of excita-tion in those part objects. In this way, he built an almost mathematical world where he kept the accounts of the excitations as if these operations provided a meaning to him. His infantile and hyperactive way of organising his life (he ran around from place to place) was supported by a particular vision of the world as being a binary world of the presence and absence of excitation in penises and nipples. The fundamental model of this vision of the world was an erect penis. Presence (erect) or absence (flaccid) was the elements of his culture of quantities and his belief in statistical data. It is the culture of the non-observation of emotional reality. In this sense, one of Ausiàs' dreams was eloquent. In this dream, some children were swinging on a penis. As happens in perverse phantasy, the testicles were missing. In the dream scene, only the necessary element for excitation (the penis) was pre-sent, at the same time that he had omitted the generative dimension (the testicles).

They were not omitted because they were peripheral, but rather just the opposite, because testicles refer to something more than just Ausiàs himself; they refer to other children, as they did previously to siblings, and would open the doors to the possibility of feeling admiration and jealousy. Whatever generates conflict is eliminated. This happened with his only sister, the fruit of his father's first marriage, as if she had not existed for him. In his mania, he had not only covered her with veils until she was blurred but had also transformed his father into a homosexual who was more interested in Ausiàs' childish bottom than in his mother.

In his struggle to keep reality under his control, he would become very anxious when he could not balance expenses and income. He would have to look desperately for some alternative to keep the balance. Because he did not want to prostitute himself to keep balance in his economy, he fantasised about prostituting his spouse whom he cared for and shaved in her most intimate parts so she would be beautiful and appealing, all the while controlling her.

Ausiàs, as we will also see with Moisés, had serious difficulties thinking. By separating emotionality from his experiences, he only paid attention to concrete information, what would be called the *fact*; without emotion, the fact is mute. It remains only as a sign that may be preceded by another sign: positive or negative. This stimulates the belief that algebra is a model for thinking. Then, to balance the accounts (be it excitations, penises, or euros), it makes sense to eliminate emotions because, since they are complicated, they make it challenging to create an exact world. Thus, thinking becomes just adding and subtracting.

Faced with a vulgar world whose value is quantity, it is difficult to discover quality.

The analytical task with Ausiàs consisted of discovering this confused and grandiose child, lost among quantities and excitations, who, at first sight, would appear to be a pervert.

3.1.3.3 Obsessiveness

Although with differences, *Moisés* shared very similar states of mind with Ausiàs. Their biographies were manifestly different. Both were well into their 30s, and each had a partner. On the horizon was the pending recognition of the combined object made up of whole objects and their private lives. This achievement delayed the clarification of their sexual identity, blocked still by fantasies and masturbatory behaviour. While in Ausiàs' family, silent and acted-out erotisation predominated, Moisés' family was divided into sexes, each one in their world. Men devoted their time to the financial world, while women spoke amongst themselves, creating a sweet, sticky atmosphere. The image that Moisés had of his parents was that each occupied themselves with an area of the family, maintaining sexual encounters occasionally but without emotion. These were hygienic encounters. When Moisés, in his relationship with his explosive girlfriend, could not reproduce this model, he resorted to bimanual masturbation with which he satisfied his unsymbolised bisexuality.

Ausiàs and Moises shared a paranoid background and an obsessive defence. Both believed that emotions were not pertinent and even that they were impertinent.

What was important were numbers. Moises complemented Ausiàs' understanding. He not only complemented him but in the supervision of Moises, I was able to listen to a unique lesson about the treatment of obsessive states such as those observed in Ausiàs. At the time, Meltzer said that…

"…the treatment of an obsessive character is really the treatment of their methods of thinking. Methods of thinking are […] concrete and based on simple dualities: yes or no, good or bad, white or black, etc. There's no place for meanings, shades, or qualities, etc. It's the mentality of a computer that is alone in having the answer: yes or no, then by multiplying the number assigned to *yes* and to *no*, you look for the answer. Moises, basically, was anxious concerning Maria—his partner—because she does not function like a computer but like a volcano. When the emotional temperature rises to a certain point, it erupts. These two have great problems thinking. She cannot think because she cannot match or put together her observations with their affective responses. It only works when it's based on emotional responses. He cannot think because he's not in contact with emotions.

One of the big problems with obsessives is that they can't work with symbols. […] Moises can't make contact with symbols that grasp the meaning of things. This is part of our current scientific education that believes that thinking and reasoning are a multiplication of data and […] will produce an emotional outcome. […] You can't make symbols for your patients if they don't bring you dreams so that you can see their ability to form symbols. […] Moises doesn't have the slightest notion that heat is emotional heat. […] These obsessive types who are not part of the human race are totally isolated in this almost mathematical attitude to everything."

What is of fundamental importance, as you were saying about your patient, is that he cannot distinguish between within our outside of the object, between the outside world, and living inside an object. These are people who continually use projective identification and live in a hierarchical, labyrinthical, mathematical world. In my experience, they are terribly argumentative. They're all lawyers. They use this method of controversy as if they were always in the courtroom, where each part of a trial says a part of the truth, and they believe that this method of argumentation is what can lead them to the truth. For me, the first aim is to introduce these people to the human race, because they are people that have a great sense of their difference, their unique character, they are grandiose, and they feel different.

Meltzer later raised the issue of the difference in the treatment of obsessive states of mind conducted by a woman or a man. Both must make the claustrophobic situation that these patients live with intolerable. The struggle to attract them to a relationship

…develops basically along linguistic lines. It consists of struggling against false logic, tricks and linguistic resources that change the value and meaning of things. A male analyst will have to face the fact that he will be an omnipotent figure in the transference. A woman analyst can allow herself to be, as Cleopatra said of women, 'soft'. Loneliness makes claustrophobia intolerable. The method I use—fighting—makes claustrophobia intolerable because it attacks grandiosity. When you attack their grandiosity, you must be prepared to defend yourself from the accusation that you are being grandiose and this seems to be centred on the idea that you know (everything) and your defence against this is that you know very well that the importance of not knowing (everything)—of negative capacity. The closest to being able to know everything is through emotions and the apprehension of beauty. The male analyst's task is to enter, with time, into contact with the maternal transference; while the woman analyst will have to defend herself from the accusation of masochism. The maternal transference in a male analyst or the accusation of masochism in the female analyst converge, and with time, both figures will converge—both parental figures will converge in the oedipal complex. The problem of establishing the combined object is a very lengthy process. I am surprised that, with patients of this type, I frequently take 8 or 9 years of analysis. The key to working with obsessives is to accept with resignation that it is a lengthy and arduous process and that perseverance is all you have. For the woman analyst, the problem is that the patient is in love with her; this goes with the patient's tenacious, clingy and demanding aspect and with the differentiation between adult and infantile sexuality…

The obsessive's struggle against the recognition of and dependence on the combined object establishes a difference in the length of treatments, comparing them with other states of mind. Thus,

> at the very same moment that the analysis enters into Oedipus everything begins to move ahead on wheels and in 4 or 5 years you find yourself at the end of the treatment. Of course, obsessive patients are all paranoid.

This statement was completed with the following:

> Obsessives are voyeurs. They believe they have this capacity to look inside the head of a person and see what there is, like when they look through a window of a house and they see what's there and what's happening: they therefore know what you're thinking and feeling. This they do on the basis of a rich capacity for paraphrasing and changing what you say, giving the meanings to your words that they want. They are very skilful at paraphrasing what you said; they know, they remember … Your defence is to tell them that you don't remember what you said because memory doesn't operate in the same way computers work. It is said that computers have memory, but they don't. They only have a register (records). The way that an obsessive paraphraser remembers the words that you have used is exactly the same as the lawyer who says that it is written in black and white and that he's got a document, as if people couldn't lie in a document. The criminal confesses but can then say that they confessed under torture, etc.

The obsessive believes in action, and you as analyst believe in meaning; therefore you are fighting with different weapons: the patient fights with a sword and you with a sickle.

The important thing about paraphrasing is that the paraphraser remembers minutely the words they have changed from what you said and can quote word for word, but what you said is not word for word, but word for word from their paraphrase. Your only defence against a paraphraser is to say, 'that doesn't sound like "my way of speaking" but sounds like "your way of speaking"'. Without dream material, you are lost; without dreams, you are dependent on the patient's anecdotal material, which is a bunch of lies because they are paraphrases, in the sense that paraphrases are lies.

In this context, a question arose about whether the number of sessions in the treatment of these patients was relevant; and starting there, other questions arose:

The frequency is irrelevant; most important is what things you pay attention to from the material the patient brings. The anecdotal material that they bring must be treated like a story about acting-out, stories from which you have to abstract the meaning of the transference that is being acted out in those performances. [...]

I think that with the obsessive patient, when you begin to argue, time goes by quickly, and you have to keep an eye on your watch because the patient has a stipulated plan to lengthen the session and invade the space of another patient. Discussing things about language is very interesting, and you will find that you're looking forward to the next round of the fight. Patients, over time, begin to realise that this continual arguing with you defends them from the natural tendency to fragmentation. They come to realize that, by arguing and arguing with you, they are held together. Later, they'll accuse you of enjoying it, but that's not true. What you do indeed like is the debate on the meanings of words and the functions words have, while the idea that patients have of arguing is the use of deceptive language mechanisms to beat their opponent. Little by little, you come to recognize these tricks and to identify them rapidly. These linguistic mechanisms are part of what Bion called the negative grid. [...] Finally, what you're going to achieve from these patients only after many discussions, is that they respect your point of view about how the mind works. [...]

We know a lot about how the mind works and how it doesn't work, and we also recognise the limits of its functioning, and those limits are very important. The basic limits that you must recognize in your work with such a patient are those imposed by language. Language doesn't only consist in saying something, but also in showing it, and what you show the patient with perseverance, patience and kindness are, eventually, your maternal weapons. The patient's complaint, with time, eventually will be that you don't love them. This isn't true; because, yes, you do love them. You love them, but in the same way parents love children. And this paternal love between parents and children has limits which are those in which the action would be unthinkable, for example, direct sexual conduct.

With this, we conclude Meltzer's masterful lesson on the treatment of obsessive people who resist reliving and symbolising their Oedipus to develop and reach emotional maturity.

3.1.3.4 On the Threshold of the Depressive Position

When *Felipe* came for a consultation, he had not been living in Barcelona for long. Barcelona was the last leg of his tour of European cities where he had tried to settle down after having hastily abandoned his native Chile. The first thing he expressed was his need to integrate here. It did not take him long to understand that he was not only referring to his longing to resolve his emigration status but also to integrate emotionally. The persistence of infantile, non-symbolised functioning tied him to compulsive behaviours that placed his work and family life in danger. In the beginning, the question of Felipe being a bidimensional personality without a home who emigrated in search of a container was one I pondered. This hypothesis was later partially confirmed, but Felipe needed to reorganise his internal container.

During the course of his analysis, different questions were eventually clarified.

In the preliminary meetings, he mentioned compulsive behaviour during the transition from puberty/adolescence concretised in the ritualised scene of mastur-bation in which he achieved orgasm by stimulating his penis between his legs. In addition to the isolation in which he lived, this scene suggested a psychotic state derived from intrusive identification with a part object/breast. The scene hinted at the representation of sadistic coitus. Repetitions in the transference and the account of his life during treatment clarified these possibilities.

In his family of origin, women were the admired objects, while his father and younger brother did not awaken his rivalry. He believed that his condition of first-born in a traditional family would provide him with an outstanding place. To his surprise, he was not outstanding in academic performance or sports. Much to the contrary, his sister was the good student who received recognition from both family and school. This provoked an envious hostility against her, and he humiliated her. The defensive response that Felipe opted for was an identification with the func-tioning of his mother; the problem, however, was that Felipe's mother appeared to be an object with serious difficulties. From Felipe's viewpoint, his mother was an impulsive woman who could occasionally get out of control, skilful in managing the concrete world, but incapable of thinking. The capacity for reverie was not her most outstanding quality.

Felipe's admiration for and envy of his sister in addition to his identification with an efficient mother led him to feel a longing to become the breast that was always available to help women out. The need always resided in others. Without actually ever functioning as a compulsive cook, he was, however, willing to give away money and do people favours. This produced a long list of people who benefitted from his generosity. It was not an aseptic generosity but depended on the mean-ing these objects had for him. If the other person was hungry/in need of money, he offered his breast/money; if the object was lacking in some resource, it was the opportunity for his compulsively generous penis/breast to offer coitus. From his nipple/penis confusion, Felipe was always willing to please his object in any erogenous zone. It was all about interchanges with part objects. This clarified the compulsive masturbation from his puberty/adolescence. What he represented in ritualised masturbation was not so much sadistic coitus but the expression of his phantasy of being the breast that fed everyone without needing anyone. He did not even need to compete with his sister because she was just a poor thing that had to study, while he was the admired object. The result of this was that she came to be a respected professional, while he permanently felt like a fraud. This is reminiscent of the feelings the inhabitants of the *Claustrum* have.

Concealed behind the defensive armour of his generosity was an incontinent child. He was incapable of waiting to satisfy his needs and desires. If he could not eat what he felt like at any given time, or evacuate when the signs appeared, he could burst into screams or hit out, in the style of his mother. In the aftermath of such explosions, he would feel ashamed and worried, thus manifesting a certain capacity to think about his acts. This capacity for thinking developed gradually in Felipe... under the protection of the analytic relationship. I say protection because Felipe felt the analysis to be the home he was looking for during his emigration. A place where he could find someone who would think with him and help him to develop his own capacity to think or, as he demanded at the start, someone who would help him to integrate. This could be seen in how he could come to analysis full of malaise, reproaches, persecutory, and confusional anxiety, and progressively calmed down as the session continued and he understood what was happening to him. This fact stimulated a dependence on the concrete person of the analyst, not only his function. After supervising the first session I presented, Meltzer said of Felipe:

...he's not fixed, he's not living in projective identification. He's a person who comes easily in and out of projective identification, especially when it concerns his sexuality and his greed. I wouldn't consider him a borderline patient or a psychopath. At first, when I saw all of that sadistic promiscuity, I considered that possibility, but none of this appears in the rest of the session. However, what does come out is the fact that he could react to any interpretation you might formulate. The interpretations that you've made have changed his mood quite radically, and this would indicate a positive maternal transference with you. I don't know what he was like twelve years ago, but at present, he's not so bad—except for the fact that he very much depends on you. This means that when he leaves a session, he probably feels quite good, and quite healthy. However, this is a state that cannot persist for very long.

In the following session, Felipe recounted a dream where represented persecutory anxieties appeared that pushed him into looking for punishment. This was enough for Meltzer to clarify that

...With this kind of patient who in external reality has caused damage, has done bad deeds, as is the case here, we see that when the depressive feelings emerge, what also appears is the temptation to stay in the paranoid-schizoid position, stuck to very suicidal ideas that would function as a sort of punishment These ideas that he has about suicide become organised as a defence against the sensation of not deserving this privileged position of being a patient of yours.

As if the patient had expressed that "one must be careful not to destroy good things". The material presented, a whole week of sessions (three sessions), prompted Meltzer to say:

> This week is very interesting, and so is his development. At the beginning of the week, he comes full of annoyance, anger, and persecution, and at the end of the week, the depressive anxieties appear. This is very characteristic of the threshold of the depressive position: the patient enters like a lion and goes out like a lamb. The patient experiences each session with great relief, as they leave him with something good inside him. When this begins to appear with consistency and the patient begins to show feelings of not being worthy of this privileged position, what is starting to take form is the situation of the end of the treatment.
>
> In some part of the material, there is the idea that someone is waiting to receive therapy and waiting for him to finish: some baby is waiting to be born; mummy and daddy are starting to speak about having another baby. And this is when the true genital oedipal situation begins to take shape. All of the other material that has previously been seen is pre-oedipal. It's not really oedipal material, but triangular material. It is important to establish the difference because otherwise the term 'oedipal' comes to be used in an exaggerated, abusive way. Pre-oedipal material is, in fact, triangular material, on a part-object level, and does not involve the jealousy of the oedipal situation but, rather, involves envy and threats of possession. When the truly oedipal material arises, the focal point that emerges is that the love that mummy feels for the baby is not the kind of love she feels for the father [...] the daddy is special, and the baby is also becoming something special: he, too, is special and must be looked after in an individual and exclusive way. This does not exclude the fact that the mother may be in love with the baby or experience the baby as an aesthetic object. Even when this happens, when the mother is in love with the baby or experiences it as an aesthetic object, what she is really in love with is not the baby's actual being but with its potential: that this baby may be miraculous—the father may be wonderful as well as the mother, but that the baby is miraculous. It's a more cosmic form of love, of being in love.

The well-being that the analysand experiences from the relationship with the analyst should evolve towards the introjection of the psychoanalytic function of the personality so that the process can continue without the analyst. That is why Meltzer suggested interpreting in the direction of Felipe connecting more with his internal objects. The stretch that was left, however, entailed resolving the oedipal conflict with all of the ambivalence that he had been unable to tolerate in his childhood. It was quite a challenge. It consisted in evolving from that representation of sadistic coitus to that of loving, life-generating coitus.

With Felipe moving towards the oedipal conflict, this completes the cycle begun by Ferrán (Section 3.1.1.1) trapped in a triangular situation: the transition from the paranoid-schizoid position of part objects to the threshold of the depressive position of more whole objects.

3.1.3.5 Synthesis: The Fate of Preconception

Marcela's immaturity relied on the dissociation of mature and infantile aspects. She did not trust the object and doubted that she could be offered something better than what she had experienced until then. There were no red lines in the relationship, but she distrusted the object's initiative. She was seeking a quiet situation in which her stability would rule, and for that reason, she avoided relationships with objects that could be upsetting to that balance. The need to respect her timing, as refers to distance and proximity, imposed itself.

The theme of stability reappears with an *Ausiàs* who was utterly committed to regulating his economy, both chrematistic and mental. Losing the hegemonic place of being the combined, regulating object of family life was unthinkable, just as such a fantasy was essential to satisfy his belief of being independent.

Moisés' inability to tolerate emotional turmoil isolated him in a closed world where he believed himself to have achieved emotional stability by appealing to bimanual masturbation. His difficulty in observing and intuiting limited his perceptive capacity to an exercise the equivalent of a rudimentary algebraic summing up of behaviours, similar to that described in relation to Ausiàs, that prevented intimacy and thinking.

Felipe was able to transition from a factual world based on excitations to a state of mind that capacitated him to begin to self-observe. To live in a world of more whole, oedipal objects allowed him to work through his jealousy.

If this clinical material is seen using the *model of the mind* implicit in Bion's thinking (Meltzer, 1993; Chuster, 2014), then these states of mind could be considered to impede the development of preconceptions. This model establishes that preconceptions seek a realisation in order to generate conceptions (thoughts) (see also Section 3.3.3). As Chuster (2014, pp. 108–109) shows,

The most important preconception for psychoanalysis is the oedipal preconception, because it includes all the others. It also proposes and delimits a field of work, which is revealed by its complexity, always more than is believed to exist within the realm of the classic application of the theory of the Oedipus complex. […] Another important characteristic of preconception is its constant reducibility to the mental. For example, the breast preconception first seeks the mind of the mother in order to arrive at the physical breast, and not the contrary. It is in the space that the mother's mind reserves to receive the preconception of the baby where a conception is created. It is in such space of creation where the baby can be fed by the rhythm of the milk with the mother's gentleness and the capacity to love. It is not difficult to understand, in this model, why some children do not succeed in taking the breast, or why there exists in many people dissociation between the material and the psychic (Bion, 1962). In the same way, the oedipal preconception seeks the mind of the parents, in order to mate the reality of the family. If this doesn't occur adequately, the individual may spend life in a state in which they feel things but don't suffer, which means also that they cannot solve their problems because they cannot reach them.

One of the ways that immature patients resist the nudge of preconception is by returning to a sensory world, taking refuge in confining oneself to bed, to the familiarity of home, or to relationships where odours and flavours predominate, as in the case of Marcela.

Another way of opposing preconception is manifested by dissociating emotion from ideas. Patients live this way, believing in a concrete, countable world where meanings are unknown. You are worth what you own. Moisés and Ausiàs exemplify this type of functioning. The other world, the one alien to their accounting, does not arouse interest. And the mother's eyes are not discovered. They are the object.

These cases illustrate the resistance to dependence on the parents—as in the case of Felipe, who was confused with a combined part object—and therefore, no development in his relationships is achieved. These patients do not suffer the pain of dependence nor the pleasure of development.

3.1.4 The Organisation of the Self and the Analyst's Interest

The complexity and heterogeneity of personal manifestations of the different material presented here demand a model capable of containment. The container-contained model offers possibilities to address them. The point of departure of this model lies in the highly complex relationship between a receptive maternal object and a needy infant seeking an object. The interplay of links and anti-links (L, H, and K and -L, -H, and -K) will determine behaviours as distinct as those based on love, understanding, envy, or intolerance to mental pain. Of all the possible links, Bion pointed out three: the symbiotic, the commensal, and the parasitic. Each one has different outcomes for the members of the dyad. One possibility would be the development of each one of the members (symbiotic relationship),[11] as opposed to those quasi-relationships where the link is not transformed even if each member can satisfy certain needs (commensal relationship), as opposed to a relationship that is destructive for both (parasitic relationship). The symbiotic relationship will make possible the development of each one of the members of the couple at the emotional and intellectual level (their capacity for thinking and experiencing an intimate relationship).

Rethinking the previous clinical material in the light of the existing type of relationship and the phantasy of projective identification as a model of the primitive relationship with the capacity to create thinking, we might be able to point out that:

1 The phantasy of projective identification, as manifested in the cases presented, did not satisfy the function of creating thinking or of being a model for thinking, whether due to: excessive and violent use of the same (for example, in Florencia or Ismael), because of the absence of an object capable of reverie (Felipe), because of the distrust in using it (Rocío or Marcela), or because of the inability to self-observe (Inés).

2 The absence or intolerance of an internal couple (the combined object of whole objects in the language of Meltzer, and the container-contained, in Bion's language) manifested itself in the cases reflecting diverse states of mind. For example, Ausiàs struggled against the couple in order to maintain the phantasy of being the combined object himself; or Ismael, who did not rely internally on a harmonious couple that could sustain him.

3 The lack of cooperation or reedition of the mother-infant or breast-baby encounters was not a resource within reach of the cases discussed here, and so, not infrequently, it was necessary to chase after patients like Moisés in order to establish a dialogue.

What happened to prevent so much potential from concluding in development? It is not my intention to name the origin of mental pain, but I cannot ignore it. I limit myself here to presenting the intricacies so that we, as clinicians, can become agents of transformation.

Most of the difficulties presented here rest on the defensive use of narcissistic identifications (projective and adhesive) that confound subject and object so that the subject does not feel separation or conflict derived from dependence on objects. Mature dependence (Fairbairn) is not easily achieved. Here I again take recourse in Meltzer (1967, p. 31), who, once having pointed out the consequences of geographical confusions, put forward the different manoeuvres that hinder the establishment of a relationship capable of developing the subject, the two members of the analytic couple, and thinking in an intimate relationship. Manoeuvres characterised, among other mechanisms and phantasies by:

> ...a tendency to diffuse genitalisation of all zones with attendant excitement and quest for sensual gratification. The second is an idealisation of the beauty of the part-objects and a quest for their exclusive possession. The third is an attempt to form a closed system of mutual idealisation with an object through idealisation of the reparative qualities of the body products.

The task of debilitating narcissism and putting the infantile parts within reach of the combined parental object encountered serious difficulties in the patients; to abandon the manoeuvres was not a safe project when distrust was present in the relationship. Defences acquired all forms possible, for example, the erotisation of language in the case of Jana or Ausiàs, Florencia's seductive exhibition, and even Marcela's or Ferrán's passiveness. These are all infantile resources to avoid adult dependence and responsibility.

Recalcitrant states of mind that imprisoned the patients to varying degrees meant that neither thinking nor the capacity for intimacy developed. Without the internalisation of a parental couple with the capacity to meet infantile demands, neither thinking nor establishing an intimate relationship is possible. Without this model, different forms of evacuation or pseudo-alternatives appear as an alternative, as seen in the following sections on thinking and intimacy.

The struggle against dependence—the root of many disorders—is not reduced to a behaviour limited to a secret and individual territory, pigeonholed, but instead involves those closest, even in the most autistic behaviours where it would seem that the mechanism of projection or that of projective identification had been surpassed or outclassed. The narcissistic organisation will search for allies in the family, among friends or even in the analyst, to remain triumphant. The therapist must persevere even when facing all the temptations proposed by the patient, in the style of the demon and Jesus Christ in the olive grove. The way to avoid succumbing to the patient's resistance pacts may reside in keeping in mind the world that the patient lives in, to find out where they might place the therapist. Meltzer always surprised us when he described *the representation of the world* that the patient had. The patient, he would repeat, creates and dramatises their internal world in the transference, and the analyst is the main object, to play the complementary role, as could be seen with Inés or Ismael. In one case as the loser, and in the other as a revolutionary. The possibility of recognising the analyst in his autonomy was remote.

In a case in Brazil supervised by Meltzer, the material of an 11-year-old boy was presented. The child showed serious social difficulties as well as difficulties at school and presented himself as the victim of poor family organisation. At a given moment, Meltzer (2008, p. 78) wondered

> what sort of world this boy inhabits and what sort of concepts of the world he has[12], because quite clearly he is in great distress and very urgently desires to be in harmony with you. Now, it seems to me that his ideas of being in harmony with you are, as I said, very bureaucratic, very military, very based on ranking, prestige and other social values.

This conception of the world and social relationships moved the boy to want to establish an intimate relationship with the analyst with the aim of being instructed on how to overcome his difficulties. Faced with this state of mind, only the analyst's attention and interest can discover the child's potential. He needed to feel that he had a place in the analyst's mind, a place that was protected from interference from his sisters. For the relationships to develop that would rescue him from a primitive concept of the world, a great capacity for the autonomous formation of symbols is demanded of the analyst, because the interpretation of routine will not affect a child like this. One must be able to think in terms of "what sort of world he's living in" (ibid., p. 84).

Discovering the representation of the world that the patient brings and offering a genuine interest in establishing an intimate relationship with him is what will permit clarifying and transforming the personality organisation of the patient who is calling at the door, whether it be Oedipus or Narcissus, but who has not had much luck in life....

3.1.5 Living in Intrusive Identification[13]

It is difficult for me to unite the term "living" with that of "intrusive identification" as I consider that the relation between both is practically exclusive. The "living" of Projective Identification is a mere reflection or a parody of the "living" in relation with the objects. "Living" being able to tolerate the conjunction of the "links of relationship" with the "anti-links"—anti-emotion, anti-knowledge, and anti-life (cf. Meltzer, 1986)—favours not only the development of the mind but also the capacity to experience love, joy, hope, pain, aesthetic pleasure, conflicts, and so on, all of which is impossible while one is "living in intrusive identification". One only *lives* outside the object. Inside the object one only *survives*, only *lives badly.*

"Living inside an object" is an omnipotent fantasy correlative to "intrusive identification" in an internal object,[14] transformed into a "Claustrum"; this fantasy differs from the communicative function of projective identification. Some of the queries that emerge from this nuclear theme are the following: Is claustrophilia[15] an omnipresent fantasy? Does the object of claustrophilia always become a Claustrum? Into which internal objects is the intrusion carried out? What is the motive that drives one to lose one's life in order to attain a pseudo-existence? What are the consequences of intrusion for that part of the self that penetrates intrusively into the object? and so on. My contribution will be centred on this latter query. I would like to present, using different material, what happens to the intrusive *part* that seeks, to a varying degree, to live inside the other. In this section, I shall show the relationship of the self with its objects, or the paralysation of the self as a result of masturbatory-intrusive attacks on the internal objects; subsequently, the state of mind of the inhabitants of the Claustrum; and finally, I shall illustrate all of this with the clinical material of a borderline patient.

Humankind has always created images and symbols in the face of conflicts that are difficult to understand, such as pain, ignorance, and death. They are representations, like myths, which have the function of supporting mental pain. In the myth of Eden, as in the myth of Prometheus, there is a representation of the prohibition of access to knowledge and the consequences of disobedient daring. When humankind attempts to attain knowledge, the secrets of life, it is punished by expulsion/scattering. In the face of the painful situation of expulsion/scattering, container fantasies arose, such as those of the bosom of Abraham or the Church (which God prepared for a long time for the reunion of his scattered children) (cf. John, 11, 52). In these representations, humankind seeks to free itself from the anxiety of scattering, but in an omnipotent way: by placing itself inside a breast-object of Church-Abraham. The quest for an object in which to take refuge and prevent pain is a defence that, to a lesser or greater degree, is used at different times in life. I remember the extreme case of an old paranoid schizophrenic, resident in a care institution for decades, who was told that he would have to be transferred to another centre. His response was: "Leave to go to another place? No way! After so many years, *I am a part of you*. Kill me if you want, but I'm not going". For him, leaving the confusion with the institution-object was equivalent to precipitating into death-fragmentation. However, *claustrophilia* is not only a defence against pain in general, or disintegration in this extreme case, but also a manifestation of envy and hatred of everything that generates bonds. One could reformulate the claustrophilic *motivation* by giving as an example a *joke* attributed to Cantinflas (a Mexican comedian): "What do we come into the world for?, to suffer?; if that's the case, we're going back!". The subjacent fantasy of return-confusion with the object seeks to eliminate pain, implicit in the differentiation subject-object. Freud himself analysed the fantasy of return to the mother's womb as a denial of castration in the case of the Wolf-Man.

To end this brief enumeration of claustrophilic motivations which, according to their intentionality and degree, are transported through intrusive identification, I would like to recall the desire to escape from his unhappy personal situation that moved Julien Green (1947) to create a character, Fabian, who could become all the satisfied people, being able to be everyone, to be someone else... but almost to the point of forgetting about himself completely. M. Klein used this character and novel to illustrate the fantasy of projective identification in the external object.

But the *price* paid for avoiding mental pain is high. Once the patient has worked their way inside the internal object, they remain trapped there. Meltzer pointed out in Jana's supervision (see Section 3.1.2.1) that once the patient had penetrated the object, she remained separate from other people by a glass division, referring to the glass divisions of the compartments where she worked, inside which she adopted the necessary social behaviour but was incapable of maintaining intimate social relations. Inside the object, one is protected from the world, but one also loses it; like the Wolf-Man who felt fortunate to have come into the world protected by a foetal lining, a veil that hid him from the world and hid the world from him. The flight from the world in intrusive identification is so great that *there is neither any contact with reality nor any idea of psychic reality (internal-external); there is a lack of the idea of nature and reality is anthropomorphised; one does not live sufficiently in the external world, therefore, access to meanings and value is banned; time, if it exists, is circular.* Meltzer (1992, p.72) enumerates other consequences of intrusion:

> ...the intruding part of the personality suffers from anxieties that are contingent on the fact of being uninvited. it is a trespasser, an imposter, a poseur, a fraud, potentially a traitor. But it is also an exile from the world of intimacy, from the beauty of the world, which at best it can see, hear, smell, taste only second-hand through the medium of the object.

The intruder feels as much a prisoner as Segismundo (Calderón de la Barca, 1635) in his tower:

"...I know so little
of the world here in this tower,
my cradle and my tomb.
I was born here (if you can call it
being born), knowing only
this rugged desert, where I exist
in misery, a living corpse,
a moving skeleton..."

(*Life is Dream,* 1st day, scene II)

Segismund's tragic and desperate situation finds a new representation in another play. I am referring to Samuel Beckett's *Endgame* (1906–1989), through which it is possible to illustrate not only the world of the inhabitant of the *Claustrum* while they remain inside it, but also the *state of the internal objects* and the consequences for the self.

The action of the play, of only one act, takes place in a dilapidated setting, separate from the external world; In the scene, we find Hamm (H), the son, permanently seated in a wheelchair, blind, with his face covered with a dirty rag (at the beginning and end of the play); his partner is Clov (C), the servant, who is permanently standing; both are devitalised and daily represent a parody. At one side of the scene in the background there are two rubbish bins with a cover; in one lives Nagg (P), Hamm's father, and in the other is Nell (M), the mother.

The imprisoned intrusive part of the self has its own representation of the world, although it is not a delusional[16] representation, with which it maintains a relationship through veils. Therefore, in *Endgame* the *external world* is represented in a paranoid way because for Hamm (15),[17] outside this room, on the exterior, there only exists death; however, this representation responds to the fact that this part of the self was never in full contact with either the external world from which he feels he has remained absent (H, 47), or with the internal world. As he resides within an object, he feels that he neither forms part of the world of objects nor of that of relations but that, on the contrary, he experiences a feeling of remoteness and surprise before daily life, which, according to him, passes by in foreign hands. He has gone into *self-exile.* The *intermediary elements* (equivalent to the senses) with the external world are represented in *Endgame* by two small windows placed in the highest part of the walls and which remain covered with curtains and through which it is practically impossible to see anything except a desperately grey landscape (C, 26). The only one who displays mobility and some possibility of looking outside this room is Clov, the servant. However, through second-hand observations, or observing through another, like Clov, very little information can be incorporated on account of the limited contact with the world and as a consequence, distorted and aberrant thoughts are produced (C, 16).

The *internal world* that correlates to this diminished capacity to observe the world would be represented, in the first place, by the same setting in which the whole play elapses: deteriorated, useless, dirty, piled-up objects. One very representative element of this anal-Claustrum-world is the *inexistence of time*, because it is always the same time for Hamm and Clov (C, 13). For them, there are never any changes; everything is always the same (C, 33), because as there is scarcely any incorporation, there is neither development nor conflict. All life is an anaesthetising and routine representation of nonsense sprinkled with an occasional haughty *boutade* that intends to simulate authority (C and H, 16). However, once the (manic) petulance deflates, Hamm (30) is able to make out that he is living down in a hole, as if he were alluding to the rectal compartment of the invaded object.

The *couple* formed by *Hamm-Clov* represents aspects of the same self.

Clov would represent the *instrumental-adapting aspects* developed through trial and error, and which are only useful in order to operate in the world of facts; for this reason, Clov has no qualms about admitting that he has never thought (C, 30). This part of the personality is characterised by *lacking authentic interests.* It is a slave to the tyrannical aspect of the self and for this reason permanently waits for Hamm to whistle to him (C, 12); he will wait forever as for Clov-Hamm time does not exist; therefore, he will never die (C, 14). As there is no concern for death, this part represented by Clov is only interested in reaching *an inanimate, devitalised, dementalised state* where all could remain still, unchanging and where the only scant pleasure arises from the contemplation of the silent, deaf, and gloomy routine.

Complementing Clov is *Hamm*, who, with his eyes all empty and white (H, 13), is not only blind but, besides this, covers his face with dirty rags (foetal lining?). Hamm would represent the narcissistic nucleus of the self that rejects contact with the objects and remains immobilised like Narcissus before the lake, but who proudly proclaims that the only life is at his side (H, 45). Hamm, superb, hates whomever draws near his haven because he could be questioned or upset and he therefore orders the extermination[18] (cf. p. 103 of the original French version) of whomever attempts to draw near his grandiose refuge. Such great hatred towards the world of objects increases his paranoid anxiety, making him fear the proximity of the people surrounding him. For this reason, he orders Clov not to come near him because he gives him the shivers (H 24, 26, 43).

Hamm's relationship with his parents illustrates the relationship of the self with its internal objects. Nagg and Nell, infantilised, degraded, with their legs mutilated, are alone in their rubbish bins. This is a way of dramatising hate towards the parents, which entails the natural consequence of the parents-rubbish falling on the ego. Therefore, Hamm (p. 89 of the French edition), after describing his parents as impoverished and dead, subsequently feels that he himself is freezing…like the destroyed objects. He will also die of darkness (48), like Mrs. Pegg, for not oiling the lamps, for not rehabilitating the objects. As a consequence of the omnipotent control exerted over the parents, whom he keeps separate, preventing them from having any kind of mutually reparatory intimacy, Hamm *cannot establish true intrapsychic or interpersonal relationships.* Hamm not only has no partner, but when he tries to get close to Clov, the latter rejects him. Clov (44) neither wishes to kiss him nor touch him (44); so then Hamm tries to defend himself by asking for his (felt!) dog. This scene suggests the isolation and the *privation of all intimacy* correlative to the attack on the parents, as the substratum of the sadomasochistic and sterile relationship dramatised by Hamm-Clov.

What is the particularity of the attack that can be described in *Endgame*? And through which means is the attack being produced? Hamm, on several occasions, directs verbal aggressions to his father, particularly those referring to the father's genitality, which is degraded to the level of fornication between scoundrels (H, 15, 35). Such is the hatred that Hamm-Clov feels towards parental intercourse and fecundity that he even reproaches him for having engendered him. The hate towards children and siblings is what leads Hamm to reproach his parents for his own birth, thus confirming what Bion (1959) claims when he refers to the hate that certain people experience towards everything that links to the couple and the fruit of this same link.

In *Endgame*, there are signs of *urethral attacks on intercourse*. There is a scene in which the parents recall their honeymoon at Lake Como and laugh remembering anecdotes… Hamm then gets furious and screams for them to keep quiet until the scene finishes with the parents shut away in their respective bins. Hamm then feels that as his anger subsides, his desire to urinate increases (H, 22). Later in an amusing scene in which Clov struggles to free himself of a flea that has got in between his genitals, Beckett makes a play on the French words *coïte* and *coite*[19] presenting the conflict that would arise if the flea were copulating instead of remaining still. It is at this moment that Hamm urinates, and Clov gives his blessing to this evacuation. In both scenes therefore *Hamm urinates when faced with references to the couple's life and intercourse*, whereby what is emphasised is the primacy of urinating over copulating and relating. In this context, urinating would have the same function as Hamm's screams before the parents' account of their honeymoon: that of interrupting the relationship.[20]

At another moment of *Endgame* and in a sad dialogue (18–19), Hamm's parents refer to their own processes of deterioration and laughingly recall that accident they had had while they were riding a tandem and they had lost their shanks. However, their laughter progressively diminishes until they both end up expressing that they feel cold, to the point of feeling frozen (19). They are frozen with sadness. Sadness that arises from the fact that in that accident *they lost autonomy*, which is what led them to living in these rubbish bins and holding themselves up on their stumps (15), as their legs were amputated in the tandem accident. The choice of this vehicle is not devoid of meaning as a tandem is a bicycle for two people who sit one behind the other. This suggests to me that *the tandem is an infantile representation of the parents' intercourse* (cf. intercourse *a tergo*), which would have been attacked intrusively through *bimanual masturbation*. The consequence for the internal object-parents is mutilation and degradation, and for the son—by identification—is paralysis: Hamm is always seated, Clov, always standing. The envious-masturbatory attack on the parental couple entails the impossibility of creating an internal and external fertile couple, Hamm-Clov being the clearest expression of the narcissistic personality that inhabits the Claustrum.

If the patrimony of the self is composed of devitalised, denigrated, controlled, etc. internal objects, the person will not be able to think, experience happiness, feel alive, or establish contact with the world of objects, but rather, on the contrary, will feel banished from life, carrying around an arrogant appearance of reality, without being able to feel emotion, with the danger of becoming fragmented, experiencing fear, feeling persecuted by hostile objects, and remaining on the fringe of time. If the lamp is not filled with oil, one will die of darkness. Darkness such as Hamm's or that of the Wolf-Man hidden in his foetal lining. It is a defeat: *Endgame* lost! (H, 82).

The blind Hamm and Mrs. Pegg died for not filling the lamp, and Segismundo knows little of the world because upon being shut away inside an object-tower, he only has access to a dismantled, barren world which makes him feel miserably dead-alive. *Knowledge is banned in all these spaces.*

Another way of representing the impoverished and blinded condition of the part of the personality which carries out the intrusion is, according to my interpretation, Plato's *allegory of the cavern (The Republic,* VII, 514 a-521 b). A parallel could be established between the sequences, motivations, and consequences established by Plato in this allegory and the fantasy of intrusive identification in the object. Just as, on account of their imperfection, the more the souls drink from the Lethe, the more deeply they fall into sensitive reality, represented by the cavern, so the part that intrudes into the object (for the different motivations mentioned above) loses the relationship with the world of objects. In both cases, there is a change of condition (from the intelligible world to the sensitive one and from the world of objects to the *Claustrum*) on account of intolerance to pain. Plato describes the immobilised inhabitants of the cavern as being asleep, *having forgotten what things are like in reality,* and who regard as true only the shadow of the objects. These inhabitants would be in a state equivalent to that which governs thinking not through observation but mediated through news agencies—looking with others' eyes and *lacking true knowledge and freedom.* The part of the personality trapped in the object, as it is unable to develop concepts, only increases its greed, while at the same time, it tries to keep away from overwhelming truth and takes refuge in the shadows[21]; so then the subject consumes but does not experience enjoyment, they accumulate but feel empty: they are only full of the shadows reflected by the others. It is the echo of the thoughts of those they idealise, but they do not know the value of ideas: they believe that the goodness of the objects resides in the fact that the other uses them. They know the best restaurants but lack a sense of "taste". They can become a presumptuous expert like that of the cavern, skilful in discerning among fleeting shadows. However, it is not difficult to discover how their grandiosity tries to cover up their boredom.

Plato considers the world of the cavern an equivalent to the hell of the Greeks, seen as a world of darkened existences. The part of the personality that lives in intrusive identification resides in a peculiar world, in a kind of distorted and pale reflection of the world of relationships between objects. The intruder is as much a prisoner of a world of words without meaning in themselves, as someone lacking in the experience of contact with objects-containers possessing the qualities pointed out by Meltzer[22] (privacy, exclusiveness, comfort, and delimitation) and who has been thrown into a closed hellish world like that illustrated by Sartre in "*Huis-clos*" (1944): a world of exiles from intimacy, who only carry a past composed of *facts*.

The analytic process of *Claustrum* patients is as painful and slow as is the liberation process of the cavern's prisoners described by Plato, because they must be freed from their chains as well as cured of their ignorance; because the grandiose specialist in differentiating the wandering shadows is nothing but an ignoramus.

3.1.5.1 Clinical Material

Some *clinical material* will illustrate the previous considerations. Jordi Pi (see Section 3.1.2.3) presented himself before me as a brilliant professional leading an isolated life centred on masturbation; he then resided in the home of a prominent politician.

In the course of the analysis, what appeared was his yearning to *establish a sensual relationship with me*, expressing desires to touch me, through his verbalisations or dreams. However, the possibility of establishing contact with me was altered by his intrusive aggression. In a dream,

> he saw a naked woman, who excited him, and there was a man who got excited with her; he saw the man's large penis, and when this man was about to penetrate her, Jordi confused himself with him, seeing in fact his own erect penis.

What soon became manifest, like in the dream, was his yearning *to penetrate the internal maternal object* through the penis-child confusion. *The part father-penis-object was only like a battering ram used to penetrate the interior of a mother, felt to be only a mediator so that Jordi could get hold of his own penis.* This was correlated with the predominance of masturbatory fantasies about small women desiring the large penises of King Kong-type men. These fantasies were fed through pornographic films which favoured his *voyeurism*, which condemned him to passivity (he lacked interests and friends and practically did not work) and to an inexistent genital sexuality. At this stage, in which the external world practically did not exist, he spent his time planning his *masturbation*. At the beginning of the analytic weekend, he would hire a pornographic film, and sitting in his armchair or lying on his bed, always covered (like Hamm?), he would reach a climax and then fall asleep. He practically did not leave his bed, remaining surrounded by the radio, TV, newspapers, and books until the following session. Jordi considered his masturbation to be a recourse which protected him from disaster. Living outside, in the world of objects, was "tormenting" (proof of this was that in his sadomasochistic outbursts, he would beat his wife). Easy as it was for him to admit his genital masturbation, it was, however, difficult to admit other equivalent manifestations. Anal masturbation was concreted in evacuation (retaining-expelling violently) and in the minute cleansing of the peri-anal zone. Another mode of masturbation observed in this patient consisted of his vomiting, which for him had become equivalent to: "I didn't masturbate, I vomited"; after provoking the vomit with his fingers his state of mind would change, he would relax and be able to go to sleep. Through masturbation, in its different forms, he changed the scene in which he was living: from living in the external world, he would enter to live in the internal world, where he would go to sleep like the inhabitants of the cavern.

Jordi could not tolerate waiting for the analyst to feed him mentally, because he feared the analyst-mommy's other baby-rivals; his desire was to eliminate them and later get into the "sensory apparatus and mental equipment of its internal object" in order to seek "the immediate emotional satisfaction of omniscience" (Meltzer, 1992, p. 76). I recall one day on which he felt very much gratified because a local leader referred to him as "a learned man". This was a satisfaction coherent with the desire he expressed to be with me "in the session in order to learn without realising it". His longing to be inside the analyst was defended tenaciously to the point of exploding violently against me if he did not feel that I was willing to let myself be colonised; he would attack my communications, breaking the link of melody-meaning; while he would gloat over the melody of my voice, he would reject the meaning of my words.

Jordi was so *far away from the world of human relationships* and from the developed feelings of jealousy that the only thing he could understand was the concrete behaviour of the analytic separations; for him, the analyst was either there or was not there, and if he was not there: "You—he said—are no longer a person, but you have become a place", *thus eliminating my reality, just as he slips towards irreality.* He denies reality, he gets inside the object, and constructs a defenceless world in which he mocks temporality and pain.

A dream allows us to understand *Jordi's relationship with objects*:

I am with Joaquín, who tells me he is going abroad and draws up a long list of people who could occupy his flat. I am suffering because I don't see my name; he realises this and writes down my name. I am worried because no one will know which Jordi it is…then he writes my surname. Joaquín comments that the flat on Olano Street is good because, from there, you can see when the police are coming as if the flat could be used to hide from police persecution. The scene in the dream changes. I am going on an excursion with colleagues from work to a lovely place, ecologically protected, with green hills and beautiful well-painted houses. I stay alone with a gorgeous girl that I knew; she speaks to me half-affectionately and half-pained because I have not taken any notice of her. I don't attach much importance to this. She then asks me whether I don't remember what she had told me, to which I answer in the negative. She says: 'that I loved you'. I answer: 'you women think that we are inside your head knowing what you think'. She feels pained and frustrated and then I say to her: 'I also love you'. In that spot, the village was celebrating a feast; from a balcony, they were pouring milk from *porrones*[23] instead of wine. I say to them: 'let's get away from here before they pour some milk on us'.

He associated that the dream was curious because that night he had gone to sleep angry because no one had noticed him.

When in the dream a separation is announced (Joaquin's departure), the immediate response is that of occupation;[24] occupation which is carried out through the *eyes* (on account of the voyeuristic overestimation of the look) and the anus (Ol-*ano* sounds like *Oh anus!*), thus managing to get into the other's list-mind, but in which a state of mind of persecution is established (the attractive object, upon being penetrated, becomes a dangerous trap). The need to clarify his name and then his surname arises because of the *loss of his identity* correlative to the invasion, which would be similar to the loss of the recollection of himself that Fabian experienced in Julien Green's novel *Si j'étais vous.*

With the verbal ability of the ambiguous politician, who changes his stance in the face of a compromising situation, Jordi slips into another scene: from the back part of the object (Ol-ano) to the front side (the beautiful hills). Here the presence of colleagues-siblings is admitted but only in order to stress his triumph: he is the one chosen by the woman, but to whom he does not pay much attention (he neither remembers nor attaches great importance to what she says). His *desire is to get inside the woman's head both to know what she is thinking, in order to attain omniscience and to have some sort of criterium (given his basic incapacity to obtain meaning from the observation of the external world), as well as to control that intercourse which gets mummy pregnant, and to take possession of daddy's penis.*

Given his extreme dependence on the object, Jordi perceives the pain inflicted on the woman in the dream and placates it with pseudo-loving declarations ("I also love you"), which leads to a manic relationship that ruins the object and renders the *"porrones"*-breasts (pouring out confusion) incompetent, thus returning to the persecutory situation.

In this case, it can clearly be seen that the main internal object of intrusion is the maternal object, through the direct penetration of the orifices, or through the intrusion in the father's penis, like in the other dream; in Jordi, there is no concern for the object but rather only the desire to dominate it and take possession of its qualities with the purpose of *being the object.* However, fortunately, as can be observed in the dream, persecutory anxiety prevents him from settling into the grandiosity of confusion.

Jordi, like the majority of the inhabitants of the *Claustrum* who approach analysis, does not reside exclusively in the *Claustrum* but oscillates between going in and coming out of projective identification, and as a result, has a greater or lesser awareness of the external world, like Hamm, who knows of the existence of the sea through the windows and through Clov. However, when from the loneliness of the *Claustrum* they approach the threshold of the external world (with the fragility of a newborn?), they suffer enormous anxiety upon being invaded (correlative to their intrusive desires), as is reflected in Jordi's dream: "I was alone in a room with thin glass walls[25] and people were looking at me, laughing around me and I felt exposed". He is exposed to violent reintrojection and, besides, his fragile mind is an easy target for the projective identifications of those looking at him. In order to go outside, he needs a mediator who may tolerate a certain degree of colonisation and who may urge him to take a look at the world, as my patient expressed:

> It's as if I were coming out of the cave and saw that it was not so dangerous and that life is pretty, but I see this through Susana's[26] eyes, not through my own eyes, and then I can't enjoy it.

Although it comes from another, he discovers the other. And he admits his difficulty: "It is difficult for me to desire her physically and spontaneously; she attracts me and I desire her but in a flat way", which means without emotional depth and without having achieved introjective identification with the father as a male.

Jordi is a borderline patient who oscillates between the external world of meanings and values and the internal world of objects into which he penetrates intrusively by different orifices. He can manifest an omniscient appearance enhanced by a great development of verbal expression in the service of seduction, but he lacks authentic interests. On account of his feeling of inconsistency, he mistrusts opening himself to the world, thus remaining totally dependent on the external objects and fearing being discovered in his true entity. The instability and immaturity of his sexual identity, his proclivity to being trapped in the voyeuristic-sadomasochistic-perversion, and the paranoid undertone distance him from intimate relationships.

3.1.5.2 Conclusion

When the intrusive part of the self "falls into the sensitive reality" of the cavern, it converts the objects into a "cradle and tomb". It then experiences feelings of strangeness for not having maintained contact with the world. A thin "glass wall" prevents the intruder from establishing contact with objects that they feel to be every time more unattainable, thus increasing their loneliness and feeling of not belonging to this community of objects, remaining excluded from all rights (to intimacy, to being recognised and remembered, to not being feared, and, on the other hand, to being loved). The trespasser wanders through the world without being in the world, and as a result, while they remain enclosed in the object, they not only escape death but also lose life. In intrusive identification, one does not live, one only subsists; one only has a life which is a "pale reflection of what things really are", and one is exiled from beauty or only looks at it through the eyes of the parasitised object.

Notes

1 When Meltzer illustrated the mechanism and the consequences of intrusive identification, he said that in some places, monkeys were captured—the monkey, a curious animal, by putting grains in a dried coconut and attaching to it a string. When the monkey puts its hand in and grabs the grains, it is then closed and the monkey is trapped.

2   The term "aspirar" in Spanish not only means to draw into the lungs (aspirate), but also to desire or wish to achieve something (aspire), and the Spanish word "aspiradora" (vacuum cleaner), an instrument that absorbs dust and gas, derives from it. The difference in meaning can be understood from the context. In English, the term "aspirated" has been chosen to name the emotional capture of another person.

3   In my paper "Living in Intrusive Identification" this patient is mentioned (see Section 3.1.5).

4   This is reminiscent of Ferrán (see Section 3.1.1.1).

5   His desire to be a father appeared in his feminine part and was expressed in the solicitous care he gave his children; this change was met by the coldness in his wife and her lack of interest in them.

6   Cap. 6 Meltzer et al. (2003).

7   With such violence that the nail, bent at a right angle that sustained it, lost the angle.

8   Active omnipotent phantasy of absorbing the object's personality.

9   The father stated that "at home we have no secrets" and "we don't close any doors".

10 In Section 1.2, reference is being made to the same patient.

11 An example of this type of relationship is the relationship between mother and son in which both grow. When the relationship has no boundaries, pathological significance ensues that usually accompanies the term. Another example of the symbiotic relationship is when "the thought and the thinker correspond and modify each other through the correspondence. The thought proliferates and the thinker develops" (Meltzer, 1978, p. 381).

12 Discovering the patient's *conception of the world* was one of the richest outcomes we learned in our supervisions with Meltzer. The patient and his material became a scene that stimulated interest. In this sense, I can concur with what happened to Vargas Llosa (2020, p. 14; my italics) when he read Borges: "...the *beauty and intelligence of the world* he created helped me to discover the limitations of my own, and the perfection of his prose made me aware of the imperfections of my own". Our notes acquired another meaning; the patient became present within a tetradimensional scene and supervision turned into an emotional experience.

13 "Living in intrusive identification", published in *Exploring the work of Donald Meltzer, A Festschrift*, edited by Cohen and Hahn, London, Karnac Books, 2000, pp. 173–187.

14 The internal objects (part, whole, combined) represent above all the parents, siblings, and persons who surround the subject in the present time (Heimann, 1942) and provide a sense of existence and identity; one of the internal objects is the superego.

15 To be understood as the anxious search of an object for different purposes; such as, to feel sheltered inside it, to deposit in it objects which one wishes to preserve, to occupy it, dominate it, plunder it, ruin it....

16 Because it has not abandoned the gravitational attraction of the objects nor has it sought refuge in the non-place.

17 Next to the letter which identifies the character, there is a number that corresponds to the page of the translation written by Beckett himself, published by Faber and Faber Limited, London, Boston, MA, 1988.

18 This expression in the English edition is omitted; however, the whole scene is an aggressive reaction (C, 49) against anyone who draws near.

19 In the English edition, Beckett replaced it with *to lay* and *to lie*.

20 Just like in the Wolf-Man where evacuation interrupted intercourse.

21 The painful flight into the shadows was represented in the following clinical material of a patient, who in a productive session, and looking at the plants which can be seen from the couch, said: "The sun is so beautiful shining on the balcony plants! How many tones of green!" He paused and went on associating:

> I had lunch at a restaurant where lorry-drivers usually go, where they serve food 24 hours a day. It was full of noise and smoke, and I was sitting at a table just underneath

the TV, so I couldn't see the screen, but I was looking at the expressions on the faces of all those surrounding me while they were watching the film.

Upon not being able to tolerate the beauty of the world, he regressed to the cavern (anal-claustrum) in order to look at only the reflections.

22 In *Studies in Extended Metapsychology*, Chapter V.
23 A kind of jar with a spout which is used for drinking wine without a glass.
24 As a child, Jordi "saw" his mother as always pregnant.
25 Remember Jana's glazed compartments (see Section 3.1.2.1).
26 A budding relationship.

Bibliography

Baranger, W. (1971): *Posición y objeto en la obra de Melanie Klein*, Buenos Aires, Kargiemn.

Beckett, S. (1957): *Fin de Partie*, Paris, Les Éditions de Minuit, 1993. Translated from the original French by the author, *Endgame,* London-Boston, MA, Faber and Faber Limited, 1988.

Bion, W. R. (1959): "Attacks on linking", in *Second Thoughts,* London, W. Heinemann, 1967, pp. 110–119.

Calderón de la Barca, P. (1600–1681): "Life is a dream", in *Six Plays*, New York, Iasta Press, 1993, pp. 287–364

Chuster, A. (2014): *A Lonesome Road. Essays on the Complexity of W. R. Bion's Work.* A construction of 21 steps towards a theory of Complexity in Psychoanalysis, Río de Janeiro, Trio Studio Bureau e Gráfica Digital, Brasil.

Freud, S. (1918). "From the history of an infantile neurosis", in *The Standard Edition of the Complete Psychological Works of Sigmund Freud*, edited by J. Strachey, London, Hogarth Press, 1966, Vol XIV, pp. 109–140.Vol. 17, pp. 1–124

Green, J. (1947): *Si j'étais vous...,* Paris, Ed. du Seuil, 1983.

Grinberg, L. & Grinberg, R. (1971): *Identidad y cambio*, Buenos Aires, Ed. Kargieman.

Grotstein, J. S. (2007): *A Beam of Intense Darkness, Wilfred Bion's Legacy to Psychoanalysis,* London, Karnac.

Harris, M. & Meltzer, D. (1976): "A psychoanalytic model of the child-in-the-family-in-the-community", in *Sincerity and Other Works*, edited by Alberto Hahn, London, Karnac, 1994, pp. 387–454.

Heimann, P. (1942): "A contribution to the problem of sublimation and its relation to processes of internalization", *International Journal of Psycho-Analysis,* 23, pp. 8–17.

Hinshelwood, R. D. (1989): *A Dictionary of Kleinian Thought*, London, Free Association Books.

Klein, M. (1955): "On identification", in *New Directions in Psycho-Analysis*, edited by Melanie Klein, Paula Heimann and R. E. Money-Kyrle, London, Tavistock, pp. 309–345

Meltzer, D. (1967): *The Psycho-Analytical Process*, London, William Heinemann Medical Books Limited.

Meltzer, D. (1973): *Sexual States of Mind*, London, Karnac, 2018.

Meltzer, D. (1976): "Temperature and distance as technical dimensions of interpretation", in *Sincerity and Other Works,* London, Karnac, 1994, pp. 374–386.

Meltzer, D. (1978): *The Kleinian Development*, London, Karnac, 2008.

Meltzer, D. (1984): *Dream-Life: A Re-Examination of the Psychoanalytic Theory and Technique*, London, Karnac Books, 2009.

Meltzer, D. (1992): *The Claustrum. An Investigation of Claustrophobic Phenomena*, Strath-Clyde, The Clunie Press.

Meltzer, D. (1993): "Implicaciones psicosomáticas en el pensamiento de Bion", *Psicoanálisis APdeBA*,2, pp. 315–338.

Meltzer, D. (1996): *Clinical Seminars in the Psychoanalytic* (unpublished), Group of Barcelona: Inés.

Meltzer, D. (1996): "Clinical seminar B", in *Meltzer em São Paulo: seminários clínicos*, edited by FRANÇA, M. O. DE A. F. & MARRA, E. DE S. (orgs.), São Paulo, Casa do Psicólogo, 1997, pp. 127–143.

Meltzer, D. (2008): *Meltzer In São Paulo*, London, Karnac, 2017.

Meltzer, D. & Harris, M. (1998): *Adolescentes*, edited by L. Jachevasky & C. Tabbia, Buenos Aires, ed. Spatia.

Meltzer, D. et al. (1986): *Studies in Extended Metapsychology*, Strath-Clyde, Perthshire, Clunie Press.

Meltzer, D. (with The Psychoanalytic Group of Barcelona & Mack Smith, C.) (1995): *Psychoanalytic Work with Children and Adults: Meltzer in Barcelona*, London, Karnac, 2002.

Meltzer, D., Castellà, R., Tabbia, C., & Farré, L. (2003): *Supervisions with Donald Meltzer. The Simsbury Seminars*, London, Karnac, pp. 91–102.

Murillo, A. (2010): "La pasión en la clínica: entre el exceso y la inmovilidad", in *De la angustia y otros afectos*, Barcelona, Grafein, GRADIVA, Associació d'Estudis Psico-analítics, pp. 311–321.

Plato (1941): *The Republic.* Translated by F. M Cornford, London, Oxford University Press.

Süskind, P. (1985). *Perfume: The Story of a Murderer*, New York, Vintage International, 1986.

Tabbia, C. (2000): "La grandiosidad en la identificación narcisista", in *El Narcisismo a debate*, Barcelona, Gradiva editorial, pp. 85–91.

Vargas Llosa, M. (2020): *Medio siglo con Borges,* Barcelona, Alfaguara.

3.2

Thinking

The psychic act of thinking has the faculty of apprehending thoughts that claim a place within the mind.

Klein started with infantile curiosity about the primary scene, and, using Freud's contributions (1920), and her own consideration of anxiety as a motor of development, "...turned psychoanalysis into the art of caring for the capacity for thought" (Kristeva, 2000, p. 14). Her discovery of the omnipotent phantasy of projective identification and her contributions to the subject of the symbolisation of the most primitive anxieties opened the doors to explore the disorders of thinking, as did Segal, Rosenfeld, or Bion.

> Following Hanna Segal—affirms Kristeva (ibid, p. 178)—for example, W. R. Bion returned to the evolution of the symbolic capacity in the young child, but he worked his way back to before the depressive position, and described the primitive thought that marks the paranoid-schizoid phase: in his view, projective identification is the first form of 'thinking.'

It will not only be a primitive thought, but also the model for thinking, as Bion (1961b) said in *The Conception of Man*: "I shall use the theory of projective identification as a model for the early development of the processes that have later come to be known as thinking". This model supposes a partner from the start: breast/mouth and later on mother/baby, with the possibility of establishing the first differentiations between object and subject. The internalisation of these differentiations and, later on, the representations and functions of the objects will be the essential elements for constructing the model of the apparatus for thinking.

In order to represent the internal apparatus for thinking thoughts, Bion uses the signs ♀♂ to mean container and contained. Nevertheless,

> ...before ♀♂ can operate, ♀ has to be found and the discovery of ♂ depends on the operation of Ps↔D. It is obvious that to consider which of the two, ♀♂ or Ps↔D, is prior distracts from the main problem.
>
> (Bion, 1963, p. 37)

DOI: 10.4324/9781003347156-10

without ignoring the fact that in the object relations model, the underlying assumption is that humans are object seekers, and depend on their objects for their subsistence and development. To not distract from the basic problem, however, it is worth pointing out the relationship of humans to thinking and thought, as Bion puts it (1967b, p. 101):

> It is convenient to regard thinking as dependent on the successful outcome of two main mental developments. The first is the development of thoughts. They require an apparatus to cope with them. The second development therefore, is of this apparatus that I shall provisionally call thinking. I repeat—thinking has to be called into existence to cope with thoughts. It will be noted that this differs from any theory of thought as a product of thinking, in that thinking is a development forced on the psyche by the pressure of thoughts and not the other way round. Psychopathological developments may be associated with either phase or both, that is they may be related to a breakdown in the development of thoughts, or a breakdown in the development of the apparatus for "thinking" or dealing with thoughts, or both.

We need to think in order to bear the burden of thoughts that we carry as humans, often without comprehension, and in general, with fear, because of its extraordinary threat: "I am thought searching for a thinker to give birth to me. I shall destroy the thinker when I find him" (Bion, 1991a, p. 38). Who possesses a sufficient container to be able to accommodate such thoughts? Our fragile mind faces the task of developing them, and also of achieving a mental apparatus suitable enough to think them. These are tasks that stir up as much longing as fear. Without introjective identification with a combined object of whole objects, offering oneself as a container is worrisome; without the aforementioned support, it is difficult to quarter emotions capable of transforming into symbols, into thoughts, and later on into language.

In Section 3.2, I will take up both the development of thinking, as well as some disorders that hinder thinking. As the expression of these difficulties, I will also present fanaticism, the inability to dream, boredom, or the coercion of the body to substitute for the mind....

3.2.1 Observation and Description in the Genesis of Meaning[1]

The field of clinical practice has expanded now with patients who consult in search of help due to their difficulties in thinking. In a world that promotes immediacy, action, immediate satisfaction of desire, which offers values such as sensuality, and considers the relativism of *anything goes* valid, these patients are stretched between subservience to fashionable slogans and suffering due to their failures in life; likewise it is hard for them to develop because they have learning difficulties, difficulties with comprehension or imagination ... that burden their lives and drag down their self-esteem.

The inability to think is different from an attack on thinking or on the mind. To attack, recourse is taken in lies, in deceptive thinking, and in ambiguous expressions that generate confusion or in the stripping of the meaning from words. In the inability to think, gaps can be filled with fabulations that become future traps... Gaps are the inability to observe facts. If facts are not perceived, meaning cannot be built from thinking about what has been observed. If one does not observe beyond what is the most apparent, conclusions will be reached that will not be able to be misrepresented, thus paving the way for ambiguities and confusion. These gaps must be the starting point for helping these patients.

These people with an incapacity for thinking lack the equipment whose tools would be "analogy, reversible perspectives, multiplication of vertices, and negative capability", which, according to Meltzer and Meg Harris Williams (1982, p. 532), are the requirements that Bion (1991a), in the first book of *A Memoir of the Future*, demands to investigate the individual-as-group. *Concrete* or *fact-oriented* people, such as some obsessives or expert speakers, are far away or find it impossible to question themselves. But who does not have non-mentalised areas of their mind-group? As I said at the beginning: the field of clinical practice is being expanded... because we all have gaps.

3.2.1.1 Language

In the clinical relationship, language can become a labyrinth. We use language to communicate, but at the same time, as a medium to incommunicate.[2] This becomes more evident with those patients that are so skilful at talking about everything and nothing at the same time. The contrast is that our therapeutic tool is language. Not infrequently, we are defenceless in the face of those who "dally nicely with words may quickly make them wanton" (Shakespeare, *Twelfth Night*, Act III, Scene 1).

Obsessive patients are, perhaps, those who most play with words. Having abandoned emotions, they work fundamentally with facts and may become abusive discussants, employing deceitful means in the use of language to vanquish their opponent. One of their resources is, for example, to change the value and the meaning of things. Obsessives cannot work with symbols that capture the meaning of things, and only use metaphors, comparisons, or differentiations, rewording, reformulations, and so on, creating a vertigo of words that aim at envelopment, and often succeed in dizzying the listener. People who operate with the alpha function in reverse also tend to produce a great number of words, often agglomerated with the symbolic thread destroyed.

The Sophists were masters at playing with words.[3] Plato, who hated them so much, presents their despicable bases in the *Euthydemus*. In the face of the Sophist production, Plato, through Socrates, said (1952, p. 401) that "you have to learn about the correct use of words", even though subsequently (ibid., pp. 401–403) he warns the astonished pupil Kleinias that the Sophists' arguments

...are the sport of the sciences—and that is why I tell you these men are making game of you; I call it sport because, although one were to learn many or even all of such tricks, one would be not a whit the wiser as to the true state of the matters in hand, but only able to make game of people, thanks to the difference in the sense of the words, by tripping them up and overturning them; just as those who slyly pull stools away from persons who are about to sit down make merry and laugh when they see one sprawling on one's back.

The games of the Sophists greatly resemble the arguments of those who seek to unseat us as analysts. We must, however, recognise that the struggle against understanding ourselves is characteristic of human nature. As Meltzer and Harris Williams (1982, p. 532),

> ...we are obliged to move on to explore the ways in which the capacity for thought may be interfered with by an equally precise misuse of language ... The obscurity of language attempting to describe the ultra- and infra-sensual is contrasted with a 'trick' language that could precisely obscure already formulated thoughts.

The opposition to the discovery of the most idiosyncratic always dark thoughts finds support in the limitations of language itself. Not only because it is a trap due to its polysemy but also because of its ambiguities and lack of precision in denoting. For this reason, epistemologists and logicians who study language, such as Cohen and Nagel (1934, pp. 224–225) warn that:

> Many of the fatuities of actual thinking take place because the inescapable vagueness of most words makes a careful check upon one's thoughts well-nigh impossible [...] To the vagueness of words their ambiguity must be added as a serious danger to accurate thinking. Serious blunders in reflective thinking occur because the meaning that a word has in some context is replaced, without the fact being noticed, by an allied but different meaning [...] the ambiguity of words may invalidate a reasoned discourse.

In the face of this vagueness and ambiguity rooted in the limitations of language, such as those cultivated from resistance to understanding, it would be wise to deconstruct them for fruitful clinical work. A suitable resource for this purpose is to ask the patient to clarify what they mean; a request that will be found irritating—as it was for Euthydemus—because their words fail to dazzle the analyst or because they feel criticised for their difficulty in expressing themself more truthfully.

The difficulty derived from the vagueness and ambiguity finds a fundamental ally in the problem of naming. Naming does not consist in surrounding an object and assigning it a degree in the belief that knowledge of it has thus been obtained. The naming of the object may induce one to think of the omnipotent act of giving a name to the objects of creation, like an Adam manifesting his lordship. Far removed from this moment is the naming of Bion's *grid*, which claims the emotional recognition of the complexity of the object as an essential requirement for its discovery. But, once again, when we try to name something, we discover anew how rudimentary and concrete our language is, especially when we try to name objects of psychic reality.

In this sense, Borges (1968, p. 40) was prescient when he said, "every state of mind is irreducible: the mere fact of naming it—*id est*, of classifying it—is a falsehood".

If language corrupts, it is possible to go to another resource to transmit emotional states. In that sense—as Wittgenstein proposed—showing can be an alternative, or, as Ungar (2000) also proposed, saying that

> ... what cannot be said should be silenced, but what cannot be said becomes a field to be shown. What is shown represents the ineffable boundary, and in my opinion, that is what is meta-communicated in the analytic attitude. It is not what mustn't be said, it is what cannot be said because of the limitations of language.

Faced with the alternative of being silent because something cannot be said, rather than silence, there is the possibility of demonstrating through behaviour. The silent presence in the face of ungrateful pain says more than many words.

Bion also suffered with the limits of language. In this sense, what Meltzer and Harris Williams (1982, p. 522) pointed out is quite eloquent:

> Throughout his later work, at least from *Elements of Psycho-Analysis* (Bion, 1963) onwards, and made explicit in the caustic *Second Thoughts* (Bion, 1982) about his own earlier papers, he has apologized for and regretted the inadequacy of language for the precise formulation of thoughts that reach beyond the sensual for their formal structure. He has often pleaded that, even given his own literary Inadequacies, the fault lies in language itself, a fault that only art can overcome.

Meltzer (1990) also considered language to be an unsatisfactory resource to describe what happens in the analytic relationship, the clinician needing to conform to using it given the lack of something more suitable, excepting what is shown with the attitude mentioned by Ungar. On occasion, Meltzer makes reference to the fact that the patient had not seen his smile or tears in his eyes (the analyst's), as a way of showing the patient a type of communication that goes beyond words.

Language evolved to name things in the external world, and for that reason, it has limitations when it comes to naming emotional states. Wittgenstein (1958) wondered "what about the language which describes my inner experiences and which only I myself can understand? How do I use words to stand for my sensations?—As we ordinarily do?" (§ 256).

Customary language—that which is used to name things in the external world—gives no guarantee that it will establish the correct relationship with what one wants to name. Wittgenstein (1958) continued, saying:

> Naming appears as a queer connexion of a word with an object [...] for philosophical[4] problems arise when language goes on holiday. And here we may indeed fancy naming to be some remarkable act of mind, as it were a baptism of an object.

(§ 38)

If it is already hard to recognise feelings, it will be even more difficult to suitably name them. That is why the need to speak exists, as does the fear of saying foolish things.[5] If we add to the natural limitations of language the difficulty of recognising emotional states of mind as well as the resistance to give those states of mind a place in our mind, the conditions are created for misunderstandings, a term that is reminiscent of Money-Kyrle. That is why Wittgenstein's proposal (1958) of assigning the therapeutic task of dissolving misunderstandings to philosophy seems very appropriate: "For the clarity that we are aiming at is indeed complete clarity. But this simply means that the philosophical problems should completely disappear" (§ 133). To such an end, he resorts to the therapeutic model stating, "The philosopher's treatment of a question is like the treatment of an illness" (§ 255). Therefore, the treatment of problems that rests on language and misunderstandings consists of managing "to pass from a piece of disguised nonsense to something that is patent nonsense" (§ 464) with the intention of fighting "against the bewitchment of our intelligence by means of language" (§ 109).

As I write out these quotes, the many different obstacles to comprehension that we observe daily in our offices come to mind. I remember once when Meltzer, in the supervision of Eduardo,[6] said: "It is true he is a great confusion creator, and it is difficult to understand what he is talking about, because he tells you that he was talking with his parents until 7:30 and when you repeat 'you talked to your parents until 7:30' he replies 'no, no'…. You really don't know what he is saying; it is important to force him to be specific about what he is saying, describe it better…" (Meltzer et al., 2003, p. 100). This hygienic task is like asking the patient to use the basic rule correctly. Reformulating Wittgenstein (1958, § 79), we could propose to the patient *that they say what they want as long as it allows us to understand what is going on.* What joy talkative patients bring us! The problem with patients like Eduardo is that they do not provide enough material for one to form a judgement, a personal opinion, but rather they speak more with the intention of programming the therapist, of directing their thoughts. This situation raises the issue of the vulnerability of the analyst, and the problem of how to overcome the siege, and reconvert it into a medium in the service of understanding.

Without moving away from Wittgenstein's thinking, or from daily clinical experience, we can confirm that the main corrective measure to avoid the analyst's vulnerability is to remain in close contact with clinical experience, distrusting general statements that may sometimes reveal the analyst's resistance more than epistemological needs. In this sense, it is useful to mention part of the *Introduction* that Terricabras (1997, p. 25) made to the Catalan edition of *Investigaciones Filosóficas*:

> …whatever philosophical statement must have as a point of reference the description of particular cases which are those that absolutely require correction […] Because the description of particular cases is the only method that can avoid hasty, general statements, or that, once made, can help to correct. It is true that Wittgenstein's method doesn't prevent anyone—not even Wittgenstein—from making false statements—the truth cannot be guaranteed—but it can help

to, at least, prevent grossly disorienting statements [...] This is, definitively, one of Wittgenstein's greatest contributions to philosophy: his precise emphasis on the importance of examples, of particular cases, which, in his view, are, in Wisdom's view, 'the ultimate food for thought'.

Reading these texts, one can only acknowledge a certain echo of Wittgenstein's thinking concerning the urgent need to base our psychoanalytic thinking on clinical facts.

3.2.1.2 Meaning

The struggle against meaninglessness does not exhaust the task of the philosopher, the scientist, or the poet. Cultivated people struggle to name the facts of our existence, and amongst them are the psychoanalysts who attempt to name the phenomena of psychic reality.

Meaning straddles the facts to be named and the names assigned to those facts. The sense of *signification* can be formulated as follows: when we consider X to be a name, it is because the meaning of X is the object denoted by X. This formulation, which could be accused of being essentialist, does not discount that the meaning of X can be determined not only by the object but also by the context, then acquiring an idiosyncratic nuance. The meaning would not be a "faithful copy" of the object but rather a creation between the object and what names it,—and in clinical practice—between the fact and the psychoanalytic function that intuits meanings from such facts.

When B. Russell (1922, pp. 7–8) wrote the *Introduction* to *Tractatus*, he said that Wittgenstein studied:

> ...the conditions for accurate Symbolism, i.e. for Symbolism in which a sentence "means" something quite definite. In practice, language is always more or less vague, so that what we assert is never quite precise. [...] The essential business of language is to assert or deny facts. Given the syntax of a language, the meaning of a sentence is determinate as soon as the meaning of the component words is known. In order that a certain sentence should assert a certain fact there must, however the language may be constructed, be something in common between the structure of the sentence and the structure of the fact. This is perhaps the most fundamental thesis of Mr. Wittgenstein's theory.

The fundamental thesis that Russell points to finds its expression in pictorial theory (Tabbia, 1970) of the early Wittgenstein, from *Tractatus*, where he proposed the correlation between world and language according to the following formulations:

> § 3.21 "To the configuration of the simple signs in the propositional sign corresponds the configuration of the objects in the state of affairs."
> § 3.22 "In the proposition the name represents the object."

§ 3.221 "Objects I can only *name*. Signs represent them. I can only speak *of* them. I cannot *assert* them. A proposition can only say *how* a thing is, not *what* it is."

Here, Wittgenstein is trying to avoid the essentialist assumptions, only attributing to humankind the function of naming objects through signs that represent the objects. That is why he says, "We make to ourselves pictures of facts" (§ 2.1). It remains to be stressed—as Anscombe (1967, p. 68) does—that "Here it is 'we' who 'give' a sign its reference". With the pictorial theory, Wittgenstein tried to avoid the infiltration of nonsense, but without sufficiently emphasising that the one in charge of establishing correlations and naming is someone who fears and/or hates the truth and is frightened or fragmented by the beauty of the object....

The later Wittgenstein considers that the primary thing in language is not meaning but use, introducing the concept of *language-games*. In these games, the aim is not to understand the meaning of words but how they function and how they are used, because each term has many meanings. This happens above all in those languages with overdetermined terms, i.e. which have a multiplicity of different meanings. The meanings can only be discovered through the context in which they are used. For this reason, for Wittgenstein, language in its meaning is not alien to those who use it. As Ferrater Mora succinctly puts it (1966, T. II, p. 37):

> A language (a language-game) is like a system of wheels. Language is justified if these wheels mesh with each other and with reality. But even if they mesh with each other, language has no basis if they do not mesh simultaneously with reality. This is why Wittgenstein has compared the philosophical language game to a wheel that turns freely, without meshing with reality, or with human activities integrated within reality.

This statement becomes more significant for psychoanalysts when language is left in the hands of the psychotic part of the personality, when the predominance of hallucinatory transformations disintegrates language, or when speech does not pretend to communicate, as in Eduardo's case.

The problem with language continues to be it having been built to run on data from external reality. It is true, as is said in *Tractatus* (§ 4.021) that "The proposition is a picture[7] of reality, for I know the state of affairs presented by it, if I understand the proposition". Wittgenstein emphasises the communicative function of the proposition to recognise the figure or picture of reality; if this function were not possible, language would be so idiosyncratic as delusional states. This statement should be completed with the distinction that Meltzer makes (1997b, p. 175) between *signs and symbols*; for Meltzer signs

> are just a way of pointing at things, using words to point. They consist almost exclusively of the conventional naming of things and functions. Now, in so far as people use signs in communicating with one another, they cannot 'mean it' because they cannot mean anything, they are simply pointing at the world.

From this distinction together with the transcription of *Tractatus* § 4.021, we could conclude that it is possible to paint pictures of the world through signs, comprehending the reality of the external world, but remaining on the margin of the emotional meaning of the experience. While there is no description of the state of mind that gives meaning to words, words remain obscure. Meltzer (1997b) acknowledges that our language is very rich in words to describe objects and functions, however, very poor in those that describe feelings. In order to achieve this, it is necessary to dispose of the symbols-not-received, but instead created from dream life and in the clinical relationship from the observation-description-interpretation in the transference-countertransference relationship, assuming the analyst has the adequate parental functions of reverie.

The dialectic of everyday life oscillates between two vertices: the non-mental vertex and the adaptative behaviourism vertex on the one hand, and on the other, the vertex of one's own mental life experienced as a private space for the generation of meanings. The creation of meaning maintains two poles that must be related: that of facts and that of words; but the fundamental difference does not reside in the possibility of establishing a pictorial relationship (early Wittgenstein) or language-games (later Wittgenstein) with only the signs that are suitable for the external world, but rather in the necessary availability to intuitively receive the meaning of internal objects. This is the basis of the generation of meaning.

3.2.1.3 Observation

There is an ever-increasing request for consultation from people with thought disorders. Thinking is not easy, not now and not previously. In order to understand the difficulties in thinking, it can be illustrative to look at what Meltzer considered to be essential components for the development of thinking: it begins with the observation of facts from which we would attempt to build meaning. The problem with thought disorders is associated with the non-observation of facts, focusing on appearance, on the surface, and reaching conclusions that cannot be refuted. Without observation, one can fabulate but not think. Thinking, therefore, begins with *the observation of facts in order to* attain *meanings*: here is an entire programme that many people disregard at one time or another.

On one occasion, Meltzer (1997b, p. 177) made use of his own experience to understand the same process: "One of the things that Esther Bick taught us was that the meaning of baby and child behaviour is not obvious. It is a matter of interpretation, and interpretation is something that grows out of careful observation. The meaning of a baby's behaviour comes as an intuition to the observer that grows out of noticing what is happening to the baby [...] the lesson is that the activity of the analyst is not primarily interpretation, but is first of all observation and description". If Wittgenstein started out from the urgent need to seat psychoanalytic thinking on clinical facts, with Bick a second step is taken, which is the development of meaning from the observation of facts.

In clinical practice, we frequently encounter behaviours and situations that make the path towards meaning impossible or that decry its failure to do so. I will refer to some of these situations or psychopathological traits in the following pages. An example is what can be observed in Florencio, a bored man. On referring to Florencio's boredom, or to the subject in general, on this occasion Meltzer (1999a, pp. 95/96) said that boredom:

> ...it might be a characterological problem that presents in those patients who complain that they don't have friends, that they feel ill at ease in social situations, or that they cannot converse in public situations. These people generally are poor observers of, both what happens around them, as well as within themselves, and as a consequence of this impoverishment in observation, a suppression of the emotional response appears. This can be seen when they describe people they encounter; they fail to describe what they see, but rather will describe stereotypes, and, of course, these stereotypes are also applicable to the perception that they have of the analyst. This would be what I call a kind of negative omniscience [...]. This type of omniscience would express itself because they describe the things that are the most evident to them, and they cannot see the details.

In the case of Florencio, his difficulty to see beyond what was the most superficial or obvious, the stereotype, was emphasised.

Other poor observers are those that elude reality by looking at what does not exist, something akin to only pointing out the holes in Gruyere cheese. Without evidence (signs, samples, or some indication), it is difficult to identify a theme, or a problem; based on negative evidence, i.e. without data, it is easy to fall into sterile theorising or infinite rationalisations. With patients who do not contribute information, that do not observe their psychic reality, the analyst is placed in the situation of having to formulate something without reference to facts or emotions, and it is fertile terrain for the analyst to become bored (see Section 3.2.4). Not infrequently, one realises that these patients, with a limited capacity for observation, have difficulties transcending a narrow margin of their sensations, considering them to be a meaning that requires neither exploration nor symbolisation.

Other more explosive, overwhelming patients cannot think either because of their inability to bring together observations with responses based on feelings of love, hatred, aggression, pain, etc., merely functioning based on their emotional responses.[8] People full of obsessionality that also cannot think due to their lack of contact with their emotions can be found on the opposite pole. Meltzer's suggestions (1998) made in reference to a patient who arrived with a pre-formed transference derived from a hierarchical family structure that exempted him from observing and thinking can be applied to patients like this:

> ...he will have to be taught to think. Before that, he has to learn to observe things so that he has something to think about [...] You have to address him like a small child who has to learn things from the beginning, and in the beginning,

children have to learn things like numbers, letters and putting letters together to make words, etc. He has to begin by observing the world and observing himself so that he has something to think about. He has to learn to observe not only the external world but also the internal world, observing his feelings, thoughts and dreams. When he brings his observations, you can teach him to think about them.

Once the patient begins to observe, you will have to collaborate with them so that things evolve from the sensual level to the point where they can be transformed into a more mental level. The nuclear movement for the project mentioned above will be the observation of the emotional experience. The alpha function Ps↔D will have to operate on the observation of the emotional experience and container-contained "to produce thoughts and develop them to higher levels of sophistication, abstraction, and complexity (The Grid, 1989) usable for thinking" (Meltzer, 1978a, p. 463).

For this emotional experience to occur and to be transformed, the adequate participation of both the patient and the analyst in the clinical encounter is required. For both Segal (1975) and Martha Harris (1984), the initial breast-baby or mother-baby pair is the model for the analyst-patient relationship. This model starts from the recognition of the constitutional factors of the baby (Freud, Klein) and from the collaboration of the mother who is sufficiently good, as Winnicott would say, and adequately containing and metabolising, as Bion would say… making possible a constant construction of the mind throughout life (Nemas, 2004). The requirement of the analytic couple, according to this model, is that the analyst have the sufficient ability of containment to give attention to the whole of the patient, instead of contemplating them as a part object, for example, or limiting themself to focusing on one aspect, even if it is that of the specific search for the meaning of the patient's associations. A partial view is always a partialisation. In this regard, I think it is appropriate to refer to the comment made by Mrs Bick to Jeanne Magagna (1997) in relation to the observation of babies: one cannot observe only the baby but the whole family, the whole scene present at that moment. The partialised gaze, without global attention, makes it difficult to have the free-floating attention to register the data of reality and to recognise its complexity: what the patient shows, what the analyst contributes, and the interaction between both.

Given the complexity of data and stimuli offered by the encounter with another person, the underlying question is about what we need to observe, without partialising, in order to gather together significant data with the aim of comprehending meanings. With that aim, Bick (1964) considered it important to observe the general behaviour of the patient within the analytic situation. An observation without interpretation. Investigating meaning comes at a later stage.

One way to observe without interpreting requires putting the anamnestic information the patient provides at a distance. Narratives are novels. They are metaphors that induce meanings "that they are not intended to convey" (Cohen and Nagel, 1934, p. 240). Freeing oneself of metaphors so as to preserve freedom of thought does not imply eliminating it as a resource. For example, it can be an initial form of very useful transformation in dialogue with children where it is introduced through the *as-if*, but recognising that it lacks the richness and the profoundness of symbols. Such a transformation is often not very different from the situation one may find oneself in when reading the reports of journalists. In this case, one is not observing the fact but rather the stories that, more often than not, reveal the journalist's perspective rather than the facts themselves. In that way, one remains more at the mercy of the vertex or the propagandist intentionality of the *news agency* than of obtaining data to think about. Many patients function as news agencies when they try to bind the analyst's imagination up in narratives by pretending to see facts *in their own way*.

In clinical practice, discovering the facts that underlie the metaphor is of interest. These facts will become such when observed in the transference. A bifocal view will therefore be needed: on the one hand, to try to understand—with a dose of scepticism—what the subject is saying and, on the other hand, to observe what is happening in the here-and-now of the transference.

In order to *observe general behaviour*, we need to use all of our senses in their specific incorporative function. To do this it is indispensable that the analyst be capable of tolerating and using their own ability to regress as much as needed so that their senses can operate as suction pads, according to Mrs. Bick's expression: "Mrs. Bick said that the organs—eyes, mouth, ears, nose—serve as suction pads like the mouth holding onto the nipple" (Magagna, 1997, p. 26) in the initial stages of infantile development. If we recover the image of the mind that Bion described to us in *A Memoir of the Future*, in which all of the parts of ontogenetic history persist and establish a dialogue, we can think that these primitive forms of connection to the world subsist in our psyche and perhaps we could call on them to be able to grasp the ineffable characteristics of our patients. An equivalent model is that of the mothers capable of knowing-auscultating-smelling-seeing their infant through the information they capture through the different senses. In terms of the perception of reality, we are currently very conditioned by verbal culture, which leads to the development of some senses more than others in perceiving the world. While I was preparing this text, I remembered the expertise of oenologists who can express (discover?) the following after tasting a reserve wine: "Intense cherry, brick-like hue on the rim, powerful aroma, rich in spicy nuances and dried fruits (figs, walnuts), candied fruits, round tannins on the palate" (Carrión, 2002). So many nuances can be picked up from taste, smell, and sight! On the other extreme, the primitive behaviour of a very regressive patient comes to mind. The patient had great difficulties using her senses, except for smell, which she used to distinguish between friends and enemies. For better or for worse, all of our senses are present in the clinical encounter and will depend on our ability to broaden our registers to be used for observation. Expressing myself like this may induce confusion as to whether observing manifest behaviour is the sole interest here. In that case, A. Green's text (1995, p. 877) would come almost as a criticism. He says: "To perceive is to be in connection with external reality. To listen is to be in contact with psychic reality". Listening to psychic reality as an alternative to the perception of the external. This thought evokes that of Meltzer (1984) when he said that one listens visually in the same way as one listens to a dream; here, he is referring to the possibility of projecting images on an internal screen to discover phantasies and meanings (psychic reality) behind the words heard. A more visual/verbal/olfactory imagination… First comes the task of perceiving the external reality, and then the mysterious alpha function of the internal objects will decode the information extracting unconscious meanings.

In this section about observation, I intend to focus on the area that is concerned with gathering information rather than interpretation or the creation of thoughts, even though I agree with Mrs Bick (1964, p. 565) when she said,

> how difficult it is to 'observe', i.e. collect facts free from interpretation. As soon as these facts have to be described in language we find that every word is loaded with a penumbra of implication […] in fact, he finds that he chooses a particular word because observing and thinking are almost inseparable.

The illusion of the objective observer perished with Heisenberg's contributions.

To be able to observe in general, and in clinical practice in particular, requires a laborious preparation as an observer prior to preparing oneself to discover the object. To achieve this ability, "the observer makes serious sacrifices, almost a purification to free their own senses: they renounce acting, speaking, moving, writing, to interpret" (Brutti and Scotti, 1984, p. 27). It is not an impossible, but rather a difficult task, because the tendency to interpret the meaning of data is as atavistic as the alertness of predatory animals. For a model of asceticism, the contributions of Bion (1970) are within our reach, for example, in *Attention and Interpretation* (see Chapter 4).

Even though it is evident, we must not fail to mention that the first requisite for observation is to sustain the subject-object discrimination. All phenomenology of narcissistic, claustrophobic, or delusional states, for example, provide enough proof that with intrusive identification, the object is lost from view, omniscience alone being possible. On the opposite pole of this phantasy is the requisite to observe, formulated as a negative capability (Keats) or as the ability to remain in uncomfortable uncertainty, without irritatingly having to seek facts, reasons, or historical explanations. This ability finds clear indications in the brief, celebrated, and highly discussed work of Bion (1967a), *Notes on Memory and Desire*. There the analyst is invited to expose themself to the experience of the potential catastrophic change in analysis, without the protection of the prejudices of theoretical training or the knowledge of their analysis patient, nor the protection that, with therapeutic zeal, would invite them to programme the clinical experience or the direction of the cure. Leaving aside our premises, we are left with greater availability to perceive those of the patient. The other contribution to the development of thought and its conditions, genesis, and uses made by Bion was his proposal of the *Grid*, with which one can observe the development of thoughts on the part of the patient, and it would serve as a self-monitoring of the analyst's functioning. When Money-Kyrle (1964, pp. 389–390) reviewed *Elements of Psycho-analysis* (Bion, 1963), he emphasised two things essential to the psychoanalytic task

> ...knowledge of an adequate number of psycho-analytic theories and accurate observation. As to the first, Bion believes that comparatively few theories should be enough, provided they are formulated with sufficient generality (see his *Learning from Experience*). But, of course, if they are not adequate, there will not be enough pigeon-holes, as it were, for all the observations. As to the second, if the observations are not accurate, they will be likely to be put in the wrong pigeon-holes in the network of theory [...] The importance of accurate observation is therefore paramount.

Another contribution made by Bion for adequate psychoanalytic observation is that of the container-contained model; without the presence of a sufficiently available container, elastic and tolerant enough to receive projections, it would not be possible to perceive data as it emerges in the analytic relationship. Therefore, the container-contained relationship will be fruitful if it is based on tolerance and patience, whereas, on the contrary, haste will be a source of prejudices and misunderstandings. The necessary availability for a fertile clinical observation finds clear expression in the following words of Di Carlo (1984, p. 32):

> ... listening means accepting the other person in their initial incomprehensibility, in the heterogeneity of meanings that we receive, remaining in the expectation that meaning will emerge in time, that it will be worked through and matured, and that the object will reveal itself with signs endowed with meaning; meanings dependent on the analyst's capacity for reverie.

I began this chapter with the mother-infant model as a paradigm of the analytic relationship and I would like to bring it to a close with a correlative reference, quoting a text from Brenman Pick (1985, p. 157): "If there is a mouth that seeks a breast as an inborn potential, there is, I believe, a psychological equivalent, i.e., a state of mind which seeks another state of mind". The equivalent in the clinical relationship is based on the patient's search for a *combined object of whole objects* available to accept the demands made by the infantile parts, willing to understand the patient's gestures and return meaning. No matter how willing the observer may be to discover the patient's inner world, they will have to be satisfied with the fact that emotional states can be intuited almost exclusively through the information emerging from dream life (Meltzer, 1984); a dream life made present in the analytic relationship.

So far, some of the conditions for psychoanalytic observation of the *whole person* with *global attention* have been named, emphasising that psychoanalytic observation is conducted not only through the sensory organs but also fundamentally with the psychoanalytic apparatus.

If one begins with the consideration of the transference as the externalisation of the image, quality and function of the internal objects onto the analyst, the countertransference will be the means of perceiving the turbulence and the alterations that this projection provokes in the analyst; in this way, it will be possible to discover, signify, and name what the patient's premises evoke in the observer. Exposing oneself as a receptive and unprejudiced medium to the transferential manifestations of the analysand makes it possible to collect significant enigmatic data that will remain in the internal world of the analyst/observer waiting to be glimpsed, intuited, described, analysed, named, etc. To this end, not only will tolerance be necessary, but also the ability to restrain one's tendency to intervene, often counter-identified with the patient's emergencies; in this sense, what Meltzer said in the Florence meeting makes total sense:

> We are all a bit hyperactive, having very little faith in Bion's internal committee[9] for exploring from all possible vertices by means of communication. If we can confine our activity to pointing and naming, to employing signs in consciousness, we give the internal 'committee' time to fashion its symbols and create the basis in dream life for understanding ourselves, our children, our patients.
>
> (Meltzer, 1997b, p. 181)

3.2.1.4 Description

Observation and description are the basis for interpretation, but what does *description* actually mean? Does it perhaps mean a lesser resource—compared to judgement—in order to say something about an object? Will it be in keeping with the devaluation that Ferrater Mora (1965, T 1, p. 426) pointed to? "The ancients already considered description at that time to be an 'insufficient definition'. One described what could not be defined, exhausting all of the essential notes in the definition". The term description, however, is ubiquitous in the writings of Freud, Klein, Bion, and Meltzer... Would that be a sign of the scientific category in which psychoanalysis falls? Will description be a lesser resource used to access the meaning of a behaviour or a work of art? Some authors consider description to be a resource that can be used to access meaning; for example, Todorov (1970, p. 105) who, while recognising that "the problems of meaning are among the most difficult in linguistics or philosophy", turns to description to access meaning by distinguishing the different planes of literary work (sounds, prosodia, grammar, semantics, and descriptive linguistics). A concrete and original meaning that arises from the relationships between different elements and contexts of the literary work. *Mutatis mutandis*, description is a suitable resource to unravel the meaning of human behaviour.

Epistemologists (Samaja, 1995) consider description to be the first stage of research of the object of study. Description is responsible for identifying the component elements of the object, characterising them, and then reworking them according to the vertex from which it is studied. Freud (1915, p. 2957) shared this opinion:

> The true beginning of scientific activity consists rather in describing phenomena and then in proceeding to group, classify and correlate them. Even at the stage

of description it is not possible to avoid applying certain abstract ideas to the material in hand, ideas derived from somewhere or other but certainly not from the new observations alone.

In order to describe something, an earlier step must be taken: that of naming. In this way, phenomena will be recovered to convert them into *facts* well differentiated from the anonymous obviousness of daily life. Starting from relevant traits of such facts, the scientist "proceeds then to a redescription, with which the search is guided in the sense of some hypotheses regarding the possible essential traits and the possible keys for functioning" (Samaja, 1995, p. 160). The new description circumscribes the object and invites us to a new exploration. That is to say, under the perspective of the vertex, we advance through new descriptions.

If, in order to describe, it is necessary to name, then the complex problem of the use of names to name things, and the problem of determining the meaning of the name arises. These are some of the most fundamental problems of the philosophy of language. Searle (1967) establishes a relationship between naming and description, considering that without description, referencing would be almost impossible. The problem emerges when references are neither pointed out nor recognised by descriptions, turning the name into a non-naming. In that case, one would enter the realm of confusion, such as "when language functions in a vacuum" (Wittgenstein, 1958, § 132). What should one do in the face of the divorce between facts and names? Terricabras (1997, p. 18) says that:

> If the way in which a philosophical problem is expressed is 'I don't know how to orient myself' (I.F. 123; cf. 125, 203), the problem most certainly won't be solved by giving explanations—even if they are metaphysic in nature—of the disorientation experienced by whomever the person in question is. The explanation reinforces and justifies the disorientation, but it doesn't eliminate it—to explain an illness does not provide a cure. What corresponds in a case like this is to find a path out of the disorientation (309). And the path that Wittgenstein proposes is that of working on a clearer, more complete description of the language-game being played, and in which one can become lost.

In the face of the perplexity and confusion of poorly thought-out issues, it is preferable to dissolve them rather than solve them, but not with explanations, as Terricabras rightly suggests. For this purpose, rather than explaining them, especially if explanation is confused with rationalisation for the enjoyment of obsessives, it is wise to observe and describe in order to find a meaning that accounts for the emotional situation. Understanding based on the explanation/description of the phantasy and personal dynamics dissolves confusion and misunderstandings. If explanations do not fit with an emotional experience, they become nothing more than a bombardment of explanations that do not enlighten anyone but only dazzle us.

From the contributions of epistemologists and the developments of Bion and Meltzer, amongst others, psychoanalysis has evolved from being a science that claimed to explain everything, to a descriptive science that does not explain anything, and that is built more as a model than as a theory.

The option of being a model and not an explicative science lies in the fact that

in psychoanalysis we are working in a non-causal system where events are factors in a field and everything is symbolic of meaning, metaphorical. For this reason it is essential that models be used for discovery and not as rules or guides to action.

(Meltzer and Harris W, 1988, p. 204)

For Meltzer (1986, pp. 221–222), theories have the value of being "merely descriptive devices for outlining the structure of the variety of internal and external experiences which manifest themselves within us as emotion". Later on, he would begin the introduction of his last work *The Claustrum* (1992, p. 3), in such an assertive way: "The thrust of psychoanalysis has moved relentlessly from a simplistic explanatory hypothesis and an optimistic aim to cure mental illnesses, towards a state of bewildered description of mental phenomena".

This is the culmination of the circle *from explanation to description* in post-Kleinian psychoanalysis. If this circle finds strength in Wittgenstein's thinking, it finds no less thrust in Meltzer's understanding of M. Klein's nuclear discovery: positions. For him, the passage from an explanatory attitude that assigns blame (typical of the schizo-paranoid position) to an attitude that tries to understand, accepting the infinite complexity of the mind and human relationships (typical of the depressive position) and the limitations to approach this task, was fundamental (Meltzer, 1986). Consistent with this assumption, he considered that focusing on the exploration of antecedents leads to assigning blame, and blame calls for punishment. Far from looking at the past, the suggestion for the clinician is to focus on the present of the transferential relationship, where the past becomes present. This presentification of the past, as Bion would say in *A Memoir of the Future*, finds an obstacle in language which, far from just describing, induces the sensation of explaining.

In the post-Kleinian circle that goes from explanation to description, a fundamental, nuclear thought exists—that of W. Bion. Approaching his considerations regarding description, one manages to advance in the comprehension of the meaning that description has for clinical practice and for the discovery of the path towards the unfathomable O. In *Transformations*, Bion (1965, p. 51) recognises that he will employ description because of the difficulty in using other means to transmit the patient's ineffable communication:

One difficulty, of those to which I referred on page 5, concerns the communication of material from an experience that is ineffable; the scientific approach, as ordinarily understood, is not available and an aesthetic approach requires an artist. Therefore, the reader will need to be indulgent if he is to grasp the meaning I wish to convey; he will find the clinical experience, if it comes his way, simpler than my description makes it appear.

Despite comparing the language of description to that of the scientist and the artist, he considers it to be the medium available to transmit the ineffable. The option for the description leads him to characterise it in several different ways that so clearly reveal his conformity with the same as his longing to make it the most suitable medium possible; some examples will be eloquent: *analytic* description (*Transformations*), *clinical* description (ibid.), *of facts* (ibid.), the *emotional background* (ibid.), *imaginative* and *oedipal* (ibid.), *strange* (ibid.), *rigorous* (ibid.), *adequate* (ibid.), *convincing* (ibid.), *correct* (*Learning from Experience*, 1962), with *scientific qualities* (ibid.), *articulated* (*Second thoughts*), that *lack rigour*, but have *definition* (*Attention and interpretation*, 1970), etc.

For Bion (1965, p. 10), description is fundamental for a transformation: "…I transform the facts I describe by regarding them in a particular way. My description is, therefore, a transformation, analogous to the artist's painting that is a product of the particular artist's approach". In order to perform this transformation, careful observation and description of the phenomenon present is indispensable, and he expressed it this way:

> …in the session I can have contact with phenomena that I have not so far observed, or have observed only partially. It is an opportunity that is not to be missed, for if it is, it can never be repeated. It therefore merits as precise a description as I can find to delineate the emotional experience to which I attach such supreme importance.
>
> (Bion, 1992, p. 214)

To carry out this transformation, observation is necessary, taking into account that the theory of transformations is one of the theories of psychoanalytic observation.

Starting from the recognition that we do not know what the objects are, what O is, we can only describe phenomena. Faced with this, the resources available to know become rudimentary, which is why Bion said in *Transformations* (1965, p. 140; my italics).

> …my reason for saying O is unknowable is not that I consider human capacity unequal to the task but because K, L, or H are inappropriate to O. They are appropriate to transformations of O but not to O. To recapitulate: Transformations may be scientific, aesthetic, religious, mystical, psycho-analytical. They may be described as psychotic and neurotic also, but though all these classifications have a value it does not appear to me that the value that they have is psychoanalytically adequate. I have chosen to write, though briefly, of transformation in hallucinosis because the *description may serve to explain* why I consider existing methods of observation, notation, attention and curiosity are inadequate….

Given the limitations of language to demonstrate facts, it is generally considered a bad remedy to take recourse in "exaggeration[10] of certain elements in order to display their significance" (ibid., p. 141). In order to salvage fact from hyperbole, it is wiser to count on the aid of the transformative and generative quality of meaning of the *container*, capable of describing and naming.

3.2.1.5 Interpretation Is a Description

When the patient's perception and description emerge from a container with a psychoanalytic function, it can be transformed into *an interpretation, which is another description*. The psychoanalyst describes within themself the invariants they perceive from the patient, and when they communicate it, they make a description "usually embodied in interpretations" (ibid., p. 11).

No interpretation encompasses the whole mystery of the internal world of a person. Confronting O, one only advances among uncertainties, formulating interpretations that describe certain zones while others remain in the dark or in the shadow caused by the interpretation itself. For this very reason, the analyst's attitude must be to explore the present in the manner of a curious and unprejudiced researcher in the hope of formulating an interpretative hypothesis that is always provisional.

In an enlightening supervision, Meltzer (1995a) described the analyst's attitude towards clinical material as similar to that of a geologist discovering a terrain:

> The ordinary process of understanding a patient's material is a process of walking through the emotions that it is stimulating in you, walking through it, walking through it until something seems to be taking shape. That is why it is so interesting, because you are not searching for gold until you say 'ah, finally I've found it. It was here', but rather, you are walking through the rocks and this process is already very interesting in itself. The rocks are interesting in themselves, not just the gold. Geology is very interesting, it is not only a science that is interested in naming and cataloguing, but the geologist is also mapping the structure of the earth and, in doing so, the movements, the displacements, the folds, etc., tell you what happened, how it happened and, also, what is happening. To be able to look at the landscape with knowledge of geology must be very nice because you can be looking then at a landscape with knowledge of the movements that have been operating there. It is a vision in action, in movement. To my way of thinking, this is the great change introduced in psychoanalysis by Mrs. Klein's work, in listening and observing something that is happening, not looking for the evidence of what happened at a time, in the past, in the way the archaeologist does, but the geological evidence of what is happening at all times, and is fundamental to describing that structure.

Describing the structure through interpretations that are always provisional; definitive interpretations can never be formulated because the geological layers of the mind ceaselessly shift. This is the optimistic view of psychic change.

Comparing the psychoanalyst's task with that of the geologist can generate misunderstanding. Psychoanalytic exploration has two protagonists capable of making exploration a shared task in a climate of "comradeship". I refer the reader to Section 3.3.1 for more on this point.

In an interview with Fisher (1995, p. 123–124), Meltzer acknowledged his masters and what he learned from each of them; he said:

> Psychoanalytically speaking. I have various masters from whom I have taken various things. From Mrs Klein, I have taken interpretation. From Money-Kyrle, I have taken patience and kindness. From Bion, thinking. But from Mrs Bick, I took observation. She was a great observer—not just of baby observation, but clinical observation.

Five years later, in a supervision in Barcelona, Meltzer made mention of how his technique had varied; on one occasion, he said,

> I was trained in the absolute belief in Mrs Klein's correct interpretation. I required various years to recover from all of this; for me, it was also a kind of disappointment. An interpretation is a metapsychological statement of a drama, a drama consisting of transference and countertransference and has relatively little to do with processes of development in history; everything happens there, in the consulting room, except when it gets out and acting out occurs.

Meltzer experienced the evolution of psychoanalysis from when it was based on reconstruction to psychoanalysis based on observation, and the evolution from the correct interpretation using the correct timing, to the consideration of the interpretation as a description of the metapsychological drama unfolding in the immediacy of the relationship. Taking up again the interview with Fisher where the subject of what to interpret was reflected upon, Meltzer (ibid., p. 121) said: "Everything that is visible in the room is available for interpretation, and by interpretation, of course, I mean mainly description. The interpretation of meaning is so implicit in the description that it really is not a separate matter". An essentially Bionian statement is reached in this way: interpretation is a description, although not all description is interpretation. The description of baby observation is not an interpretation because what characterises psychoanalytic interpretation is the description in the transference-countertransference, which is observable in the analytic relationship.

Both in clinical practice and baby observation, one relies on the complex and mysterious instruments of psychoanalytic description and intuition. In this sense, Apprey (1997) was mistaken when he requested that Meltzer be censured for stating that interpretation was a description. I believe that Apprey's mistake was to confound phenomenological description (cf. Husserl) with psychoanalytic description because, as Meltzer (1997a) himself replied,

> but if one supposes that any disciplined description can do more than touch the surface of what has been observed, one has not understood the depth and

complexity of unconscious processes nor the limitations of consciousness as an organ of attention" (p. 131).

An area of the symbolic problems of certain clinical practice has been traversed. The limitations of language in naming have been recognised as well as the limitations of the subject when confronting their own truths, as well as those of the external world. It has also been mentioned that one of the problems observed is that of those people who state what they did not see and who are assertive about the unknown, getting lost—without being clinically psychotic—in a world of words that dazzle only fleetingly. One of the initial and fundamental resources in clinical work is that of accompanying the patient in the discovery of the objects of the world, collaborating in developing the patient's capacity for observation, without which they would remain excluded from the symbolic dimension. When the analyst possesses an adequate capacity for reverie, then with their observations, descriptions and interpretations, they can contain the rudiments of meanings to offer them to the analysand, in the hope that at a future time, they will be taken up, and that this will contribute to the development of the symbolic function of internal objects. To walk such a mysterious and enigmatic path, like a passionate geologist, the analyst must tolerate the turmoil of the detailed description, managing fear of the unknown. They must be endowed with patience and poetic capacity to sustain the catastrophic leap or change from the sensitive to the intuitive. A leap that demands the analyst's availability to observe the patient globally, beyond the text of the words, almost more attentive to silences and rhythms than to semantics in order to access meaning. I believe that the recommendation of an old master remains valid: "to develop clinical intuition, read poetry".

3.2.2 Fanaticism, Identity, and Thinking[11]

Many of the painful moments that humanity is going through now are linked to the vindication of the first beliefs and traditions or the return to the religious origins of the organisation of existence. In the name of God, ideologies are organised that defend the purity of the first texts and principles. These claims are present in terms such as fanaticism, fundamentalism, terrorism, integrism, and orthodoxy; terms that need to be differentiated. This task is presented below:

'Fundamentalism' is a term of Anglo-Saxon origin with which it was catalogued in protestant churches and organisations that insisted on the divine origin and the infallibility of the Bible. It refers, in general, to everyone who postulates a return to foundational beliefs and the fundaments of any religion. In this term's adaptation to Islam (Islamic fundamentalism), the petrified religion of the Koran is turned into an ideology(...). 'Integrism' is a word of French origin that appeared in France in 1910, during the quarrel between intransigent Catholics and modernists. When applied to Islam, fundamentalists are those who make a literal and rigid reading of the sacred texts and declare themselves opposed to any interpretation or modification of them. Islamic fundamentalism would also be the dogmatic and authoritarian radicalisation of the Islam of the desperate believer, a kind of religious fascism in whose name, moreover, the most extremist groups arbitrarily and indiscriminately kill all those who oppose their postulates and their ideal model of society, based on the ironclad principles of Islam. [...].

(Escribano, 2001, p. 17)

These hostilities in the name of principles caused the Tunisian poet Abdelwahad Meddeb (2003) to state that "If fanaticism was the sickness in Catholicism, if Nazism was the sickness in Germany, then surely fundamentalism is the sickness in Islam" (p. 1), although not only of Islam. The term fanaticism refers to a rigid attitude that admits no variations. Fundamentalism, integrism, fanaticism, dogmatism, and sectarianism are different manifestations of a radical intolerance to any new vertex in the name of the defence of an idea that aims to be eternal. The slogan of loving God or homeland above all else may characterise fanaticism and distinguish the fanatic from the person who enthusiastically loves their country, culture, or traditions but is capable of not attributing to these objects and values the exclusive and superlative character of *above all else*. Blind faith in an idea, and the belief of being in possession of the truth, justifies and predisposes towards acting in the role of the conductor, the leader, the *Führer*, evangelist, or preacher, in the style of a particular leader of a political and religious movement that aspired to establish an Islamic republic in Iraq, and who upon arriving in Iraq from Iran proclaimed, "Our duty is to point the Iraqi people in the right direction and give them everything they need for political, economic and social reconstruction" (Marirrodriga, J., 2003, p. 5). These very words could be found in the mouths of the Catholic missionaries who came to America along with Christopher Columbus to point out the exact path. These drivers can defend their point of view but have serious difficulties understanding and sharing other *points of view*. What is ours and what is not ours can become simple elementary arguments for fanatics.

3.2.2.1 The Context of Fanaticism

What is foreign can be a stimulus for the development of symbolism and knowledge, and for the exercise of non-intrusive curiosity, but it can also trigger the desire to transform the other according to *my* own way of seeing reality. When one lives focused on oneself, there is a tendency to believe that everyone thinks alike. If the opposite seems to be true, one may feel the desire to *convert* everyone to one's own *truths*. Sometimes it is difficult to draw the line between offering one's own point of view to stimulate thinking and orchestrating a campaign to direct how others think. Advertising may exemplify attempts to stimulate obedience, but more subtle forms seek to *convert* the public and thus create directed thinking. For instance, in the name of *widespread volition*, the interpretation of laws is often modified (for example, by lengthening sentences for prisoners soon to be released). Laws are also changed in the name of *social demand*. In Spain, the penal code has been reformed every year, as if in response to criminal acts that generate social commotion, as a reassurance for the citizenry. Perhaps it is not understood, however, that the citizenry's concern is not only motivated by a thirst for vengeance but that it can also be stimulated by the economic needs of the press. Scandals sell well. Comparing the population of Spain and Finland, there is less prison population in Finland than in Spain, which is attributable to the fact that in Finland, newspapers are sold only by subscription. This makes it unnecessary to create alarmist headlines to increase sales. Headlines create *public opinion* that later puts pressure on lawmakers[12] and on courts of law. Dishonest politicians are also skilful creators of half-truths and outright lies[13] that try to create a domesticated form of public opinion. Maintaining *one's own opinion* is a task that everyone is not always in a position to perform, especially under the conditioning information of those who act like the pied piper. The spotlight technique[14] is a simple means of conditioning thought. The fanatic circumscribes one part of reality and, by the use of repeated slogans, attempts to create a following. In contrast to the Cartesian maxim—*I think, therefore I am*—the fanatic says: *follow me*. This invitation becomes tempting in a world in crisis, in a world that continues to lose its narcissistic infantile worldview: humanity is no longer the centre of the universe. It does not descend from divine clay, nor is it governed by reason. On the one hand, it cannot become human outside of the group, nor is there any ideology that frees it from anxiety. On the other hand, certainties are crumbling at the pace of scientific progress, and not even consumerism is a safe haven… In contrast to the old ideologies or worldviews, today, "destiny has been replaced by design", as Rubert de Ventós ironically put it, and so we are drifting towards an anxious scepticism. In times of crisis, someone usually appears, offering to lead the way to the true path,[15] even if it means throwing the dissidents out of aeroplane windows, like that sinister saviour, General Videla, did in Argentina. He believed himself capable of distinguishing true Argentines from traitors because fanatics believe they possess the acute smell of ferrets to detect traitors, whom they are always chasing. Because

> …traitor—says Amos Oz (2002, p. 28)—is the one who changes in the eyes of those who cannot change and would not change, and hate change, and cannot conceive of change, except that they always want to change you. In other words, traitor, in the eyes of the fanatic, is anyone who changes.

and therefore becomes a dangerous tumour to be removed. This surgical recourse arises because, for the fanatic, the truth is one, just and eternal.

> The Pope repeated, very consistently—said the philosopher Gianni Vattimo (2009, p. 41,42)—that there can be no negotiating with truth. Does this 'fundamentalism' characterise Catholicism only, or Christianity too? […] Look at the frequent interreligious dialogues that take place everywhere in the world, where the participants are almost always 'officials' of the different confessions. They do not engage in dialogue with the view of proposing any change; dialogue is just a way of reconfirming their authority on their respective groups.

And if truth is non-negotiable and different cultures are mutually dangerous, it is possible to slide into violence—Hanna Segal (2003) stated, "to destroy the work of the Devil (represented by Soviet Russia)—Armageddon being God's war to cleanse the earth of all wickedness, paving the way for a bright, prosperous new order", following the "just and true" model. With these words, psychoanalyst Hannah Segal described the danger posed by Christian fundamentalists entrenched in the US government in the Bush era.

In periods of instability, not only does the need for *eternal truths* arise, but also the questioning of one's own identity increases; this need to define the terms of one's own identity can be seen, for example, in a particular urgency to construct the family tree when parents die, or the question of identity that erupts with the hormonal revolution of puberty, which has led to adolescence being considered the *philosophical age*.

The question of identity also arises at the social level when the concept of *proximity* is not enough to define community membership. Proximity is associated with place, with neighbourhood; neighbour (from the Old English, neah "near" + gebur "dweller")—defined by the Merriam-Webster dictionary as "one living or located near another"; and is also "fellow man". In the neighbourhood, social roles are usually predetermined, and the whole group is affected when something alters this predetermined order. Geographical, informational and technological isolation favours the feeling of proximity, which is modified when roads and information arrive (especially through information technology) or when needs lead to emigration or the reception of immigrants. In the stability of close groups, people tend to acquire an identity derived from place rather than from individuality. In rural Catalonia, the *renom* (nickname), or house name, identifies almost more than the surname. Questions are raised when foreigners appear: What family are you from? Where are you from? Are you Freudian, Kleinian, Lacanian? Questions that try to congeal anxiety with an answer. Not infrequently, one may feel that "Hell is other people", as Sartre (1944) said in *No Exit*, but without these others, one lacks identity because identity is "an effect of the other's gaze on me, a gaze that is and makes me a mask, a person" (Morey, 2007, p. 36). Just as in neighbourhoods, identity is acquired and coexistence is guaranteed through a predetermined order, neighbourhoods can also become *hell*, exploding in different ways. In a small village in the Catalan Pyrenees, the patron saint's day is still celebrated in two different places, barely a hundred metres apart, joined by a bridge over a small river; a separation necessary to keep the resentment of two groups in check, one with its origins in the UGT and the other in the CNT, who fought each other to the death during the Spanish civil war. Left-wing trade unionists who killed each other over ideological nuances.

The struggle for the defence of group identity is manifested in multiple ways. The struggle between different factions for identity during the period of national reconstruction in France evolved with each side wielding:

> …in defence of smaller, local languages, memories, customs and habits against 'those in the capital' who promoted homogeneity and demanded uniformity—as

well as in the 'cultural crusade' waged by the advocates of national unity who aimed to extirpate the 'provinciality', parochialism, *esprit de clocher* of local communities or ethnicities. National patriotism itself deployed its troops on two frontlines: against 'local particularism', in the name of a shared national fate and interests; and against 'rootless cosmopolitanism' that viewed and treated the nationalists in just the way the nationalists viewed and treated the 'narrow-minded provincial bumpkins' because of their loyalty to ethnic, linguistic or cultic idiosyncrasies.

(Bauman, 2004, p. 77)

The battle for identity usually arises from considering that the river, as in the small village in the Pyrenees, has only one bank: *ours, the authentic one*, whereas the other bank, that bank that belongs to *others*, is foreign, untrustworthy, and therefore dangerous, ignoring the fact that the bridge can unite different worlds, although not so different. Occasionally, some people with certain personality limitations can become the most vehement defenders of identity, or of the excellence of *this shore*, and are usually the ones who suffer most with what is different, especially in a changing, globalised world, like the one described in a poster of the streets of Berlin in 1994, which according to Bauman (op. cit., p. 27)

poked fun at loyalty to frames no longer able to contain the world's realities: 'Your Christ is a Jew. Your car is Japanese. Your pizza is Italian. Your democracy is Greek. Your coffee is Brazilian. Your holiday is Turkish. Your numbers are Arabic. Your letters are Latin. Only your neighbour is a foreigner.'

The insecure person, usually quite humourless, is not prone to mocking what is different, except when they do so out of paranoid anxiety, because it is precisely what is different that is found to be so disturbing and threatening. If one's sincere and authentic right to have a stable cultural community, enriched by contributions from other ways of life, is not easily attainable, amid fears of being exposed to abandonment, then the conditions exist for refuge to be taken in rigid ideas or ways of understanding things. When social instability is widespread, the yearning for authoritarianism increases at the pace, for example, of the rise in unemployment… In extreme situations

…no wonder that for many people the fundamentalist promise of 'being born again' into a new warm and secure family-like home is a temptation they find hard to resist. They might have preferred something other than the fundamentalist therapy—a kind of security that does not require effacing their identity and surrendering their freedom to choose—but no such security is on offer. 'Constitutional patriotism' is not a realistic choice, whereas a fundamentalist community looks seductively simple. And so, they will immerse themselves in its warmth right now, even if they expect to pay for the pleasure later.

(Bauman, op. cit., p. 47)

The price is, however, not excessive if the feeling of safety and superiority that certainty grants, or that of being a privileged participant of the community of the wise, can be enjoyed. Certainty and superiority can also be considered other simple ingredients of fanaticism, along with the radical dissociation between one's own, the *fanum*,[16] and the *pro-fane* or the *outsiders*; everything the community rejects can be expelled and deposited in the latter, turning into devalued objects everything that is suitable for getting rid of, until they are eliminated. History provides ample examples; for instance, the Jewish holocaust in central Europe, or the Hutus in Rwanda. The enemies of the community and the country are determined from a narcissistic vantage point, and for that reason, they can be fought. This is "the typical fanatic claim: if I think something is bad, I kill it along with its neighbours" (Oz, op. cit, p. 25). This arrogance prevents reparation and, on the contrary, feeds the persecutory guilt that calls for more punishment. But the need for punishment is solved by turning it outwards, towards the pro-fane, which generates an infernal circle of defences that prevent learning from experience and rectifying. The trick for not avoiding rectification is to always find another enemy. Hanna Segal (2003) noted that, after the end of the cold war,

> NATO went in search of a new enemy to justify its continued military power. When visiting western capitals, George Kennan[17] was shocked to discover that despite the disappearance of the supposed Soviet threat and our supposed reason for keeping a nuclear arsenal, the western countries could not even conceive of nuclear disarmament. It was, he said, like an addiction. Nuclear firepower was constantly on the increase.

To escape persecutory anxieties or to alleviate the confusional ones, destructible enemies to compulsively denigrate are needed. Addiction anaesthetises thought. Both doubt and questioning stun the confused and irritate the paranoid, just as independence of judgement threatens the fanatic, which is why they are often so keen to gain adherents to their own cause, their own way of thinking. Somewhat ironically, probably to soften the harshness of his comment, Amos Oz (op. cit., pp. 31) said:

> The essence of fanaticism lies in the desire to force other people to change. The common inclination to improve your neighbour, or to mend your spouse, or to engineer your child, or to straighten up your brother, rather than let them be. The fanatic is a most unselfish creature. The fanatic is a great altruist. Often the fanatic is more interested in you than in himself. He wants to save your soul, he wants to redeem you, he wants to liberate you from sin, from error, from smoking, from your faith or from your faithlessness, he wants to improve your eating habits, or to cure you from your drinking or voting habits. The fanatic cares a great deal for you, he is always either falling on your neck because he truly loves you or else he is at your throat in case you prove to be unredeemable [...] One way or another, the fanatic is more interested in you than in himself, for the very simple reason that the fanatic has a very little self or no self at all.

The aim of the apostolic vocation of the fanatic is to build up a homogenous group of like-minded people who are simple, pure, that provide help to the other bank of the river, to this perfidious world (disloyal, unfaithful, treacherous, lacking in the true faith) as sects proclaim with the following messages: "this new culture remains pure because it doesn't allow anything strange or soiled to enter that may contaminate it. One must forsake all to form a part of the new culture" (Quesada, 2009, p. 8). The condition for purity is to put everything dirty outside, and the price is the abandonment of one's own thinking. The defence, however, always leaves a margin for uncertainty and the insecurity that the strength of faith or ideological certainty does not cover the whole of existential anxiety. Thus, a fundamentalist Christian family went into turmoil when the father lost his job. Through social media, they connected with their family and friends, saying that "the hand of God was present in this situation" and asked everyone to pray as they relied on the power of prayer to "open new doors of work".

The "hand of God" and the "world of men" is a binary organisation of the world, as simple as that of Luis, a young patient that suffers a physical malformation from birth, burdened by almost delusional interpretations that, at times has a schematic cosmovision, like the worldview of some fanatics. In a session, he expressed his anger with his father, who came into his room and contaminated it. Luis used to say that his father, walking on the pavement next to a school, could smell the odour of the pupils who are "illegal immigrants, undocumented"—Arabs who have germs that his father later contaminates his room with, thus "contaminating the Spanish scent". I will leave to one side the dimension of Luis' positive oedipal conflict (his jealousy of his parents' sexual life: the father who enters the room), his negative oedipal conflict (the desire to be loved by his father) and his jealousy of possible pupils/siblings; I will limit myself to showing the binary organisation of the world (Arabs-Spaniards) and the admiration that he felt for the leaders of this binary organisation: Hitler and Franco. Luis would say, very pridefully, "Franco, who was a friend of Hitler, was Spanish, and under his rule, no *pateras*[18] tried to enter the country, and he was the leader of all of Spain". Luis, like many fanatics, believes that a strong leader will avoid disintegration and will protect the borders (that in psychic reality represent different sphincters). Luis could express that

> Hitler hated the Jews, homosexuals, people with handicaps, immigrants of all kinds, the mentally ill, and people with Down's syndrome, and he sent them all to the gas chambers or he had them executed. He also hated drug addicts. Hitler wanted a superior race, not inferior, but rather supermen.

But he identified with the feared aggressor and rejected Arabs to deny his terror that he himself would have been eliminated. Thus, it was that at a particular moment in time, he relaxed, arguing that "I was born in the 80s, and this happened in the 40s". His fanatical schematics, however, did not free him of the suffering that contaminated him like germs. When faced with these germs that represented the Arabs "that are scum, bastards that set off bombs and take away our work and invade us like the plague", Luis uses obsessive defences like washing, showering, using air-fresheners and pesticides, and deep down inside would like to eliminate them; like many fanatics, he believes that *apartheid* is the (final?) solution.

3.2.2.2 The Group

While this patient can express his pride at being Spanish and reject the Arabs, he defends himself from his feelings of insecurity, vulnerability, and fear of the future. He registers, at the same time, a false sensation of power associated with the fact of forming part of a large group—called Spain—with an idealised, vertebrated leader—Franco. Although Luis avoids contact with the outside world where skin-heads live, it tranquilises him to feel a part of a horde led by a father with certain primitive, erotic, exciting, and terrifying primitivism. Luis' ambivalence of his father is similar to the "civilized man" who "has traded in a portion of his chances for happiness for a certain measure of security" (Freud, 1930, p. 42); but Luis' degree of dependence was so great that few rebellions could take on this so greatly needed, loved, powerful father. His tendency to isolate himself kept him from associating with and joining groups that would allow him to participate in this characteristic common to all groups: the capacity to unite and form crowds eager for action and impatient vengeance for grievances. As Freud (1930, pp. 41–42) said,

> It is clearly not easy for people to forgo the satisfaction of their tendency to aggression. To do so makes them feel uneasy. One should not belittle the advantage that is enjoyed by a fairly small cultural circle, which is that it allows the aggressive drive an outlet in the form of hostility to outsiders. It is always possible to bind quite large numbers of people together in love, provided that others are left out as targets for aggression. I once discussed this phenomenon, the fact that it is precisely those communities that occupy contiguous territories and are otherwise closely related to each other—like the Spaniards and the Portuguese, the North Germans and the South Germans, the English and the Scots, etc.—that indulge in feuding and mutual mockery. I called this phenomenon 'the narcissism of small differences'—not that the name does much to explain it. It can be seen as a convenient and relatively innocuous way of satisfying the tendency to aggression and facilitating solidarity within the community.

As long as there are Arabs on whom to unload one's limitations and hostility, Luis will be able to perceive himself as a Spaniard, a member of a superior race. But if this feeling of superiority is shared by a group fused to a leader who sanctions and accredits action, the conditions are ripe for the greatest crimes to be committed in the name of an ideal, a homeland, a flag, or a god. Crimes that make more than obvious the failure of the group to contain and modulate the most primitive anxieties, allowing them more innocuous and constructive forms of expression. It is surprising that, in the face of financial crises, people think of the responsibility of leaders and their inability to solve problems. The model in which leaders are responsible is implicit in this way of acting, without recognising that groups create their leaders with the task of putting words to their unconscious desires. The leader is a function of the group, and for that reason, the group coerces the leader to submit to its silent will, at risk of being dismissed, or made into a scapegoat if they do not obey.

When Amos Oz (op. cit, p. 30) says that "the cult of personality, the idealisation of political or religious leaders, the worship of glamorous individuals, may well be another widespread form of fanaticism", I believe that he is referring to the forms of expression of fanaticism, but not of his creation; it was not Hitler who created Nazism, but rather a people at a specific time in history. I believe it is a mistake to condemn leaders and acquit their followers, establishing in this way a deceitful and dangerous dissociation. It usually occurs that when a tragedy occurs, the leader is pointed to as the one responsible, with the old model that states that by getting rid the dog, you get rid of rabies. Hitler was chosen, but another fascinating and destructive leader could have also been named, like David Koresh, the self-proclaimed reincarnation of Christ, who, at the helm of the Seventh-day Adventist Church, called for the massacre in Waco, Texas, in 1993, known as the Davidian massacre. The tendency to take a part for the whole indicates a serious restriction in the ability to think, in addition to being a technique to hinder any sort of change, in the style of *The Leopard*.[19]

Belonging to a group implies benefits and sacrifices. The benefits come from the utilisation of the institutions by "their individual members to reinforce individual mechanisms of defence against anxiety, [...] and the expression and gratification of libidinal impulses in constructive social activities" (E. Jaques, 1979, p. 478); the benefit, however, is counterbalanced by the dose of obedience demanded by the institutions. It is important to keep in mind here that fanaticism usually gains ground when

> we submit—says Segal, (op. cit.)—to the tyranny of our own groups. If we project too much into our group, we surrender our own experiences and the group tyrannises us; we follow like blind sheep led to the slaughter. This does not mean that we should insulate ourselves and enjoy some superior ivory tower of our insights; we are all members of some group or other and share responsibility for what 'our group' does. Even when we are passive and feel detached, our apathy abandons the group to its fate.

Responsibility for groups one belongs to is exercised through participation in working groups and defiance of basic assumptions; this means holding on to a *point of view* even if it is an annoyance to the group, which is often satisfied when there is a false sense of well-being "*amongst ourselves*".

Group life and group thinking do not go well together. Freud (1921), in *Group Psychology and the Analysis of the Ego*, illustrated how the increase of affect and the inhibition of thought are the basic facts of group psychology. Bion, starting from the hypothesis that it is the absent object that stimulates the emergence of thought, considers group life as the *enemy* of mental activity because there is no absent object in the group: one is continuously surrounded by present objects. The continuous presence of objects, as happens in group life, prevents mourning and internalisation of *absent* objects and, in turn, by locking the subject into uniform thinking through group life and facilitating two-dimensional imitation, hinders the development of the imagination.

3.2.2.3 Imagination

The fanatic finds it difficult to imagine something different. They cannot harmonise with the text of John Lennon's *Imagine*. They cannot imagine anything because they neither observe nor look; they cannot imagine that there is no heaven or hell, but instead claim that things can only be one single way. There are no individuals or unusual people in the world, but only categories, and that is why reality is made up of classes or sets: blacks, Arabs, Arians, Rumanians, thieves, rich people, immigrants, mestizos, etc. People are part objects, samples of a class, and for that very same reason, immigrants who "take away people's jobs" can be looked down upon in contempt, as Luis liked to say to me, perhaps not realising that he was talking to an immigrant. Without observing the particular, one cannot imagine. Faced with the fanatic's lack of imagination, Oz (op. cit., pp. 32–33) harbours "hope, albeit a very limited hope, that injecting some imagination into people may help cause the fanatic to feel uneasy. This is not a quick remedy, this is not a quick cure, but it may help"; he believes "that a person who can imagine what his or her ideas imply [...] may become a less complete fanatic, which is a slight improvement", i.e. if Luis had realised that he was insulting his own analyst, perhaps he could have been less myopic, less fanatical. But he was not talking to an immigrant because he was looking from *his* vertex, and I was *his* psychotherapist, because one can demand that all immigrants be expelled, except *my* maid![20]

An antidote to fanaticism is observing reality's complexity from all possible angles and viewpoints. This requires the ability to step outside of oneself to venture into the unknown of the object, but for this adventure, it is necessary to be intrapsychically integrated and sustained in whole, complex, and interrelated internal objects; this infrastructure will sustain the richness of the imagination and enable the discovery of meanings. Meaning [see Section 3.2.1] is generated in the interrelation of iconographic[21] elements present, for example, in dreams or poetry. John Lennon's song acquires its meaning in the interrelation of the elements, which is impossible in a fanatical person. This impossibility arises from the inability to imagine what is going on in another person's mind. When the fanatic performs the exercise of imagining what another person is thinking, they usually see what they have attributed. The fanatic's curiosity is more possessive than probing; they are interested in counting thoughts and possessing them, and they do not care about invading the private spaces of others. It is an intrusive curiosity.

If, at the peak of symbolic development, we find creative non-zealous imagination, aesthetic experience, and intimate relationships (see Section 3.3), one could point to the non-mental reflex arch as its opposite. In order to evaluate the difference between both poles, it would be wise to listen to Meltzer's proposal (1980b, pp. 141–142) where he points out the regressive path that goes from imagination to the non-mental; his proposal says that regression begins with

> …withdrawal from the depressive position to the paranoid-schizoid position; it continues in the second step: from the withdrawal from the whole object to the part object (i.e. from an object with an individual identity to an object with a class identity); the next step is: from the object relation to narcissism (i.e. from the family-type relation to the *gang*-type group); finally, it is the withdrawal from the narcissistic to the basic assumptions group. It is here that the passage from three-dimensionality to two-dimensionality takes place: it seems to me, in fact, that in the basic assumptions groups, the modality of identification is adhesive, consisting of the imitation of the behaviour of the other members of the group. […] The next step is isolation, as we can see in the autistic child. Then we have autistic dismantling, i.e. the one-dimensionality of autism itself.

This regressive road from an object with interiority (tri-dimensionality) where meaning is generated, to a dismantled object, a pure surface, creates the basis for a fanatical attitude because it is easier to attribute meaning to an object reduced to exteriority, upon which banners can be hung based on skin colour or intonation. In this sense, Luis' way of functioning suggests an adhesive identification[22] with his father, a person skilled in handling objects but with little capacity for imagination, reliant on concrete indications for action, and who does not always understand. Luis' mother seems more intelligent but, suffering from a long post-natal depression, she was unable to relate to him, leaving him more in the hands of his father and grandmother. Luis' vital impulse found evasive, concrete answers, which prevented complex symbolic development that would make it possible to go beyond a world of *Arabs* and *high-bred Spaniards*.

The failure in parental reverie and the absence of imaginative observation is the stimulus for remaining on the surface of objects and, therefore, far from the meaning of the experience and the facts; but remaining on the surface or with a sole aspect of the phenomenon, dismantled as it were, tranquilises the fanatic because it avoids an encounter with mysterious and contradictory aspects in the object that might bring them closer to a situation of conflict and of change. Before risking learning from experience, they prefer to fill their mind with objects built from elemental schemes and poor imagination. The fear and the difficulty involved in resolving the conflict with the outside of the object, or what can be seen, and the enigmatic interior, their intentions, and desires lead them to take refuge in a world of certainties built on the basis of simple generalisations. Meltzer (1980a, p. 138), in his conference "On symbols", differentiated between imagination and fantasy, saying that "imagination is the function whereas fantasy is the product of imagination" and, following upon this, Martha Harris added "imagination can be talked about only from the moment in which an internal object exists with the ability to be used to produce images and to contain the experience of the imagination". If imagination is reliant on the internalisation of an object capable of producing images and representations and containing the experience, then people like Luis and other fanatics have but meagre possibilities because having two-dimensional internal objects that are able to function operationally in the world of facts they are nevertheless, unable to function in the world of complex meanings; with *Arabs* and *Spaniards*, a simple and sufficient organisation of the world is constructed. For the fanatical family or institutional group, there is, without a doubt, heaven and hell, and all the rest are dangerous imaginings or nonsense that do not deserve to be considered.

One way in which the development of imagination and thinking could be encouraged is by stimulating observation from different angles so that each member can look at phenomena from different perspectives; this would require overcoming the tendency towards homogenisation that comes from operating based on basic assumptions.

3.2.2.4 Abstraction

Just as the continuous presence of objects and the inability to think about the mysterious interior of these present objects, or to transcend the epidermis of experiences, can hinder the development of thought, in the same way, the absence of relationships hinders the emotional experience of apprehending reality. Having a grasp of the objects and their interrelationships makes the development of knowledge possible; apprehension is dependent on the process of abstraction. This consists of indicating and separating elements or properties of an object or several objects or sets, and of the relationships that these objects have with each other, to induce/deduce common characteristics from which to construct a concept. An optimal process of abstraction correlates with a greater grasp of variables in phenomena.

To be capable of abstract thought, a series of data revealed as essential must be observed, along with the necessary intuition to take the risk of formulating a concept; a risk, a leap into the void that is not always tolerated; thus, some people are always waiting for new data, they never have enough to draw a conclusion, and are therefore unable to formulate an opinion or create a concept. Also, the fear of paralysis, as happens to some obsessives, can push them into hasty opinions.

The fanatic, having difficulty with imaginative observation, often chooses to generalise from a partial experience that has been little explored; this, together with haste, enhances prejudice rather than judgement based on observation and abstraction. As Bion (1962, p. 59) said, contact with "sweet, bitter, sour objects" is necessary to abstract "sweetness, bitterness, sourness", but for this, it is necessary to tolerate the turmoil that contact with the object creates; if the object can satisfy the baby's demands and if we assume the baby has a "capacity for abstraction, the infant can feel that from the total experience he can detach an element which is a belief that an object exists that can satisfy his needs" (ibid., p. 60); this belief is the result of the repeated experience of finding, for example, the object/breast when it was needed. Translating this into the language of logic would be if *p. q therefore r*; this means that if the state of necessity finds a feeding object/breast, then the emotional experience of satisfaction ensues. Therefore, abstract thinking means revealing the *relationship* (of conjunction [represented by the period] and consequence) between *elements* (p. q). In fanatical functioning, however, it is almost impossible to establish this relationship because the elements are placed at such a distance[23] (see Section 3.3.1) from each other as to impede the construction of a *gestalt* and make a comparison; in this way, what a fanatic says can remain out of space and time, becoming eternal. Generalisations and slogans become unquestionable, unverifiable, and unprovable. Just as the psychotic is trapped in concrete thought and bizarre objects, the fanatic, by dismantling objects and the experience of time and space, levitates above reality; by contrast, the poet has the capacity to take an adequate distance from concrete things to make "a discovery of relations between them possible" (Morey, op. cit., p. 310). One might ask whether the destruction of victims by fanatics, when they dynamite the bodies, is not, in addition to the triumph of hatred, a perverse, concrete, mental way of realising the fantasy of decomposing objects to such an extent that any synthesis or identification becomes impossible.

Tolerance for frustration is an essential condition for apprehending reality, just as omniscience can become a drug to anaesthetise the pain of the conflict before the present object. Bion (1962, p. 65) expressed it in the following manner: "If the learner is intolerant of the essential frustration of learning, he indulges fantasies of omniscience and a belief in a state where things are known.", but in reality "knowing something consists in 'having' some 'piece' of knowledge". But some *piece of knowledge* refers to the fact that reality is broader than what has been named so far. The fanatic, far from seeking knowledge, appeals to the belief that they *obviously* possess it, a belief that arises from arrogance and is based on omniscience. The fanatic neither interrogates nor questions themself because they are confident that reality is as they have defined it and are ready to defend it with all kinds of weapons, dialectical or explosive, although they often interrogate, even sadistically, those who think differently.

In order to avoid pain when facing the apprehension of the unknown, the fanatic appeals to an *absolute abstraction*; with this term, I would like to mention the strategy used to disarm the object and keep it superbly disarmed at a distance, paralysed, without allowing it to join or reunite with anything. One might wonder whether, in the last stage of Joan Miró's painting, there might not be something of this absolute abstraction because the level of abstraction in his works is so high that only an integrating mind can intuit the object that is the origin of the first transformation. But there is an essential difference between the artist and the fanatic: the artist can abstract and make metaphors by creating an object capable of awakening evocations in the spectator, whereas the fanatic immobilises both the initial object and attempts to paralyse and omnipotently control the spectator.

The interior of the fanatic, as is the case with the autistic patient, is organised like a non-interactive museum; this interior was clearly described by Shirley Hoxter (Meltzer, D., et al., 1975, p. 177) upon informing about Piffie, a child with residual autism:

> The failure to achieve introjection and integration of dynamic living objects was a major difficulty in Piffie's therapy. His elaborately developed internal space was

organised like a museum of specimens, each scholastically identified, each isolated in its own case, to be kept and remembered forever—but never to be used.

This pretension of taking eternal control over the object and the yearning for im-
mobility expressed in the primitive obsessive controls sustains "the fanatical con-
victions that emerge not only to avoid a catastrophic change, but rather to maintain
a cold, isolated, dead, split off and deteriorated world of fanaticism in its purest
form" (Sor and Senet, 1993, p. 49). In an eternal, immortal world where everything
always occupies its own spot, there is no place for doubt but rather only certainties. "The uncertainty principle (Heisenberg) or negative capability (Bion) have no
place in the fanatic wasteland", as I said elsewhere (Tabbia, 2007, p. 24).

If one could formulate a concept out of a normal abstraction that conserves
the essential notes of the original object, in the *fanatical non-transformations*, as
Sor and Senet proposed, a concept is produced that welds together elements that
maintain "a reinforced coherence with total disregard for facts, vertices or articulations"; disregard means non-observation, arbitrary generalisation that gives rise to
"a set of not necessarily coherent ideas that remain 'welded' so to speak, resisting
any onslaught coming from logic, reality or emotions. The origin of this phenomenon lies in the mechanisms of splitting and isolation" (Sor and Senet, 1993, p. 57);
consistent with this formulation, they state that "a fanatic necessarily emerged from
an autistic structure" (ibid.).

The fanatic's discourse is brimming with absolute terms like the watchwords
("homeland", "nation", "what's ours", "we are workers whereas those who come
from the south live at our expense"; "the Arabs steal our jobs" Luis would say),
and contains slogans that become unquestionable beacons that do not stand up to
scrutiny. As Sor and Senet (op. cit.) say, the concept of *Maximal Idea*,[24] which designates a simple idea, isolated from all relationships and impossible to submit to
contrast with other ideas that, in this way, become an unquestionable concept and
backbone of the argument. It is organised as if one of the iconographic elements
of the symbolic field had separated towards an infinite and solitary space where it
would eternally reign, as usually occurs with fanatical movements that withdraw
from the world to create their own reality. The fanatical idea, the *maximal idea*, and
the catchword are like shadows: they pass over water without getting wet. This idea
can be transmitted from generation to generation undeterred, like family secrets.
The skilfulness in remaining eternal and unchanging consists of transforming it
into an entity in itself disconnected from its context. An example of this disconnec-
tion can be illustrated through the prohibition of eating pork in Semitic cultures.
What was originally a hygienic measure became a religious concept to be rigor-
ously followed even in societies capable of refrigerating food thus preventing its
decomposition as was wont to happen initially, threatening the health of potential
consumers. As I said elsewhere (Tabbia, 2007b, p. 25/26),

> Fanatical or Maximal ideas usually refer to themes related to domestic life. That
> is to say, the original world of *fanum* or *domus*: race, the homeland, values, reli-
> gion, etc., and are projections of primitive relationships derived from the life of

the *domus*. The Lares deities regulate food, the relationship between the genders and the relationship with the ancestors who have become gods. Their function is to guarantee the continuity of life and of the family group that sustains the denial of death itself. These ideological organisers, turned into dogmas, are incorporated into our lives simultaneously with the smells of family food. The smell of our mother's nipples and eyes constructs the goddess Gaia that engendered and contained us. If such eyes later become a mysterious conflict-generating stimulus, then the child can develop as a psychic subject; otherwise, the process of humanisation stops. When the mother and the family function as an instrument in the service of transmitting the Maximal Idea, then questioning, differences, or opposition will not be tolerated, and for the sake of the Maximal Idea, attempts will be made to force the child back into the fold. Seduction, coercion, physical violence, blackmail, reproach or bribery are all ways to ensure that the child does not alter the family ideology.

The antithesis of fanatical functioning is reflected in Bauman's comment (op. cit., pp. 14–15) where he said:

George Steiner, an acute and most insightful cultural critic, named Samuel Beckett, Jorge Luis Borges and Vladimir Nabokov as the greatest contemporary writers; what in his view united the three otherwise sharply distinct authors and made them tower above the rest was that they all moved with ease in several different linguistic universes[25]. That continuous boundary transgression allowed them to spy out human invention and ingenuity behind the stony and solemn facades of seemingly timeless and indomitable creeds, and so gave Identity 1 5 them the courage needed to join in cultural creation knowingly, aware of the risks and pitfalls that notoriously mark all boundless expanses.

The stony, solemn facades of seemingly timeless and impregnable fanatical creeds were it not for the fact that they can become malignant, violent, or exclusionary, would cause astonishment, smiles, or blushes, and perhaps even a dose of longing for those times when we believed in Father Christmas or that the stork brought children....

3.2.2.5 Identity

Fanaticism is a challenge for every psychoanalyst. In the face of "the obvious", "the natural", "the customary", it questions meaning and also believes in psychic change. One of the fundamental psychotherapeutic tasks is to modify the superego; this is achieved by modulating emotions and creating or rehabilitating internal objects. Rehabilitation consists of permitting the objects their autonomy so that they repair themselves and develop in their own way, and not according to the way the children want them to; if these objects are given their freedom and enriched, they can become inspirational for the self. The concept of objects as models for the self can be misleading if one believes that these objects are to become concrete models of identification; it is not a matter of copying the concrete characteristics of objects but of achieving partial identifications with the functions exercised by these objects. A well-constituted identity is based on partial identifications of characteristics and functions of the different internal objects (parents, siblings, teachers, etc.).

In fanatical groups, you find people with *petrified* identities. In family groups organised around an unquestionable ideology, they take great care to ensure that their members follow the domestic model. Carefully chosen schools, monitored friendships, recommended reading, etc. ensure that nobody wanders off the chosen path. The subject is left with the task of internalising the models offered by the fanatical group or constructing their own objects and models. A fanatic is the result of the internalisation of objects that have entered their psychic apparatus without modification; a consequence of such introjection is that the characteristics of the object become embedded within the subject. What is embedded, however, is the concrete characterisation of the objects but not their functions; what is incorporated is not, for example, the ability to cook, but the meticulous and eternal imitation of a particular dish which must always be the same.

Incorporating concrete objects into the psychic apparatus results in a rigid superego and a petrified identity. Bassols et al. (1985, pp. 182/183) clearly expressed how the internalisation of objects and concrete models create rigid people with a false identity, as can likewise be observed in fanatics; they stated:

> We believe that the ability to structure a flexible identity open to new experiences and permeable to all influences that affect it, so as to have the ability to modify itself adequately and sustain continuous development throughout life depends on the type of internalisations that took place in early infancy. Objects may take on a stifling quality when they are poorly linked to the ego, when they remain as embedded objects from which orders and prohibitions emanate, and demand emulation in everything. They force the ego to conform with complete submission to their decrees. In these cases, a similar situation arises concerning values. These are rigidly internalised and installed values which have to be served in an inflexible manner, and despite the fact that circumstances may change, that new elements of judgement and confrontation may appear, without the autonomy of thought and one's own capacity for appreciation counting. Then, we find subjects with an identity that seems to be solidified, impervious to new experiences, and stubbornly clinging to what they have acquired in childhood. We believe that this type of identity—which, in reality, is a false identity—is found when the concrete contents have been internalised as aims and ideals to be served and to which one has to direct oneself, that is, as schematic ideas and values totally ascribed to certain patterns of action or relationship. [...] The key to this question lies in the fact that, in order for permeability, appropriate development in accordance with the times, and the assimilation of everything new that life brings, what the infant internalises must not be concrete content, objectified ideas, etc., but functions and symbols. Thus [...] it is not any one truth that needs to be incorporated, but the love of truth, the search for

it, honesty in the face of truth; or, not this or that way of behaving towards children, but the function of fatherhood and motherhood, the ability to be a father or mother, to make children grow up, to nurture them. In this case, the subject will […] have the ability to pursue the truth wherever it is, to cherish it and remain faithful to it as a tribute to parents who have instilled in them this love of truth.

Paternal love manifests itself when, from the parental function, it accompanies the child's development without pretending to lead them along a single, true path. The claim that the child should follow the same path as the father, rather than a fervent desire, would be considered an expression of the death drive. These thoughts are also valid for exercising the psychoanalytic function.

In contrast to the fanatical model that there is one truth which has not only been received and is protective, but also constraining, there is also the model of the personality which develops through the task of constructing its own truths in reflexive contact with the world, far from subjugation and adhesive imitation of the concrete characteristics of objects.

In the face of the various manifestations of a radical intolerance of any new vertex, and for the sake of the defence of an idea that claims to be eternal, a dose of humour is needed, such as the desacralising humour present in Fernando Botero's painting which, by exaggerating (see Section 3.2.1, note 10) features, reveals the absurdity of certain pretensions.

3.2.3 Difficulties in Dreaming

In the Shakespearian tragedy *Macbeth*, Shakespeare does not speak only of the royal ambition of a partner, nor of Lady Macbeth's resentment about not having children, nor of the reproachfulness towards Macbeth for his sterility, nor even of the murder of the host and cousin, king Duncan, etc. He also speaks of another murder with devastating consequences … he speaks of the murder of dreaming. In act II, scene 2, Macbeth is troubled and says to Lady Macbeth:

I heard a voice cry, "Sleep no more!
Macbeth does murder sleep"—the innocent sleep,
Sleep that knits up the ravel'd sleave of care,
The death of each day's life, sore labour's bath,
Balm of hurt minds, great nature's second course,
Chief nourisher in life's feast-;

Later, Lady Macbeth, disturbed, invites him to not *"think so brainsickly of things"* (p. 5954). Lady Macbeth's worry is not related only to her ruthless ambition or frustrated maternity but also the fear of going mad if the murder of dreams is committed because such a crime is equivalent to the murder of life itself. Without dreams, there is no self-care and no repair of the wounds inflicted during wakefulness. Neither are consumed energies restored, nor can life's pleasures be enjoyed because they are not grasped nor symbolised. This second service or opportunity afforded by nature that we use several hours a day, totalling up to a third of our life, is used to physically restore us—as is the case with all animals—and to properly develop human capacities linked to the world of desires and symbolic development. If this human dimension is killed, then dreaded delusional thoughts may appear, just as the fragmentation of the personality threatens the ability to sleep and dream.

Later, when the king is murdered, Macbeth claims,

> For mine own good all causes shall give way. I am in blood stepp'd in so far that, should I wade no more, returning were as tedious as go o'er. Strange things I have in head that will to hand, which must be acted ere they may be scann'd.

Lady Macbeth replies: "You lack the season of all natures, sleep". And Macbeth accepts the proposal: "Come, we'll to sleep" (Act III, scene 4, p. 6006). Shakespeare shows Macbeth driven by impulse, by repetition, unable to reconsider, unable to think, and caught up in action. Faced with the strange things that want to be put into action, Lady Macbeth reminds him of the natural remedy to restrain impulse: sleep; so Macbeth accepts the invitation to sleep.

To introduce the difficulties of dreaming in the context of the murder of the father king in *Macbeth* is not an exaggeration because it is in the sphere of dreaming that the greatest murders can be committed and the most exalted creations can be realised. For such destructive and constructive acts to be committed, however, in the dream, a well-constructed psychic apparatus is needed, in which repression has been able to operate, and tolerance of the loss of the object has been able to give way to symbolisation. This apparatus must be elastic enough to contain the natural turmoil of psychic life. I refer to turmoil because in the territory of the dream, we encounter "strange things" that can astonish or frighten us with disparate results. If astonishment leads to symbolisation, we will develop in our personality. However, if it overwhelms us, we could avoid dream work and opt for action, hallucination, psychosomatic disorders, the functioning of basic assumptions, or the non-place of the delusional system. As regards dreaming and sleep, we can feel as much uneasiness as that expressed by the expert, General Banquo: "A heavy summons lies like lead upon me, and yet I would not sleep. Merciful powers, restrain in me the cursed thoughts that nature gives way to in repose!" (Act II, scene 1, p. 5944). Sleep is to give words to strange things, to noble desires, to resentments and evil thoughts, etc.; in this sense, the request of Malcolm, the son of the murdered king, is very significant: "Give sorrow words. The grief that does not speak whispers the o'erfraught heart, and bids it break" (Act IV, scene 3, p. 6050).

Giving words to free the heart from devastating pain means making tolerable the unresolved pain that contradicts the pleasure principle. One of the functions of dreaming is to make desires bearable by negotiating with censorship and binding unconscious excitement in order to discharge it and preserve sleep. But it would be impoverishing to reduce the function of dreams to a kind of useful trickery for those who have been able to repress and organise their psychic apparatus. On the contrary, its significance is amplified if we recognise in it a symbolising function. It is not only the repressed that needs to be symbolised (Jones, 1916), for there are other states of mind that have not been able to access repression, the working through of mourning, successful dream work, or symbolisation. As Segal (1981, p. 91) says, "the capacity for nonconcrete symbol formation is in itself an achievement of the ego–an achievement necessary for the formation of the kind of dreams covered by Freud's theory". Giving words to pain, desire, and emotion is to symbolise, just as the transformations into images or the organisations in myths and dreams are narrative forms in which the outlines of thoughts are interwoven. This introduction shows a choice for a conception of the dream within the unbounded world of dreams. This choice is guided by the post-Kleinian representation of personality, heir to the models of Freud, Klein, Bion, and Meltzer.

3.2.3.1 The Models

In the following brief presentations of the different models, nuances will be omitted because their intention is only to outline the framework from which to observe and describe the difficulties of dreaming.

The model of the world that *Freud* presents us with is that of a subject with a constant yearning to free themself from the excesses of stimuli that bombard them. At the same time as they fight against such stimuli, they also fight against the deadly tendency to rest. In the second model of the psychic apparatus, the personality appears as a negotiator before uncomfortable masters: the drives, the external world, and the superego. According to Bléandonu (2000), Freud built his dream theory largely on the material provided by a well-mentalised neurotic patient and conceived this theory from the experience of satisfaction in this patient. He assigned dreaming the task of satisfying repressed infantile desires as well as protecting sleep. He considered bad sleepers to be those who woke up without having been able to dream in order to avoid waking up (cf. Freud, 1900, vol. IV, note 2). Whereas dream theory is inextricably linked to wish fulfilment, Freud does not exclude other functions: "Our first dream is the fulfilment of a wish; a second one might turn out to be a fear come true; the content of a third might be a reflection; whereas a fourth might merely reproduce a memory" (ibid., p. 623).

Melanie Klein's discovery of an internal world is a fact full of consequences. We do not live in one world but rather in two, the internal world being the place, the theatre, where all meaning is generated that will transcend the external world. Unconscious phantasies that took place in psychic reality extend, when we sleep, to dreams, allowing a continuous flux of unconscious phantasies during wakefulness and sleep. The subject's development requires the presence of a maternal object that will satisfy needs; the internalisation of such an object and its later identification with him will be the basis for future development.

Bion's model is that of a mind that builds itself by digesting emotional experiences, which allows it to change into another, with different capacities from the previous ones. The mind—with the available equipment—goes out—like Oedipus—in search of truth. The object to be internalised during infantile helplessness is not so much that of a gratifying mother—as Klein believes—but that of a mind that understands and creates meanings that are returned to the infant. The alpha[26] function that the mother exercises for the child is to collect the confusion and offer the child sufficient discrimination to differentiate the elements of the conflict, making them tolerable. When the alpha function has been internalised, it will transform conflicts into elements suitable for developing thoughts in the manner of a neurotic personality. When the alpha function fails, and instead of working-through frustration, it expels it, we would be in the realm of psychotic personality functioning. For Bion, dreams are essential to the task of digesting experiences. He does not consider that the dream seeks the fulfilment of desires

> …within an instinctual economy dominated by sexuality. Dreaming is part of the process of 'digesting' truth, which is as necessary to emotional development as food is to the body. Bion challenges Freud's view that a dream is analogous to a hallucinatory satisfaction of a wish, since hallucination is largely aimed at unburdening the psyche of what it cannot tolerate. Consequently, the dream work works in the opposite direction—towards containment, conservation and memorisation.
>
> (Bléandonu, 2000, p. 324)

and available for the $Ps \leftrightarrow D$[27] process.

Meltzer considers unconscious phantasy to be an adequate concept for describing the dream process, believing "dreaming to be as continuous in the mind as is digestion in the body. but concentrated more fully on its task when the other mental processes of dealing with the outside world are in abeyance during sleep" (Meltzer, 1984, p. 88). He considers—following Bion—that, in accordance with the digestive model, three processes should be taken into account: the digestion of the experience in order to dispose of what is truth, the evacuation of elements irrelevant to emotional experiences, and the evacuation of falsehoods which are considered to be poison to the mind. In the struggle against truth—because it inflicts pain—and against falsehoods—which invade everything—are the dynamic elements present in dreaming. In the dream process, one can study the consideration for figurability (which, for Meltzer, means the formation of symbols and the interaction of symbolic and linguistic forms) and the work of dreaming (or the operations of phantasy and the thought processes by which the solution to emotional problems and conflicts is sought).

We thus approach that great stage of the "generative theatre of meaning" that Meltzer proposes and that Bion allows us to intuit in *A Memoir of the Future*, in which the different parts of the personality interact and generate meanings and lies, sometimes solving problems and sometimes failing to solve them. Faced with this theatre as the analysand displays it, the analyst is invited to "transform the evocative descriptive language into the verbal language of the description of meaning" (ibid., p. 52) as a necessary step towards the manipulation of thoughts through rational processes.

We began with the dream conceived of as the realisation of desires, and within a drive model of the mind, to reach the point of thinking of the dream as a privileged resource for the creation of thoughts and necessary for the development of the personality. This was a journey initiated by a brilliant neurotic who, in his self-analysis, discovered the psychoanalysis of dreams. Now, on the other shore, we encounter others who have researched psychotic functioning of the mind and have expanded psychoanalysis into largely unknown areas, such as schizophrenic disorders, hallucinations, psychosomatic disorders, actings-out, and basic assumption functioning, that all oppose the working through of psychoanalytic work. Using this as a background, we can explore difficulties in dreaming.

3.2.3.2 Difficulties in Dreaming

When Macbeth is distressed because the strange things want to take action, Lady Macbeth proposes restful sleep, an invitation accepted by Macbeth, who then proposes to go to sleep. However, they go to sleep together, as if he needs the company of Lady Macbeth in order to sleep. Some people *cannot fall asleep out of fear*, needing to stay awake, or they demand the presence of the other or put the radio on. For some people, going to sleep causes them as much anxiety as open spaces cause an agoraphobic. When there is no internal container, an internal object possessed of the *reverie function* that works so that the sleeper participates in this second opportunity to work through/digest, the subject will avoid sleeping. The absence of a containing object refers to a serious mental disorder, albeit without a frank, observable psychosis, but always referring to people with great depressive and, therefore, paranoid anxieties, and a clear presence of maddening objects (García Badaracco, 1986). The following example[28] illustrates this: a seven-year-old girl who could not sleep, even with the regular presence of a parent, would awaken startled and distressed from her brief, always light sleep, expressed on sheet 1 of the CAT (Children's Apperception Exam), onto which phantasies of a nurturing mother were regularly projected, phantasies that three children had been abandoned by their parents, and that a ghost was living inside the house, soiling her homework, ruining the garden, etc. The presence of a terrifying anal object in her inner world became more evident in what she had to say about sheet 10 of the CAT: two people lived inside the bathroom where they were locked up; the mother hit the boy because he was to blame for them being confined there. The mother killed him, digging her nails into his eyes. She was an evil witch who had actually adopted him. God cast a spell on her and killed her; the two people ended up dead. So much for the story. This child, far from feeling protected by a sort of maternal guardian angel, was pursued by an incontinent internal object that could not metabolise experiences for her. Consequently, the child had to remain alert and awake and, therefore, unable to sleep.

As opposed to those who do not sleep, there are *those who do not dream*. Many executives, businessmen, and people who are generally successful in managing the concrete world will boast that they do not dream. In reality, these are people who are incapable of playing at *as if*, or pretending, and suffer from a serious dissociation from their emotional life. One might think that they do not dream because the dreaming apparatus has been expelled or evacuated or, perhaps, that apparatus never fully developed. As Lía Pistiner de Cortiñas (1999, p. 61) says,

> They cannot gain access to their psychic reality because they cannot discover it, and they do not succeed in discovering it because they do not 'dream' it. It could be said that, for them, even their dreams are sensuous experiences that they cannot narrate, or, if they do, they cannot produce any kind of associations, not even in the analyst.

These people who do not dream or do not remember their dreams make the heart speak until it breaks, as Malcolm said. They often suffer from major muscular contractions (see Section 3.1.2.1), repetitive headaches, hypertension, and digestive disorders, thus turning their body into a dramatised dream through their organs and the disturbed functioning of the latter. Although they often consult many specialists, they feel unable to go to the psychoanalyst whom they fear, especially for fear of developing dependent attachments. These patients need a long time to develop trust in the figure of the therapist and, if the relationship continues, they can dream on the condition that the analyst can provide metaphors, stories, witticisms sewn with figurative language in their almost non-mental world.

There are also people who may start dreaming until their sleep is interrupted, as in panic states (Segal, 1991), nightmares, or sleepwalking. These alterations have different meanings depending on the dreamer's age and state of mind, as the discrimination between the internal and external world, the organisation of the psychic apparatus, and motor manifestations of behaviour differ according to each stage of development. For example, just as sleepwalking and night terrors are frequent in childhood, sleepwalking is usually of greater significance when it manifests itself in adolescence, indicating neurotic or psychotic emotional disorder. Night terrors in adolescence often indicate deficits in the differentiation of the internal and external worlds, the fragility of defence mechanisms, and the threat of psychotic breakdown. These disturbances have in common the onset of painful emotional states that interrupt sleep and dreaming, and trigger motor behaviours.

What is the meaning of interruptions in sleep and dreaming within the psychic economy? A response is the failure in dream work in order to contain an overload of stimuli. Motivated by an interest in understanding patients suffering from somnambulism, I was able to establish (Tabbia, 2001) that

> ...the phantasmatic poverty of patients with somnambulism, in whom I could observe, for example, that the scenes of the dream's manifest content often take place in the same spaces, with the same characters and with situations very closely linked to the immediate moment. The failure in the dream function produces dreams that, in extreme cases, seem like a photographic repetition of the waking state, evidence of a deficient alpha function. I also agree with the failure of the preconscious to fulfil its function of preventing access to motility.

Interruptions in dream work—in the form of motor behaviours in somnambulism or painful feelings in night terrors or nightmares—occur when the psychic apparatus fears becoming overwhelmed by a thought or desire. When the alpha function of the internal objects fails to *digest* or transform the initial outlines of thought because a catastrophic change may happen, and the container fears breaking, the evacuative task of overloading the muscles with persecutory and painful stimuli is then transferred to the muscles. A brief exposition of clinical material will illustrate the scarce level of transformation of the dream contents in somnambulistic actings-out. The patient in question, who has been in my care for a long time, suffered repeated affective abandonment, although he was always taken care of physically. He has been unsuccessful in working through the loss of the placenta; he longs for a strong union with a mother he can never satisfy, and he did not resolve his mother's following pregnancy... In the transference, any trace of another patient is felt as an offence and a betrayal, and his body would tense up, ready to attack or defend himself. He recounted the following: "I didn't know who was sleeping next to me, whether it was my older brother or a woman, so I said, 'let's change places' and I got up, went to their side and pushed them". He said he could not tell, in that state between sleep and wakefulness, when he pushed. The session continued in other directions until near to the end, he reported that a child had been born to his younger brother, i.e. a child with the same surname as him. I suggested that the patient's jealousy made him function explosively, pushing and longing to expel the newborn. His brother, like his nephew, represented the father who had to be removed-pushed out for two reasons: because of his desire to take the place of the brother-nephew-baby and stay with the mother, and also to take the place of the father (the same surname facilitates the displacements). He wished to stay with his mother and to separate himself from the father-king Duncan, whom he felt was like a stallion who overwhelmed the mother with so many children, confining him to the children's attic (see Section 3.1.2.3). The patient usually accepts the interpretations that show him his oedipal conflict as long as he is not confronted too much with his murderous impulses towards the reproductive father, the cold mother and the brother who was born after him, and towards whom he experienced a great ambivalence. In somnambulistic behaviour, he would benefit from that "great perturbation in nature—as the doctor in *Macbeth* said—to receive at once the benefit of sleep and do the effects of watching" (Act V, scene 1, p. 1617). The patient satisfied his desire for aggression by pushing, without the responsibility or fear of perceiving his own aggressiveness. At the same time, he managed to excuse himself through the exculpatory formula of the impossibility of distinguishing between being asleep and awake. This patient sought help for his explosive behaviour. I believe that the eruption of motor behaviour during sleep could be conceptualised as an *aberrant change*, as Bion (1961a) proposed in *Experiences in Groups*, because an external element (the muscles, in this case) is introduced to dissolve an emotional conflict. I have observed in patients with somnambulism that, as a result of analytical work, produce dreams with the same meaning, but kept within the symbolic sphere.

Difficulties in waking up are also part of the difficulties in dreaming. Many patients report that they find it difficult to wake up and need some time, a coffee, a cigarette, etc. to return to waking life. I believe that this correlates with the place (psychic and emotional) where one has gone to sleep and the way in which one has entered sleep. I am not referring to the external space but the internal space; if the patient goes to sleep within an internal object in which they are installed, and if the way of entering is intrusive-masturbatory, there is a loss of self-identity because time is needed to get out of that object in which they have been in during sleep. Functioning on the basis of intrusive identification is not restricted to wakefulness and results in an impoverishment of the subject as well as damage to the object. I refer to a patient to illustrate this; the patient is a young man in mourning who cannot wake up in the morning, a behaviour that is causing him to lose time in life as he misses university classes… A few days ago, he associated his bed with a coffin, which he gets into and stays in.

3.2.3.3 Other Difficulties in Dream Symbolisation

I must refer now to the difficulty in dreaming dreams that are specifically symbolic. It would seem to be a contradiction, but that is only in appearance. In the same way that there are dream thoughts[29] every night even though we do not have, or do not remember, the contents of a dream, there are also dreams with different symbolic levels, although all dreams are transformations that represent objects and relationships. A symbolic dream is that which allows for an almost inexhaustible investigation of meanings for the dreamer, and that will allow them to transcend themself and advance towards a comprehension of the human being in general. I imagine symbolic dreams to be like those that permit a kaleidoscopic view, discovering new combinations. These are dreams with a high level of condensation that appear in the analysis and to which one usually returns because they acquire new meanings at different moments of the analytical process.

Evolution in the symbolic quality of dreams is a suggestive measurement of the evolution of the therapeutic process—an evolution in the level of dream symbolisation that I will present in the following paragraphs.

A paradigmatic case is that of certain people who *repeat the same behaviours in sleep as during wakefulness.* I remember the suffering of a person who worked cleaning houses, and the few hours that she could sleep were spent dreaming the same thing that she had done during the day without undergoing any kind of modification. Never has it been better said that the worst nightmares are those that resemble reality. For Fain and David (1963), the dreams of operative patients are non-existent or poor, reduced to the representation of memories of daytime life, restored as they are, or almost are, without having been worked through by dream work. These dreams seem to have escaped the pull of the unconscious and the force of censorship as if the victim had not been desire but the psychic apparatus that had been stripped of its function by the overwhelming presence of a waking experience. This type of dream could be conceptualised as a coagulation of beta elements, as impressions of reality that do not find an intrapsychic container capable of adequately transforming them. In reality, the transformation has been insufficient because it has only allowed it to be remembered, presenting itself as a mute dream. The absence of psychic life in these non-mental people is indicative of the malfunctioning of the alpha function and the contact barrier (see Section 3.2.2, note 13) and demonstrates a major disturbance at both the psychic and, later on, the organic level. These dreams that reproduce life awake can be said to have the function of recording a problem (C3 of Bion's "Table") with a possible and almost sole evacuative function (C6). Just as these dreams are dependent on the possibility of finding a transforming container, recurrent *traumatic dreams* that conform to the waking model can also be conceptualised as beta elements awaiting the alpha function.

In the mental life of *psychotic personalities,* we find different levels of symbolic functioning and, therefore, of dream production. Within their mental functioning, it would be necessary to differentiate between evacuative hallucination from the psychotic part of the personality that some patients conceal by saying instead that they had a dream, from dream production originating in the neurotic part of the same subject. When suffering increases and the threat of a break in equilibrium between the two types of functioning is disturbed, a crisis can develop with a number of different outcomes; one of the possibilities is asking for help. This would be the case of a patient who asked for help in understanding his outbreaks that were not only concrete (throwing books) but also, later on, I understood that these explosions were the expulsion of aborted dreams. The patient allowed me to observe his hyperactivity, psychosomatic disorders, and irritability, which he unconsciously related to the loss of his Thai masseur, all in the first meeting; at this time, I thought about the failure of the container object and waited, while thinking about his expectation of a maternal container. In our second meeting, he spoke to me about his dreams with static, photographic-like images, without actions; in the third meeting, he brought an eloquent dream. It was a dream that had been produced by his neurotic part that perceived an imminent peril:

> I was in an area of my country and was speaking with a man that I wasn't acquainted with, and we were walking in the same direction. In front of us, there was a dustbin lorry or a lorry carrying many things, and we had to arrive in the city first. The road was between a sea and a lake. The image was bright with colours, and the man looked like a Van Gogh painting.

In this context, we began treatment. I gradually learned the meaning of the dream. The patient was in a cul-de-sac (in his country of origin, one would say, "between the devil and the wide blue sea"), having to face an agglomeration of beta elements (the dustbin lorry). He began to feel overwhelmed: he threw objects around and shouted. He began breaking out in eczema and saw objects on the ceiling of my office. The photographic dreams, static, bi-dimensional, stripped of all meaning, could be illustrated with a dream that consisted of "a vertical piece of iron, bound together with another U-shaped piece of iron with a pane of glass". The major problem was that sometimes the patient did not treat what he said as symbols but rather as facts. That is why when I said something simple like, "upon losing your feelings, you have turned into ice", he thought it was really like that, in the same style as the concrete dreams that Segal speaks about (1986). The fulcrum for containing this crisis was the reference—in the dream—to the city he was going to, which could represent the idealised maternal transference. To get there, I had to overcome several obstacles—the father was one of them—unless he could be as brilliant and psychotic-omnipotent as van Gogh (idealised paternal transference). My ally was his arrogant and competitive but emotionally capable child side. Shortly after starting treatment, his wife asked him to leave their shared home, and in addition, he also lost his job. Thus, he suddenly found himself alone in a foreign country with no money, home, or family… With him, it was necessary to distinguish between dreams, concrete dreams, and transformations into hallucinations and to use very simple language to prevent him from emptying out abstract language of emotional meaning. A danger was that intolerance to the pain of transformations would cause the *evacuation* of the rudiments of dream thoughts (Grinberg, 1981). The antithesis of evacuative dream functioning would be the *elaborative* one, which would be based on introjective identification with the psychoanalytic function of the analyst and allow for the development of a genuine interest in dreams and the acquisition of a higher level of abstraction and condensation. In my foreign patient, therefore, neurotic, working-through dreams alternated with evacuative-psychotic dreams.

I now want to refer to dreams in terms of their greater or lesser readiness to approach more indeterminate meanings and, in so doing, be exposed to catastrophic changes in the Bionian sense of the term. They will also demand a proportionate tolerance of the emotional turmoil and pain implicit in the search for truth from the dreamer. To this end, I establish a gradation between narrative, allegorical, and condensed symbolisation dreams.

I will begin by contrasting *narrative dreams* with *condensed symbolisation dreams*. I cannot deny the symbolic character of narrative dreams, but I believe that because of their function, they can be easily distinguished from condensed symbolisation dreams. *Narrative dreams* are usually long, with little condensation and with little symbol formation. In order to become more symbolic, they need to be worked through again from the countertransference. These dreams are comparable to topographical surveys in which the constituent elements of the present object are described. If they were placed in Bion's "Table", they would be between row 3 (notation/memory) and row 4 (attention) with the function of pointing out the selected fact that at that moment becomes evident to the analyst and the analysand. I discovered the naming of the narrative dream in a supervision with Meltzer, and it was because of the following dream, which I will now share. The patient (see Section 3.1.2.2) lived with her parents and her brother, and she was having problems in her relationship with her partner at the time; she dreamt that she

> was with two boys and a third one wanted to attack me, but I wouldn't give the attacker anything. I don't know if it was by tricking him or because I had

nothing; the assailant wanted to stab me with a knife. There was a long argument between the four of us who were there about him not stabbing me with the knife. We are in a flat; the assailant pretends not to be there, but he may try to plunge the knife into me at any moment.

The patient interrupted her account of the dream to comment on how men always stalk women and that women must defend themselves, and then continued with her narrative of the dream:

there is a struggle, and the knife falls to the ground; the assailant becomes per-plexed, and she says: I am the victor, but I don't know where the knife went; the knife had fallen near the window and, since the assailant is more agile, he was able to grab it. At the end, between the three of them, they take the assailant captive and put him out on a balcony. The night is ending, and there is already light in the sky. There are more people on the balcony. There's a couple; there are no guard rails on the balcony, and the assailant slowly falls down, collapses and hurts himself.

She went on to say: "I was very active in the dream". Meltzer (1991) at the time commented:

It's a kind of dream that includes different themes, and it's going to take months to work through them all. On the one hand, it has to do with her relationship with the nipple, because she is confused with her boyfriends and her boyfriends' pe-nises. On the other hand, it has to do with her brother's jealousy when he sees her attached to her mother's breast. It may also have to do with parents who have to protect children from killing each other. Not much can be said about this dream, except that the baby is encountering the nipples, with all the confusion that ensues, and the question of what is going to happen in this analytic family. In such long, narrative dreams, there is very little condensation and, therefore, very little sym-bol formation. This indicates that not much can be done with them immediately. It is quite different in *condensed symbolisation dreams* because these are dreams of insight and show that a problem has been worked out and can now be understood. Whereas a narrative dream usually simply talks about a problem and names that problem but does not find a condensed symbolic representation.

The characterisation of narrative dreams is particularly pertinent in thinking about dreams that people with great oratory capacities narrate, as is the case with some obsessives. In the measure that these people use concrete modes to think in a binary style, like computers, and work based on facts, "they cannot work with symbols that grasp the meaning of things, because they can only use metaphors, comparisons or differentiations" (Meltzer, 1999b) and analogies that are ways to simulate think-ing. These patients use words a lot, but the words are not symbols, but rather signs, conventional signs, allowing them to talk about everything without understanding the meaning or value. Therefore, narrative dreams can be an organised union of signs but alienated from emotion and condensation, their meaning is marginalised, or they can be reduced to the naming of a situation awaiting further transformation.

Just as narrative dreams can limit meaning, so *allegorical dreams*[30] can constrain the symbolic dimension of dreams. Allegories are representations of some idea through different languages. On the one hand, when the dream becomes an allegory, it could be said that it is imprisoned by the function of explaining something through "the rather ingenious substitution of known elements for what is mysterious and unknown; it is a kind of cheat because it pretends to bring the unknown within the sphere of the already-known" (Meltzer, 2000, p. 36). On the other hand, dreams that contain symbols or in which there is symbolic formation always leave open paths that are unapproachable and unfathomable. As Meltzer says: "A symbol carries with it the gift of humility; you know perfectly well you will never understand it completely" (ibid.). One *dream of condensed symbolisation* is that brought by the patient mentioned before. Rocío said I had

> a strange dream that I barely remember, only one scene. There was a group of people, and we had to go through various tests; we had to take our clothes off; we were naked and were not ashamed. One of the tests was a trail that led to a place that was in the centre of the earth—hell. We walked down stone steps, an increasingly narrow tube, like an inverted cone; we descended, and in the corner, there was a kind of trap, and we couldn't get out; perhaps I put the steps there afterwards. It was a deadly trap; we would die there. It was a space. There were excrements;

directly afterwards, the patient said she had had more than one dream with excrements all over the place and that she had not told me, and she picked up the narrative of the dream again:

> so there we were. We couldn't get out; it was a kind of trick. I tried to remember it. I tried to fix it: once down there, another escape could be attempted, but since we were naked, we didn't have anything we could use; perhaps we could dig a tunnel upwards. I went a long time without sleep. I spoke again with Santiago (her partner). He was very unhappy... the relationship is confusing. I have the doubt that, because I am ill, the relationship is ill because of me.

In the supervision of this material, Meltzer considered it to be a dream of *condensed symbolisation*, an *insight* dream. Zonal confusion is observed there. Deception seems to be at the centre of the dream. The deception is realised through the undressing that allows her to drive the relationship with her partner to an *impasse*. The deception may consist of stripping words of their meaning, reducing their function to that of occupying and controlling the space. It can also allude to the relationship between the psychotherapist and the psychiatrist treating the same patient at the same time, and that, like her parents, had supposedly invited her to a sexual relationship, but instead of developing in the mother's genitals, would have been displaced to the anus from where it could be expelled into madness. That is why the deception would have to be related to anal masturbation that initially provokes an exciting sensation which, however, leads irremediably to the faeces in which she gets caught (anal claustrum). On the way to the centre of the earth, they discover different levels of the meaning of deception that she interprets in all of her relationships and which prevents her from differentiating between nipple and penis, food and excrement, development and impasse, trust and manipulation, etc.

The narrative dream takes inventory, the allegorical dream uses complex terms to give an account of known themes, and the dream of condensed symbolisation invites unlimited research. All three contribute to symbolic development, although to different extents, always linked to the tolerance of emotions and tolerance of the absence and presence of the object.

Those dreams in which something new is always discovered from the inexhaustible mystery of the object as if we were discovering different geological eras or different types of mental functioning are reminiscent of the "navel of the dream" formulated by Freud: "There is at least one spot in every dream at which it is unplumbable – a navel, as it were, that is its point of contact with the unknown" (1900, Vol. IV, p. 111). However, by its very nature, a navel always refers back to previous generations and, as such, is a condensation of a moment in the evolutionary history of the human species; from that navel, one can travel multiple associative paths which, depending on the level of tolerance to mental pain, would lead to thoughts without a thinker (Bion).

Shakespeare's universality lies in the fact that his symbols are inexhaustible, to the point that Harold Bloom (1998) called him the inventor of the human. In a sense, the analyst is also an inventor of the human in the analytic encounter, with the addition that in the relationship, both members of the couple are transformed, without knowing each other's direction. Different transformations take place in that relationship, which is why I will end by quoting Shakespeare again. When Duncan, the king of Scotland, greets his general Banquo, he says to him: "let me infold thee and hold thee to my heart". Banquo replies: "There if I grow, the harvest is your own" (Act I, scene IV). General Banquo's recognition of his king coexisted with his ambitions; both affections went together until Macbeth's ambition killed his rival Banquo. Within one heart, antagonistic affections coexist. The continent does not guarantee their quality. From the way *Macbeth* unfolded, one can well admit that within a welcoming parental attitude, like the analytical relationship, very different objects are harvested, and truths and lies unfold. It all depends on who governs the organ of consciousness.

3.2.4 The Boredom of the Adolescent and the Analyst[31]

Boredom has no dates, nor does it belong to a particular developmental age; boredom is a state of mind that may silently appear without warning. Everything depends on a state of mind. It always has the same effect: it causes oppressive discomfort; it is a station that can be reached but where nobody wants to stay. Jankélévitch (1963, p. 113) masterfully described boredom in the following manner:

> …it is not despair, i.e. the underside of the high relief and the tragic perspective, but indifference, inappetence, absolute irrelevance. When becoming is no longer magnetised, oriented and polarised by the magnetism of the future, space loses its voluminousness, and the fiery flashes of desire disappear. 'My soul, says Kierkegaard, is like the dead sea, over which no bird can fly'. Boredom is calm disgrace. The sea of oil. The opposite of the exhilaration of departure and impetuous morning winds. Even if we later see it as a passing thing, it seems eternal as long as it oppresses us. It debases everything it touches because its function is to despise and devalue, as love is the preferential predilection. It is the most terrible solvent for values, it attacks them and decomposes them in silence, like a veiled acid; it takes away our appetite wherever it passes, the qualities become faded and become anodyne, insipid and odourless… but, above all, colourless.

If I may add something to Jankélévitch's excellent description, I would point out that rather than seeking to devalue or depreciate, in boredom, there is no value or anti-value to be found in anything. It is all the same. Nothing arouses interest; nothing is found attractive. There is no light that stimulates tropism. No feelings, fantasies, or meanings, that is to say, no psychic reality.

In a certain sense, it resembles catatonic states but only in clinical phenomenology. In these, internal objects are present either with a destroyed quality or with a highly persecutory valence. The person defends themself against terrifying objects, with which they maintain a stubborn fight. The object is present.

In states of boredom, what is produced is a stubborn desire to cut off all contact with the world and cultivate nothingness; a state that the Granadan poet Antonio Carvajal—in his sonnet *He closed his house off from the world: nobody, nothing*—describes how to close oneself to the world to seclude oneself in a quiet darkness where neither flowers nor trills fit … until one day it seems more dead than alive.

The individual who is bored is not dead but wishes they were in order to feel nothing. They only want to close off their life to the world. No days, no sorrow, no whispers. Rather than a struggle, it is a withdrawal from conflict. Here what is of interest is not so much the world, nor anyone's reality, but rather how to enclose oneself not to feel anything and instead achieve a state of indifference. Nirvana? In adolescents, this is impossible. On the one hand, their drive throws them out into the world, whereas on the other, when they become confused, they long to close themselves away and shut their eyes to the world … until curiosity gets the better of them. A puzzling state is thus created. As disconcerting as an oil slick that silently extends itself over the sea, soiling everything it touches. Parents wonder about their child. What has happened to this boy who shone full of illusion, or with that little girl that always made us smile? Puberty arrived! The world of these children changed; they are now in another place, in another time. The world that they once longed for but now do not understand. Their parents do not understand either. Bewilderment takes over everyone. Oil covers life. The sea is left with no waves. The adolescent grows silent. They isolate themself, dazed and confused. What has happened for these children—so full of impetus—to become vagabonds in a strange world?

3.2.4.1 The Adolescent and Boredom

The world of the adolescent is no longer that of childhood. Their world is now disturbed by emotions and hormones clamouring for a new space, and previous schemes or modalities are no longer accepted. Infantile apparel becomes tight as the body expands. The adolescent thinks: What is happening to me, is that me I see in the mirror? And what has happened to my parents? They don't know everything anymore, they can't do everything, they don't even know what's happening to me, and they look at me in bewilderment... Besides, they're old... A vision of the world is progressively generated in which, on the one hand, "...there is the world of adolescents, full of life, sexuality and pleasure, and this adolescent sexual world is surrounded by an old, destroyed, envious and desexualised adult world that observes their sexual activities and wants to stop them..." (Meltzer and Harris, 1998, p. 158). Two worlds are becoming antagonistic in the adolescent mind. One is that world that was built in childhood, and the other is the one that emerges with the first tremors of the pubertal volcano. The world of childhood is not far away and was quite comfortable, as described by Freud (1909, pp. 1987–1988):

> For a small child his parents are at first the only authority and the, source of all belief. The child's most intense and most momentous wish during these early years is to be like his parents (that is, the parent of his own sex) and to be big like his father and mother. But as intellectual growth increases, the child cannot help discovering by degrees the category to which his parents belong. He gets to know other parents and compares them with his own, and so acquires the right to doubt the incomparable and unique quality which he had attributed to them.

The discovery of other realities and other families makes the comfort of old pale as the turmoil increases when oedipal rivalry appears and the process of separation from the parents begins. Pain begins to strike the child, in pace with the necessary development of the individual and of society, as Freud said (ibid.):

> It is quite essential that that liberation should occur and it may be presumed that it has been to some extent achieved by everyone who his reached a normal state. Indeed, the whole progress of society rests upon the opposition between successive generations. On the other hand, there is a class of neurotics whose condition is recognizably determined by their having failed in this task.

A normal state of mind[32] requires separation from the previous generation. Freud showed how some became neurotic because they had not achieved separation from their parents. Others become neurotic or develop other disorders when their obsessive latency defences crumble, and they feel tossed about by turbulent confusion. Nobody reaches the adult state of mind without having first successfully transited the crossroads of Oedipus—that moment when all longings and confusions become reactivated. The emotional negotiation of this moment will have consequences for the recognition of psychic reality, the basis of personal autonomy and identity, or for the lack of recognition of the aforementioned reality, the basis of boredom. I consider, therefore, that the adolescent's boredom is the outcome of their opposition, with all possible gradients, to any conflict related to the necessary loss of infantile states of mind, thus closing the "*house to the world*" of psychic reality.

The adolescent who resists abandoning idealisations, above all those referring to their parents will fight with all their strength to oppose experiences of disappointment that would allow them to humanise their parents and build an internal image much more in accordance with the reality of their external objects. To an excessively abusive degree, the schizophrenic anthropomorphises[33] the world before recognising it to be a separate and distinct reality from themselves. With this aim, dissociations[34] and idealisations, conveyed by projective identification, are adequate means to deny reality. This comparison is merely an attempt to illustrate the arrogance of the adolescent and manifests itself, to the highest degree, in the schizophrenic. They believe they are capable of building a better and bigger world than the one they have found. The impossibility of the adolescent approaching objects and observing them is based on omniscience and on the fact that they "*lack the imagination to imagine that there are things they cannot imagine*" (Meltzer and Harris, 1998, pp. 322/323). Another consequence of this know-it-all attitude is the mental restriction that will only allow them to see what is within their limited worldview. This *denial as a defence* baffles and irritates parents and teachers who are unable to get the attention of the adolescent who is immersed in *their* world. For this reason, it is not uncommon for them to accuse adults of being invasive when they are in their own world. Retraction aims at regulating the amount of information that reaches them. This does not mean that adolescents are not curious; quite the contrary; they are eager to know, explore, and discover, but the pace at which they can go about having such experiences is limited by their capacity to incorporate them. When an emotional experience—which always implies some change, mourning, castration—is felt as a threat or offence, they may resort to the defence of boredom which, like a "*veiled acid*", makes psychic reality disappear.

3.2.4.2 Language and Groups in the Life of an Adolescent

At no other time in life is the group as necessary as in adolescence. This can be put in another manner: the adolescent that suffers the most is the isolated adolescent (see Section 3.3.5). The bored person finds it very difficult to participate in the life of a group. Thus, the adolescent need to act and to speak, both of which are essential for progressing towards an adult state of mind, is diminished.

Children and adolescents talk and talk... But what do they say? Talking makes sense when it is about exchanging information and communicating emotional states. The intention here is not to name and discriminate all of the communicative variables that make up juvenile conversations. However, it could be affirmed that in their communication, the exchange of information, the communication of emotional states, and the evacuation of excitement coexist. Moreover, another differentiation could be established in terms of the quality of the conversation depending on the predominant emotional state; thus, in the pubertal groups, where identity is as blurred as in dancing schools of fish, noise is almost more important than words. By contrast, in adolescent groups, where individuality is more predominant, and sexuality is finding a more intimate space, words, and dialogue have greater depth. It cannot be denied, however, that youthful chatter generally serves more to feel part of a group than for communication. It would have the same calming effect that listening to the sound of running water in the fountains had on the Arabs. For bored adolescents, this noise, rather than alleviating them, increases their discomfort and makes them feel impenetrable.

Below, I will refer to the meaning of language and the group in the life of the adolescent in terms of spaces needed to work through the transition.

The child believes in language; words mean a named object. Moreover, since adults are the ones who master language the best, adolescents believe in them as if they were powerful and protective gods. Despite the faltering of this belief with the arrival of puberty, the young person continues to believe in language; they still have not let go of the magic power of words and eventually will be able to use them like projectiles in arguments. For language to become the representation of an absent object, the young person has had to let go of their dependence on the present/concrete and venture into the development of observation and abstraction.

Some people have great difficulty observing their own interior to access introspection because their internal and external realities are not differentiated, and they continually alternate in what becomes an oscillating confusion: what is inside is outside, and what is outside is inside. This confusion, occasionally exciting but frequently persecutory, nudges them into living in a closed world to avoid feeling overwhelmed. Thinking about their emotional experiences is not a project for these individuals. In this manner, they may pretend to be in an analytic session as if they were at the beach or at work, as happened to me once when a patient stretched out on the couch asked me to serve him a fizzy drink. This adult/latent, possessing almost exclusively an exoskeleton, the fragile container of a gaseous personality, did not use words to name an internal reality but a *concrete* resource to organise his concrete life. Introspection was not a word in his vocabulary. In addition, the references made to the transference relationship were felt to be comments about the external world. He yearned only for me to lead him. Boredom was his normal state.

It is frequently difficult to differentiate between words that emerge from observation that express one's own thoughts from those that are merely clichés or slogans. These products are not our own creations but rather repetitions of what has been absorbed from the environment. One only has to listen to adolescent conversations to see that they are often echoes of dialogues, with a few glimpses of originality.

Indeed, the level of culture and mental health establishes important differences in the type of dialogue and language, but it is undeniable that one of the benefits of belonging to a group is that it offers words and models that exempt one from the task of observing, abstracting, and formulating. The group offers a pseudo-identity but does not stimulate one's own thinking. The healthy adolescent has the possibility of entering and losing themselves in the group, enjoying the excitement and anaesthesia that group life offers and then leaving; on the contrary, there are others who struggle to perpetuate their permanence in the group, wrapping themselves up in its jargon, because the group is the *only skin* that will contain them, and outside there is only loneliness, isolation, and boredom awaiting them.

The almost exclusive use of clichés, slogans, and letting themselves be guided by fashions are signs of an unstable personality and of a certain thinking disorder; these are fragile terrains where boredom develops. Faced with this "anodyne, insipid, odourless, and above all, colourless" terrain, many different types of reactions can arise. Alejandra, on the one hand, said: "When I'm bored, I eat" and José said: "I masturbate". Pedro, on the other hand, rides 30 km on his bicycle. Behaviours may vary, but they have one thing in common, which is that they all revolve around the stimulation of sensoriality. Anything is good for eliminating this emotional state. In this way, the circle of non-mentality, generator of boredom, closes. This is so because the bored person cannot symbolise when quickly fleeing from this state and rushing into evacuation. They cannot because they lacked a containing object to decode, or because they did not trust their ability to overcome the distance that separated them from the object. Not infrequently, the swimmer gives up on reaching the other shore because they are afraid of being swept away by the current. To safely reach the other shore requires the presence of an object that can sustain the subject in their initial steps; in this sense, we have only to observe the conduct of animals to see how their progenitors accompany and encourage their offspring to leave the nest. Along with the repeated experience of finding a containing object, trust is developed with the capacity to tolerate frustration and feel gratitude. Not infrequently, basic distrust can arise from a certain inability to integrate experiences and objects. This inability can be correlated with the difficulty in carrying out adequate splitting, which is the first step of future integrations. Difficulties in splitting, integrating, abstractions, and naming prevent the creation of thinking and encourage conforming with the productions of the groups and with fashionable language. An added problem is that, instead of venturing onto the other shore, the young person fills themselves up with words and theories; Javier, aged 17, used to say that he "still hadn't had sexual relationships because he hadn't found the right girl with whom to establish a serious relationship". By inventing stories and rationalising, Javier filled his emptiness and put his fears at a distance. I am not belittling the stories, fictions, or theories so frequently encountered in adolescents, but rather merely would like to point out those stories, fictions, and theories that aim at "closing off the house from the world".

When I refer to fiction, I am not thinking about literary creation, which is based on a great deal of work of symbolisation, but rather on that which arises from the poor or null recognition of external or internal reality and the effort necessary to create thoughts. In this sense, we could differentiate between the production of words, fictions, and narratives that occur from a paranoid-schizoid way of functioning, or a depressive type of functioning. From the former type of functioning, a creation/fiction emerges with predominantly part objects, which are generally not respected, much in the style of poems written with no punctuation, containing hyper-abstractions and references that could be said to be almost delusional and incomprehensible to the reader, as well as generating a sensation of crowding. In more "depressive" creation, not only would the reality of the object/theme be recognised, but also that of their possible relationships, with a degree of symbolisation, abstraction, and formulation that allows the reader to feel that they have been taken into account during the artist's production. This does not mean that what has been created was done so complacently or condescendingly. In this sense, creation has become an evocative bridge, even if it requires work to understand poetic language. From these considerations, we can say that the bored adolescent is incapable of producing a poem in either of these two modalities because of their limited capacity to make differentiating splits. The bored adolescent is just suffering, feels paralysed, and probably angry. Violence grows in the confusion-filled back room. Danger is present. When adults try to make them talk, it only worsens. I have referred here to behaviours that are employed to put boredom at arm's length: taking refuge in sensoriality (the door to addictions), and evacuation through language. Another recourse could be the taking of refuge in electronic gaming. The fascination that adolescents feel with computers is not only related to the universe that opens before their curiosity, but also rather the omnipotent phantasy of dominating the world, in the same fashion as latency children who, on learning the word that names an object, believe that they can already construct and manage it. A curious adolescent will take advantage of computers to broaden their world, establish relationships with other young people, and even develop programmes or create games. A more withdrawn adolescent might reduce their world to bellicose or action games with little contact with other young people. A more bored adolescent will lose all interest in this world within their grasp. This is the child that suffers most, because, isolated, they can only find refuge in superficial or resentful/aggressive ideas, toying with the possibility of freeing themself through suicide or practising self-harm or being aggressive with others, even to the point of murder. Carvajal used to say that "he closed his doors to the world" and "went by a corpse and it was his own". In the face of such destructive ends, however, one could consider the alternative, which would be the flattening out of the adolescent locked in their war games that can last as long as necessary until the need to go out into the world arises. I recall Ivo (now 16 years old), who spent nearly two years enclosed in his room playing war games… until he felt bored and locked up in his cave which pushed him back out into the world. Ivo recounted how the support of a health team and his family, who did not abandon him, helped him to go through the door and out to the street without being stifled… He has now begun a degree in computer science… I believe that shared language and gaming are a valid recourse for isolated and bored young people because the virtual players become progressively more real, creating a *permeable* community that is definitely *impermeable* to the adult world.

The meaning of the group for the adolescent resides in the fact that it offers a space where the separation from parental objects can be worked through. The adolescent's disillusionment with the receding world of childhood finds an antidote in the group. When adolescents and teenagers get together, they tend to displace some of the emotionality derived from family life onto the group. Nevertheless, not all adolescents benefit equally from group life; for example, the adolescent who does not feel part of the family group and is unable to be part of an age group becomes isolated and stuck, as though there was no way out. At this crossroads, distrust and despair emerge, and when the emotional struggle is abandoned, boredom appears: "…it is not despair, […] but indifference, inappetence, absolute irrelevance" (cf. Jankélévitch). Many adolescents feel incapable of being part of a group. I consider that group life is like a *patera*[35] that rescues the young person and allows them to move from childhood to adult mental life… But to be part of a group and to benefit from this experience, one must be mentally healthy enough not to fear the experience of dissociating oneself and placing parts of the self in the components of a group, which is also necessary to experience a relationship with a close friend. I think that the group has a therapeutic/containing ability because it facilitates the interplay of dissociation and identifications.[36] The fear of confusion can anchor the young person to the periphery of a group. The experience of opening oneself up to the group implies counting on a feeling of confidence that allows the adolescent to go beyond the limits of their own perimeter without the fear of losing themselves or of being rejected. Frequently, we hear the painful story of a young person who felt that everyone laughed at them in a group and wanted to disappear. It happens that, while swimming in a turbulent journey, mirrorings grow and fears increase… When I refer to the benefits of group life, I do not have in mind gangs[37] with psychopathic leaders, but groups where one can live out different roles and functions, and experience emotions (love, hate, curiosity) with the unconscious goal of enabling enriching reintroductions of the personality. The bored adolescent does not risk being part of a group because they are not only afraid to open up and come out of their confinement but also because they are afraid of their own emotions, especially their own aggression and that which emerges from the group.

Once an adolescent, especially a bored adolescent, has been able to become part of a group (in general, a same-sex group), they will have to newly confront pain when this group begins to break up. This moment is set in motion when the longing to form couples emerges. When the young person who has found refuge in the group begins to feel the wrench of separation, then danger increases. Some may derive from the group's limited therapeutic functioning, whereas others are the consequence of the young person's limited capacity to participate in the emotionality of the group.

Boredom, that dense "oil slick", is not something that affects only the person who suffers it directly or their family but also those that participate analytically with patients who are, to a greater or lesser degree, anchored in this state of mind. It has a particular impact because boredom is a "terrible dissolvent of the values" of psychic reality. This is the aim of psychoanalytic work; it is a silent and veiled danger that turns our work "anodyne, insipid, odourless and colourless". This possibility grows in response to the deadly decision to deny psychic reality. The adolescent is not always willing to explore their internal world and does not feel very comfortable exposing themself to the adult; it is also not rare for them to employ defences more proper of the latency child,[38] as occurred more than once with Ivo, whom I mentioned earlier, when I went to his house to care for him because he was opposed to leaving his house and going out on the street. More than once, I had to go to him, both of us in silence, while he played his war games on his computer. At times like those, I was left, as Meltzer would say,

> with no means except those of our own imagination and countertransference for the creation of a dramatic scene in our minds that will account for such action and behaviour, and in that way be able to go on seeing some kind of meaning.
> (Meltzer and Psychoanalytic Group of Barcelona, 1995, p. 74)

not infrequently, nevertheless, I was overwhelmed with discouragement and boredom, and I wondered what it meant to go to his house and spend so many moments without understanding what was happening to him. Perseverance[39] made it possible for a bond of trust to develop that allowed him to begin to communicate and to offer opposition to his parents' proposal to interrupt the therapeutic relationship.

3.2.4.3 The Analyst's Boredom

To understand boredom and emotion, it would not be superfluous to recall the fundamental premise that all transference by the patient corresponds to the analyst's countertransference. "Every transference situation provokes a countertransference situation [...] These counter-transference reactions are governed by the laws of the general and individual unconscious. Among these, the law of talion is especially important" (Racker, 1968, p. 137). Anguish, hatred, and feelings of guilt in the countertransference can be considered fundamental, technical problems because they affect the availability and the work of the analyst. If, however, we recognise boredom to be deleterious for emotional bonds in general, it can be affirmed that it is so to an even greater degree for transference-countertransference relationships because, in this way, it can dissolve the specific means of making therapeutic interventions possible. Now, being aware of the significance of all these affects towards the therapeutic relationship, it is worth asking, in this particular case, why the analyst gets bored. I intend to present some elements of understanding in the following pages.

3.2.4.4 Some Answers from the Analyst

Beginning with the premise that the unconscious functions on the basis of its own laws, Racker (1968, pp. 169–170), considers that when boredom and sleepiness are frequent and even regular, it is usually:

> …unconscious talion responses in the analyst to a withdrawal or affective abandonment by the patient [...] the patient withdraws without going away, he takes

his emotional departure from the analyst while yet remaining with him [...] This partial withdrawal or abandonment expresses itself superficially in intellectualization (emotional blocking), in increased control, sometimes in monotony in the way of speaking, or in similar devices. The analyst has at these times the sensation of being excluded and of being impotent to guide the course of the sessions. It seems that the analysand tries in this way to avoid a latent and dreaded dependence upon the analyst. This dependence is, at the surface, his dependence upon his moral superego, and at a deeper level it is dependence upon other internal objects which are in part persecutors and in part persecuted. These objects must not be projected upon the analyst; the latent and internal relations with them must not be made present and externalized. This danger is avoided through various mechanisms, ranging from 'conscious' control and selection of the patient's communications to depersonalization, and from emotional blocking' to total repression of any transference relation; it is this rejection of such dangers and the avoidance and mastery of anxiety by means of these mechanisms that lead to the withdrawal to which the analyst may react with boredom or somnolence.

If the patient abandons the analyst for different reasons, for example, in order to protect the analyst from their own hostility, or because the patient does not tolerate dependence or emotions (love, hatred, knowledge), making them feel helpless, then the analyst could unconsciously take revenge through their own boredom. Speaking about the analyst's boredom must not prevent us from thinking that the process could be just the opposite: that the patient becomes bored with a deficient and bored analyst. Boredom becomes obvious when one of the two actors is not in contact, or only partially, as may happen in social encounters when the other person presents themself in such a discrete fashion, friendly, prudent, I would say reactively prudent, that this person ends up awakening a disinterest because this type of behaviour cools down any passionate encounter to the point where it is preferable to break off an unbearably tiresome relationship!

Another way of provoking boredom in the listener is when the person speaks only self-referentially and is incapable of the slightest curiosity about the other. Such a self-indulgent but essentially defensive position may inadvertently provoke an aggressive response from the listener, angry with the narcissistic, solipsistic talker! The countertransference reactions of emotional distancing of the analyst from their patient are exacerbated in the relationship with narcissistic and borderline patients against whom the analyst would defend themself with characterological defences. This is studied by Kernberg (1975, p. 62). He starts from the identification that the analyst makes "with the patient's aggression, paranoid projection and guilt", which in turn generates a secondary defence: withdrawal or narcissistic distancing. The defence entails "that empathy is also lost, and the possibility of continuing an analytic approach with that patient is threatened". This defensive and aggressive behaviour (both for the patient and for the analyst themself) emerges from countertransference reactions to patients who are determined to deny the existence of the analyst as an independent person and whom they try to control and devalue. Control would manifest itself through withholding information and could be accompanied by something similar to "an unconscious attempt to put the analyst to sleep, or at least to maintain him in a state of chronic frustration created by monotonous repetitions" (Kernberg, p. 305); this would place the analyst in a lethargic, boring situation that could awaken the countertransference reaction of talionic boredom, according to Racker's original idea, and which would entail the loss of interest in the patient. One might, however, question whether the analyst's talionic boredom is only a consequence of the countertransference or whether it is also a deficit in the organisation of the analyst's personality.

Leaving the analyst aside is neither necessarily nor exclusively aggressive behaviour. It all depends on which part of the analysand we are referring to: the infantile-immature part or the negativistic-narcissistic part. In the normal process of development, the object acquires presence only after an arduous process. For example, the construction of an object with the capacity to contain the projection of pain, what Meltzer (1976) has called the "toilet-breast", requires a long path of interplay between self and objects. Moreover, on the one hand, for the psychic economy, external objects, even if they collaborate a lot with the baby, are at that moment only valued and needed, but still not loved. On the other hand, the adult, when they have identified with the parental functions, assumes that their task is to let themself be used as long as the baby needs them. This is a task that Joseph (1989) assigns to the analyst during the analytic process, that of allowing their availability to be instrumental in the reconstruction and symbolisation of the history, the phantasies, and the content of the defences. Up to this point, we are referring to the adult's willingness to take charge of the infantile parts that demand full attention. In some situations, the analyst may be upset at being treated as an object; but if this discomfort becomes an obstacle to their work, we would have to think that it is more a personal problem of the analyst. The right to be treated with respect is not incompatible with being available for the patient's inner world to manifest itself. In the analytic situation, the analytic function is more important than the analyst's individuality, especially with primitive personalities. It is not surprising that the analyst feels lonely and bored if they are expecting to be treated as a subject rather than for their function. This is why I believe that boredom takes on a different, non-retaliatory meaning if understood according to the patient's state of mind. It can be stated without difficulty that it is part of the analytic task to experience boredom when treating narcissistic patients, or people who were not stimulated enough in their early childhood, who have not found a "sufficiently beautiful" (Meltzer, 1988) and available mother. However, referring in particular to narcissists, Kohut (1971, p. 271) points out that when the specular transference sets in, these patients only recognise "the presence of the analyst to a limited extent: they are aware of the analyst insofar as the latter fulfils their functions with regard to the patient's narcissistic needs". Therefore, if the analyst does not tolerate the narcissistic patient's display of self-grandiosity, they may react with

boredom, lack of emotional involvement with the patient, and precarious main-
tenance of attention (including such secondary reactions as overt anger, exhor-
tations, and forced interpretation of resistances, as well as other forms of the
rationalized acting out of tensions and impatience).

(ibid., p. 246)

However, if the analyst withdraws, becomes bored, or defends themself because
they do not feel that they are the object of the patient's interest, we could presume that they are frightened of "feeling drawn into an anonymous existence in
the narcissistic web of another person's psychological organisation" (ibid., p. 276).
Consequently, these reactions could hinder them in their therapeutic function. To
the contrary, if they understand the processes of confusion-individuation, they will
be more "able to mobilize and maintain their empathy and cognitive involvement
with the therapeutically activated narcissistic configurations of their narcissistic
analysands" (ibid.) and of the narcissistic cores of the other patients. That is why I
believe that if the analyst loses empathy and becomes bored, it is due more to the
persistence of insufficiently analysed narcissistic nuclei in the same analyst than to
a problem of transference. How difficult it would be for this analyst to analyse a
patient who asked to be served a fizzy drink!

The analyst's experiences can be felt to be strange. The analyst can feel like the
victim of a situation that traps them. In the same way that the identification with
an isolated patient can generate the countertransference feeling of boredom in the
analyst, receiving the projective identification of an internal, isolated object, impoverished or bored, can be disturbing. The concept of projective counter-identification
(Grinberg, 1976) gives account of the force and the efficacy of the patient's projective
identification to affect the analyst's emotional economy. An example will illustrate
this: the patient, who had experienced different types of affective abandonment in his
boring infancy, is currently worried about the future of his own children. He feels it
to be so unbearable to approach his infantile suffering, and his resentment towards his
parents is such that, not infrequently during the session, I find myself trapped in fantasies of being alone, looking at public works or buildings under construction without
being able to get out of this situation that, initially was attractive to me, and then
later became enormously boring. The defining characteristic of this situation is that
it appears suddenly, and I cannot free myself until I have experienced being locked
up, abandoned, bored, and feeling the loneliness and suffering, which then stimulates
me to look for a meaning. When I analyse my emotional state, I discover it to have
been an unconscious reaction to the penetration of the projective identification of this
patient who trusted in my ability to be able to tolerate his abandonment and boredom.
What is surprising about this reaction is the force with which it became installed
in my mind, the tenacity of it, its seductive onset given my interest in architecture,
and the sensation of imprisonment, as if it were a strange object that dominated me
and made me feel lonely and bored, in the midst of repeated scenes with no escape.
Returning to my patient, I was able to confirm that my emotional state responded
to his desperate attempts to free himself of unbearable states of mind. It would be

impoverishing for me to remain only in this aggressive consideration of the patient's projective identification because I would lose sight of its communicative function, even if it were annoying. My boredom allowed me to discover his. The violence of this communication is often experienced with patients who have not been cathected libidinally, who have not been considered as subjects, who have not aroused parental interest, or who have been "trained" rather than stimulated in their thinking. The analyst, in becoming bored, may come to understand the loneliness, emotional poverty, and symbolic emptiness of his patients.

3.2.4.5 Your Boredom Bores Me

Another way of understanding the analyst's boredom is to consider it a consequence of the patient's severe defensive attitude. According to M. Wang (1979, p. 524), "boredom occurs when fantasy and fear hold each other in balance when the courage to face either is lacking"; this is the moment in which the swimmer will drown, but in this case, becomes bored. The struggle to keep in balance exhausts the people that must

> …chronically prevent the emergence of fantasies. Fantasies that at any time (especially in social situations) would lead him to feel threatened. He therefore must keep himself hidden. He cannot allow us or himself to know what might excite him […] and therefore become interesting to us. Inevitably, and because of his inhibition, he also becomes a bore for us; that is to say that he is as much a bore for devoting his efforts to covering up his conflicts as he is a bore for the analyst to whom he closes the doors of investigation. One can thus see how boredom and boring the analyst are interrelated.
>
> (Khan, 1996, p. 11)

This text by Masud Khan would seem to be an explication of Carvajal's poetry. But boring the analyst by intending to alter their phantasmatic activity, leaving them to believe only in the truth of technical or operative objects, could become a form of retaliatory persecution of the analyst against the patient in the form of boredom (Gutton, 1996, p. 69). The problem is magnified when the analyst feels guilty about feeling bored with the patient because boredom is often accompanied by drowsiness, evanescent fantasies, and disinterest; all this together can fill the analyst with discomfort because it violates the promise made to their patients to listen to them attentively.

According to Kohut, the analyst's unpleasant boredom could be related to a certain deficit in the constitution of the analyst's self-esteem. According to Racker and Kernberg, it could be a retaliatory consequence of the patient's desire to ignore the analyst. Meltzer (2004) offers another perspective, considering it a countertransference consequence of negative transference. He does not consider negative transference in terms of lack of trust or hostility, but as avoidance of an emotional. His starting point is the attachment model proposed by Bion. In analysing the characteristics of negative transference according to the bond, Meltzer proposed the following names for negative transference:

- the anti-link of love (-L) he termed puritanism or the superiority of pure love
- the anti-link of hate (-H) he termed hypocrisy or the denial of hatred
- the anti-link of knowledge (-K) he termed philistinism, which is to say opposition to thinking which entails a contempt for thinking, for art, for beauty, and for spiritual values.

I will now present the countertransferential affects that Meltzer proposed as a response to each of these negative transfers.

The "countertransference of puritanism" is confusion, almost the very absence of countertransference itself, and derives from an attitude of going after the patient by complacently accepting their discourse. This understanding of the countertransference of puritanism resembles the concept of countertransference submission, formulated by Racker (1968, p. 170), in which the analyst would have the tendency "to avoid frustrating the patient and would even cause the analyst to pamper him".

The "hypocrisy countertransference" is also characterised by a feeling of incomprehension, but with an attitude of superiority and criticism towards the patient.

The "philistinism countertransference" is again characterised by incomprehension, inability to think and understand, and where the patient is perceived as if they were stupid.

Having said that, Meltzer (Meltzer and Racker Group, 2004, p. 19) states:

...all these negative links and the countertransference that follows have one aspect in common: the lack of fantasy and of imagination. This inability on the part of the patient refers to the inability to understand the nature of the positive links, of the true meaning behind words such as love, hate, and knowledge. The patient is not in a position to understand the true meaning, and for them, they are just meaningless terms. They do not know what it means to love, to hate, or to be interested in another. What are the consequences of this? When the analyst perceives the patient's inability to imagine, and to understand, a common element is created: boredom; the therapist's boredom in relation to the patient, or the patient's boredom in relation to the therapist.

He then raised the following question: What is behind or underneath this boredom? His response was that it is "the absence of interest that causes boredom" (ibid., p. 20). I would add that not only does the absence of interest cause boredom, but also rather the very absence of curiosity itself.

It is a shared experience to feel discomfort with people who have repeated difficulties in understanding and who, moreover, are often assertive in their comments. The analyst may feel despair at expressions of concrete thinking that are stated as obvious, or at people who are unable to use metaphors, or who do not transcend the realm of the anecdotal, and get caught up in the insubstantial details of routine and everyday life. This is why Meltzer, on another occasion, said that it was "material of a very shallow kind, superficial and boring, that has lost all value as communication" (Meltzer and Psychoanalytic Group of Barcelona, 1995, p. 70). In such a field sown with incomprehension, boredom develops rapidly.

3.2.4.6 Boredom Created by a Lack of Contact

Boredom is not merely a reaction to the patient's negative transference; it may also be the consequence of the failure of the analytic dyad to connect deeply. Let us look at a session with a young engineer who at the time of the consultation was not sleeping, not dreaming, not working, and was isolated and bored. He was a young latency-type man, although his chronological age was around 30, who walked as if he was not looking. The sessions used to begin by him asking me: "Where did we leave off last time?"; he used to express that he did not know what he was coming for and demanded that I lead him. After a year, he recognised that, without knowing the cause, he now slept regularly, had dreams, and had gone back to work again. His concrete thinking, nevertheless, continued to manifest itself in bizarre behaviour during the session, such as asking me to serve him a fizzy drink. In the following brief material, it will be seen how my rush to combat his depersonalisation moved me in quite the wrong direction.

> *PATIENT:* He enters and gestures towards the furniture that forms a casing around the radiator, saying, "That's new".
> *THERAPIST:* I point out to him that his eyes have opened and that, in fact, that object had always been there.
> *P:* I almost didn't come. I'm a bit dizzy. He crossed his arms and legs. I'm not thinking about anything.
> *T:* You looked at the radiator casing, you've come into contact with an object, and you react by withdrawing. You almost didn't come, you cross your arms and your legs, and now you say you're not thinking about anything.
> *P:* Uneasy: What do you mean? You're saying it for a reason. You reach a conclusion I don't reach.
> *T:* If you open your eyes, you see something, but after that, you isolate yourself. It seems that that exchange is somewhat dangerous.
> *P:* He says he's not thinking about anything and remains silent.
> *T:* I question that.
> *P:* He says he has fleeting thoughts that he cannot catch, and that it makes him feel too lazy to think. [...]
>   The session continues until a complaint is made about his boss, who doesn't do much work in exchange for earning a high salary, and he says:
> *P:* I don't work because he doesn't generate any work for me, and I get bored.

The beginning of the session illustrates a failure in the analytic encounter due to the analyst's error by making a complacent intervention, reinforcing it: "*you have opened your eyes*"; my intervention was directed at a neurotic level of contact with an object, when in fact the most interesting thing to point out would have been the patient's desire for a warmer relationship (the radiator) and that this relationship would generate "something new" that would take him out of paralysis and boredom. However, despite his doubts, he came to the session, hoping that the analyst would offer him something new, something he did not know. It was a desire to be satisfied by the analyst, and that is why he came, but I did not understand it, and interpreted it as a manifestation of his desire to function according to the dependent basic assumption on an individual level: to receive something without working for it. By not satisfying his desire, he felt persecuted ("*What do you mean? ... You reach a conclusion I don't reach*"). In his statement, "*I don't work because he doesn't generate work and I get bored*", several meanings coexist. On the one hand, he was bored because he had dissociated his capacity for generating projects, and he put it (projective identification) in his boss and in me in the transference; in this way, he established a demanding dependent relationship that became persecutory for me and that, in addition, I did not understand what new thing had to be produced. On the other hand, he perceived that if he did not work, he got bored. That is to say; he did not think or take in thoughts, limiting himself to demanding that I free him from his suffering, like a child who functions according to the pleasure principle. Also, at this time, he did not usually pay my fees on time, even when he had no economic difficulties. In this context, I felt threatened: I would not get paid if I did not produce anything. It was as if the talionic law presided over our relationship. He would frustrate me by not paying me because he felt frustrated by not receiving new thoughts from me that he needed, and I would take revenge by not understanding him. In addition, danger followed on my heels because I could return, unmodulated, the persecution that he generated in me by his justified demand: his reason for coming was so I would accept his warm approach to me and so that I would give him some new ways to think about himself. However, when I did not interpret him correctly, he felt frustrated, cheated, and withdrew more, increasing his rejection. Our lack of communication increased before my half-blind eyes. Even though the climate of persecution would have seemed to revitalise our relationship, in my countertransference, my dismay and confusion were on the rise, and in the meantime, I perceived that I felt increasingly more distant from the patient, as if in a boring desert. Underlying this encounter was resentment against his parents, which was denied through idealisation, and an affection towards me that I did not fully grasp, making it seem more like a social encounter than an established analytic situation. My boredom and his were frequent visitors. In this field sown with misunderstanding—if the analyst did not work, he got bored—the boredom only grew. We did not understand each other, and we got bored.

3.2.4.7 Approaches to Boredom

Beginning with the premise of a paper written by W. Baranger, where he considers the countertransference to be essentially constituted by affects, Sirota (1998) posits that affects such as boredom, drowsiness, distrust, or special interest as responses to the patient, are a starting point for questioning and towards interpretation. This is because, as E. Tabak de Bianchedi (1998, p. 618) said, emotions move us, differentiate us from machines and are "the breeding ground in which the seeds of our rational and irrational thinking capacities and of our creative or poetic capacities develop". These affects become the starting point for understanding once a genuine interest in discovery and investigation develops, as opposed to a complacent attitude. Furthermore, in relation to boredom, the first requirement for the development of the yearning to discover and name things is, paradoxically, to find boredom itself interesting. In that sense, it would be appropriate to recall what Bion (1977, p. 14) said about a patient of his who was so boring that he became fascinated by the idea of how he managed to bore him: "How could this man converse with me in a way that came closer to what I would call 'pure boredom' than anything else I had ever experienced? That's why it's fascinating, it arouses curiosity".

With this aim, and until becoming fascinating, it will be necessary to tolerate the weight of boredom and discover interest in the bored patient. It will be necessary to surpass the level of anecdotes of the external world to be able to focus on the investigation of the phenomenon of boredom, emptiness, and laziness as it manifests itself in the transference relationship. To study this phenomenon, it may be useful to take up the suggestion made by Meltzer (1991, p. 19) for dealing with adolescents:

> The general attitude with the adolescent patient is to take an interest in everything that happens, in everything the adolescent says, and to resist the temptation to interpret until there is a clear transference meaning. Nor do you have to interpret things from the outside world, which is perhaps what attracts you in the first place.

This implies tolerating the frustration of not understanding and bearing the pressure of producing something new according to the patient's will. I believe that the analyst's interest manifests as an exploratory attitude to discover and describe, in the richest possible language, the present and hidden elements that will pave the way for the interpretation. This exploratory activity stimulates the bored patient's capacity to ask questions, which helps to dislodge the boredom that occupies the place of the desire to know (Fernández, 1995). The tolerance of paranoid anxiety, complaints, and aggressive outbursts latent in boredom makes possible the unfolding of the epistemophilic drive, which, like the Tramontana winds, will sweep away the clouds of boredom.

To sweep away these clouds of adolescent boredom, it is necessary to be careful enough not to assume with our interventions the image that the adolescent has of adults; for adolescents, we adults are the ones who fight to maintain our privileges (money, sexuality, home…), and therefore, our interventions will have to be tactful enough to interpret without losing sight of adolescent characteristics. Moreover, because the adolescent "is so tied to the group and the fashions generated by the group and the media, it is difficult to establish the transference" (Meltzer and Harris, 1998, pp. 326/327); this obliges the analyst to pursue the transference and bring it into the analytic situation, clearly differentiating between internal and external reality, as well as speaking clearly enough to dispel their belief that what the adult really wants is to manipulate the adolescent. That is why with Ivo, I accepted all of the conditions that he set out for me: to remain silent, watching him playing on the computer, listening to the music he had recorded, talking about his fantasies when he so desired, not criticise his aggressive behaviour (putting his fist through his bedroom door, blackmailing his parents), looking at the erotic photos of a female friend ... I took in everything, with few comments. Just enough to make him experience a relationship of understanding and interest, far from a critical attitude. The requirement is to let oneself be used until the internal world manifests itself, then, as far as possible, give meaning back to the patient. Few interpretations had a favourable outcome. I saw Ivo once a week because he would not accept more than that, and I went to his house weekly for months.

My experience was consistent with that of Bradley (2015), a specialist in adolescence at the Tavistock Clinic. Bradley proposed preparing to face the encounter with his patients, also seen on a weekly basis. He called it his "attentive waiting". Not infrequently, I found myself wondering while on my way to Ivo's house, far away from my practice, what would happen that day. Would he open the door for me? Sometimes the family was not there. Every day was a surprise.

Bradley employed three resources to guide his work: to be clear about the kind of space that existed between him and his patient; to express thoughts in the adolescent's own language; and, third, to avoid referring to previous sessions unless the adolescent had done so first. I agree with these three requirements, which deal with therapeutic distance, the vocabulary used, and tolerance of the adolescent's pace and initiative. I consider these to be essential and generous requirements that arise from a respect for the complex and conflictive nature of adolescents. These resources arise from two essential elements to guide the treatment of adolescents, or adults, with different levels of personality development: interest in the patients and passion for the psychoanalytic method.

In conclusion, I will retransmit the thinking of an exceptional musician. His comments on music can be applied both to the clinical work of the psychoanalyst as well as being an approach to boredom. The Latvian cellist Mischa Maiski (Riga, 1948) said he did not see the future of classical music to be as bleak as some of his colleagues predicted:

> *There is no need to lower the standard of quality* in order to reach new audiences. There will always be an audience as long as the artist leaves his soul in the performance of his work. You can change the costumes and the presentation of the concerts, but in the end, what captures the audience is *the energy of the artist on stage.*
> (El País, 3-3-2005, p. 41; my italics)

In the same way as a lack of emotional commitment leads to the dismantling of the patient's attention and interest, rendering their capacity to symbolise and think more difficult, it is the emotional commitment of the analyst which promotes the identification and restructuring of the psychic apparatus, thus making possible the surging up of thoughts in the middle of the desert.

3.2.5 Writing with the Body

At no time in a human being's life is their body not present.[40] We are body, and nothing about humans is foreign to that body, whether it is to enjoy, suffer, damage, or symbolise. Evolutionary moments, with all their longings, passions, and miseries, of which the body is a part, have been represented by great artists in different moments of history and a variety of circumstances. I will only mention two artists for whom the body is the protagonist: the divine bodies on the ceiling of the Sistine Chapel painted by Michael Angelo and the ages represented by Vigeland in the sculptures in the Oslo park. In both masterpieces, the mute body simultaneously speaks because "is the stage where each subject's life is played out, where their emotions and affections are expressed and experienced, the struggles between their desires and the impositions of society. It is the site of pleasure and suffering" (Fischbein, 2010, p. 19).

Not only one but infinite human bodies exist, filled with stories, geographies, ages, and social classes, as perspectives of study. It is not the same body that the pathologist examines, not that of the athlete, the fashion designer, the adolescent or the elderly, nor that of the happy or the sad… But the body is always at the basis of the feeling of identity. Grinberg Leon and Rebeca Grinberg (1971, pp. 55–56) state it clearly: "Everyone experiences themself as inextricably linked to their body […] one's eyes, hands and in general one's face and genitals are the most significant areas for the recognition of one's own and other people's bodies". It is the basis of the feeling of identity for a double reason because the integration and synthesis of the different representations of oneself, including the representation of the bodily self, creates a feeling of identity that is reaffirmed, in turn, in comparison with other people. A paradigmatic example of the significance of the body in the construction of identity is evident in the pubescent and adolescent when they insistently look at themselves in the mirror or selfies, which are often shared, over and over again as if they did not recognise themselves in their reflected image. Another, more painful example is seen in disorders of body identity and depersonalisation of borderline or schizophrenic people.

Of all the possible bodies and all the meanings assigned to them, this book will only deal with those heavily laden with functions, i.e. the bodies forced to speak, to express words without other alternatives. Instead of writing with words, these patients write with their bodies. There are not always enough resources available for the most primitive and the most evolved part of the ego to coexist, as Freud said in *Civilization and its Discontents*. Coexistence can overflow to the point of forcing the body to speak. Not only do these words, which could not find a way to express themselves in the mind, fall back on the body, but also the body can be understood as an essential ally of the subject, overcoming the effacing Cartesian dissociation. With Bion's contributions, among others, the scope, function, and significance of the body have expanded, as Pistiner de Coriñas (1993, pp. 340/341, my italics) puts it, the Bionian conjectures

> ...about pre-natal and post-natal states of mind, together with his strong hypothesis about the synchronous existence in the personality of different modes of mental functioning, opens up another perspective on how to conceive of the body. This approach makes it possible to approach the soma-psyche relations in terms of anticipation, simultaneity, different registers, communication/incommunication, etc. [...] From Bion's imaginative conjectures, it is possible to think of certain bodily manifestations as somatic anticipation, adequate bodily equipment, which will make possible what will later manifest itself as functional operations of the mind, *and not only as functions that indicate a failure of mental processing*. From these conjectures, some somatic manifestations could be conceived as pre-emotions (in the same sense as innate preconceptions), pre-natal emotions: which *have not yet had a psychic birth*, which have not yet undergone a psychic transformation and which precede meaning and symbolisation...

It seems appropriate to me to differentiate here between failures in symbolisation, the origin of pathologies and thought disorders, and those thoughts that have not yet found a suitable container to become such. In an intermediate situation between the failure of symbolisation and another in transit towards it, I would point to somnambulism (Tabbia, 2001); although it can be considered a hysterical dissociation, I think it can also be related to flight towards motility when dealing with unconscious content that was about to enter consciousness.

To understand what the body, its words, its thoughts, and the successive and simultaneous aspects of the personality write, it is enough to approach the fascinating and complex world presented by Bion (1991c) in *A Memoir of the Future*. There, the different ages of the body speak and claim a place in the dialogue between the different parts of the personality and confront the arrogant supremacy of the mind. The mind-body opposition was one of Bion's great concerns, to the point that he presents them as "our two enemies Soma and Psyche" (Bion, 1991b, p. 565). This opposition and the desire to establish a diaphragm that *separates and unites* both realities moves Bion (1991b, p. 551) to declare, ironically:

> P.A. ...Amongst the many and frequent dangers of psycho-analysis none is more dangerous than the experience of the coming together of the pre-natal and the post-natal personalities. It can be easily appreciated that the danger is associated with anything whatever—psycho-analysis, music, painting, mathematics— which could remind those two personalities of their continued and continuing 'contact' with each other in the same body and mind.

It is contact, but in a very uncomfortable cohabitation that is not exempt from mutual disparagement.

> BION In the meantime—if I may join in the discussion—his premature personality continues its life in uneasy proximity with his post-mature lodger in the same physical soma. Sometimes the psycho-somatic partner demonstrates his soulful qualities; sometimes his soma-psychotic demands acknowledgment and recognition of his physical and psychotic gifts. I describe the situation in naively pictorial terms. There are other descriptions, but most of them have been impregnated with pejorative connotations.
> ALICE Such as 'hypochondria'?
> BION Yes; or 'crazy', or 'insane', or 'difficult', or 'tiresome'.
>
> (ibid., p. 564)

The reality and presence of the body in mental dynamics demands attentiveness, i.e. that the mind be listened to and spoken to:

> BION ... the feelings, absent or aroused, have powerful physical accompaniments.[...]
> P.A. ... what language must we talk to the body? I think we must talk our own native language, ordinary articulate conscious speech, as correctly as we can. The speaker must also be free of the need to silence his body. If he is talking, the conversation must not be interrupted by the need to silence his hands, or his feet, or his facial muscles, or his eyes. For that matter he has to be free to talk even without fear of what lies his tongue may communicate. I have known analysands who could talk perfectly but who were nevertheless disturbed by the thought that they would stammer; that one of the 'two' people present would be the mouthpiece of a third even though invisible and inaudible.
>
> (ibid., p. 567)

If the fear that something hidden appears and causes anxiety and states of alarm, it would be wise to create something that would be capable of collaborating in the overcoming of the dissociations within the person and between human beings themselves as well as with the rest of the animal kingdom. For this reason, in Bion's *A Memoir of the Future*, a

> 'committee' is set up—a 'talking shop', a 'parliament' of the personality on the model of psychoanalysis, to try to 'do something' by avoiding action and concentrating on the problems of language and discrimination. This 'committee', the work group, is the 'foetal idea', and its task is to try to allow the 'meaning to get through the barrier' between mind and body.
>
> (Meltzer and Harris Williams, 1982, p. 542)

The possibility of success that the meaning permeates the barrier will depend on the predominant state of mind; when the infantile part of the personality governs the interchange, then serious difficulties to permeate it exist because an immature state of mind uses the body more than language and symbolisation do (Bleger, 1969; Grassano, 2001); for that reason, people who speak through their bodies have been called infantile personalities. This does not imply a discrediting of the body, but instead of the use made of it. Much to the contrary, and picking up what has been said, there is no humanity without body. Because of this, I agree with Lombardi (2012, p. 110) when he states:

> The reference to the body appears to be central in the work of Bion in the measure that it is the body that provides the prime material destined to be transformed into psychoanalytic elements; the experience of the body participates, in addition, continually to the making of thoughts, passing through the dimension of what is felt, of myths, and passion. This incessant movement in thinking, in which the bodily experience is a central stop…

And the first stop is the one fulfilled by the senses as a gateway, to the point that Bion (1966, p. 10) considers "an object to be sensible to psycho-analytic scrutiny if, and only if, it fulfils conditions analogous to the conditions that are fulfilled when a physical object's presence is confirmed by the evidence of two or more senses". While the senses accomplish their incorporative function, they are so wholly unperceived as they are scandalous when they expel or simply do not register. This last aspect is the introduction to the world of psychopathology. In this paper, Bion will reference different ways of using the body to express or conceal alienating states of mind (those that precede the minus sign), which will be illustrated with the clinical material of a young adult.

In the same manner that states of mind vary, the vertices to observe, listen to, and decodify the *body's thoughts* have also changed throughout the course of the history of psychoanalysis. A fundamental variation occurred when the vertex moved from the axes placed on the repression to that placed on the *split*. Thus, "the early success of the concept of repression", says Meltzer (1995b), "has largely blocked the research and understanding of these other ways in which the body and its functions come to participate in the symptomatology of mental disorders". And in order to investigate the messages sent by the body, it is essential to resort to the concept of splitting. The notion of splitting of the ego shows us that

> …within the ego, there may be different logics superimposed on each other which give rise to thoughts based on very different principles. The ego splits according to its inability to tolerate the reality principle; it therefore renounces a part of itself so that the other part can survive. Two very different cognitive types of logic are thus generated; one takes the reality principle into account, the other disregards it.

(Lutenberg, 2000, p. 129)

Splitting is not only a defence mechanism but also a fundamental resource to establish structuring differentiations. In relation to the subject of the splitting of the mind and the body, however, it can be pointed to as an extreme defence that "... marks the appearance of states in which what is mental can be momentarily suspended, and the soma responds biologically" (Grassano, 2001, p. 159).

If it is assumed that there are as many bodies as there are people and as many vertices to be studied, then it is necessary to specify which body is being referred to in each case. Circumscribed to the world of clinical practice, an initial differentiation can be made between bodies charged with meaning (conversion) and mutebodies or body-things[41] of somapsychotic states (Fischbein, 2010). If states of mind are characterised by who commands the organ of consciousness, it is appropriate to distinguish meta-psychologically between symptoms in order not to remain a prisoner of symptomatology, in which case it is possible to distinguish, without claiming to make an exhaustive classification, between the manifestations derived from

> ... a narcissistic reaction of projective identification with a sick object, in which a part of the body is identified with the sickness and weakness of the object (as in *hypochondriasis*); or it may be a response based on the failure of symbol formation (on the side of *psychosomatic* reactions), or it may be a situation in which a part of the self is experienced as inhabiting a certain area of the body, constituting from there an enemy of the self (*somatic delirium*); or it constitutes the symbolic representation of an emotional conflict that is referred to the body, as a theatre of symbolisation (*conversion hysteria*).
>
> (Bermann, 1996, pp. 19–20)

These differentiations, especially hypochondriacal phenomena, somatic delusions, and conversion hysterias, highlight the effectiveness of intrusive identification in altering the organs as representatives of internal objects. The projective/intrusive identification dynamic will be presented at greater length in the different psychopathological states.

3.2.5.1 Alterations to the Organism

Starting from the concept that any alteration of the organism is psychosomatic, it is worth questioning the distinctions between the various psychopathological manifestations in which the body is involved.

Attempts have been made to differentiate psychosomatic states according to the predominance of the central or autonomic nervous system. Thus, somatisation has been linked to the autonomic nervous system and conversion to the central nervous system (Grassano, 2001), but this distinction is not very consistent because, as Coderch (1975, p. 143) objects

> ...certain signs and symptoms that have traditionally been included as part of conversion hysteria, such as vomiting, syncope and nausea, are based on

disturbances of the autonomic nervous system. On the other hand, psychophysi-ological responses can also, similar to conversion reactions, be non-verbal and symbolic communications expressed in the language of the organs. Finally, in psychophysiological reactions and conversion symptoms, an impulse kept un-conscious by the effects of repression may present itself transformed into a so-matic disturbance or dysfunction.

The differentiation according to the predominance of one nervous system or an-other does not provide any specific clarification. What is more widely agreed, es-pecially among writers and psychoanalysts, i.e. among people interested in psychic reality, is that the body speaks when issues cannot be expressed through the sym-bolic, as Shakespeare said: "Give sorrow words; the grief that does not speak, whis-pers the o'erfraught heart and bids it break" (*Macbeth*, Act IV, scene III). In this sense, it is accepted that the alterations to the organism become alarm signals that speak of a split between the mind and the body. Faced with this split, it will be nec-essary to identify the meaning of the signal that becomes visible in "a conversive or hypochondriacal or somatic body" (Rappaport de Aisemberg, 1998–1999, p. 208).

The alarm signal, like the distress signal, is a device triggered in dangerous situa-tions to avoid the development of overwhelming anguish and suffering. The capac-ity to develop anxiety or to emit signals will depend on the degree of development of the personality; in this sense, McDougall (1983, p. 932) says, referring to a case, that her patient could not use repression as an effective defence because he would lack "'psychic capital' to work through those primitive impulses: partial drives that have not been able to fuse to the genital drive, and thus submit to successive repres-sion". It lacked the necessary ego resources to implement the appropriate defences stimulated by the anxiety signal.

Anxiety in hysteria has been understood in different ways, and as the processes of splitting and projective identification developed, it led to hysterical manifesta-tions being included within the hysteria of distress

> and all this, taken together, finally disappeared within the concept of signal dis-tress [...] The general concept of conversion has gradually moved in other di-rections, particularly in the development of the concept of hypochondriasis and the development of the concept of somatisation and psychosomatic disorder.
>
> (Meltzer, 1995b)

The analysis of conversion hysteria in terms of repression merited a precision made by Meltzer the very same day:

> The question of repression itself is also much more complicated than the me-chanical model of this marvellous toy described by Freud, according to which there is a pushing of things from the preconscious to the unconscious level. In reality, it seems that it is not so much a repression of memories as a repression of objects, and therefore a repression of the memories related to these objects. How

this happens varies greatly from patient to patient. However, what seems fundamental is that the object is killed in psychic reality; fortunately, dead objects can be brought back to life[42] in psychic reality. However, objects are not only killed in psychic reality but also locked up, not incinerated, but buried-in-the-faeces.

In this way, the approach shifts towards the treatment of the object and signals a change in the understanding of the phenomena expressed in the body. In this text, I would like to emphasise the reference to the possibility of revitalising and rehabilitating objects in psychic reality, the starting point of the psychoanalytic task.

Meltzer thought that there are currently very few cases of conversion hysteria, except in underdeveloped and highly eroticised societies, but one might wonder whether this might not be linked to the presence of religions that censor sexuality. He went on to add that

"…at the time Freud was working, conversion hysteria was a real and frequent occurrence, based on a process which he called repression but which today we would see in a rather more complicated way. Today we would think of it in terms of splitting processes, in terms of movement in and out of projective identification, in terms of attacks on internal objects and the damage done to these internal objects, all of which leads us to link it to hypochondriac types of states."

The focus of hysteria shifts from *repression* to *splitting*. Pathological splitting becomes essential to understanding psychosomatic disturbances, revealing, for example, "the appearance of states in which the psyche is momentarily suspended and the soma responds biologically. The bodily demands fail to become alarm signals, significant indicators that can prevent the psychosomatic equilibrium from breaking down" (Fischbein, 2000, p. 159). Engaging the body in this way may be considered by the patient as a balm, or minor damage when dealing with mental pain linked to intra- and inter-subjective conflicts. This is why *fibromyalgia* patients—stubborn defenders of the organic basis of their suffering—seem to feel relief when the body emits pain signals. It seems that their greatest threat comes from mental pain, e.g. sadness and frustration. In a way, they function as if they were empiricists who only recognise 'facts' and have great difficulty recognising psychic reality.

They prefer language that talks of synapses and neurotransmitters instead of depression or neurasthenia, which was the classical name for the symptoms now grouped under the term fibromyalgia (Ramos García, 2004; Martinez Ferraro, 2010; Sales, 2010).

3.2.5.2 Hypochondria

Hypochondria refers to the relationship with internal objects, but not just any type of relationship, but rather a relationship based on introjective identification with a damaged object or its function. In order to understand hypochondria, it is necessary to refer to how the object was introjected. For that, it would be wise to determine if a cannibalistic introjection predominated (which would seek to wrest parts or functions from external objects) or an intrusive identification (as if to overpower the mind, the body, or the attributes of the object), with the state of mind of the hypochondriac being the natural consequence. As Meltzer (1965, p. 14) put it:

> The projective identification with both internal figures, which accompanies bi-manual masturbation, damages the internal objects because of the violence of the intrusion into them and the sadistic nature of the sexual relationship attributed to them. Thus, hypochondriasis and claustrophobic anxieties are to some extent an invariable result.

This state of mind can be manifested in various bodily or verbal manifestations, as I observed in a young man with severe pain in his legs and/or in the back of his neck. He was willing to undergo aggressive operations on the bones of his legs following the recommendation of a bone specialist. This young man, at that time, had a state of mind derived from the identification with internal/parental objects experienced as insubstantial, in particular his mother who, with a manic-depressive structure, triumphantly exhibited a diagnosis of *fibromyalgia* with which she obtained a work disability. His internal objects were fragile, pierced, bitten, crushed, evanescent... This young man related to the external world from a desperate desire to eat and catch something, manifesting himself as a baby with no intrapsychic support and who demanded to be cradled. In his phantasies, actions, and verbalisations, the desire to eat me piece by piece so that I would be his alone appeared. He also expressed the need to look at me in order to aspirate me with his eyes. His insatiability also manifested itself in the area of his sexuality: he could have sex without ever losing his erection, even after three or four orgasms, as if he suffered from a certain degree of emotional priapism. Voracity could drive him to eat junk food[43] or steal small amounts of money, with drugs being a permanent temptation. The phantasy that his penis was equivalent to a mouth appeared several times. For him, each of his erogenous zones could take on oral functions. Once these phantasies were analysed, i.e. once he understood his irrepressible longing for the object in order to deny separation anxiety, individuation, and his restrained violence, his emotional state automatically changed. If he had arrived at the session desperate, with muscle spasms, and full of pain in his limbs or in the back of the neck, he would leave instead calm and grateful, that is to say, differentiated from the object. He would also leave relieved because the inevitable retaliatory phantasies of being dominated or devoured by the analyst had not been fulfilled. If he arrived non-mental and full of bodily sensations, he would leave my office as a subject. This change is the consequence of having understood his internal relations to be mental rather than physical events and of having been able to analyse the intense ambivalence in the transference where the analyst can be intensely loved and hated.

Although hypochondriasis could be thought of as a release of unmetabolised emotions that end up driving the body mad, as happened to the young man whose damaged objects were retained in his legs, it seems wise to me that attention is directed to the treatment of the object that is being retained in the body. Meltzer (1990) used to ask when diagnosing, following Freud, who the one who was ill was, and what they were suffering from, and then he would inquire as to whose pain it was. These questions seek to clarify whether the sufferer is ill or has become the most capable of sustaining the unsustainable pain of a family group. The interrogation would then be directed at discovering which damaged object, for example, the subject had identified themself with. Once the damaged object had been located, it was time to explore where it had been projected. In melancholia, it is placed in the mental area, whereas in hypochondria, the damaged and, therefore, persecutory object is projected onto the body (as in the young person's legs), from which point it then directs its hostility against the subject, who laments their misfortune, and seeks any solution, such as having their legs operated on. In this sense, Meltzer (1978b, p. 205), following Klein, says that

> ...hypochondria stood very close to melancholia through identification with damaged objects and that the struggle had to do with the way the identification processes altered emotionality, so that instead of feelings of guilt on the one hand, or persecution on the other, the person tended to feel self-pity, projected as clamorous demands for reparation of the self, or to be rid of the damaged object by surgical means...

as can be observed in borderline-psychotic personalities that succeed in having repeated operations in the secret hope of killing and removing the persecutory object deposited in their body. Once, in a psychiatric hospital, I made the acquaintance of a patient who had managed to be surgically operated on at a dozen different opportunities with no real organic need. In a dialogue with her, references to bombs from the Spanish civil war always appeared as if it were a contemporary conflict that, in her hypochondriacal delusion, she had tried to remove surgically. If this is an extreme case, however, perhaps we could establish a certain resemblance to some cosmetic surgeries, as if with these surgeries, the subject were attempting to remove the signs of the passing of time, deterioration, or even death itself in a very nearly manic attempt at self-reparation.

The identification with an object resulting in identity confusion characteristic of hypochondriasis can be observed, for example, in *hypochondriacal anorexia*. Meltzer (Meltzer and Harris, 1998, p. 126), in discussing the case of Debbie analysed by Martha Harris, distinguished *hypochondriacal anorexia* from *symptomatic anorexia*; at the time, she was referring to Debbie's claim to control what she ate:

> ...starving the objects themselves and maintaining an omnipotent control over the sexual relationship through which they are nourished. Symptomatic anorexia is characterised by bulimia or vomiting, which is greed for the object and then refusal of food as a consequence of envy.

In my experience, this is a moment in the analysis when Debbie moves from hypochondriacal anorexia to symptomatic anorexia. Hypochondriacal anorexia consists of identification with the object that has been deprived of its sexual nourishment. Basically, it is the breast that has been deprived (is starved) of semen. Symptomatic anorexia consists of the infantile behaviour of alternating avid eating and vomiting with envy and contempt for food in the form of vomiting or diarrhoea.

It seems to me an important therapeutic goal to have transformed a hypochondriacal anorexia into a symptomatic one, because this enables the abandonment of massive projective identification, identity confusion, and the overcoming of massive projective identification as a primary defensive modality.

I believe this distinction to be fundamental because in hypochondriacal anorexia, the subject is almost detached from the suffering of the object imprisoned in its own body, with whom the subject imagines themself to form a symbiotic unit that would make both space and time disappear (Lutemberg, 2000). In symptomatic anorexia, however, once identity confusion has been overcome, the subject is exposed to sensations of separation, want, jealousy, and rivalry. For Meltzer, symptomatic anorexia "is the one that oscillates between bulimia, vomiting, obsession with gaining weight, breast reduction… and it is the one that really deserves the name of anorexia nervosa" (Meltzer and Harris, 1998, p. 225).

When facing a situation of need or of want, the bulimic person

enacts the bulimia by eating up all the food and not leaving any for the other children. He goes to the refrigerator and eats all there is until there is absolutely nothing left. Then he vomits in order to spoil and ruin the food that should have been for the others.

(Meltzer and Psychoanalytic Group of Barcelona, 1995, p. 80)

Here, the control and destructive mastery over the object is both in the service of jealousy and of perversion.

Meltzer's further understanding of anorexia nervosa is that the structure of anorexia nervosa is characterised by splitting. He differentiates between the state of mind of the anorexic and the bulimic part. The anorexic part would function as if it did not need anything, as if it wanted to gratify itself with an idealised self-image based on the remains of identity confusion, behaving as if it were a vain little princess who does not need to feed and care for her body, whereas the bulimic part would function as someone who feels so little that she is capable of accepting any treatment or mistreatment, as often happens to some girls who lend themselves to sexual relations where they are sexually used, and no affection is offered. But both the anorexic, as well as the bulimic part are characterised by a feeling of loneliness, a state of mind of orphanhood, and having great difficulty in establishing a good relationship with good objects. Whether they despise food or will swallow just about anything, the person is much hindered in emotional growth and development, and suffering is guaranteed. This is less evident when projective identification is of such intensity as to generate identity confusion, as in hypochondriacal anorexia, because the subject lives outside themself and enjoys the grandiosity derived from the identificatory part of the projective identification.

3.2.5.3 Psychosomatics

It would appear contradictory to place psychosomatics in the set of psychopathological disorders because the normal or healthy state is psychosomatic, i.e. a state in which psychosomatic unity is integrated and remains as such. Using the term "psychosomatic" within the field of psychopathology, however, means the "somatic expression of an emotional conflict that precedes meaning and symbolization" (Meltzer, 1993, p. 335). In this sense, the body must again do something it is not supposed to do. The use of the body to express meaning is not the same across the full spectrum of disorders; thus, for example, in *conversion hysteria*, the body expresses an already created meaning, whereas in *psychosomatic disorders*, symbolisation has not been sufficiently developed nor has it "achieved a degree of dreaming, thinking and of conscious emotion" (ibid.).

In a sense, psychosomatic disorders can be compared to miscarriage in that something that began was interrupted. At this moment, I believe it would be opportune to remember the concept of Bion and attacks on linking because what characterises psychosomatic disorders, much like psychotic disorders, "is the tendency to rid oneself of those functions, either embryonic or not, that make possible the contact with 'facts' (experiences). Psychosomatic manifestations would be a consequence, a vestige of these types of functioning" (Pistiner, 1993, p. 348). In relation to attacks on linking, Lombardi (2012, p. 103) differentiates between those attacks shown by Klein and those formulated by Bion:

> The attacks on linking do not refer to the bond between the baby and the mother's breast / mother's object, as the sadistic attacks on the breast described by Melanie Klein had been, but above all to the bond between thoughts, and furthermore to the bond between the specialised sense organs of the body and consciousness, that is to say to the bond between body and mind.

It is a fair and suggestive differentiation. It is fair because, in Klein, it is the envy of the object that promotes its destruction, whereas, in Bion, the object of attack is the linking functions. In both experiences, a primitive intolerance of object dependence is expressed. By integrating the object and its functions, this differentiation would not become insurmountable. Meltzer (1967), in the classic Psycho-Analytical Process, formulates the development of the object in terms of toilet-breast first and feeding-breast later. These are two ways of naming the infant's primary object, differentiating functions. Klein referred to the breast, using the language of children, to refer to the emotions towards the first object. With Bion's contributions, one could think of the breast as an object available to be linked to the baby's needs. The attack on the sense organs would have, among other things, the intention of preventing, either through envy or because of the overwhelming and complex character of the object, the apprehension of reality, symbolisation, and responsibility... in the manner of Oedipus who attacked his own eyes—in a psychotic act—in order not to see his tragedy.

In order to refer to the interruption in the process of symbolisation, Rappaport de Aisemberg (2005, p. 277) uses the concept of a short circuit, making a metaphor of the psyche's defence in the event of a surge in power:

> The short-circuit to the soma is one of the destinations of the investiture of primitive sensory traces, potentially traumatic, pre-psychic traces inscribed between soma and psyche, which have not been able to follow the path of psychic processing, the translation into a mnemic trace and representation.

She points out the interruption in the process, which prevents the pre-psychic or pre-mental traces from transforming into memory traces and, therefore, into representation.

Psychosomatic disorders, however, are not always the same in their manifestations but instead share the same motivation: to avoid a situation that is overwhelming for the psyche. This possibly overwhelming situation can be interrupted at different moments in the development of symbolisation, and it is interesting to discover at what moment and with what outcomes the short circuits occur. In this sense, Meltzer (with Harris Williams, 1988, pp. 230/231) in *The Apprehension of Beauty* formulates three moments in which the emotional experience is hindered or the symbolising linking function is attacked, moving towards evacuation

> ...instead of thought, memory, judgement, action.
>
> First would be the raw sense data, rejected as material for alpha-function, namely what Bion calls beta elements. Second, we could describe varying stages in the condensation of the discursive myth; and finally, we could expect to find fragments of the formed symbol, attacked and dismembered. The first of these, the raw sense data might be conceived in terms of perceptual processes, already organized as precepts in the sense of gestalten, both of objects of external and internal sense, and perhaps glistening with an aura of incipient significance endowed them by the organ of attention, separated out from the general bombardment of sense data. We could imagine that such stimuli, organised only minimally, could be shunted, for evacuation, directly into the innervation of the organs.
>
> The second category, fragmented mythic constructions, bits of stories about emotional experiences, could not be directly shunted. Because they contain a narrative structure, as fallen columns of a temple contain architectural qualities, they would lend themselves to evacuation through quasi-social actions. This is the significance of Bion's category of 'Beta Screen' as a designation for compulsive meaningless speech. We can add to this a similar beta-screen of action, as seen in the hyperactive child. [...] clinically speaking, we could describe this form of evacuation under the heading of automatic obedience/disobedience.

In the third category of phenomena of evacuation of fragmented, cannibalized symbols we would want to include the whole range of phenomena called hallucination: both normal, in the sense of incidental, and pathological, in the sense of an organized defensive posture. This would include Bion's category of Transformations in Hallucinosis as an aspect of character. [...] One can easily see that this makes immediate sense of the sequence of events of withdrawal symptoms, commencing with hyperactivity and eventuating in unbearable psychosomatic phenomena.

Short-circuiting can occur when attention began to highlight some data from an indiscriminate set, when that data has started to become myth, or when the data has reached an intolerable level of significance. Some forms of evacuation can be expressed by innervating the organs, or by speaking or moving irrepressibly, in the style of those who cannot stop speaking, or through expulsion by means of the senses; these are different forms of discharge that necessarily carry the threat of generally violent reintrojection.

The interruption or short-circuiting of the generation of meaning can find refuge in the protomental (basic assumption functioning, transformation into hallucinosis or psychosomatic disorders).

I would not like to forget to mention another contribution, in this case, that of McDougall (1983, pp. 919/920), in reference to the possibility of using data from external reality for dream life, or of not using it. She refers to the motivation of her patient Paul to:

> ...to move away from their phantasmatic life, and which are perhaps the same ones that feed what is called 'psychosomatic personality' or 'operative thought' and which motivate an apparent lack in the dream life of this type of patient. Daytime remnants are not stored. These subjects 'dream' awake; the perceptions of the sensitive world are altered without being recovered by the attribution of a new meaning, i.e. they are not remodelled by a psychotic thought that would explain this projection of internal reality outwards. Instead, certain 'operative' dispositions and the foreclosure of both the representation of the affect and the representation of the unbearable idea appear, and thus a lack of psychic compensation becomes evident. These multiple avoidance manoeuvres undoubtedly contribute to the appearance of the so-called 'operative' phenomenon.

In this case, the idea was to avoid "unbearable ideas" that generate threatening anxieties, but the expulsion of the representation of the affect or the idea prevents available elements from remaining for the production of dreams. This difficulty in constructing data apt for dream life encounters another example in the hyperrealism of dreams derived from the failure of the alpha function; with this, reference is made to people that produce dreams that are an unmodified copy of the facts of waking life (see Section 3.2.3). Others produce "interminable" dreams that are, more than a communication, an evacuative action. Referring, however, to psychosomatic personalities, it may be the case that some have the inability to produce daytime remnants, as McDougall points out, and thus to dream, just as others may produce dreams but are denied any significance during wakefulness; in that case, obsessional defences work to protect against psychotic, primitive anxieties, such as those of disintegration or breakdown. A woman patient suffering from multiple sclerosis produced dreams featuring great anxiety content but struggled desperately not to become aware of the menace in which she was trapped; she defended herself against any interpretation by trivialising it or resolving it in terms such as "I am just like my father" or "my sister is just like my mother". She could not approach her anxiety of death and only relied on pushing it away and inoculating it in a sensitive sister who accompanied her, or in me.

McDougall used to say that "daytime remnants are not stored away", and the reason for this incapacity may reside in an initial difficulty in connecting with reality, and, therefore, producing them. When Bion (1979, p. 253) suggests "three principles of life" against "two principles of mental functioning" formulated by Freud, he proposed that the first principle is feeling. Beginning with the fact that feeling is perceiving sensations coming from one's own body or an external stimulus, it is natural that the first vital principle is feeling. When perception is not altered, data apt for thinking can be produced. This data can become daytime remnants of dream life and, as with all such data, can suffer any of the attacks described by Meltzer to interrupt the process of symbolisation. The damaged or unused data lead to evacuation as opposed to thinking, memory, judgement, and action.

The main victim of psychosomatic personalities is *thinking*. Stating that people with a predominance of psychosomatic functioning have difficulties in doing their own thinking does not mean that they are non-mental, but rather that

...they manage—says Grassano (2001, p. 79)—with an apparent grasp of the symbolic order, which is underlain by an incapacity for metaphorical linkage, which is expressed in serious disturbances in their thinking.

We suggest an approach to psychosomatic illness in which a constant conjunction is established between: chronification of bodily illnesses and over-adaptation to reality, which takes as the only vector of the response to the environmental world 'the ought to be', ignoring desire, possibility and need. They lack the capacity to grasp essentially human needs, both in intersubjective contact and intrasubjectivity.

From the point of view of judgement and sense of reality, we observe that rigid, unquestioning conformity, together with the fact that these patients constantly encourage others to offload responsibility onto them, is the vector on which the nodule of pathology lies. The second vector, the illness in the body, is the 'somatic protest', which denounces the procrastination to which the bodily and emotional self is subjected.

The rigid adaptation to reality, in which the Principle of Reality is dissociated and in open opposition to the pleasure principle, led us to affirm that these patients 'suffer from sanity'.

This characterisation can be complemented by the concept of "normopathic" patients described by McDougall (1978). Adapting to reality, or mimicking reality, is the technique for avoiding conflict. Another technique is de-mentalisation (Meltzer). These "sane" people capable of "adapting to the rules" are often well regarded in communities where obedience is demanded, but when this personality breaks down through an organic symptom that signals over-adaptation, drugs are used to re-establish the hierarchical order established by the one at the top of the pyramid. Some of the concepts formulated so far will find expression in the story of Arnoldo and his vicissitudes.

3.2.5.4 Arnoldo's Vicissitudes

I have been able to treat Arnoldo in different moments of his life; in the first stage, which was in his mid-20s, he came for consultation because of problems related to his difficulty separating from his family and organising a future of his own. Subsequently, he came due to different life circumstances. This has allowed me to understand the disorders suffered by a person whose body often speaks and writes.

As a way of presenting Arnoldo's states of mind, it can be said that the symptomatology that prompted the consultation request was linked to his father's deterioration.

Much work had to be done to overcome Arnoldo's difficulty in symbolising his paranoid anxieties, difficulties that were supported by the overvaluation of scientific thinking, based on data and statistics. Paranoid anxieties found different objects on which to rely, finding, in the body, a large territory where, if not respiratory problems, then a freckle, a wart, or prostate issues were experienced as the tip of the iceberg foreshadowing tragedy. Hypochondriacal and psychosomatic problems coexisted and alternated with neurotic states of mind, which at times acquired the characteristics of an inverted Oedipus, becoming aroused by powerful men while at the same time idealising and denigrating women.

To begin to refer to Arnoldo, I must mention the following text by Winnicott (1951):

> It is to be noted that psyche-soma growth is universal and its complexities are inherent, whereas mental development is somewhat dependent on variable factors such as the quality of early environmental factors, the chance phenomena of birth and of management immediately after birth, etc.

I take up the concept of the "quality of the early environment", because one of the fundamental conditions for good development consists in having a suitable mother which, in Winnicott's terms, is that of an ordinary "good" mother. It is this good mother that Bion takes up from the point of view of the development of thought and formulates it in terms of the reverie. It is also taken up by Meltzer (Meltzer & Harris Williams, 1988) as stated in the introduction of his paper *The Apprehension of Beauty*: "To our own and all ordinary beautiful devoted mothers we dedicate this book". Without this first object, the physical and emotional survival of the human infant is not assured. In Arnoldo's case, several circumstances came together that did not create a suitable container to sustain him. When Arnoldo was born, his mother had just lost a daughter, which may have stimulated an over-dedication to the bodily care of her son. The father was a German researcher with a discreet professional career who did not achieve economic status, a situation that wounded his self-esteem and which he concealed with scientist arrogance and authoritarianism. In identification with this father, Arnoldo struggled to make amends.

The request for a consultation coincided with the beginning of his father's deterioration, which Arnoldo considered the trigger for his malaise. The reasons for the initial meeting, however, were no more than the first presentation of a person in whose psyche-soma almost all of the manifestations derived from difficulties in thinking had passed and spoken. His body was the scenario where metaphors slipped. Symbolisation and development of the psychoanalytic function of the personality were not a project for Arnoldo.

To start referring to Arnoldo by introducing his parents does not imply that we assume the position that the environment determines the subject because, as Winnicott (op. cit.) said "mental development is somewhat dependent on variable factors such as the quality of early environmental factors". Even if the environment was arranged in the best of conditions, the way in which the baby receives and deals with the opportunities received, mainly from his parents, also counts. In this sense, not only forced *splitting*[44] (Bion) is used to receive something from the object without acknowledging or thanking it, but also to make the best of the object even if it does not function as an "ordinary mother" (Meltzer) and acknowledging that the baby "becomes able to allow for her deficiencies" (Winnicott, 1951).

A symptom was present from the beginning of the analysis and the first years of his life: *asthma*. Even today, although more as a threat than a symptom that detracts from his autonomy, and he does not lose sight of his inhaler. If I have begun by presenting the symptom, asthma, it is because it is a reflection of the conflictive relationship that the child experiences with its first object: the mother.

Of all possible mothers, each child has their own original mother. There are loving mothers who are attentive to the demands of their baby, and from a position of respect based on intuition, they adapt to the infant's needs. There are others that fear the baby's emotions and, instead of metabolising the baby's demands, they respond by inundating the baby with an extra dose of their own anxieties, returning *a nameless dread* (Bion), or a bomb, as Liberman et al. (1986) said. Others exist that are incapable of accepting the baby's demands and become impermeable to the projective identifications, although they might be capable of responding with *material* efficiently to the baby's demands but leaving the emotional dimension to one side. Liberman called them "bouncing mothers", and Meltzer "efficient mothers". There is also another type of mother who needs the child to complete her identity deficit by turning the child into a phallic object, an object to be used to complete herself. None of the latter offers the best response to infant needs, but the child cannot renounce their mother because of their absolute dependence, which is why it is often necessary to resort to a certain type of dissociation, similar to forced splitting. The counterpart of this agreement/disagreement is that instead of optimal development, psychopathological alternatives arise, such as what Winnicott called the *false self* and Meltzer called *pseudomaturity*, or other more harmful types such as those characterised by schizoid, autistic, etc. withdrawal. Examples of such agreements/ disagreements are abundant in the borderline world.

The reason for pausing to make a certain characterisation of Arnoldo's mother lies in the need to understand the symptom of asthma. As far as I could observe, Arnoldo maintained an absolute dependence on an idealised mother ("she did everything well"), but she, from an ideological position, did not enjoy bodily contact with the baby, and at the same time opposed "the manifestations of infantile sexuality" (Zusman de Arbiser, S., 1999, p. 338). Far from enjoying Arnoldo, she encouraged in him a particular differentiated position in relation to the daughters, like that of an administrator in their service. This is reminiscent of "Mother Courage" (B. Brecht).

In intrauterine life, the baby lives through the placenta, and at birth undergoes major circulatory and respiratory changes. From then on, it is dependent on air and the maternal object, both of which are indispensable. The extreme dependence on air and the mother for survival becomes even more significant when analysing asthmatic patients. In this respect, Arbiser and Zusman de Arbiser (1978, p. 164) have found

> ...in the asthmatic, there is a mother-air equivalence, and for this reason when the mother becomes persecutory and also demands to be accepted, she creates in the child and then in the adult, the obligation to be retained, in the form of 'bad air' which fills the lungs. Air that must not be eliminated, for which the unconscious ego of the individual contracts its bronchiolar muscles, thus provoking an asthma attack. They cannot relax these muscles because this means becoming independent of the 'bad mother', which their maternal superego forbids them to do. This difficulty is sustained by the asthmatic's conviction that to free themself from the persecutory inner mother would imply matricide.

Neither with her nor without her; Arnoldo was trapped, suffocated.

Without suffering from a severe symptom such as asthma, I was able to observe in another adult, imprisoned in a symbiotic bond with his mother whom he loved/ hated, a tendency to have breathing problems and to suffer from a certain impossibility to cry, reducing his painful expressions to small sobs as if they were broken spasms, which the patient called "my cry". Arbiser and Arbiser also recognise this in the asthmatic access, that of being: "...an equivalent of a child's cry for its mother, an expression of pain, despair and despondency" (ibid.).

Both in this patient who cannot cry and in Arnoldo, the problem lies in not being able to expel the *bad object/mother*; when I say bad object/mother, I refer both to the inability to care for the child and to overprotection to the point of suffocation. But this object becomes even worse when the child deposits their own damaged objects in it or when the child mistreats it. When this internal object is expelled, occasionally manically, and a certain reintroduction occurs, a talionic sense of suffocation can ensue, a cruel revenge of an offended object. However, the longing for life is pressing, and the desire to get rid of the retained object increases, creating a spiral of longing and guilt that is suffocating. This discomfort is exacerbated when the object, the mother, or another person in the patient's environment, such as the wife or girlfriend, does not recognise the experience of despair while feeling suffocated. What is to be done with so much suffering and despair? Where do you unload it if there is no possibility to symbolise it? One scenario appears as an alternative: one's *skin*. Here the papyrus is full of rabid overlapping scratches.

The inability to tolerate ambivalence towards the needed-loved-hated mother prevented him from internalising an object with which to identify and assume a separate identity. If he was an object (phallus) of the mother, and she was a necessary object for the son, the phantasy of a single identity, a single body, a single skin, was created through mutual identification. Arnoldo's ambivalence was written on the suffering skin, in a desperate struggle to acquire an identity, as McDougall (1989, p. 153) says:

> What should have been supplied from internal sources (that is, some introjected image of the maternal environment that would restore to the infant a feeling of corporeal limits and of the capacity to contain painful emotional states) has to be sought in the suffering body itself.

Atopic eczema and the need to *scratch* until he bled was the way Arnoldo sought his limits and alternatively expressed his ambivalence towards the first objects or his own family. The anxieties of dispersal due to the absence of a containing internal object experienced by Arnoldo confirmed Mrs Bick's (1968, p. 114) view when she suggested that

> in its most primitive form the parts of the personality are felt to have no binding force amongst themselves and must therefore be held together in a way that is experienced by them passively, by the skin functioning as a boundary.

In one of Arnoldo's sessions, you can see the relationship he has with internal objects and the manifestation of the state of mind through the treatment of his own skin. He looked like a ship full of leaks as he desperately tried to stop the flooding and bleeding. His skin did not function as an internal/external boundary. This is the second of his two weekly sessions. The movements or sounds he makes while stretched out on the couch will be highlighted in italics.

3.2.5.5 A Session with Arnoldo

PATIENT: He remains in silence for about three minutes while *clearing his throat*. There are moments when everything looks black to me, although perhaps I'm exaggerating. Things are not going well in my life, and I don't know how to improve it. I'm dissatisfied; it's variable. I can go from one place to another. My crises with Rosa—his wife—have not resolved themselves. We really want to fix it. *He clears his throat. Meanwhile, with his right hand, he scratches his right eye and chin; then his head, his right eyelid, his head, under his right eye, his chest…* At the same time, I find it difficult to cope with my son… He gets distracted and becomes dispersed. When he goes back to school, the problems return. He told me that he did badly because he came last… I get demoralised. The problem was not solved. I don't tell him off. I tell him that I feel bad that he is the last in the class. *As he speaks, he scratches his left hand on his chest, under his left eye, scratches his chest again, his beard, his right eye, his left eye, his chin, his chest, and his left eye.* He is impressed by my reflections. It's a mental problem that he won't get until he matures. But I still want him to change overnight. He goes to psychotherapy once a week with his mother; after that, they will propose a treatment of two or three sessions. It's a lot of money, plus school, sports (to prevent him from watching TV)… *Meanwhile, with his right hand, he scratches his left arm, his right eye, and his chest, puts his hands in his pocket, scratches his chest and then his elbow.* I feel I am between a rock and a hard place. If I object to the treatment and he grows out of it… *He clears his throat.* I'll have a guilty conscience for not having given him treatment when he was little. I feel a bit lost. *He scratches his left eyebrow.* I'm going under, but I can't cope. It's as if you had an abnormal child and what he's suffered! *He scratches his chest, his right cheek, and his right chin.* All these things together: the relationship with Rosa, the problems with my son, create a tough situation; it makes me not want to start working.

THERAPIST: What you communicate is that the things that worry you generate a fear of going under, although perhaps more exactly, it's the sensation that you can explode as if your skin were to open up and your internal world were to come out of you. You've been continually touching your body as if to check for wounds. It's as if you had the sensation that your problems could ooze out of your pores. (While I speak, he stops touching and scratching himself almost completely).

P: I'm itchy. Especially my lip and my eyes. A tremendous itch. *He scratches the nape of his neck, and then he combs it.* When you spoke, I thought that those things concern me and that I carry them deep inside of me. I was thinking that the other night I went to talk to Juan (a friend) and I didn't tell him either of the two things: what's going on with Rosa, and the thing with my son. I remembered but didn't feel like it. I didn't feel like talking. I don't feel Juan is that close to me. They're intimate things you only tell someone you're very close to.

T: On the one hand, you can feel scared that your conflicts are so overwhelming that they slit open your skin, break your mind, but, at the same time, you feel a strength that allows you to reserve for yourself the intimate things in your life. You go back and forth: between fear that your problems break you and the ability to keep them to yourself and choose when and with whom you speak about them.

P: *He clears his throat, thrusting both hands in his trouser pockets.* This thing about not talking to anyone except here gives me an isolated feeling. I have increasingly less trust in people, and I have fewer friends. *He scratches his left eye and then his chest.* It's nice to tell your friends things. I've distanced myself from people now (and he names a few). Silence. *He scratches his left, lower eyelid.* I was just thinking about Rosa and her uncle (a widower). Today we're going to go to pick up some boxes. I don't remember if I mentioned it here. *He touches his arm and his chin.* He's made a huge change: from being really nice while the aunt was alive, and when she died, he withdrew; as if he wanted to distance himself; he was out of sorts with Rosa for no reason. *He touches his face and scratches his right eyelid.* She told him to get lost because of a refusal. It really upset me; Rosa is upset. She doesn't deserve it. I'm afraid I'll shoot my mouth off and tell her everything. Stop her in her tracks. *He smiles.* I run the risk of getting angry. Rosa asked me to go with her. There's information that sets me against him. He changed my aunt's will; he was able to convince her, and he took her to the notary a month before she died. She let herself be tricked. *He scratches his left arm.* He's a deceitful man; who went from being nice to rejecting. I got angry with him. It was a big disappointment for me, like a betrayal; that's why I'm worried about getting angry with him. *He scratches his left shoulder, then his chin. Silence.* I even remember (*he clears his throat*) the sculpture that my aunt made for Rosa and that he didn't want to give to her. He's not much of a person. *Silence. He clears his throat. He scratches his right cheek, the right side of his forehead and the left side of the back of his neck.* Everything I said! The subject of health, itches, and the thing about my anus. The doctor said I'd end up in the operating room because the fissure is becoming chronic. It'll be a short operation with a day in the hospital and then some rest. That's a whole new set of things to add to everything, although today, my spirit is better than it was days ago. I feel more hopeful. *He clears his throat.* Maybe yesterday I felt like this, and I was able to talk to Rosa; it's a bad time, but yesterday I recovered a bit. She is also going through a bad personal moment: she's sad, hysterical, and nervous; she doesn't feel understood by me. She says I don't appreciate what she does and that I complain about everything.

T: Independently of Rosa, what you're saying is that when you're here, you can receive an explanation and you feel listened to. That makes you have hope of feeling better, that things can heal and not necessarily become chronic. On the other hand, when you're alone, waiting, you feel that enormous irritation: that everything is taken away from you, that you be stripped—like the change in the will—that they'll cut you off. As if I had become a frustrating mother who progressively takes everything away from you; but when you can hear me and understand something, you feel calmer and more hopeful.

P: Of course, but what you say upsets me (*he scratches both eyes*) a lot: I have no solidness alone. You're here. I understand. I'm better, but when I'm left alone I feel worse. That's the way it is. It upsets me. It makes me angry and I feel sorry. What little solidness I have when I'm alone! And if I add to that the number of years of treatment I've had, and all that I should have learned, and the stability I could have (*he clears his throat*) and seeing myself so weak; if I'm in the session, yes, but outside of here I go down, I fall apart, I'm afraid; it demoralises me. I don't only think like that now, but other times too; this dependence on the therapy is like vitamins (*he scratches his nose*) but with the aggravating factor that when you stop taking them you feel nervous exhaustion again. It makes me angry; then I think that maybe I should finish this therapy so I won't have this support (*he scratches his right arm*). On the other hand, I see myself with my ten thousand problems (*he smiles*) that are now one hundred thousand, and then I see myself in trouble, all in a mess. Carry on: a lot of need of treatment, to understand it all more, and I've got this ambivalence; there are times when I think that I should break it off (*he scratches his left arm*) and other times that I should reinforce it. (*He clears his throat*). Deep down, I'm a dreamer, very innocent (*he scratches his right shoulder and the left-hand side of his chest*). I still have the fantasy that I'm going to change, like with my son that I will suddenly change and I'll have a softer temperament and I'll be stronger, more mature, pleasant with magnificent relationships. Everything that I'm not. I get angry about how unhappy I am in my skin, in all senses of the word (*he smiles*). Some people are just so fine that they don't ever see reality, but I'm at the other extreme (*he scratches his head. Silence. He clears his throat*). I feel too much in these sessions, like stabilising elements; they're points that stabilise me, with new perspectives that I value a great deal but so much time to be so little! It's defeatist. I'm better now, but what a weakling I am! (*He scratches behind his right ear*). Just look how frightened I am, how little I'm worth. Wow, what a temper I have! (*He smiles and clears his throat*). I was thinking about Juan: that at the moment I was incapable of expressing any of this to him, I rather talked about anecdotes, about holidays, politics… On the other hand, on another day, I talked a lot with him and with Jordi.

T: Again, the idea of limits appears: your skin may be leaky, a skin that doesn't feel comfortable. You may have a feeling that you can slip through your skin and be emptied out, weakened, without consistency, but you say you can decide at every moment what to say or what not to say. You may feel like a watering can—full of holes, the anal fissure, the itching—but finally, you can choose what to talk about, what to say; and you can distinguish between what the relationship with me in treatment is from what the relationship with a friend is.

3.2.5.6 Interpretations of the Material

In this session, the verbal and the para-verbal speak at the same time and can be read from different points of view. There are two scripts: one with words and the other with gestures, both directed from the unconscious. These scripts admit different readings, depending on the angle chosen. On this occasion, a first reading will be made taking into account how Arnoldo is linked to the analyst; a reading that suggests the following sequence:

First, he begins by expressing his despair: "everything looks black to me", a despair that makes him feel "between a rock and a hard place" and "lost" to the point of sinking, faced with the projected "abnormal" situation... As soon as the therapist speaks to him, he seems to reorganise himself and the reference to intimacy appears: "They're intimate things you only tell someone you're very close to". That is, he recognises an intimate relationship with the analyst who has told him something, as if the feeling of going under were beginning to subside. After making a somewhat hysterical scene regarding the fear of such intimacy, he refers to a triangular/oedipal situation: the conflict with the uncle and aunt and the inheritance problem. There is a conflict of distrust: the parents promise, but then go their own way, to the point that he speaks of "betrayal" as if the primary objects cannot be trusted. Perhaps the betrayal has been twofold: the mother had more children, and the father did not give her all his potency/penis/phallus. All his resentment could be held in his anus, become chronic, waiting to be cleansed, perhaps, by another powerful penis/phallus, the analyst. Approaching a more oedipal problem allows him to address the issue of his treatment of women, probably devalued from an inverted oedipal position. When he is shown his great dependence on another person, he becomes irritated as if he feels denuded, and does not want to recognise it, for at that moment he scratches both eyes, which necessarily prevents him from seeing. He lists his many ills in detail, and refers back to his friend, as if to acknowledge that he needs a healthy male to rescue him. Because he is satisfied to have a male figure to help him close so many pores, he smiles.

Behind this reading from a neurotic vertex lies another, more associated with primitive anxieties. In this sense, touching and scratching communicate as much as verbalised speech. Both languages express fear and the need to reassure himself that disintegration has not taken place. Hence, when the therapist speaks, he does not feel the need to touch himself because the voice and the meaning of the interpretations reassure him that he is not disintegrated, but whole. He experiences the analyst as present[45] and fulfilling the para-excitatory function, a function that his primary objects should have offered him, and that he would have been able to introject. The capacity to put distance from his anxieties through words is evident in the fact that Arnoldo can choose what he talks about with his friends; earlier on, with less capacity for self-containment, he needed to unload verbally in long conversations, not exempt from eroticisation, with them, which functioned as phallic support. The possibility of choosing what to say at any given moment is the result of the type of transference (maternal and paternal) that he develops and which allows him to distance himself from what attacks him directly from within. A transference fraught with distrust, hostility, reproaches, threats… but which, when sustained and analysed, could serve to build a bond of collaboration and trust.

The difficulty in building an internal container to sustain emotions can be related both to the failure of the maternal function and the compulsive need to scratch himself to expel, according to the model of projective (evacuative) identification, the feelings and bad objects. In the material it can be observed how Arnoldo has projected his suffering and fear of disintegration into his oldest son, along with his own identification with a deteriorated father. This defence is, however, insufficient, and he tries to expel his malaise through his scratching. This situation encounters a complement to the *enuresis* that he suffered from up until puberty, and that is where the metaphor of the watering can comes from, in which through multiple holes, like pores, he can satisfy sadistic and erotic phantasies. Sadistic because they attack the object that pursues him. Erotic because of the sensory/masturbatory pleasure that he achieves. The problem becomes more encompassing because the more he scratches himself and more self-erotic satisfaction he achieves, the more he fears that his body will be (ship) wrecked, and that is the reason for the reference to a boat, because his relief is always fleeting and the threat of disintegration does not disappear.

Understanding the meaning of somatisation, i.e. that his body expresses intolerable mental contents, has been fundamental in order to discover Arnoldo's internal world. It felt intolerable to him to recognise and accept his *ambivalence* regarding his first object: his *mother*; the idealisation of this mother concealed a distant, cold, pragmatic, and overprotective mother who, in turn, received all of the discharge (through projective identification) of Arnoldo's damaged objects, building a persecutory maternal object. In the material, we can observe how when he scratched his right side, he spoke about his wife, and when he scratched his left side, he spoke about his son, even though his irritation and scratching could pass over "from one side to the other". Thus, by scratching or tearing his skin, he builds an incompetent internal object, incapable of containing his son. A pierced mother does not sustain the desires and needs of a son, and the son cannot build, by introjective identification, a containing object. That is why the identification with a deteriorated father remains a useless alternative to stop the fear of psychotic disintegration because he cannot count on either an internal, trustworthy mother or father. He cannot build an internal family around which his life could revolve and in which he could feel protected.

The concern he expresses for his eldest son refers to difficulties at school, to difficulties linked to learning. I think that in this way, Arnoldo was giving an account of his own difficulty in symbolising and learning, even though he had finished his degree in a short time. The question remained with me as to his ability to learn, whether it was based on the introjective incorporation of knowledge or on an adherence to content, as sometimes adhered to by people. This question could be extended to his use of the treatment, whether he is introjecting a containing analytic function, or if he is using it like vitamins that have a momentary effect, while he is in the company of the therapist. A situation that evokes the relief he would have felt when he was given creams to cure or soothe his atopy, which must have felt like caresses. This could be related to the smiles that appear towards the end of the session, although they could also express triumphant smiles with respect to the jealous sisters who were not in their mother's arms. The references to how bad things are sound like a justification for staying longer in the maternal arms of the analyst, as if expressing the desire never to be separated. And for that, on the one hand, he has so many organs and pores (up to 100,000) to use, that he could be guaranteed many years of care: he can tear his skin, he can make an anal fissure, he can have an asthmatic attack; in short, he has many anchor points to make somatic conversions… "he will always have sensitive skin that will talk" said McDougall when we discussed this material. On the other hand, when I discussed this material with Alberto Hahn, he suggested the image of the buttons on a car radio: "you press a button and a station appears, you press another and another station appears…". Arnoldo had many pores to claim maternal and paternal care.

When Arnoldo says that he feels like "he's between a rock and a hard place", I believe that he is expressing how *trapped* he feels In his psychic reality, between a maternal object off whom things bounce like a wall, and a jealous paternal object who threatens him because of the close relationship that he has with his mother whom he beckons to him since the first months of his life with his eczema and whom he imprisons with his multiple illnesses. The trap, though, was that he could only get care through being ill.

But this expression, "between a rock and a hard place" may also refer to his oedipal fantasies and conflict with male and female figures. This more neurotic problem manifested itself in some episodes of *impotence* and the need to appeal to stories of other men's sexual experiences in order to become aroused. It was a way of introducing a man who would free him from the fear of being absorbed and trapped inside a woman. A woman perceived ambivalently. However, in addition to this complex image of women, this young man's sexuality was so confused between the various erogenous zones that anal evacuations forced him to ask for forgiveness through *rituals*, as if anal arousals made him feel that he had tainted the idealised and pure woman, as if at the same time, he had torn off the penises of the powerful men he needed to become a man. By being around powerful men he been dizzied, that is, momentarily lost his own identity. From a feminine position and through anal masturbation, he retained the penis in the anus, although he then felt persecuted in the form of an anal fissure: a sword pricked him, as it could prick him anywhere on the skin; as if it were the revenge of the father retained in the anus.

The expression "to feel unhappy in my skin" does not express only the desire to change, but rather the desire to give up identification with a manipulative and controlling father, not to mention jealous, as he expressed, with displacement on to the uncle that made the aunt change her will. Arnoldo's wife complained about his controlling attitude and that she felt humiliated by him. I believe that the absence of a good, non-idealised, maternal object, did not offer Arnoldo the support necessary to rescue him from identification with an arrogant father in a deteriorating process. His ambivalence about internal objects was verbalised and updated in the therapy when he said,

> A lot of need of treatment, to understand it all more and I've got this ambivalence; there are times when I think that I should break it and other times that I should reinforce it. Deep down, I'm a dreamer, very innocent I still have the fantasy that I'm going to change, like with my son that I will suddenly change and I'll have a softer temperament and I'll be stronger, more mature, pleasant with magnificent relationships. Everything that I'm not.

With regret, he thus expressed that he was still not a mature person, with an identity based on introjective identification with maternal and paternal objects that live passionately and in harmony. At this time, Arnoldo still could not find the limits of his identity in psychic reality, but rather in the periphery of his speaking skin. In this, I endorse McDougall's (1989, pp. 152–153) conclusions with regard to his polysomatising analysands, in that

> … There was clearly a breakdown, as with many poly-somatising patients, in the early introjection of a soothing and caretaking mother image (Krystal, 1977, 1978a, 1978b) with which to identify. The positive investment in bodily suffering is reminiscent of those babies with incoherent mothering who bang their heads relentlessly on the sides of their cribs, as though to find confirmation of their body limits while distracting themselves from painful emotional states. What should have been supplied from internal sources (that is, some introjected image of the maternal environment that would restore to the infant a feeling of corporeal limits and of the capacity to contain painful emotional states) has to be sought in the suffering body itself.…

for example, by *scratching*, as Arnoldo does. But he scratches not only to find his own limits, but also to keep his erotic satisfaction hidden or to rid himself of his ambivalence towards the first objects, especially the mother, who, in her ideology, rejected erotic pleasure. As Winnicott (1934) pointed out:

> The obsessive quality of the scratching is an indication of the child's fear of loss of a pleasure-system, and the self-mutilating that is so common corresponds exactly to the cruel element that in obsessive onanism is directed at the self, although in the accompanying unconscious phantasies it is fundamentally directed towards an object in the environment…

In studying papular urticaria that stimulates the urge to scratch all over the body, Winnicott (1934) said that such urticaria is

> ...more closely related to anal than to genital onanism and is, so to speak, a spread-out over the whole skin of a special sensitivity of peri-anal skin and anal mucous membrane; the reason for this spread-out is largely repression in connection with actual anal sensation and the passive fantasies that go with it, though factors may be operative in the direction of encouraging general skin excitement (unsuitable underclothing, infestation, an attack of scabies, a skin experience such as vaccination, chicken-pox, impetigo, and so on).

> If the condition under consideration is related to genital masturbation, it is to the obsessive variety, rather than to ordinary normal genital excitability and fantasy accompaniment. The obsessive element indicates a lack of satisfaction as a form of gratification, and points to an anxiety drive. It is well known that there is a lot of cruelty in (neurotic) obsessive genital masturbation, showing both in the physical treatment of the genitals and in the fantasy accompaniment, and the obsessive quality is related to underlying anxiety.

If the different anchoring points of Arnoldo's erotic self-satisfaction are brought together, it will be observed how the itching of eczema, anal itching, and the various forms of masturbation, not always directly communicated, have come together; this suggests that anxieties linked to subject-object discrimination and autoeroticism come together in the skin.

Faced with the intensity of Arnoldo's scratching in the session, I could not help but feel a certain discomfort which, according to Winnicott (op. cit.), could be related to censorship of his own pleasure because...

> We all retain a potential skin erotism, as for instance when the sight of someone scratching himself makes us itch to scratch too. In certain emotional states we are more sympathetic in this respect than we are in others. The social prohibition of scratching illustrates the universal guilt over skin erotism, and presupposes skin pleasure. Any irritating skin lesion is apt to reactivate our skin erotism, and the following instances may be cited: chilblains, anal pruritus...

Many other questions could be formulated when considering Arnoldo's material, one of them being the following: why does the scratching decrease as the session goes by? Probably he is not only encountering containment in the dialogue with the analyst who frees him of the compulsive need to monitor the integrity of his skin, but also that he has been able to transition from the initial auto-erotism to the satisfaction of an encounter with the object. That is why, in the measure that his scratching diminishes, a smile appears, and he no longer needs his body to write for him.

Notes

1 Published in *Revista de Psicoanálise* da Sociedade Psicanalitica, Porto Alegre (Brazil), December 2004, XI(3), pp. 489–518.
2 "Most of our mistakes are fundamentally grammatical. We create our own difficulties by employing an inadequate language to describe facts. Thus, to take one example, we are constantly giving the same name to more than one thing, and more than one name to the same thing. The results, when we come to argue, are deplorable. For we are using a language which does not adequately describe the things about which we are arguing" (Huxley, 1938, p. 133).
3 In the preliminary note to *Euthydemus* by Plato, J. B. Bergua (1968, p. 189) enumerates the bases of the word games:

> purely accidental amphibologies, sometimes due to a particularity of syntax; the double meaning that certain words naturally often have; confusion of the word with the reality of the thing expressed; arbitrarily established relationship between two attributes of the same object.

4 Wittgenstein affirms in *Tractatus Logico-Philosophicus* § 4.003, "Most propositions and questions, that have been written about philosophical matters, are not false, but senseless. We cannot, therefore, answer questions of this kind at all, but only state their senselessness".
5 It must be said that I use a word, the meaning of which I don't know. Does that mean that I am speaking foolishness? Say whatever you want, as long as it doesn't prevent me from understanding what is happening. (And when you see it, you won't say certain things" (Wittgenstein, 1958, § 79).
6 Eduardo (see Section 3.1.2.4) and in D. Meltzer, R. Castellà, C. Tabbia and Ll. Farré: *Supervisions with Donald Meltzer*, Karnac, 2003.
7 It can also be translated as *image* or *painting*.
8 On establishing differentiations between affects and emotions is no simple task, not only for impulsive people, but also for clinicians. Feelings can be added to a broad conception of "affects" (Valls, 1995). For example, the terms "sensations", "feelings", and "emotions" found no discrimination nor definition in Bion. For him, "Sensations, feelings, affects and emotions are the phenomena that manifest themselves during an analytic session". (Sandler, 2005, p. 728). He considered reality to make itself present, and with this presence, the possibility of a scientific truth when, in the analytic relationship, a "feeling" emerges that he thinks of as an internal, sensual stimulus. This is the way he expressed this idea in *A Memoir of the Future* when the character P.A. says, "The nearest that the psycho-analytic couple comes to a 'fact' is when one or the other has a feeling" (Bion, 1991b, p. 536). A feeling that will become alpha if it encounters a function that will transform it. This is a situation that some impulsive people have never encountered.
9 Meltzer refers to the *committee* of the third book of *A Memoir of the Future* (Bion).
10 On occasions, the hyperbolic forms of language confer relief to the facts, as occurs with Valle Inclán's esperpento (1869–1935) or the paintings of Botero (1932–).
11 Published in *Intercambios, papeles de psicoanálisis,* number 26, June, 2011, Barcelona, pp. 17–29, and in *Revista de Psicoterapia Psicoanalítica* de la Asociación Madrileña de Psicoterapia Psicoanalítica, Number 22, September, Madrid, 2017, pp. 9–35.
12 After completing this book, I came upon a text: *Contra el populismo penitenciario* (El País, 17 de julio de 2010, p. 27) by Ramón Moles Plaza, director of the Centre de Recerca en Governança del Risc of the Universidad Autónoma de Barcelona, where it says,

> In ten years, crime has remained stable and at low levels, public perception of crime is also very low, however in twenty years prison populations have doubled. What

can be the cause of such incoherence? It appears that successive reforms of the penal code as a response to what is being called 'social alarm' could partially explain this fact. I have the conviction however, that there are more profound reasons that have to do with the 'penitentiary populism' of a political class that reacts to surveys, in turn fed by mainstream media that tends to increase social alarm which, every so often, justifies the demand for tougher penal rules despite the very high cost of this populist model based on parliamentary testosterone.

13 One of the pernicious consequences of fake news is that it increases suspicion about the information received by any media and this can diminish interest in social and political phenomena.

14 The spotlight technique consists of illuminating one part of reality or of someone else's discourse, leaving the rest in darkness, the context being what would give meaning to the illuminated part.

15 Faced with a panorama saturated with insecurity, Cardinal Ratzinger denounced the *dictatorship of relativism* during the 2005 Conclave and emerged from it elected Pope, taking the name Benedict XVI, in honour of St. Benedict who fought for the recovery of the Christian order in the decadent West of that time.

16 The Latin term *fanum* is the name of sacred places; people organise geography, circumscribing what is sacred (temples, cementeries) and other places that acquire non-sacred or profane character where everything considered not honourable can be deposited. This organisation of spaces can be observed in animal behaviour that usually keeps the nest clean while excrements are evacuated outside.

17 US diplomat.

18 Precarious boats used by migrants to illegally access European shores.

19 When faced with a conflictive situation, *the Leopard* (in the Visconti film of 1963, and based on the novel by Giuseppe Tomasi di Lampedusa) suggests changing something so everything will continue on as before.

20 Domestic staff.

21 The elements acquire another meaning when they mix with others, similar to the creation of violet by the combination of cold red and blue.

22 In a note that Michel Haag made on Bick's paper (1986, p. 66), he raises a difference between Bick and Meltzer regarding the concept of adhesive identification. In that note he says:

> In her oral teachings, E. Bick explained to us that she preferred 'identiTY' over 'identiFICATION' because the latter implies a whole mental process to become identified with the person, while adhesive identity is limited to a 'STICKING' TO SOMETHING WITHOUT MENTALIZATION, like someone touching wood supertitiously. E. Bick pressed her hands together, one against the other, palm to palm, without interlinking her fingers, to make herself well understood. Consequently, she disapproved of D. Meltzer's saying 'adhesive identification'.

One might ask whether it is possible to construct an identity without any symbolic process, without any identification. The difference between them, according to Meltzer (ibid., p. 77), responds to the fact that she "later preferred to speak of *adhesive identity* rather than identification, because the intellectual implications and the obstacles for the formation of symbols did not interest her", as they did Bion and himself. Michel Haag was not convinced by this argument.

23 Adequate distance is a fundamental condition for the development of thoughts. The Rubin Vase allows us to discriminate distances. A neurotic may oscillate between seeing a vase and two faces directly opposite one another. A psychotic will see only one of the two options—a vase or two faces. The fanatic won't see either because they will place

the two lines facing one another at such a distance that no gestalt can be organised, like the two banks of a river that never come together and cannot be compared. So, just as the fanatic sees dismantled objects, and, therefore, the parts of these objects lose the possibility of articulating themselves to create an object, in psychotic functioning the loss of distance predominates through massive projective identification that gives rise to bizarre objects; the example mentioned by Bion (1967) is eloquent: the patient who had projected aspects of their apparatus to look at the gramophone and then felt that the gramophone was watching them.

24 Sor and Senet de G. (1993, p. 249), referring to the Maximal Idea, understood

a dogmatic or mono-idea, whose main characteristic is that of lacking articulations with other ideas. It is not a problem of quantity but of obstinacy based on isolation. It is not the fact that it is 'a lot' but that it is 'concentrated'. It does not accept plurality or coexistence, it obviously rejects exchange, it does not change, it does not transform itself, it never enters into crisis.

25 Vargas Llosa (2020, p. 29) referring to Borges' work says that

his fantastical stories, which take place in the Pampas, in Buenos Aires, in China, in London, in any place of reality or unreality, show the same powerful imagination and the same formidable culture as his essays on time, the language of the Vikings....

26 With this term, Bion (1962, p. 37) names the function that "transforms the sense-impressions related to an emotional experience, into alpha-elements, which cohere as they proliferate to form the contact-barrier" that separates and distinguishes conscious and unconscious elements. In the face of the baby's incapacity, it will be the mother who exercises this function. "The mother and her mind (experienced by the baby as her breast), has to perform the function of thinking for the baby. She returns to the baby those disturbed parts of itself in a state that enables thinking" (Meltzer, 1984, p. 43). This function has to be introjected so that the subject can continue to construct alpha elements suitable for thinking.

27 For Klein the evolutionary process was teleological: from the paranoid-schizoid to the depressive position. Bion takes it up and integrates it into the theory of thinking that oscillates between fragmentation and integration through the alpha function of a thinker. The double arrow indicates that every thought can be the starting point of another, in a reversible movement of dispersion and new coherence.

28 I thank M. Elena Sammartino Rovirosa for the material on this girl.

29 "We have dream-thoughts every night, but we do not have dream-content every night" (Nunberg and Federn , 1974).

I have already, in another place, suggested that the real difference between a unconscious and a preconscious idea (thought) consists in this: that the former is carried out on some material which remains unknown, whereas the latter (the preconscious) is in addition brought into connection with word-presentations.

(Freud, 1923, p. 22)

30 "Allegory, or *continuous metaphor* as Aristotle called it, proposes a series of descriptive or narrative elements that individually correspond to the various specifics of the idea it means to signify [...] If the allegory differs from the metaphor by its extension and continuity, then it cannot be identified with the symbol either. Allegory has a mechanical, symmetrical character which the symbol does not participate in. Allegories, however, like symbols, can offer the possibility of a double or triple understanding and never propose figures that can be univocally exchanged with abstract substantive names" (Diccionario enciclopédico Salvat, 1981).

31 Published in *Controversias en Psicoanálisis de Niños y Adolescentes*, APdeBA, Buenos Aires., 2018, Number 23, pp. 43–65.

32 This is not the place to establish the limits of the polysemy of this term, but M. Klein's (1960) "*On mental health*" could give sufficient significance to the term.

33 It anthropomorphises because by attributing meaning to material reality it becomes "humanised": that stone hit me!

34 I am not referring to the primary splitting that allows for inside/outside, self/object, good/bad differentiation that impacts on differentiation and personality development, but to the pathological splitting that leads to severe disorganisations and directly undermines symbolic development and fosters paranoid and confusional states.

35 See note 18.

36 It allows both the excision of childish, immature or confused parts, and their projection onto the group, and the reintrojection of one's own aspects that return metabolised by the permanence in the repositories and allow the feeling of identity to be reorganised.

37 Even in that case, it seems preferable to me to join a gang than to remain isolated. The work of Carlos Ríos (2000): "El adicto y sus grupos" (The addict and their groups) illustrates the significance of groups in the lives of young people.

38 For example, playing with their back to the analyst so how the game is constructed cannot be seen.

39 Meltzer said that perseverance and interest is the only thing that cures…

40 "… *everything begins and ends in the body*, and there is—therefore—no behaviour (normal or pathological) that does not have organic causes, i.e. in which there are no modifications of the organism. But *the body, considered only* at its biological level of integration, is *not strictly speaking the body of the total human being*, because in the latter, all its manifestations are also and always psychological, insofar as we consider it as an area of behaviour" (Bleger, 1969, p. 162).
"BION: In the relationship I have been describing—pre-birth ↔ post-birth—the individual often behaves as if his wisdom and intelligence would be contaminated if he allowed himself to recognise that his *body thought*; conversely, that *his physicality would suffer if he allowed his body to know what his mind thought.*" (Bion, 1991c, p. 566). My italics in both texts.

41 "We can speak of the body-thing, i.e. the organic, the object of study of biology, up to the body-representation, which is dealt with by psychoanalysis. Within this second option, we refer to various categories. We speak of the body of psychosis, the body of hypochondria and the body of hysteria. This is certainly not an exhaustive list. […] In hysteria, bodily expression occurs in the erogenous body, in the body of psychosexuality. It is a body at the representational level, which is distant from the body of the anatomist. In contrast, when bodily expression comes from the soma, we are confronted with a body corresponding to the biological plane, lacking in symbolism and psychic transformation" (Fischbein, 2010, p. 21).

42 Meltzer's expression merited a comment by Hahn (2020), which I transcribe here for clarification. Regarding the expression "dead objects can be brought back to life", Hahn specified that "an attempt can be made to repair or rehabilitate damaged objects, but the dead are irreversibly dead unless we are dealing with a manic, denialist, omnipotent personality". Hahn added that he did not believe Meltzer would claim "resuscitation as a resolution of guilt and loss. What is recovered are experiences, memories of moments of intimacy and affection and/or more negative aspects of relationships with a version of living internal objects".

43 High-calorie food which made him fat.

44 With this term, Bion (1962, p. 10) describes a primitive defence associated with

> a disturbed relationship with the breast or its substitutes. The infant receives milk and other creature comforts from the breast; also love, understanding, solace. Suppose his initiative is obstructed by fear of aggression, his own or another's. If the emotion is strong enough it inhibits the infant's impulse to obtain sustenance.

Asolution to continue receiving food is a forced splitting, as Bion says: "fear of death through starvation of essentials compels resumption of sucking. A split between material and psychical satisfaction develops" (ibid.). The impossibility of recognising the object that nourishes prevents gratitude together with the experience of satisfaction and the experience of being loved. Then,

> The need for love, understanding and mental development is now deflected, since it cannot be satisfied, into the search for material comforts. Since the desires for material comforts are reinforced the craving for love remains unsatisfied and turns into overweening and misdirected greed.

(ibid., p. 11)

Aclinical example of forced splitting is observed in bulimic personalities who do not achieve the experience of satisfaction and remain trapped in unsatisfactory consumerism.

45 This suggests the experience related by Bick (1986) of a baby who shivered when his mother took off his clothes to bathe him, but did not shiver with cold because he stopped shivering as soon as she touched him with a piece of wet cotton wool; Bick hypothesised that "this touching derives its power from its significance as an adhesion, as a re-establishment of feeling stuck on to mother".

Bibliography

Anscombe, G. E. M. (1967): *An Introduction to Wittgenstein's Tractatus*, London, Hutchinson University Library.

Apprey, M. (1997): "When disciplined description precedes interpretation: Slowing Dawn Meltzer´s account of *sincerity* to reinsert description in post-Kleinian phenomenology", *Journal of Melanie Klein and Object Relations*, 15(1), pp. 91–130.

Arbiser, A. & Zusman de Arbiser, S. (1978): "Contribuciones al estudio del paciente asmático", *Revista de Psicoanálisis*, XXXV(1), pp. 163–171.

Bassols, R., Beà, J. & Coderch, J. (1985): "La identitat i els seus límits", *Revista Catalana de Psicoanàlisi*, II(2), pp. 173–188.

Bauman, Z. (2004): *Identity: Conversations with Benedetto Vecchi*, Cambridge, Polity Press.

Bermann, L. (1996): "La histeria: Entre Klein y Bion", in *Homenaje a Freud: La histeria 100 años después*, Barcelona, GRADIVA, pp. 13–20.

Bick, E. (1964): "Notes on infant observation in psycho-analytic training", *International Journal of Psychoanalysis*, 45, pp. 558–566.

Bick, E (1968): "The experience of the skin in early object-relations", in *Collected Papers of Martha Harris and Esther Bick*, edited by Meg Harris Williams, Scotland, The Clunie Press, 1987, pp. 114–118.

Bick, E. (1986): "Further considerations on the function of the skin in early object-relation", *British Journal of Psychotherapy*, 2(4), pp. 292–299

Bion, W. R. (1961a): *Experiences in Groups and Other Papers*, New York, Tavistock Publications Limited.

Bion, W. R. (1961b): "The conception of man", in *The Complete Works of W. R. Bion*, edited by Cris Mawson, London, Karnac, 2014, Vol. xv, pp. 9–30.

Bion, W. R. (1962): *Learning from Experience*, London, Karnac Books.

Bion, W. R. (1963): "Elements of psychoanalysis", in *The Complete Works of W. R. Bion*, edited by Cris Mawson, London, Karnac, 2014, Vol. V, pp. 1–86

Bion, W. R. (1965): *Transformations*, London, Karnac, 1984.

Bion, W. R. (1966): *Elements of Psychoanalysis*, London, Karnac Books, 1984

Bion, W. R. (1967a): "Notes on memory and desire", *Psychoanalytic Forum*, 2(3). Published in *Revista de Psicoanálisis*, APA, XXVI (3), 1969, pp. 679–682.

Bion, W. R. (1967b): *Second Thoughts*, London, Karnac, 1984

Bion, W. R. (1970): *Attention and Interpretation,* London, Karnac.

Bion, W. R. (1977): *Bion in New York and Sao Paulo*, edited by Marisa Pelella Mélega, London, Karnac Books, 2017.

Bion, W. R. (1979): "Making the best of a bad job", In *Clinical Seminars and Other Works,* edited by W. R. Bion, London. Karnac Books, pp. 321–332 Bion, W. R. (1991a): "The dream", in *A Memoir of the Future*, London, Karnac Books, pp. 1–218

Bion, W. R. (1991b): "The dawn of oblivion", in *A Memoir of the Future*, London, Karnac Books, pp. 427–578

Bion, W. R. (1991c): *A Memoir of the Future*, London, Karnac Books.

Bion, W. R. (1992): *Cogitations*, London, Karnac Books.

Bion, P. (1994): "Las estructuras mentales escondidas", *Psicoanálisis*, APdeBA, XVI(1), pp. 7–21.

Bléandonu, G. (2000): "Las transformaciones según Bion", *Psicoanálisis*, APdeBA, XXII, 2, pp. 315–332.

Bléandonu, G. (2000): *Wilfred Bion: His Life and Works 1897–1979*, New York, Other Press, 1994.

Bleger, J. (1969): *Psicología de la conducta,* Buenos Aires, Centro Editor de América Latina.

Bloom, H. (1998): *Shakespeare: Invention of the Human*, New York, Riverhead Books.

Borges, J. L. (1968): *Collected Fictions*, London, The Penguin Press, 1999.

Bradley, J. (2015): "Watchful waiting in psychoanalytic work with adolescents" (unpublished), Conference *Doing Things Differently. The influence of Donald Meltzer Psychoanalytic Theory and Practice*, Tavistock Clinic, London.

Brenman Pick, I. (1985): "Working through in the counter-transference", *International Journal of Psycho-Analysis*, 66, pp. 157–166.

Brutti, C. & Scotti, F. (1984): "Osservazione – conflitto – bisogni", in *Quaderni di psicoterapia infantile/4: L'osservazione*, edited by C. Brutti, & F. Scotti, Roma, Ed. Borla, pp. 23–28.

Carrión, I. (2002): "Narices de oro", *Madrid, El País Semanal* (1329), pp. 31–38.

Carvajal, A. (1943): Sonetos Poetas Españoles Siglo XX. Foro Poético Libertario. Available at www.airesdelibertad.com

Coderch, J. (1975): *Psiquiatría dinámica,* Barcelona, Ed. Heder.

Cohen, M. & Nagel, E. (1934): *An Introduction to Logic and Scientific Method,* London, Routledge & Kegan Paul LTD.

Di Carlo, A. (1984): "Osservazione e apprendimento", in *Quaderni di psicoterapia infantile*, op. cit., pp. 29–41.

Diccionario enciclopédico Salvat (1981): Barcelona, Ed. Salvat.

Edmonds, D. & Eudinov, J. (2001): *Wittgenstein's Poker: The Story of a Ten-Minute Argument between Two Great Philosophers,* New York, Ecco.

Escribano, L. (2001): *El fundamentalismo islámico*, Madrid, Acento editorial. ISBN 84-483-0572-8.

Elvira, O. A. (1999): "Sobre el soñar en los pacientes psicosomáticos", *La interpretación de los sueños, 100 años después*. XXI Simposíum y Congreso interno, APdeBA, T. I y II, pp. 259–273.

Fain, M. & David, Ch. (1963): "Aspects fonctionnels de la vie onirique", *Revue Française de Psychanalyse*, 33, pp. 241–399.

Fernández, A. (1995): "Aburrirse=aburrarse", Ric. Rodolfo (Comp.): *Trastornos narcisistas no psicóticos*, Bs. As., Paidós, pp. 205–216.

Ferrater Mora, J. (1965): *Diccionario de Filosofía*, T. I y II, Buenos Aires, Ed. Sudamericana, 1966.

Fischbein, J. (2000): "La clínica psicoanalítica y las enfermedades somáticas", *Psicoanálisis, APdeBA*, XXII(1), pp. 157–182

Fischbein, J. (2010): "Las súplicas del cuerpo", *Psicoanálisis, APdeBA,* XXXII(1), pp. 19–35.

Fisher, J. (1995): "Donald Meltzer in discussion with James Fisher", in *Intrusiveness and Intimacy in the Couple*, edited by S. Ruszczynski & J. Fisher, London, Karnac Books, pp. 107–144.

Freud, S. (1900): "The interpretation of dreams", in The Standard Edition of the *Complete Psychological Works* of Sigmund Freud, edited by J. Strachey, London, Hogarth Press, 1966, Vol IV, pp. 1–338

Freud, S. (1909): "Family Romances", in *The Standard Edition of the Complete Psychological Works of Sigmund Freud*, edited by J. Strachey, London, Hogarth Press, 1966, Vol IX, pp. 235–244.

Freud, S. (1911): "Formulations on the two principles of mental functioning", in *The Standard Edition of the Complete Psychological Works of Sigmund Freud*, edited by J. Strachey, London, Hogarth Press, 1966, Vol XII, pp. 218–226.

Freud, S. (1915): "Instincts and their Vicissitudes", in *The Standard Edition of the Complete Psychological Works of Sigmund Freud*, edited by J. Strachey, London, Hogarth Press, 1966, Vol XIV, pp. 109–140.

Freud, S. (1920): *Beyond the Pleasure Principle*, New York, W. W Norton & Company, 1961.

Freud, S. (1921): *Group Psychology and the Analysis of the Ego*, New York, W. W. Norton & Company, 1990.

Freud, S. (1923): *The Ego and the Id*, London, The Hogarth Press Ltd., 1949.

Freud, S. (1930): *Civilization and Its Discontents*, U.K., Penguin Books, 2004.

Garcia Badaracco, J. (1986): "L'identification et ses vicisitudes dans les psychoses. L'importance de la notion d'object qui rend fou", *Revue Française de Psychanalyse*, 5, pp. 1317–1337.

Grassano, E. N., (2001): "Diálogo entre distintas perspectivas teórico-clínicas en psicosomática", *En Revista de la Sociedad Argentina de Psicoanálisis*, 4, pp. 77–95.

Green, A. (1995): "Has sexuality anything to do with psychoanalysis?", *International Journal of Psychoanalysis* 76, pp. 871–883.

Grinberg, L. (1976): *Teoría de la identificación*, Buenos Aires, Paidós.

Grinberg, L. (1981): "Función del soñar y clasificación clínica de los sueños en el proceso analítico", in *Psicoanálisis. Aspectos teóricos y clínicos*, edited by Leon Grinberg, Buenos Aires, Paidós, pp. 171–186.

Grinberg, L. & Grinberg, R. (1971): *Identidad y cambio,* Buenos Aires, Ed. Kargieman.

Guiraud, P. (1971): *La semiología*, México, s. XXI editores, 1979.

Gutton, P. (1996): "La morosidad: más bien el hastío que la barbarie", *Psicoanálisis con niños y adolescentes* 9, pp. 61–77.

Hahn, A. (1993): Personal correspondence.

Hahn, A. (1997): "Contratransferencia" (unpublished), Seminario "Teoría de la Técnica", Barcelona.

Hahn, A. (1999): "Técnica de interpretación de los sueños" (unpublished), Seminario "Teoría de la Técnica", Barcelona.

Hahn, A. (2020): Personal correspondence.

Harris, M. (1984): "L'individuo nel gruppo: apprendere a lavorare con il metodo psicoanalitico", in *Quaderni*, op. cit., edited by C. Brutti, & F. Scotti, Roma, Borla, pp. 79–98.

Harris, M. & Meltzer, D. (1976): "A psychoanalytic model of the child-in-the-family-in-the-community", in *Sincerity and Other Works,* edited by Alberto Hahn, London, Karnac, 1994, pp. 387–454.

Harris Williams, M. (1983): "'Underlying pattern'in Bion's Memoir of the Future", *Revue Française de Psychanalyse,* 10, pp. 75–86.

Harris Williams, M. (1997): "Reply to Dr. Apprey's paper", *Journal of Melanie Klein and Object Relation,* 15(1), pp. 133–134.

Hinshelwood, R. D. (1989): *A Dictionary of Kleinian Thought*, London, Free Association Books.

Huxley, A. (1938): "Breughel*" in Along the Road,* London, Chatto & Windus, 1948, pp. 133–152

Jankélévitch, V. (1963): *La aventura, el aburrimiento, lo serio*, Madrid, Taurus, 1989.

Jaques, E. (1979): "Social systems as a defence against persecutory and depressive anxiety", in *New Directions in Psychoanalysis*, edited by H. Klein & R. Money-Kyrle, London, Tavistock Publications, 1955, pp. 478–498.

Jones, E. (1916): "The theory of symbolism", in *Papers on Psycho-Analysis,* London, Balliére, Tindall and Cox, 1918, p. 181

Joseph, B. (1989): *Psychic Equilibrium and Psychic Change,* London, Routledge.

Kernberg, O. (1975): *Borderline Conditions and Pathological Narcissism*, New York, Jason Aronson Inc.

Khan, M. (1989): "Introducción", en Winnicott, D.: Sostén e interpretación, Buenos Aires, Paidós, pp. 9–30.

Klein, M. (1960): "On mental health", In *Envy and Gratitude and Other Works 1946–1963,* edited by M. Masud and R. Khan, New York, The Free Press, 1975, pp. 268–274.

Kohut, H. (1971): *The Analysis of the Self*, The International Universities Press, Chicago, 2009.

Kristeva, J. (2000): *Female Genius. Melanie Klein,* New York, Columbia University Press, 2001.

Langer, S. (1962): *Esquemas filosóficos*, Buenos Aires, Ed. Nova, 1971.

Liberman, D. et al. (1986): *Del cuerpo al símbolo*, Buenos Aires, Ed. Trieb.

Lombardi, R. (2012): "Il Corpo nella teoría della mente di Wilfred R. Bion", in *Consecutio Temporum, Rivista critica della postmodernità*, Roma, Anno IV n 7, Novembre 2019, pp. 96–111; ISSN 2531-8934.

Lutenberg, J. (2000): "El cuerpo, el inconsciente, los pensamientos y el pensador", *Psicoanálisis*, XXII(1), pp. 109–134.

Magagna, J. (1997): "Three years of infant observation with Mrs. Bick", *Journal of Child Psychotherapy*, 13, pp. 19–39.

Mancia, M. (1996): *Del Edipo al sueño. Modelos de la mente en el desarrollo y en la transferencia,* Madrid, Biblioteca Nueva.

Marcelli, D., Braconnier, A. & Ajuriaguerra, J. (1986): *Manual de Psicopatología del adolescente*, Barcelona-México, Masson.

Marirrodriga, J. (2003): "El poder de El Seminario (Al Hausa)", in *Domingo 18-5-2003*, Madrid, El País.

Martinez Ferraro, P. (2010): "Fibromialgia: Una nueva enfermedad… o una antigua conocida", *Informaciones Psiquiátricas* – S. Boi de Ll. Barcelona, Primer trimestre 2010. Número 199, 19–38.

McDougall, J. (1978): *Plea for a Measure of Abnormality*, New York, Brunner/Mazel, 1992.

McDougall, J. (1983): "Cuerpo y metáfora", *Revue Française de Psychanalyse*, XL(5–6), pp. 915–943.

McDougall, J. (1989): *Theaters of the Body*, New York, W. W Norton & Company.

McDougall, J. (1993): Personal correspondence.

Meddeb, A. (2003): *The Malady of Islam*, New York, Basic Books.

Meltzer, D. (1965): "The relation of anal masturbation to projective identification", *International Journal of Psychoanalysis*, 47, pp. 335–342.

Meltzer, D. (1967): *The Psycho-Analytical Process*, London, William Heinemann Medical Books Limited.

Meltzer, D. (1968): "A note on analytic receptivity", in *Sincerity and Other Works*, edited by Alberto Hahn, London, Karnac, 1994, pp. 166–169.

Meltzer, D. (1973): "Routine and inspired Interpretations: Their relation to the weaning process in analysis", in *Sincerity and Other Works*, edited by Alberto Hahn, London, Karnac, 1994, pp. 290–306.

Meltzer, D. (1976): "Temperature and distance as technical dimensions of interpretation", in *Sincerity and Other Works*, edited by Alberto Hahn, London, Karnac, 1994, pp. 374–386.

Meltzer, D. (1978a): "A note on introjective processes", in *Sincerity*, op. cit London, Karnac, 1994, pp. 458–468.

Meltzer, D. (1978b): *The Kleinian Development*, London, Karnac, 2008.

Meltzer, D. (1980a): "Del simbolo", in *Quaderni di psicoterapia infantile*/5 Simbolo e simbolizzazione, ., edited by C. Brutti, & F. Scotti, Roma, Borla, pp. 127–141.

Meltzer, D. (1980b): "Sulla immaginazione", in *Quaderni di psicoterapia infantile*, Roma, Borla, 1984, pp. 132–169.

Meltzer, D. (1981): "The Kleinian Expansion of Freud's Metapsychology", *International Journal of Psycho-Analysis*, 62, pp. 177–185.

Meltzer, D. (1984): *Dream-Life: A Re-Examination of the Psychoanalytic Theory and Technique*, London, Karnac Books, 2009.

Meltzer, D. (1986): "Clinical seminars in the Psychoanalytic Group of Barcelona" (unpublished).

Meltzer, D. (1990): "Conferencia pronunciada por el Dr. Donald Meltzer en APdeBA", *Psicoanálisis*, APdeBA, XII(1), pp. 123–134.

Meltzer, D. (1991): Clinical seminars in the Psychoanalytic Group of Barcelona: Gerard (unpublished).

Meltzer, D. (1992): *The Claustrum. An Investigation of Claustrophobic Phenomena*, StrathClyde, The Clunie Press.

Meltzer, D. (1993): "Implicaciones psicosomática en el pensamiento de Bion", *Psicoanálisis, APdeBA*, XV(2), pp. 315–338.

Meltzer, D. (1995a): "Clinical seminars in the Psychoanalytic Group of Barcelona: Elizabeth" (unpublished).

Meltzer, D. (1995b): "Hysteria". Clinical seminars in the Psychoanalytic Group of Barcelona (unpublished), Oxford.

Meltzer, D. (1997a): "Reply to Maurice Apprey's paper", *Journal of Melanie Klein and Object Relation*, 15(1), pp. 131–132.

Meltzer, D. (1997b): "Concerning signs and symbols", *British Journal of Psychotherapy*, 14, pp. 175–181.

Meltzer, D. (1998): Clinical seminars in the Psychoanalytic Group of Barcelona: Luis (unpublished).

Meltzer, D. (1999a): "Diálogos clínicos con Donald Meltzer", *Psicoanálisis*, APdeBA, XXI(1/2), Monographic number.

Meltzer, D. (1999b): Personal communication.

Meltzer, D. (2000): On symbol formation and allegory. Available at http://www.appliedpsychoanalysis.com

Meltzer, D. (2002): "Considerazioni attuali sull'autismo", in *Transfert, Adolescenza, Disturbi del pensiero. Mutamenti nel metodo psicoanalitico*, edited by Gruppo di Studio Racker di Venezia, Roma, Armando editore, 2004, pp. 158–162.

Meltzer, D., Castellà, R., Tabbia, C. & Farré, Ll. (2003): *Supervision with Donald Meltzer. The Simsbury Seminars*, London, Karnac.

Meltzer, D. & Harris Williams, M. (1985): "Three lectures on W. R. Bion's A Memoir of the Future", in *Sincerity and Other Works,* edited by Alberto Hahn, London, Karnac, 1994, pp. 520–550.

Meltzer, D. & Harris Williams, M. (1988): *The Apprehension of Beauty: The Role of Aesthetic Conflict in Development, Art, and Violence*, London, Karnac, 2008.

Meltzer, D. & Harris Williams, M. (1998): *Adolescentes,* edited by L. Jachevasky & C. Tabbia, Bs. As., Spatia, ed.

Meltzer, D. & Psychoanalytic Group of Barcelona (1987): "Clinical seminars in the Psychoanalytic Group of Barcelona: Victor", in *Psychanalytic Work with Children and Adults – Meltzer in Barcelona*, edited by Psychoanalytic Group of Barcelona, London, Karnac, 2002, pp. 21–44

Meltzer, D. & Psychoanalytic Group of Barcelona (1995): *Psychanalytic Work with Children and Adults – Meltzer in Barcelona*, London, Karnac, 2002.

Meltzer, D. & Racker, G. (2004): *Transfert, Adolescenza, Disturbi del Pensiero*, Roma, Armando editore.

Meltzer, D., et al. (1975): *Explorations in Autism: A Psycho-Analytical Study*, London, Clunie Press.

Meltzer, D. et al. (1986): S*tudies in Extended Metapsychology: Clinical Applications of Bion's Ideas*, London, Karnac, 2018.

Merriam-Webster. (n.d.). "Neighbour", in *Merriam-Webster.com Dictionary*. Available at https://www.merriam-webster.com/dictionary/neighbor

Money-Kyrle, R. (1964): "Review", in *Collected Papers of Roger Money-Kyrle*, edited by D. Meltzer, London, Karnac Books, 1978, pp. 389–396.

Morey, M. (2007): *Pequeñas doctrinas de la soledad*, Madrid, Ed. Sexto Piso.

Muñoz Vila, C. (2011): *Reflexiones psicoanalíticas,* Bogotá (Colombia), Editorial Pontificia Universidad Javeriana.

Nemas, Cl. (2004): "El concepto de mundo interno y la teoría del duelo", in *Melanie Klein en Buenos Aires, Desarrollos y Perspectivas*, edited by APdeBA, Buenos Aires, APdeBA, pp. 139–143.

Nunberg, H. & Federn, E. *comp.* (1974): *Las reuniones de los miércoles: Actas de la Sociedad Psicoanalítica de Viena,* Buenos Aires, Nueva Visión.

Oswald, I. (1990): "Terrores nocturnos y sonambulismo", in *Avances en la investigación del sueño y sus trastornos*, edited by G. Buela-Casal & Navarro Humanes, J.F. comps. 1990, Madrid, Siglo XXI de España Editorial, S. A., pp. 345–349.

Oz, A. (2002): *How to Cure a Fanatic*, London, Vintage Books, 2012.

Pistiner de Coriñas, L. (1993): "Psique-soma- diálogos y cesuras", *Psicoanálisis, APdeBA*, XV(2), pp. 339–358.

Pistiner de Cortiñas, L. (1999): "Dreams and lies: The discovery of psychic reality and the aesthetic dimension of the mind", in *The Aesthetic Dimension of the Mind Variations on a Theme of Bion*, edited by APdeBA (Asociación Psicoanalítica de Buenos Aires), London, Karnac Books, 2009.

Plato (1952): "Euthydemus", in *Plato IV Laches Protagoras Mend Euthydemus*, translation by W. R. M. Lamb, edited by T. E. Page, E. Capps, W. H. D. Rouse, L. A. Post, and E. H. Warmington, Cambridge, Harvard Unity Press., pp. 373–505.

Plato (1968): Platón: Eutidemos. Traducción, noticias preliminares y Estampa Socrática de Juan B. Bergua, J.B. En: Diálogos Segundo Hippias-Protágoras-Eutidemos-Gorgias, Clásicos Bergua, Madrid, Quinta edición, Madrid, Clásicos Bergua.

Quesada, J. D. (2009): "Una tribu bajo sospecha", in *Domingo*, 15-03-09, Madrid, El País, pp. 8–9.

Racker, H. (1968). *Transference and Counter-Transference*. New York, International Universities Press, Inc.

Ramos García, J. (2004): "Fibromialgia: ¿la histeria en el capitalismo de ficción? *Revista de la Asociación Española de Neuropsiquiatría* 89, pp. 2933–2946.

Rappaport de Aisemberg, E. (1998–1999): "Más allá de la representación: los afectos", *Revista de Psicoanálisis*, APA, Número especial internacional 1998–1999 62(2), pp. 197–214.

Rappaport de Aisemberg, E. (2005): "Trauma, pulsión y somatosis", *Revista de Psicoanálisis*, APA, LXII(2), pp. 273–280.

Ríos, C. (2000): "El adicto y sus grupos", *Psicoanálisis*, APdeBA, XXII(2), pp. 483–506.

Russell, B. (1919): "Descriptions", in *Meaning and Reference*, edited by A. W. Moore, Oxford, Oxford University Press, 1993, pp. 192–207.

Russell, B. (1922): "Introduction", in *Tractatus Logico-Philosophicus*, London, Kegan Paul, Trench, Trubner & Co.

Sales, L. (2010): "Dolor corporal y afectos. A propósito de un caso de fibromialgia", in *De la angustia y otros afectos,* Barcelona, Gradiva, pp. 379–390.

Samaja, J. (1993): *Epistemología y Metodología. Elementos para una teoría de la investigación científica*, Buenos Aires, EUDEBA, 1995.

Sandler, P. C. (2005): *The Language of Bion, A Dictionary of Concepts*, London, Karnac.

Sartre, J.-P. (1944): "No exit", in *No Exit and Three Other Plays*, New York, Vintage, 1989, pp. 1–46

Scharovsky, L. (1999): "*Construyendo la* Vía Regia", in *La interpretación de los sueños, 100 años después,* op. cit., pp. 585–597.

Searle, J. R. (1967): "Proper names and descriptions" in *The Encyclopedia of Philosophy*, edited by P. Edwards, MacMillan, Nueva York, pp. 487–491.

Segal, A. (1975): "The psychoanalytic approach to the treatment of psychotic patients", in L*iving on the Border: Psychotic Processes in the Individual, the Couple, and the Group*, edited By David Bell and Aleksandra Novakovic, London, Routledge, 2013, pp. 1–10.

Segal, H. (1981): "The Function of Dreams", *The Work of Hanna Segal A Kleinian Approach to Clinical Practice,* Northvale, Jason Aronson Inc, pp. 89–100

Segal, H. (1991): *Dream, Phantasy and Art,* London, Tavistock/Routledge.

Segal, H. (2003): "The mind of the Fundamentalist/Terrorist. Not learning from experience: Hiroshima, the Gulf War and 11 September", The Institute of Psychoanalysis, News & Events, Annual Issue 2003.

Shakespeare, W. (1606): *Macbeth,* Cambridge, Cambridge University Press, 1997.

Sirota, A. (1998) "Afectos y efectos de la contratransferencia", *Buenos Aires, Psicoanálisis APdeBA*, XX(3), pp. 777–786.

Sor, D. & Senet de Grassano, M. R., (1993): *Fanatismo*, Santiago, Chile, Ed. Ananké, ISBN 956-7152-04-7.

Strawson, P. F. (1950): "Sobre el referir", in *La búsqueda del significado*, edited by L. Valdés Villanueva, Madrid, Ed. Tecnos, 1991, pp. 57–82.

Tabak de Bianchedi, E. (1998): "El psicoanalista apasionado o aprendiendo de la experiencia emocional", *Psicoanálisis*, *APdeBA*, XX(3), pp. 617–629.

Tabbia, C. (1970): "La correlación entre mundo y lenguaje en la teoría pictórica según el *Tractatus Logico-Philosophicus* de Ludwig Wittgenstein" (unpublished).

Tabbia, C. (2001): "Sonambulismo. Cambio catastrófico y actuaciones durante el dormirsoñar", Barcelona, AEPP (Asociación Española de Psicoterapia Psicoanalítica) Rev. 4/5, pp. 81–92.

Tabbia, C. (2005): "L'avorriment: l' emoció anul.lada", Barcelona, *Revista de Psicoteràpia psicoanalítica*, ACPP 8, pp. 189–207.

Tabbia, C. (2007a): "Resistenza al cambiamento nel funzionamento fanatico", in *Il fanatismo. Dalle origini psichiche al sociale,* edited by F. Spadaro e C. Tabbia: Roma, Armando editore, pp. 13–33.

Tabbia, C. (2007b): "El aburrimiento y la belleza del mundo", in *De un taller psicoanalítico, a partir de Donald Meltzer,* edited by The Psychoanalytic Group of Barcelona, Barcelona, *Grafein* editores, Colección GPB, pp. 263–286.

Terricabras, J. M. (1997): *Introduccio* a las *Investigacions filosòfiques* de L. Wittgenstein, (1958): *Investigaciones filosóficas*, Barcelona, Edicions 62, 1997, pp. 5–46.

Todorov, T. (1970): "La descripción de la significación en la literatura", in La *semiología*, edited by R. Barthes, C. Bremond, T. Todorov & C. Metz, Buenos Aires, Ed. Tiempo contemporáneo, pp. 105–114.

Ungar, V. (2000): "Transference and aesthetic model", *Psicanálise* (Journal of the SBP-dePA), 2(1). Available at http://www.virginiaungar.com/wp-content/uploads/Esthetic-Model.pdf

Valdés Villanueva, L. (ed.) (1991: *La búsqueda del significado*, Madrid, Ed. Tecnos.

Valls, J. L. (1995): *Diccionario freudiano*, Madrid, Julian Yébenes, S. A.

Vargas Llosa, M. (2020): *Medio siglo con Borges,* Barcelona, Alfaguara.

Vattimo, G. (2009): "Solidarity, universalism and the interreligious dialogue", in *Solidarity and the Crisis of Trust*, edited by Jacek Kołtan, Gdansk, European Solidarity Centre, 2016, pp. 37–50.

Wang, M. (1979): "Some psychoanalytic observations on boredom", *International Journal of Psycho-Analysis*, 60, pp. 515–526.

Winnicott, D. (1934): "Papular urticaria and the dynamics of skin sensation", *British Journal of Children's Diseases*, pp. 5–16. *International Journal of Psychoanalysis*, 16, pp. 104–105.

Winnicott, D. W. (1954). "Mind and its relation to the psyche-soma." *British Journal of Medical Psychology*, 27(4), pp. 201–209.

Wittgenstein, L. (1918): *Tractatus Logico-Philosophicus*, London, Kegan Paul, Trench, Trubner & Co, 1922.

Wittgenstein, L. (1958): *Philosophical Investigation*, Oxford, Blackwell.

Yankélévitchi, V. (1963): L' Aventure, l'Ennui, le Sérieux, Parìs, Champs essais. Madrid, Taurus, 1989.

Zusman de Arbiser, S. (1999): "Sobreadaptación y enfermedad psicosomática en niños y adolescentes. Distintos abordajes terapéuticos", *Revista de Psicoanálisis*, LVI(2), pp. 335–353.

Intimacy

In a documented work about intimacy, the philosopher José Luis Pardo (1996) presents a fruit theory on the subject which he considers to be a prejudice. On page 13, he says:

> This is the origin of what we might call 'the fruit theory of intimacy', a prejudice implicitly shared by psychologists, sociologists and philosophers: the person would be like an avocado; the outer skin would be the advertisement, the protective, shiny if somewhat rough and indigestible layer (not in vain does it hold the monopoly over violence), which is seen from the outside and which protects the inside; the nutritious and succulent meat (always one step away from corruption) would be privacy, the zone of maturity where individuals enjoy the treasure of their property safeguarded from public voracity by the law that protects their freedom (the only sphere that, despite terminological abuses, sociologists can talk about); and intimacy would be the opaque, solid, impenetrable bone, nuclear heart and germinal seed that has neither taste nor shine.

I will not refer to prejudice or ignore the fruit metaphor because, beyond criticism, it is possible to recover essential ideas for understanding intimacy. First, it is worth questioning whether there is anything as marvellous and fascinating as a seed, that prodigy of nature. This tiny object—even if it is the size of an avocado seed—has the potential to give rise to other living beings. In a sense, it has a certain equivalence to the intimacy that, under the right circumstances, in fertile soil and protected from siege, as Klein would say, a personality can develop. Therefore, rereading Pardo's text, I do not discard the fruit metaphor. Without this seed, complex in its structure and with great potential, we could be thrown into profound loneliness. Certainly, the analyst's office may have different textures, some as rough or as shiny as the skin of the avocado, all of them available protection from prying eyes. But it will be the containing function of the analyst, working as a team with the patient, which will produce that nourishing pulp that will allow the development of an intimate relationship. Rather than defining intimacy, I will now focus on describing the conditions for the establishment of an intimate relationship that will enable the birth and development of a new state of mind.

DOI: 10.4324/9781003347156-11

3.3.1 The Concept of Intimacy in Meltzer's Thinking[1]

When Freud (1930) replied to his friend Romain Rolland that

> ...Our present ego-feeling is, therefore, only a shrunken residue of a much more inclusive—indeed, an all-embracing—feeling which corresponded to a more intimate bond between the ego and the world about it. If we may assume that there are many people in whose mental life this primary ego-feeling has persisted to a greater or less degree, it would exist in them side by side with the narrower and more sharply demarcated ego-feeling of maturity, like a kind of counterpart to it.

he mentions that deep desire to unite with the surrounding world, to establish an intimate communion with other people, a longing to merge with objects; but these longings and feelings take on different nuances depending on whether it is the desire of an infant or an adult, since the limits of the ego differ in both states of mind. However, when Meltzer (1971) mentions the yearning "...to come to grips with this mystery of intimacy that breaches the solipsistic loneliness of individual mind and renders it tolerable", he is referring to the pain of the isolated mind, trapped in sterile solipsism. I think that in the tension between the longing for communion and isolation lies the terrain of intimacy. Freud exchanges ideas with his friend Romain Rolland; Meltzer claims to solve the mystery of intimacy. In this intimacy that develops between friends and between collaborators, they try to unravel mysteries of the mind. One of them, perhaps the greatest, is that of the development of the personality, and within that mystery, another: that of intimacy.

Meltzer has always been interested in the subject of intimacy, his work speaks of it and his contributions have arisen from a longing to understand himself and others. Intimacy participates in the mysterious character that underlies every relationship. Intimacy is a strange encounter with the other, which astonishes and challenges, moves and resists, and makes us long for it, which we often seek but do not find, and which we suddenly find, like a flower on the road, without having foreseen it. At the base of our self is that old longing for union, for intimate common-union with the world and with ourselves, with our first objects and with the community that engendered us. These were some of the themes, the questions that stimulated Meltzer's psychoanalytic thinking; let us then look at some of his contributions to the understanding of the mystery of the intimate relationship.

He (1993, p. 317) said that

> Psychoanalysis has concerned itself with those areas of the personality involved in the intimate relationships which enable both family life in the external world and the building of an internal family. Psychoanalysis, initiated by Freud's work on the neuroses, has been mainly concerned with emotional and intimate relationships, both because of its peculiar method and because of its interests and its therapeutic capacities....

Emotional and intimate relationships become a fundamental theme of psychoanalytic thought because they are the ones that make it possible to unveil the process of the construction of the object and the constitution of the subject based on the group and family model of the mind. By referring to different areas of the personality involved in the construction of the internal and then external family, Meltzer is thinking of the emotional interplay of links and anti-links and of whole and part objects that will make possible the construction of a family with the capacity to function as a work team that generates the development of the personality of its members, which will transcend in the construction of the community (Tabbia, 2003). But the centrifugal direction from intimate relationships to the construction of the external family and community is complemented by the centripetal direction of intimate relationships that has the function of making the solipsistic solitude of the individual mind tolerable (cf. Meltzer, 1971) and unravelling the depths of each one; at the base of both directions lies the mystery of intimacy. The mysterious character of intimacy refers both to the inner thoughts, affections or affairs of a person, family or community and to the unconscious dimensions that make it possible. For Meltzer and Harris (1976), "intimate" means something "*essentially internal, and unknowable to anyone except himself*" (p. 435), but the intimate (from Latin: *intimus*: "innermost") can only be known through the mediation of an internalised other. I think it is no exaggeration to say that attempts to answer the question of what is deepest within ourselves and to unravel that very close relationship we call intimacy run through the history of psychoanalysis.

Intimacy, which enables the creation of the inner family, which allows us to discover ourselves, which is sustained in dialogue with internal objects, and which is not offended by the privacy of others, is nourished by emotional experiences and the containment of conflicts between subjects and objects. In speaking of emotions and conflicts, I want to avoid the possible confusion of believing that intimacy is defined exclusively by loving, tender feelings, as can happen between lovers; such a conception would indicate an omission or denial of the interplay of links and anti-links, as formulated by Bion. A more precise characterisation of an intimate relationship is one in which both participants constitute themselves as mutual containers, which through reverie make possible the development of the bond that makes them grow as persons and as a couple (conjugal, paternal-filial, scientific, analytical, friendly, etc.); that is why I believe that the intimacy that allows the development of the personality and of interests that transcend the couple itself is the one based on *aesthetic reciprocity* with a predominance of the K link.

This way of understanding intimacy differentiates it from casual relationships or activities constrained by contracts or the constraints determined by the basic assumptions (Bion); i.e. protomental functioning where personality development is not possible. It is likewise necessary to differentiate between intimacy and *complicity* because in the reciprocity of intimacy, development is aimed for, whereas complicity refers to the triumph of a third (external or internal) who is marginalised. Once again, intimacy differs from *collusion* because the latter is an unconscious defensive organisation in the service of avoiding the reintrojection of split-off aspects that have been deposited in the other couple member.

Although psychoanalysis has dealt with the areas of personality involved in intimate relationships, with exceptions such as Erikson's (1950), these have not been given a prominent place in research, which is why I was surprised when Meltzer[2] proposed intimacy as one of the three dimensions for understanding the structure of personality (see Section 3.1). To visualise structure, he proposed a *first dimension* that included structures characterised by denial of psychic reality and living in the external world incapable of introspection and thinking; structures characterised by splitting processes; those defined by the use of intrusive identification; those characterised by uncontrolled and objectless emotionality; and perhaps one could also include people trapped in the delusional system, outside the world of objects, such as schizophrenics. The *second dimension* of defining structure considers the degree to which people live in intimate relationships, tied to the family structure or, conversely, to analyse whether they are people living in groups, in a diffused group identity, operating by tropism and oscillating between basic assumptions. The *third dimension* investigates thinking and its disorders, i.e. whether thinking can be used to relate to others. I think Meltzer would agree that the third dimension is a derivative of the first. But, this proposal, which gives a prominent place to intimacy, made me wonder whether the dimension of intimacy might not be a significant and powerful sign of adult development and might encompass the other two dimensions.

In order to better understand the world of intimate relationships, it is useful to contrast it with those relationships characterised by group functioning in which the subject neither uses thought (third dimension) nor feels responsible (first dimension). As Freud (1921) explained in Group *Psychology and Analysis of the Ego*, responsibility is placed on the group and the leader is given the task of leading, whether they are general or a cardinal. The unconscious aim is to achieve results according to the pleasure principle, i.e. without effort, without work, without pain; that is how groups governed by the basic assumptions function. However, when the family is presided over by responsible internal objects, it functions as a working group. In contrast to that mode of functioning, the family gang operates as vandals presided over by intolerance of frustration and a thirst for revenge. Another example of a group with defensive functions is the pubertal same-sex group, where, through mutual projective identifications, the fragmentation of the self is sustained. A common feature of these different groups is that symbolic development, as well as intimate relationships, are severely hampered. One of the conditions for these groups to function, as driven by negative tropism, is the absence of clear boundaries between the components of the group, sustained by the massive use of narcissistic identifications.

3.3.1.1 Distance

Boundaries and distance are fundamental conditions for intimate relationships. If the distance between two objects is excessive or non-existent because they overlap, it is impossible to establish a relationship. In the gestalt combination of Rubin's vase, we doubt between seeing two faces or a vase, but if the lines were superimposed or excessively distant from each other in such a way as to prevent comparison, we would have no doubts. Doubt, like relationships, needs distance; and for intimacy, isolation is as damaging as fusion, for "*these two limits, more like east and west than the ends of a spectrum, tend to meet at the antipodes, since fusion in one direction imposes isolation in all others*" (Meltzer, 1971, p. 261). In order to relate to each other, it is necessary to find the proper distance so that neither dissolving fusion due to too much proximity nor freezing in isolation due to too much distance occurs. Schizoid patients are an example of the difficulty of finding the optimal distance. Those who cannot separate themselves from degraded internal objects also suffer, as expressed by Felipe, an adult who spoke to me about his panic about women whom he desires but who, when they approach him, feels them to be like giant bats[3] that stick to his chest, terrifying him; this condemns him to impotence and loneliness. Those who have been sucked into the madness of paternal objects also suffer, unable to develop an intimate life because an omnipotent and omniscient father controls the family's movements. We also observe the importance of distance during the clinical encounter, for example, when we move in our chair and this causes our voice to move towards or away from the patient, and the patient responds as if feeling invaded, raped, beaten, or abandoned, etc.; this is why some patients do not tolerate the couch or vigilantly stretch out, interpreting the slight variations that often go unnoticed. Meltzer also used the concept of distance as a technical device to differentiate between areas of the patient's personality when he spoke to

> the adult part of the patient's personality or one or more infantile structures, or a more generalized class of object of which some part of the patient is a member (men, children, babies, etc.), and these may be referred to in the past, present, or future.
>
> (Meltzer, 1976, p. 380)

Optimal distance, adequate proximity, and geographic contiguity are names that point to conditions for the development of intimacy. The name proposed by Meltzer (1971, p. 262) of "geographic contiguity" suggests the geography of the earth and the organisation of borders between continents and states. The construction of borders and gateways has valuable consequences for psychic reality; we could almost say that this would be the greatest achievement of any process of growth and development, among other reasons, because only by respecting borders can we establish authentic relationships. But all relationships in the external world are contaminated as a consequence of projections, just as internal objects are affected when "their boundaries of inviolable individuality and privacy" (Meltzer, 1992a, p. 59) are not respected. When these boundaries are transgressed, confusion emerges, as happens with babies who have

> difficulty in constructing their boundaries if their space of intimacy is not respected, since jouissance, like pain, when boundaries and thresholds are crossed, have in common the fact that they lead to confusion and not to the required process of separation and individualisation.
>
> (Schaeffer, 2006, p. 145)

Crossing the boundaries of our intimate space as well as our bodily intimacy creates confusion because, for every person, adult or infant, the orifices of the body are sacrosanct "because we attribute to these entries the significance of portals to the internal world" (Meltzer and Harris Williams, 1988, p. 68). By projection, the borders of states take on the significance of boundaries of the self that are felt to be invaded by all those who enter uninvited, such as illegal immigrants, easy support for the projective identification of the rejected aspects of the self.

In the organisation of the personality, there is an object with a special, foundational significance; I am referring to the combined object of whole objects functioning as a working team (Bion) (see Section 1.2). Achieving introjective identification with this object will be the result of a long process, leading to an adult structure of the personality in which this identification will precede the self in its capacity to think, will be the basis of creative mental functioning and a model for intimate relationships:

> Gradually, owing to the mysterious process of aspiration towards the excellence of these evolving internal objects, the adult portion of the personality—says Meltzer (1991)—may emerge and manifest itself in the area of its passionate interests and in the desires of its intimate relationships. Its joyousness takes shape in the work of building the family of private life and contributing to the gradual evolution of the human family.
>
> (p. XVII)

Such joyousness, accompanied by a certain fear for the split immature aspects, is present in the relationship of comradeship[4] between the parental objects. To understand what "comradeship" means, we can turn to what Meltzer describes when referring to the relationship between analyst and patient in the therapeutic alliance; for him, it means "to abandon themselves to the adventure of pushing beyond therapy for the patient's psychopathology into the unknown of character development for both" (Meltzer, 1973b, p. 304); for me this is comradeship, something that goes beyond pragmatic goals, the achievement of benefits, to venture into the discovery of new aspects of the life of the mind. I think that image gives a sense of the way in which internal objects continue to evolve as long as their comradeship is lovingly respected and their intimacy and mystery are not interfered with by those outside the chamber (cf. Meltzer and Harris Williams, 1988, p. 83).

Conflict arises when the envious, jealous, and negativistic infantile parts do not tolerate the comradeship of the combined object; then

> when this love is lacking and the mystery and privacy are seen as secrets of power, the chamber becomes a fortress [...] The place of this creative intercourse, so prosaically called the parental bedroom, is the locus of awe and wonder in the internal world.
>
> (Meltzer and Harris Williams, 1988, p. 83)

Thus, this mysterious place where meaning is generated is degraded and comes to be considered by the infantile parts as the seat of an aristocratic and unjust conspiracy. Then, the private world ceases to be synonymous with intimate space, preserved from curiosity, and becomes a space governed by the concept of property, with the owner being able to dispose of it without any consideration for the external or internal object. Soon the sinister place of the cloistered family appears on the horizon, according to which everything is permitted within the walls of private property. Recognition of the combined object and its privacy, with the stubborn claim that the only reality is the external one, is distant. Gone, too is the child's task of deciding why the parents have closed the door to their room, whether they have done so "for reasons of secrecy or privacy" (Meltzer and Harris, 1998, p. 326). Far away is the need to look inside oneself and, through imagination, decide the reasons for privacy and so unravel the secrets of the meeting between the parents.

Children's curiosity about sexuality, intimacy, and parental privacy is revitalised by hormonal development, and when puberty arrives, the task of resignifying the sexual, private, and intimate life of the parents has to be faced once again. I believe that the mystery of the Holy Trinity, of such significance for Western Christian culture, reflects the founding conflict of the psyche: that of the child versus the mystery of the parents. Resolving it is a pretension with uncertain results. But even if the adolescent feels them to be the master of sexuality and from their possession sets out to solve the mystery, "the secrets of the sexual life of the parents can only be discovered through falling in love, and you can only fall in love through processes of identification" (Meltzer and Harris, 1998, p. 326). Such a process involves renunciation and mourning, and that offends adolescent omnipotence. So, if instead of "relinquish an object of desire in the external world and make a move towards internalization" (Harris and Meltzer, 1976, p. 440), one turns to concrete, sensual experiences and soon discovers that the resource of excitement is insufficient to conquer the impregnable bastion of the longed-for intimacy. Thus begins a class struggle against those who are considered to be the undeserving private owners of goods (house, money, sex, etc.). This pushes the adolescent into "the political concept of family life [...] which conceals a complete confusion between privacy and secrecy. This constitutes the core of the denial of psychic reality" (Meltzer, 1989, p. 199). The recourse to masturbatory arousal and invasion obliterates the difference between private-intimate and secret along the way. The confusion arises from the failure to distinguish that secrecy, like complicity, refers to a public, external space, and the belief that secrecy would be something that parents would wear to arouse the child, subjecting them to passive contemplation. The private-intimate, however, refers to functions of the inner world (cf. Meltzer and Harris Williams, 1988, pp. 83–84), and the inner world is only accessed by the abandonment of the object and by identification. The border of the inner world requires mourning as a passport. With arousal, secrets are meant to be discovered, but the secrets of the privacy of the parental objects are only discovered through the imagination; for that reason, with the invasion, psychic reality is lost (cf. the first dimension for understanding the structure of the personality).

We began with the need for boundaries for the recognition of the object's privacy and a condition for intimacy, and we are in the space of rebellion where the object ends up being invaded, its merits denied, and creating a climate of confusion in the style of a *claustrum* where intimacy is not possible.

3.3.1.2 Emotions

Nothing is lost in our inner world; moments may be eclipsed, but the old longing for fusion with the object subsists alongside the most generous feelings. As Freud (1930, p. 6) said, "Our present ego-feeling is, therefore, only a shrunken residue of a much more inclusive—indeed, an all-embracing—feeling which corresponded to a more intimate link between the self and the world around it". We are seekers of objects and relationships… and the paths and results depend on many variables. One of the first conditions for true relationships is that "*the possibility of emotionality be fully experienced or accepted*" (Meltzer, 1971, p. 265). But experiencing emotions is not always a tolerable experience, as illustrated in *Aesthetic conflict*. This is why Meltzer (1992a, p. 57) suggested that

> …our innate response to the beauty of the world, that is, aesthetic receptivity, contains an integration of these three, positive links, L, H, and K, but that the pain of ambivalence combined with the need to tolerate uncertainty, makes it very difficult to hold these links together. The processes of unfolding bring relief by unfolding the links to separate objects, thus also splitting the self in its emotional capacities and experiences.

However, the dissociation of the self in order to tolerate contact automatically diminishes the quality of the encounter. If dissociation is extreme, if intolerance to conflict leads to renouncing the world of objects and taking refuge in the non-place of the delusional system, the conditions for the most absolute loneliness are created. Communication also ceases when a part of the self penetrates inside an object because the "disparity In the geography of phantasy, one inside and one outside an object, precludes understanding" (Meltzer, 1971, p. 262).

In the *Claustrum*[5] model, one can observe the ravages experienced by the parts of the self that invade the object. The consequences are different according to the colonised compartments, but they all have a common denominator: the absence of intimacy, "*an exile from the world of intimacy*" (Meltzer, 1992a, p. 72). Perhaps, it is the inhabitants of the rectal compartment who suffer most from "*the retreat from emotional links with other humans; the world of intimate, and therefore basically family, relationships*" (ibid., p. 151). These inhabitants, alienated from relationships, are trapped in pornographic objectification and anal quantification, with the parameters of money, time, age, and frequency of sexual relations, for example (cf. Harris and Meltzer, 1976, p. 21); but without any possibility of intimacy as illustrated in Beckett's play (1957): *Endgame*,[6] in which the central character, locked in a dingy room and cut off from the world, is terrified when the servant approaches him, or filled with rage when his parents, separated and locked in dustbins, show some mutual affection. As intimacy is excluded, when intrusive identification mediates, for Meltzer, there is also no intimacy within the head/chest compartment with all its omniscience, control, and possessiveness; there is no intimacy there, as illustrated by Oblomov (Goncharov, 1858), unable to fall in love or care about the external world, and only devoted to enjoying soft armchairs... In the genital compartment, the party is reduced to celebrating the phallus, which exhausts itself in the discharge and ends up depressed.

Lack of communication gradually arises when emotions are not tolerated and when whole or part objects are invaded, with the result that freedom, joy, symbolic development, etc. are sacrificed. Faced with this situation, Meltzer said "*the term 'intimate' human relationships, on the other hand, is the realm I wish to reserve for the emotional experiences that set thought in motion*" (Meltzer et al., 1986, p. 18). Consistent with his family model of personality development, he placed intimate relationships as the basis of the generation of meaning:

> An emotional experience is an encounter with the beauty and mystery of the world which arouses conflict between L, H and K, and minus L, H and K. While the immediate meaning is experienced as emotion, maybe as diverse as the objects of immediate arousal, its significance is always ultimately concerned with intimate human relationships.
>
> (ibid., p. 17)

Only in emotional and intimate relationships is it possible to find meaning in the interplay of emotions. To summarise, we could say that the predominance of intrusive functioning leads to impoverishment of the self, damage to the object, and disruption of symbolic development, as in symbolic equations (Segal), whereas the tolerance of emotionality and aesthetic conflict within an intimate relationship creates the right setting for the birth of symbol, thought, and adult personality development.

Just as we speak of the parts of the self that are removed from intimacy because they are installed in objects, we must also point out the opposite movement, when working to recover the lost aspects of the self. Not infrequently they are recovered in moments of rest and holidays or when we have temporarily left our usual spaces, occasionally burdened with immature, infantile projections. I agree with Meltzer (1971, p. 263; my square brackets and italics) when he says that

> ...intimate contact is often made through sallies outside the accustomed sphere. Bad parts of the self all too often invade the sphere of good objects, especially during times of separation or stress, to subvert and lead astray the infantile parts of the personality. Conversely, sallies for reclaiming the apostate [the parties that abandoned fidelity to the good objects] *or converting the heathen* [those who still do not believe in good objects].

When we separate ourselves from the usual place and tolerate distancing ourselves from issues that had absorbed us, new vertices can be found to un-cover the object that had been lost or blurred; but distance is not achieved only by putting kilometres in between. We can also rethink the complicated initial subject in a new light in the space of the dream world, in conversation with a friend, in dialogue with a supervisor, or by letting the issue rest.

3.3.1.3 Trust

The task of recovering lost or not yet achieved aspects, that of discovery, or that of thinking, etc. entails a heroic attitude that can only be accomplished if there is firm support, solid trust in the internal objects that encourage us in the endeavour; moreover, such a task can only be accomplished under their inspiration. It takes courage not only to recover lost aspects but also to go out to meet another person, to shed the protective armour of intimacy, to undress oneself for the encounter with that other who is always unknown in their mystery and intentions.

> one of the chief items in men's distrust of the aesthetic impact of women relates to the motivation behind their 'beautifying'. Is it a manifestation of vanity? Is it predatory? Or can it be trusted as a function of their generosity?
>
> (Meltzer and Harris Williams, 1988, p. 74)

this reminds me of the suffering and fears of Felipe (see Section 3.1.3.4; see Section 3.3.1, note 1), my patient, who claims to have "antibodies to intimacy" because he is always afraid of being abused; he fears both women, whom he feels are like blood-sucking bats, and men, with whom he avoids any relationship. But these fears are frank projections because he is a person who, under a strange and compulsive generosity, often functions as a vampire. Perhaps, his fear of being invaded drives him to be an invader, but the result is always the same: living in terror and isolation. I believe that this fear is not exclusive to men, nor is it always as exaggerated as in my patient, but I consider it to be a question that arises regarding the mystery of any object. It is true that we do not cease to be

> …intelligent herd animals trained from birth onwards through our aptitude for primitive identification processes (imprinting, adhesive identifications, mimicry, etc.), and are thus creatures encased in a social armour of great conservatism
>
> (Meltzer et al., 1986, pp. 14–15)

that distrust new objects. But to further pursue the experience of intimacy and of a new object entering this world we share, we need a state of mind capable of tolerating ignorance and what Bion (1970) called a negative capacity. When one lives in darkness, any light whatsoever dazzles us. Accompanied by an object, however, we overcome the fear of walking down unknown paths. What sustains the search for an object and the aspiration towards intimacy is what M. Klein (1959, p. 248) called unconscious oneness

> based on the unconscious of the mother and of the child being in close relation to each other. The infant's resultant feeling of being understood underlies the first and fundamental relation in his life.

However,

> ...the amount of trust derived from earliest infantile experience—says Erikson (1950, p 224)—does not seem to depend on absolute quantities of food or demonstrations of love, but rather on the quality of the maternal relationship. Mothers create a sense of trust in their children by that kind of administration which in its quality combines sensitive care of the baby's individual needs and a firm sense of personal trustworthiness.

In Felipe's case, the maternal function that brings together sensitive care with trustworthiness was lacking, as the maternal object has appeared in his associations as an irrational, impulsive woman, capable of biting her son or hitting him with sticks. However, when the experience of the maternal object has been acquired or recreated, enriched by the link with the paternal object, and the feeling of trust was made possible, then the basis for communication and the adventure of discovery was created; because, as Meltzer said "the aegis of trust that the internal breast raises in psychic reality evokes an aspiration and a striving in friends and lovers towards unreserved communication" (Meltzer, 1971, p. 280) just as it happens in intimacy, where there may be plenty of words, but where there is always time to unveil new mysteries and develop new bonds. I believe that the trust in the first object, the introjective identification with the combined object, plus the aesthetic experience in the K link entail

> ...a very powerful impulse to share—says Meltzer (1987, p 560)—the apprehension of beauty with at least one other mind. For this reason, the emotionality of the K link has the same generative power with respect to the work group as L and H have to the formation of the family. When the K link arises within the parental couple linked by L and H, their relationship to the children takes on a new observatory and thoughtful quality, which makes the family into a work group and protects it from its tendency, under stress, to revert either to a gang or basic assumption organization.

As I have already pointed out, when the attributes of the combined object have been solidly established in the internal world, it becomes a model of intimate relationship; that same object pushes to emulate it; that is, it stimulates a relationship as intimate and creative as that of the combined object.

The longing to share, the fear of getting lost in the vehemence of the intimate encounter, and the danger of isolation recall Erikson's (1950, p. 237) formulation when in *Childhood and Society*, he described the vital crisis between "Intimacy and isolation" in the following terms:

> Thus, the young adult, emerging from the search for and the insistence on identity, is eager and willing to fuse his identity with that of others. He is ready for intimacy, that is, the capacity to commit himself to concrete affiliations and partnerships and to develop the ethical strength to abide by such commitments, even though they may call for significant sacrifices and compromises. Body and ego must now be masters of the organ modes and of the nuclear conflicts, in order to be able to face the fear of ego loss in situations which call for self-abandon: in the solidarity of close affiliations, in orgasms and sexual unions, in close friendships and in physical combat, in experiences of inspiration by teachers and of intuition from the recesses of the self. The avoidance of such experiences because of a fear of ego-loss may lead to a deep sense of isolation and consequent self-absorption.

I believe that this description of the intimate bond of the young person who embarks on the experience of forming a couple and a family captures the terms that characterise intimacy:

- "*fuse his identity with that of others*" although without becoming confused with the other, but rather maintaining discrimination.
- "*commit himself to concrete affiliations and partnerships*" i.e. transcend the pure and passionate encounter[7] that to a certain measure would be expressed in the intimate and erotic encounter, to give oneself over to the adventure of a mutual discovery.
- "*to be able to face the fear of ego loss in situations which call for self-abandon*", relinquishment and tolerance of persecutory anxiety as opposed to the desire to share.
- letting oneself be led or the "*inspiration by teachers*" in the form of the combined object that one wants to emulate.

3.3.1.4 Intimacy in Infantile, Perverse, and Adult States of Mind

We have looked at the pillars on which intimacy is founded: the subject-object differentiation, the introjection of an object that is sustaining, and the introjective identification with the combined object that incites us to recreate its intimacy. I believe that we are now in a position to take another step forward, and differentiate what is meant by intimacy according to the predominance of infantile, perverse, or adult states of mind, bearing in mind that there is a bit of a saint and a madman in all of us; as Klein (1959, p. 262) reminded us: "nothing that ever existed in the unconscious completely loses its influence on the personality".

The most central concept related to infantile states that differentiates them from the adult state of mind is their very close relation to the body with its sensations

and urges or Impulses. Sensuality and action are therefore their most characteristic modes of experience and participation in the world.

(Harris and Meltzer, 1976, p. 438)

this formulation gives words to a fundamental characteristic of infantile mental
functioning: that of seeking sensual gratification without any consideration for the
object; for that reason, infantile parts often confuse intimacy with sensuality. Such
confusion leads to object-seeking for direct sensual/sexual gratification, ending
when the goal has been achieved. In infantile functioning, the object has value
as long as it is present; if it comes immediately, if it satisfies the infant, and if it
withdraws without asking for anything in return. However, intimacy does not take
place when only the pleasure principle regulates the encounter with the object. The
immediacy of the relationship with objects is illustrated in Alex's suffering—an
adult homosexual who suffers from not being able to establish a relationship with a
partner; he is trapped in a childish mode of functioning that depresses him because
he feels less and less desire, and the search for excitement through pornography
increases his uneasiness, while the impossibility of intimacy increases his despair.
Alex believed that "intimacy could be measured by the intensity of sex" and complained that using condoms in *fellatio* does not increase intimacy because it "takes
away from senses and smell"; he demanded his partner's orgasm on his face to
"find intimacy". Alex's desperate search for intimacy is thus driven by the infantile
model, whose very base is sensorial, immediate, and quantitative.

In the *latent* state of mind, it would seem that great intimacies would develop,
but in reality, it is almost impossible for intimacy to develop because of the great
difficulty in experiencing and accepting emotionality. In the face of inner conflicts,
the latency child—says Meltzer (1971, p. 265)—is

being-unable-to-mean-anything-in-particular. It is the bourgeois position,
which, if we were to speak sincerely, would have to say, 'I'm in favour of the
winning side' [...]—Meltzer continues saying, with irony, that this—can be the
basis of very great intimacy, as one sees in groups, religions, political parties

because in this state of mind, hypocrisy reigns, and the outcome is societies with
little space for intimacy, weighed down by snobbery, and so hierarchical and arrogant, where the world is organised into two opposing realities: us who are so cool,
and them, so beneath us.

The feeling of fusion—as observed in *pubescent* groups—is a consequence of
projective identification, in which the boundaries of the ego disappear, and one has
the feeling of forming a union with the other, an extraordinary intimacy; this is observed, for example, in the emotional state following intensive psychotherapeutic
group experiences from which one emerges with the feeling of having extended the
boundaries of the self to the point of feeling that one is part of a "wonderful us" or
that one has created great friendships or had profound, intimate encounters. Didier
Anzieu (1975) calls it "the group illusion"; such encounters are nothing more than

an illusion and far removed from an experience of intimacy. It is rather an experience of excitement resulting from the momentary loss of the limits of the self, which widens until it encompasses everyone and creates a confusion of identity based on mutual projective identification, something akin to a *folie-à-deux*.

For "understanding to exist, direct contact is necessary" (Meltzer, 1971, p. 262), whose condition of possibility is the overcoming of geographical confusions, for, without direct contact and differentiations, there is no intimacy. This is a feeling from which the parts of the personality that live in intrusive identification, such as the inhabitants of the *Claustrum*, are excluded.

> ...the part of the personality [...] in its life in the claustrum [...] in its unhappy state, faced with problems of survival, devoid of trusting and intimate relationships, shorn of the capacity for autonomous symbol formation and therefore of the ability for creative thought, in constant danger of being detected as an interloper and arraigned for trial and expulsion into "nowhere", the ensconced part of the personality must balance this misery with certain pleasures.
>
> (Meltzer, 1992a, p. 121)

The pleasures of the intruder are grandiosity (Tabbia, 2000a) and the belief that emotion is excitation; that is why in *perverse* states of mind, the aim is to achieve intimacy through excitation, as is revealed by some homosexuals that become depressed when they discover that love or intimacy were only passing excitations. Triumphant complicity and the illusion of "unity of mind" (Meltzer, 1973a, p. 111) in the perverse experience do not let more than disillusionment and despair pass through, because once we go through the door, the trap closes behind us.

The *adult* part of the personality arises from introjective identification with good objects and therefore it is natural that the greatest degree of adult intimacy manifests itself in relationships where dialogue made of words and silences, generosity, respect, non-violence, freedom, the ability to share pain and joy, interests, and curiosities and where losses are tolerated predominate. Intimate discourse between parents, and between parents and children, dialogue between friends, or the dialogue between patient and analyst are all based on two pillars: "*identification with the combined object of psychic reality and the realization of a suitable partner for conversation*" (Meltzer, 1971, p. 281) with no limits. This identification has a double outcome. On the one hand, it is the condition of the possibility of adult sexual intimacy, as Meltzer (1973a, pp. 67–68) says:

> The foundation, in the unconscious, of the sexual life of the mature person is the highly complicated sexual relation of the internal parents, with whom he is capable of a rich introjective identification in both masculine and feminine roles. A well-integrated bisexuality makes possible a doubly intense intimacy with the sexual partner by both introjection as well as a modulated projective identification which finds its place in the partner's mentality without controlling or dominating.

The other consequence of the identification with the functions of the internal parents is that it constitutes the condition of possibility of symbolic development insofar as both objects function as mutual containers of emotions, as a function of reverie. The identification with the combined object will have very significant consequences for the adult structure of the personality because it will be a source of inspiration (ego ideal), allow the development of thought, give psychic bases to sexual identity, be the foundation of mental stability, make the work group possible (Bion), and manifest itself in adult intimacy.

3.3.1.5 Julio's Dream

This introduction to intimacy that I have given up until now is not far from being considered a criterion for mental health and the development of the personality in the direction that Meltzer (1967, p. 22) showed in *The Psycho-analytical process* when he said that

> the resolution of this configuration of object relations stands as the border between mental illness (psychosis) and mental health, just as the resolution of the obstacles to the dependent introjective relation to the breast traverses the border between mental instability and mental stability, and as the passing of the Oedipus complex leads from immaturity to maturity.

The second dimension that Meltzer proposed in order to visualise the structure of the personality has great diagnostic and prognostic implications; he said that it should be described whether people live in intimate relationships, linked to the functions of the family structure, or, to the contrary if these are people who live in groups, in a diffused identity within the group, operating by tropism and oscillating between basic assumptions. I believe that a person who is able to have intimate relationships under the parameters we have outlined will be able to orient their life under the aegis of the combined object that suggests the way, and that they wish to emulate; they will be able to develop an internal family, transcending the community. On the contrary, a person who has serious difficulties in achieving such introjective identification will lack genuine criteria elaborated in internal dialogue and will be at the mercy of the slogans provided by propaganda, depending on the environment to orient themself in life, with the danger of disintegration if they lack another to serve as a model to imitate or reject. The world of fanatics, cults, fashion consumers, and the pubescent/adolescent community often walks in the partial light provided by an enlightened one. The fear of catastrophic change paralyses them and holds them in a pseudo-mature existence, as it did for Julio.

Julio was a young man who was organised around a verbal capacity with which he seduced, but which ended up generating boredom because his words lacked real meaning; his gestures and precisions seemed professional; but so much pseudo-maturity made him feel like an object in the hands of an older couple with phallic characteristics, based on solid and recognised scientific knowledge.

Julio's loneliness was remarkable. His parents had separated many years ago; the father had been trapped in a sterile, aristocratic mentality that prevented him from managing his own economic reality; the mother, however, was able to reorganise her emotional and working life. Most of the therapeutic work with Julio consisted of dismantling his pseudo-mature armour, always supported by some idealised part object that served to sustain him by means of making demands; thus, he was able to organise a strike in his workplace, fight for the recovery of missing children, or promote the strengthening of cultures in possible decline. His demands were not absurd; on the contrary, the way he committed himself was absurd. A healthy infantile part allowed him to find support in parental objects that rescued him.

The revitalising of the paternal object went through diverse stages that, worked through in the transference, allowed us to analyse from his oedipal rivalry to his feminine position. The differentiation between reality and fantasy with respect to his father permitted him to achieve a more adult-like relationship with him.

Julio found himself in a compromising situation in the middle of a long-term crisis in his relationship, and divorce was under consideration when his wife became pregnant, which precipitated the return of both members of the couple to their country of origin, his wife departing first. For the duration that he stayed in this city (Barcelona), he ran into (on the internet) his first girlfriend from adolescence, a girlfriend who had frustrated him sexually, and brief but torrid moments of cybersex were established over the distance separating them.

Julio's dream was as follows:

> I was in a room with high ceilings similar to those in my office, where Carlos and Eva were. In front was a television and something else that was turning rapidly, like a spinning top, that, as it slowed down, looked like Ménem[8]; Julio, who was standing behind next to Carlos and Eva, pointing at the TV said to them, 'that's Ménem, what a moron!', with a great deal of anger.

Let us look at some facts and associations to comprehend this dream better. Carlos and Eva, a couple, were friends who generously and supportively took him into their home, where Julio felt at ease.

When Julio was a teenager, he had ambivalent feelings about Ménem because, on the one hand, he admired him for the women and cars he had and for the *dolce vita* he lived, while on the other hand, he rejected him because he had ruined the country. Julio explained that in Argentina they do not call Ménem by his surname because it is said speaking his name brings bad luck, so to refer to him, they use Julio's surname, which I will leave out for discretion's sake. I think Carlos and Eva represent the parental function of the analyst. Carlos is my name, and I think Eva represents the maternal function. It should be noted that Julio came to therapy through his mother's efforts. The reference to the generosity of his friend's partner referred to the feeling of gratitude to the analyst who was able to accommodate his finances in order to make treatment possible for him.

The dream can be understood as two conflicting models of intimacy.

The revolving image that appeared on the television represents the self-exciting, masturbatory resources (oral—a talking tongue—anal, and genital), which deceptively contained him as in an autistic spinning that generated a perimeter (an external border) and prevented him from spreading out, but which, in reality, impoverished and isolated him, as if he was inside a glass tube (television screen); I believe that this functioning we see, based on arousal, represents the image of intimacy that the adolescent has before falling in love. At that moment, intimacy is excitement and exhibition, presided over—"President" Ménem—and sustained by part objects represented by cars and women. This motor and autoerotic defence was first transformed into a visual image which could then be "named" and given a surname—"Ménem"—but, that name connected him with an object that was still partially devalued and gave him "bad luck": it ruined his country-mind.

I believe that the couple made up of Carlos and Eva in the dream represents the adult level of functioning as manifested in the capacity to observe and wait for both objects differentiated and interrelated in an intimate and creative bond.

The internalisation of the combined object—Carlos-Eva—which is placed between the stimulus (on the television) and Julio's mind, allowed him to differentiate between his immature adolescent aspects and the mature ones, these being represented by the friends who took him in, in external reality, and the analytical relationship.

The confrontation between the two types of functioning—adolescent/adult— was linked to the doubt between returning to an old story with the first girlfriend and thus avoiding facing paternity, or assuming it, something he was also looking forward to. Ménem, also called Carlos, condenses the name of the analyst and Julio's surname, supporting the denigrated paternal transference, becoming a threatening internal object. Ménem would then be the anti-Carlos/analyst, representing the combined couple's adversary. Thus, an intimate relationship of collaboration-creation (Carlos-Eva) is contrasted with that of a possible filicide[9] (did Ménem-Laius have his son murdered?). This conflict makes it difficult for him to assume paternity (will he be like Carlos/Eva or Carlos Ménem/Laius?) and pushes him into his pseudo-mature defence: making speeches about his upcoming paternity, which sound more like rationalisation than the reverberation of a sincere desire.

In Julio's dream, two forms of tropism appear: the excitement and vertigo of the cars, as opposed to the K-based tropism of the combined object; between the two, there is tension. It is the tension derived from the danger of the permanent threat to the relationship of intimacy by the irruption of the Ménem parts, that part of the object that is not in a link with the combined couple but, split and projected, remains in the breech, like the psychotic or perverse parts, always ready to eclipse the combined object. Just as the relationship of intimacy can be threatened by the possible irruption of split parts, like Ménem in the dream, there would be another way of eclipsing that relationship, and it is the one that would manifest itself in those in which there is an absence of tension or denial of distrust; this could be seen as a perversion of intimacy such as the one that would manifest itself in some analytic relations, in which the analyst does not exercise their function, but creates an illusion of proximity, ending up in disillusionment and boredom. On the contrary, an authentic analytic encounter is often both astonishing and frightening because, in the interplay of links and anti-links, an intimate, passionate relationship emerges, for which courage is needed. As Meltzer (1971, p. 280) put it, the psychoanalytic method

> ...which dares to throw two strangers together in the expectation of their having a thousand or so hours of Intimate, spontaneous, emotional conversation, not to mention therapeutic benefit to patient and scientific or technical advance for the analyst. And the wonder of it is that they do eventually achieve a dialogue of endless interest, which must finally be relinquished by both of them.

A dialogue of endless interest that surprisingly takes place in a corner of the working group in an atmosphere of comradeship, where, as I said, there is generosity, respect, non-violence, freedom, the ability to share pains and joys, interests, and curiosities, where losses and limits are tolerated, and where longing is welcomed. Such a dialogue of endless interest is possible in the context of intimate relationships, founded on the resolution of the conflicts intrinsic to the first and third dimensions proposed by Meltzer for the study of personality. I believe that we can now take up the three dimensions and affirm that they not only serve to understand the structure of the personality but are also fertile, as he said, to understand the psychoanalytic therapeutic method, which, by studying transference and counter-transference moves in the direction of psychic reality, thought and communication, and intimate relationships.

3.3.2 Passionate Kindness[10]

At the beginning of this volume, García Márquez's (1985) novel *Love in the Time of Cholera* came to mind, in which he narrates Florentino's perseverance in love; I believe that the association arose not only because of the reference to the necessary perseverance when it comes to affection, but also because of the reference to the time of cholera and, among several questions, it stimulated the following: is it possible to love in times of cholera? I distinguish cholera from anger, but it becomes particularly difficult to develop loving relationships in both cases. More precisely, I wonder if it is possible to love in difficult times, in times characterised by relativism and confusion of values. When young Pablo says "in my generation there are no strong bonds and everything is uncertain", he expresses the same sorrow and scepticism as Rosemary in *A Memoir of the Future* (Bion, 1991a, p. 178): "I believed a man and his promises once. I don't now, but I did once. I didn't die, but something died in me–mentally". Pablo refers to his generation as being as disenchanted as Rosemary; both share in the disenchantment despite belonging to a generation that has had few restrictions on experiencing relationships, although more appropriately, it could be said that they have been able to consume more sexuality but, perhaps, have not experienced as much intimacy as they would have wished;

sexuality has often been divorced from love. So much so that some adolescents and young people, Pablo among them, may feel sex—in Meltzer's words (Meltzer and Harris, 1998, p. 331)—as something

> ...so undervalued and disappointing that they no longer fall in love. That's why their relationships, even when there is marriage and children, have a strong fla- vour of impermanence. The tolerant attitude towards sex confronts them with a method of selection of the companion that, in a certain sense, is a checklist method; it is cold, and it is an accommodating arrangement, which contributes to its provisional nature.

When relationships and sexuality are overrated, reiterated frustration is all but guaranteed because, perhaps looking for love, they find only excitation, discharge, sensual pleasure. This does not prevent them from searching, but suffering repeated disappointments that increase their distrust and despair. Bauman (2003, p. viii) describes this clearly when he says:

> ...are men and women, our contemporaries, despairing at being abandoned to their own wits and feeling easily disposable, yearning for the security of togeth- erness and for a helping hand to count on in a moment of trouble, and so desper- ate to 'relate'; yet wary of the state of 'being related' and particularly of being related 'for good', not to mention forever—since they fear that such a state may bring burdens and cause strains they neither feel able nor are willing to bear, and so may severely limit the freedom they need [...] to relate....

They are as fearful of committing to a relationship as being left out of them. This can translate to an avid search of relationships with a variety of different results depending on the state of mind of whoever is doing the exploring, which would leave room to discriminate "where the line is between licence and freedom", as Robin questioned (Bion, 1991b, p. 409). Thus, in a certain sense Meltzer (Meltzer and Harris, 1998, p. 321) would respond to Robin by pointing out the need to dis- tinguish, in these difficult times

> ...between freedom and licentiousness. The relatively healthy teenager feels free to experiment with sexuality; the more disturbed teenagers feel that 'any- thing goes'. 'Anything goes', as in Cole Porter's famous 1920s song *Anything Goes*, the era of girls with short skirts and hidden breasts who thought only of having fun.

Nevertheless, fun in these choleric times where "anything goes" does not necessar- ily lead either to joy or to falling in love; on the contrary, it often leads to despair, as what happened to Pedro, who longed for the encounter with Antonio back in Madrid, with whom he quickly made love, but then declaring: "now I feel tired, I go to bed at 5 p.m., I'm very fragile, perhaps an encounter with another man upsets me a little, but with Antonio I was so happy; the second day I met him I told him 'I love you'". The urgency of the encounter is called love. The same urgency to establish relationships is frequently observed in desperate patients, who often experience an intense dependence in the transference and on external objects. In this sense, what happened to Raúl is eloquent—Raúl who, showing the lack of unity of mind and the ferocity of his greed during the psychoanalytic session, could express desires to take possession of the object that was present by expressing with words, fantasies, and gestures the desire to take possession of me, the desire to eat/bite me, to suck me up through his eyes, to penetrate me anally with an ambivalent penis as, occasionally, he could carry a sharp sword inside him, or to tear off/eat my penis/nipple so that it would be his alone and not be given to any other patient, etc. But all these fantasies could alternate with requests or pleas to be held as if he were a child about to disintegrate… anything was possible when it came to the anguish of feeling or being left alone. The longing for a possessive fusional relationship, and thus the avoidance of a personal relationship, can also make evident his fear of an intimate relationship with an object that is present. Anything goes to avoid an intimate relationship, as Meltzer points out (Meltzer and Harris Williams, 1988, p. 29, my italics):

> The impact of separation, of deprivation—emotional and physical, of physical illness, of oedipal conflict—pregenital and genital, of chance events, of seductions and brutality, of indulgence and over-protection, of family disintegration, of the death of parents or siblings—all of these derive the *core of their significance* for the *developmental* process from their contribution as aspects of the underlying, fundamental process of *avoidance of the impact* of the beauty of the world, and of *passionate intimacy* with another human being. It is necessary for our understanding of our patients, for a sympathetic view of the hardness, coldness and brutality that repeatedly bursts through in the transference and countertransference, to recognize that conflict about the *present object* is prior in *significance* to the host of anxieties over the absent object.

In this sense, the impatient Raúl preferred to eat the object that was present, rather than relate to me and then digest the thoughts that had been produced during the analytic encounter, which alternates with necessary and painful separations. In these difficult times, with so much loneliness, longings, and fears present in our meetings, many questions arise, some of which are: what are some of the conditions for a "passionate intimacy"?, and why is it so hard to fall in love?, and, approaching the realm of psychoanalytic practice, what becomes of the emotions between both participants of the analytic hour? An initial approach to such questions might involve adding others, such as: from where do we set out to look for objects? Now depending on the starting points, we will find objects that will make development possible or, to the contrary, that will guarantee frustration and disappointment.

"We are animals activated by curiosity" (Bion, 1991a, p. 177) because we are always struggling to find meaning in our lives and because we need to know where the objects we will need to feed us, love us, and/or transcend us are. We seek objects that occupy the place that our unconscious assigns to them. In this sense, right from the start, we seek someone who is able to satisfy the need for infantile dependence. This need, because it is attached to impulses and basic needs, may cause us to lose objectivity, stimulating us to look at objects more in terms of what benefit they can provide us with than sincere interest in discovering the other, that other's internal world, or its mystery. Being anchored to needs, the infantile past, or resentment, can eclipse the understanding of the present because of the mind being "...so stuffed full with 'memories' there is room for nothing more" (Bion, 1991b, p. 393). An outcome of a biased look at the past can confuse the domain of psychoanalysis, as mentioned by the character

> P.A. ...my party is not past times. Always the mistake of thinking that the past is the property of psychoanalysis; the past is the property of Regret. Regret is a guest at the psychoanalytic party, but it is not the host; nor is psychoanalysis the domain of regret.
>
> (Bion, 1991b, p. 406)

Stating that psychoanalysis does not belong to the past does not mean denying its importance. Quite to the contrary, the fundamental tool of psychoanalysis would be lost: the transference; with such a statement, the aim is to demonstrate the need to explore the transference with the end result of being able to explore the "foundation of truthfulness in our relation to the world" (Meltzer and Harris Williams, 1988, p. 205). For this veracity, which makes us adult subjects, to be achieved, the transference must be seen as

> ...an externalization of an internal object or situation, [that] falls into two great categories, infantile and adult. In analytic work we are concerned chiefly with the infantile transference. But there are no inconsiderable number of people who, in the course of childhood, have accepted the disillusionment in their omnipotent-omniscient expectations of parents without a significant loss of love for them. What has happened is that the infantile transference has been replaced by an adult one, whose maintenance the parents must continue to deserve by their actual qualities.
>
> (ibid., pp. 38–39)

When the infantile and adult transferences are recognised, "the creative potentialities residing in the structure of the mind, with its basis in 'thy will, not mine'" (ibid., p. 205) will be able to develop and therefore an investigation of the relation to the world of people and objects can become passionate, taking into account

> ...Wilfred Bion's great formulation of the emotional links, of their origin in the impulses to love, to hate and to know our objects, and ourselves, rescues us from the impotence of quantitative modes of thought about emotions. It enables us to see that passion is not a matter of intensity, but rather of integration of these three impulses when confronted with the impact of objects, and, again, of ourselves.
>
> (ibid., p. 205)

Passion becomes the condition of the possibility of discovering our true relationship to the world, whereas anti-links will create pandemonium—that world where confusion and coldness reign.

When passion is mentioned (see Section 3.3.1, note 5), it is often compared to falling in love, but it should be pointed out that passion can coexist with love as well as with hatred or knowledge; in this sense, the passion of the scientist and the hatred of the paranoid person are clear examples. Passion is an intense inclination or great liking for a person or thing, but when referring to love, it is important to establish its relationship and differentiate it from sexuality because they can be considered synonyms. In this sense, in *A Memoir of the Future* (Bion, 1991a, p. 183, my italics) the following point is made:

BION   ...Becoming sexual is part of physical maturation. *Real love* is not a *function of the thing loved, but of the person loving.* That is part of psychical or mental maturation and is not obstructed by *accidental features* of the thing or person loved.

MYSELF Amongst these features that you call 'accidental', are you then including that which we call the *sex* of the person?

BION *Certainly*; sex applies to anatomy and physiology and, as is usually the case when we talk of the mind, has been taken over by the psycho-analysts because we have to make do with a language invented for physical life or 'sensuous experience'. *'Passionate love'* is the nearest I can get to a verbal transformation which 'represents' the thing-in-itself, the ultimate reality, the 'O', as I have called it, approximating to it.

ROLAND Then you think Alice could love me?

BION If she is correct about loving Rosemary, she is *capable of loving you*. That does not mean that she would want to be with you, either for an ephemeral episode or for life, or for anatomical or physiological purposes.

The person who loves is *capable of loving* an object irrespective of its accidental features, among which the sex of the person is mentioned. But the capacity to love passionately will have the limitations inherent in the characteristics of the person who loves; it is therefore worth questioning the different types of intimate and loving relationships because, for example, the utilitarian relationship centred on the search for objects that meet unconscious needs is not identical to the loving relationship of someone who is more concerned with the well-being of the object while at the same time repulsed by the slogan of *anything goes*.

3.3.2.1 Intimate Relationships

A criterion useful in differentiating between different types of intimate relationships in which love also can develop is that which is based on "infantile", "narcissistic", or "adult" states of mind. The coexistence of direct manifestations of these states in the very same subject, independently of their chronological age, or in a couple, makes the description of a broad range of feasible relationships possible. Implicit in this type of discrimination is the supposition that, the greater the dependence on internal objects, the greater the subject's autonomy, whereas the opposite translates into a person greatly lacking an adult state of mind being more dependent on external realities, just as could be deduced from the opinion of "P.A.: ... If she cannot depend on herself, she would be unwise to depend on anyone else" (Bion, 1991b, p. 400).

Both love and intimacy characterise a close relationship that develops in privacy, i.e. within the sphere of private life that one has the right to protect from any intrusion. Love, like intimacy, is dependent on the type of relationship established between the objects and the quality of the objects themselves; this implies that there are different types of loving and intimate relationships dependent on the dominant personality structure, and bearing in mind that beyond structures and momentary evolutionary states "nothing that ever existed in the unconscious completely loses its influence on the personality" (Klein, 1959, p. 262). It is therefore appropriate to differentiate various personality structures, because depending on these, it will be possible to discriminate between different forms of relationship.

In order to designate *infantile* functioning of the personality, from birth till adolescence, a time in which the subject is greatly dependent on the family group, it would be wise to point out that the world is organised around idealised objects— the very same family, in the centre of which are the parents. The periphery and strangers are assigned the function of a repository for the bad aspects of the split ego and objects. This organisation of the personality is characterised by its instability,[11] where the processes of projection and introjection fluctuate in accordance with the tolerance to pain, and that

> ...since infantile structures, unlike the adult self, are bound directly rather than indirectly (through identification) to the impulse life and its primitive emotionality, eschewing of psychic reality produces the matter-of-fact, reality-bound, calculating, and adaptive quality of character that we read as 'shallow' for its lack of imagination, insensitivity to others' feelings, and materialism.
>
> (Meltzer, 1971, pp. 201–202)

When this type of attachment (materialistic, concrete, utilitarian, pragmatic, superficial, etc.) to objects predominates, a type of communication tends to occur that can be characterised as

> ...urgent, direct, and sincere communication, both of emotion and concerning emotion. But since the part in control [of consciousness] changes very rapidly, taken over a period of time the communication may seem so full of contradictions as to approximate hypocrisy.
>
> (ibid., pp. 264–265)

which generates surprise at the fluctuating nature of communication. This state of mind produces a kind of passionate and intense encounters like flares that burn out in a short time and—once the passion has passed—are forgotten in an instant. This leads to searching for and consuming encounters that could be described as bulimic functioning. Just as happened to Pedro with Antonio, to whom he confessed his love on the second day, but soon after, he was alone again, longing to find another man with whom he could repeat those passionate encounters... This urgent need for objects does not characterise a true intimate relationship where the other is loved and towards whom there is a feeling of fidelity in affection, but rather it designates a relationship based on the imperious need to alleviate a momentary situation. This does not exclude that the child can feel real loving feelings towards the figures on whom they depend, but the ambivalence generated by dependence itself, as well as the choice of object makes loving feelings and intimate relationships unstable.

We could name various ways of elude infantile anxieties associated with loneliness or the feeling of helplessness that could result in the denial of psychic reality and emotional life itself, which is conducive to a type of relationship that is far from the experience of intimacy as Fisher (1995, p. 87) states: "This denial can lead to a flattening of emotional experience and a relating to the external world as well as to the partner in a 'matter of fact' way". This can be observed in some couples that do not seek psychotherapeutic help "to regain some contact with each other emotionally, but for assistance in re-establishing the denial of emotional reality, which has somehow broken down" (ibid.). Some couples tolerate cohabitation while a relationship based on pseudo-intimacy is maintained. This could repeat itself in psychotherapeutic relationships where the patients' messages are not recognised or taken up by the analyst.

In contrast to the transience of infantile states of mind anchored in oscillating projective identifications, one can mention the "stability" of states derived from identity confusion, characteristic of *narcissistic* states of mind. The pleasurable (manic) sensation derived from identification with idealised aspects of the object, as manifested, for example, in omniscient states, carries as a guaranteed counterpart the impossibility of the experience of intimacy. This is because the prerequisite for experiencing intimacy is that of subject/object discrimination, a differentiation that is prevented when the relationship is based on narcissistic identifications. Any authentic contact with the world is hindered when one lives in a state of intrusive identification (Tabbia, 2000b) because by living inside another, one only has contact with the world through the invaded object, as one discovers in the pseudo-existence of the snob. But, the manic state of mind derived from narcissistic identification functions as a defence against the fear of dependency implicit in all loving and intimate relationships. Living intrusively entails the impossibility of experiencing first-hand events and generating a sense of certainty and omnipotence. People with these sensations can dazzle and fascinate subjects anchored in infantile states of mind. Combinations of both functionings can lead to "very close" couples, who seem to live an idyllic intimacy, but in reality, each member of the couple lives in another emotional world, where the defence against loneliness and intimacy is collusively agreed upon. An example of this type of bond is that of those couples who live in their own and others' idealisation, among which we could point out those that Meltzer (1971, p. 262) named as a *dolls' house* type relationship where each one feels wonderful, loves themself, and feels loved: "I love me, and you love me". Another type of relationship that would appear to be intimate is one where one partner lives in intrusive identification with an idealised object, which allows them to function as a secure, firm, authoritative yet non-mental person, while the other partner remains fixed in a dependent, infantile type of functioning, behaving obediently, albeit with a secret life, but calling their partner *mummy* or *daddy*. This is not to be confused with the functioning of couples where one partner functions as a container for the other partner's anxieties. The digestive function of one of the partners, capable of metabolising the anxieties of the other, does not characterise a narcissistic relationship, as long as this functioning is temporary, since it is characteristic of a truly intimate relationship to function as a mutual container.

The relation between container-contained is a good model to illustrate an intimate relationship where in an alternating and flexible manner, the members of the couple carry out a mutual function of reverie. But to achieve *adult* functioning and become capable of establishing an intimate bond, a requirement would be that the personality structure rest predominantly on introjective identifications with whole objects. A couple develops an intimate relationship when both of the members allow themselves to become inspired by the combined object of each one of them. When I say predominantly, I am referring to the fact that identifications temporarily predominate, even though I would like to point out that integration is a process in continual construction/reconstruction, functioning with internal objects acting as lights on a never-ending path. The sense of identity, although recognisable, is in constant transformation, as can be seen from the following text: "…the adult sense of identity derives from the introjective identification with parental figures and is fundamentally bisexual, although an individual's *integration* may not *have proceeded so far as to enable* bisexuality to be *experienced and acknowledged*" (Meltzer, 1973a, p. 86; my italics).

In intimacy, based on a relationship characterised as typical of the depressive position, the other is respected and recognised as an object to discover. Counterposed to the belief in omniscience that claims to know what is happening with the other person, in the depressive position, the other is always a continent full of mystery, like the unconscious of every subject. The person who renounces omnipotence, omniscience, and control of the object also experiments feelings of gratitude and humility before the possibility of being surprised by the mystery of the other person, this mysterious thing-in-itself. This does not mean that one cannot take recourse in communicative projective identification to investigate the object's states of mind, but far from the goal of domination and exploitation. From the state of mind of someone who feels calm in their innermost being, they tolerate, in turn, the curiosity of others and the inevitable turmoil in intimate encounters because they are confident in the foundations of their personality.

At this point, we can take up again the following text: (Bion, 1991b, p. 400) who said: "P. A.: …If she cannot depend on herself she would be unwise to depend on anyone else", to say, inversely, that the condition for adult dependence is that of depending on internal objects… which makes access to the experience of love possible.

3.3.2.2 On Love

Nevertheless, in speaking about passions, it would seem necessary to define *love*, a challenge which exceeds this book. An approach, however, to the subject can be taken through some of the dialogues between characters in *A Memoir of the Future*.

Based on previous differentiations, we could consider that in *narcissistic* relationships, two situations come about: on the one hand, a debasement of the object, while on the other, the pleasure of perceiving oneself to be idealised would exist. Thus ROSEMARY (ibid., II, p. 365, my italics) could possibly feel that ALICE "… *weighs heavily—dependent—* as if she looks to me for help […but at the same time states:] I find *her fascination very agreeable*".

From this narcissistic position, it is difficult to establish a relationship of trust, in much the same way that dependence becomes intolerable, as can be seen from the dialogue between ALICE and ROSEMARY (ibid., p. 367, my italics):

ROSEMARY […] Did you trust Roland—with me I mean? […] I wouldn't have trusted him an inch…
ALICE I was young—and in love.
ROSEMARY My Mum warned me that if ever I was such a damned fool as to fall in love, she'd chuck me out of the house. […] Fancy thinking I would be in love with Man—or her! She hasn't learned that *love makes clear thinking impossible.*

But just as amorous passion would prevent thinking, the subject—infantile/narcissist—has to be vigilant in order to keep control of the world: "I can't—says ROSEMARY—*waste time on her—I have enough to do to keep Man in his place. It's asking for trouble to let him get the upper hand*" (ibid.), appealing, for that goal, to whatever lies and pretence are necessary, as ROSEMARY goes on to say: "I shall be *terribly* upset of course" (ibid.), blaming Man for his own sterility.

It is easy to be manipulated when you have low self-esteem. In that state, you can become confused about your feelings, as happened—according to P. A.—to ROSEMARY and ALICE who "…was hungry [for love] and you were hungry, so it was not surprising that you were both vulnerable—susceptible to the seduction of physical sex […] Neither of you knows the slightest thing about love…" (ibid., p. 368).

Hearing this, ROSEMARY reacts with hurt feelings and the following dialogue is established between them (ibid., p. 368, my italics):

"*ROSEMARY* Excuse me, I do. I know a lot more about it than you do. I know what you and Roland and Robin and that boy thought they were teaching me. I learnt that their love was not worth much.

P.A. Yes, you may have learnt what 'worthless' love is, *but that isn't love*. In the catalogue it may go for love [...] No doubt your collection of predators go for 'lovers'; your love may be of much the same *predatory* kind. You haven't said or done anything / call love.

ROSEMARY You are a stickler for good English. *How do you define 'love'?*

P.A. I don't. [...] 'Love', in so far as it relates to the past, is a ghost of a memory; as to the future it is a hope casting its shadow before. 'The thing itself—

ROSEMARY Yes, I hoped you would get to it in time—

P.A. I must disappoint you. As a psycho-analyst I cannot aspire to success where the Saints, Philosophers, Artists of every kind have not succeeded.

ROSEMARY You can try.

P.A. I know what you mean, but it is not a domain in which 'effort' is applicable. [...]

ROSEMARY Do you think mankind will ever achieve it?

P.A. It has nothing to do with Past, Present or Future. *'It' has been, is, and will be.* Psycho-analysis, or preaching, or painting, or music are not 'it'—they are *'about' it*.

In this dialogue, love is differentiated from predatory relationships, attributed—from a resentful and narcissistic position—exclusively to men. But although love cannot be defined, as philosophers, saints, and poets have failed to do, it is an experience that can be accessed through identification with parents who have been able to love each other, and from this past, project light and shadows onto the future. In order to discover what love is, it will be necessary to give up the childish belief that adults can do everything[12] (as expressed in ROSEMARY's challenge: "You can try"), which is why P. A. suggests that in this field, neither effort nor voluntarism is worthwhile, but that *the mystery of love can only be discovered through passionate experience*. The distinction between *the experience of love* and speaking *about love* is thus established. This distinction is valid for all passions: it is one thing to talk about them and another to experience them.

In the same way that ROSEMARY's mother warned against the experience of falling in love, threatening to throw her out of the house, falling in love continues to be a universal and unpostponable need, but it is necessary to differentiate between *love based on interest in the other person, and the bestial love* that ROSEMARY described (Bion, 1991a, p. 38):

> I couldn't stop your beastly husband making what he, in his beastly way, called "love"—his "beastly" love—to me. I used to laugh at his horrible, mawkish, shop-soiled, left-over love, though of course his public school education, his gentlemanly education made it impossible for him to conceive that his skivvy—your skivvy—could see through both of you.

Bestial love, cloying, and incapable of recognising the object's intelligence can be translated in many ways, although in all of those, ignorance and the lack of respect for the object coexist. An instance of this type of relationship is in *Jerónimo*'s dream, a wealthy adult who, at the time, usually missed sessions with no awareness of the meaning of his actions, which often were reduced to something concrete. In this dream "he entered some houses through a window and robbed men's watches; in a room, there was someone in the shower, who had no idea what was going on, so he robbed watches". Although he could hear my interpretation, he could not comprehend that the payment of the session was not enough to be responsible for the treatment he was giving the relationship. The meaning of mistreatment in the setting, degraded and turned into a kind of anal orifice that he could penetrate with no respect, could not fit in his mind; it was impossible for him to understand that the temporary container of the sessions had been debased. In the dream, however, he warned that someone in the house was not aware of what was happening, surely referring to the fact that I was not sufficiently aware of the pillage that the analytic relation was undergoing and that therefore if anyone were responsible for the theft, it would be the distracted analyst. The association between ROLAND's cloying love and Jerónimo's dream arises because, in both, objects are abused and disregarded as if they were only toilets where he could relieve himself.

Faced with ROSEMARY's mother's distrust, or ROSEMARY's own contempt for certain manifestations of love, or the invasive conception of the relationship present in Jerónimo's dream, one could counterpose the *passion of the adolescent* capable of *venturing into love* with an incipient depressive background that makes them capable of loving even the object's faults, of forgiving them, and even heroically trying to fix them. This is reminiscent of the case of another young man who fell in love with a girl who was in a symbiotic relationship with her mother and who, in love, threw himself, without success, into rescuing her from such a prison. I will transcribe below a dialogue between Meltzer and Martha Harris because it describes the experience of love in adolescents, something that could be generalised to any love relationship, regardless of the age of the participants; Meltzer (Meltzer and Harris, 1998, p. 140, my italics) begins by saying that

> One of my preferred ideas, in the measure that we are taking into account the depressive anxiety of these adolescents, is that they participate a lot, not only in the pain, but also in the suffering of others. They are, therefore, in a certain sense, constrained in assuming a therapeutic role in relation to the depressive anxieties of others, as with their own. When this happens, it would seem as if they'd assumed the role of the jester. These people possess a *great capacity to love, and they persist in their lives and development* faring quite well. One of my ideas concerning adolescents, and in connection with their capacity to love, is that they experience it as a position of extreme vulnerability—as concerns humiliation, and they consider that whoever falls in love is stupid. *The adolescent who can tolerate feeling stupid for having fallen in love is at the beginning of their adult life. [...]*

Martha Harris asks Meltzer "if the adolescent's suffering—that means forgetting their own self-esteem in order to *place themself at the disposition of all*

of the suffering that's implicit in loving someone or something—is the essence
of the depressive position. This would suppose abandoning omnipotence and
omniscience and leaving control of the object to one side.

D. M.: The ethics of this group of adolescents is to concern themselves for
those who suffer, that were not successful, that don't take risks, because the
depressive position is being in contact with the tragic element of life".

The vulnerability of ALICE and ROSEMARY, who could succumb to seduction
because they lacked love, was pointed out above; now vulnerability is again mentioned in relation to the fear of venturing into love experiences..., but those who
do not feel vulnerable may be moored in childish/narcissistic omniscience and
omnipotence, or because they are anchored to internal objects. Introjective identification with whole objects generates the feeling of confidence that allows for the
adventurous and free experience of love, sexuality, and hopefulness in groups; for
this very reason, those adolescents who are capable of falling in love are in solidarity with the suffering of those who do not yet venture into love experiences.
Just as the adolescent on the road to adulthood is capable of taking an interest in
the other, giving up omnipotence and omniscience, and abandoning "object control", as Martha Harris used to say, the *healthy* adolescent is capable of venturing
into love, that indefinable emotion before which philosophers, saints, and poets
have stumbled. But even if it is difficult or impossible to define love, this is not an
insurmountable obstacle to mentioning some of the *effects of love*.

3.3.2.3 The Effects of Love

One of the consequences of love is that it *transforms* people who are in love, just as
Alice states in dialogue with the character BION (Bion, 1991a, p. 183):

ALICE: (looking at ROSEMARY) I've been transformed into something, and this,
    if you'll forgive me for saying so, would depend on me saying: 'I'm in love'
BION: Or maybe you've managed to be loved.
ALICE: No, I love Rosemary.

Love transforms relationships, like the one that ALICE and ROSEMARY established, because it has the ability to transform something strange into something
extraordinary. This is how Meltzer (Meltzer and Harris Williams, 1988, p. 39) tran-
scribes what he considers to be the marvellous description that Stevenson gave of
falling in love, and the transforming effects it has in the lives of those who have
fallen in love:

Falling in love is the one illogical adventure, the one thing of which we are
tempted to think as supernatural, in our trite and reasonable world. The effect
is out of all proportion with the cause. Two persons, neither of them, it may be,

very amiable or very beautiful, meet, speak a little, and look a little into each other's eyes. That has been done a dozen or so times in the experience of either with no great result. But on this occasion, all is different. They fall at once into that state in which another person becomes to us the very gist and centre-point of God's creation, and demolishes our laborious theories with a smile; in which our ideas are so bound up with the master-thought that even the trivial cares of our own person become so many acts of devotion, and the love of life itself is translated into a wish to remain in the same world with so precious and desirable a fellow creature.

Being in love has a certain diffusive capacity because it moves one to feel that everybody should be in a similar situation, as if wishing to transform it, improving everything one does to the point that "the lover begins to regard his happiness as beneficial for the rest of the world", in Stevenson's words (ibid., p. 40).

Both the experience of *loving* and that of *being loved* provoke in both partners the desire to know the other, because love encourages *reciprocity* based on the relationship between different elements. This means that the other becomes a mysterious continent that one wishes to discover and fears invading. This raises the choice, not always clear, between knowing through imagination or unknowing through intrusion. A shadow that hangs over those in love is that "deeper knowledge of oneself will inevitably cool the passion of one's beloved" (ibid., p. 39), as if the doubt of being worthy of being loved lingers. Although these fears may coexist, nevertheless, what produces "…the (most pleasant) surprise (in the world) is that being in love has an astonishingly ennobling effect on one's character, that is, on one's view of the world and fellow human beings" (ibid.); to this, I would add that it *ennobles* one's view of oneself by feeling chosen by the loved one, by receiving that love. Furthermore, as well as ennobling, it *revitalises* because it is quite possible that, in the choice of object, there has been an attempt to repair early traumatic situations, to repair the ravages sometimes created by the pathology of the paranoid-schizoid position. Just as feeling loved ennobles and allows the transformation of the subject's own state of mind, repair based on love stimulates *creativity* which, at the same time as it repairs the external world, repairs the internal one. The *diffusive* effect of falling in love *repairs* both members of the couple, whether it is a couple in love, a maternal-filial relationship, therapeutic, or of another nature.

Revitalisation and reparation introduce *hope* in those situations where no horizons were in sight. Love would be—as I have already mentioned—the antidote for those

> …men and women, our contemporaries, despairing at being abandoned to their own wits and feeling easily disposable, yearning for the security of togetherness and for a helping hand to count on in a moment of trouble, and so desperate to 'relate'.
>
> (Bauman, 2003, p. viii)

An antidote because love rescues the beloved from anonymity and makes them extraordinary. What is revitalised, revalued, and recovered is the potency that was hidden, perhaps, under depression and the fear of feeling discarded.

I would not be able to end this limited enumeration without mentioning that love awakens feelings of responsibility towards the beloved, just as the fox told the Little Prince that one must be *responsible* for the rose one has tamed (cf. Saint-Exupery, 1943).

A synthesis could be made to differentiate loving relationships from circumstantial relationships, based on infantile or narcissistic mental functioning, which could be stated as "goodness, beauty, strength, and generosity replace in esteem the initial enthralment to size, power, success, and sensuality" (Meltzer and Harris Williams, 1988, p. 1). The former characterise parental functions, where the integration of bonds allows the development of *passion*, that passion which has to be made "available for all the suffering that is implicit in loving someone /or something" (Meltzer and Harris, 1998, p. 140), whereas the latter (size, quantity, etc.) respond to the dissociation that hinders the development of passion and facilitates more infantile, concrete functioning.

3.3.2.4 The Clinical Relationship

Psychoanalysis is based on a relationship in which links and anti-links interplay and are updated in the space of the clinical encounter. In that territory, each member of the encounter lives a particular experience, similar to what Meltzer conceptualised as *aesthetic conflict*,

> most precisely stated in terms of the aesthetic impact of the outside of the 'beautiful' mother, available to the senses, and the enigmatic inside which must be constructed by creative imagination. Everything in art and literature, every analysis, testifies to its perseverance through life.
>
> (Meltzer and Harris Williams, 1988, p. 22)

In "every analysis", in every clinical encounter, the conflict between obtaining data through the senses and/or through the imagination is re-enacted. Of all the impacts experienced in the aesthetic conflict, I am interested in focusing on certain conditions that the analyst must have or sustain in order to carry out their clinical work.

It can be assumed, legitimately, that the person who requests a consultation comes with the need to rediscover or find a path that leads to the development of their personality. What is the psychoanalyst looking for, or what do they bring to the encounter with this stranger in front of them? What is required of the analyst? It is assumed that the analyst is identified with the parental functions (see note 20) and that they are willing to lend themself to an interaction that makes such a development possible, allowing themself to be used to "help them with their anxieties" (Joseph, 1989, pp. 111–112). But letting oneself be used with intentions? In this respect, Meltzer (2004, p. 443, my italics) thought that the psychoanalyst is not being asked to

...have any ambition in relation to the patient; nor are they expected to experience any conquest made by the patient as a reward. All that is required of them is to pay attention with *interest* and to tolerate the uncertainty, the disappointments of the patient. The burdens imposed on the analyst are the sacrifices of parenthood in this particular form.

Described in this way, it becomes quite clear that what is required of the analyst is that they work with *passion*, passion for the work. And that is not the same as passion for the patient. It is merely a passion that generates a kind of imaginative relationship with regard to the patient and the patient's development. It is not even necessary that the analyst like the patient. However, it is necessary that they be able to imagine the patient becoming a kind and admirable person in the future. That is all that is demanded of parents: that they are able to make a kind of *selfless sacrifice for the sake of the development* of their children, based on the *imagination of their growth and development.*

Working with passion within an imaginative relationship that transcends anecdotes is something that becomes a pole of attraction for the patient. If this disposition meets the states of deprivation and orphanhood that always remain as a consequence of the ambivalence of the first relationships, or the need to re-work problems of more adult dependency, then the conditions for a clinical relationship are created. However, one of the problems that arise is the degree of the analyst's readiness to establish a *passionate relationship*, in which their feelings are engaged. In this respect, Meltzer (ibid., pp. 446/447, my italics) said that

...for many years, until very recently, analysts tended to believe, or at least to say, that the analyst should not show their feelings to the patient. The fact is that they cannot avoid showing both their feelings and their lack of feelings to their patients. Moreover, either the feelings they show or the lack of feelings they show are an *immensely important factor in the analytic relationship*, just as they are in any human relationship. If we want to panic a baby, it is enough to look at it with dead eyes. To provoke panic in a patient, all that is needed is to talk to them in a dead voice. Prolonged silence has the same effect as talking to them in a dead voice. Then there really is no possibility of hiding feelings, or the lack of feeling, from the patient. Clearly, the conclusion is that the analyst has to pay close attention to feelings, recognising that they are communicating them.

...This causes a terrible difficulty: distinguishing between showing feelings as *action* and showing feelings as *communication*, and this differentiation is very difficult to make in relation to oneself or anyone else. The differentiation really lies in the *motivation*. When feelings are shown in order to make an impact on the other person, you are not communicating; you are doing *propaganda*. Furthermore, of course, it is a great danger for the psychoanalyst to lose the position of communicating and end up doing propaganda for the patient.

Working passionately implies being so in touch with the feelings derived from transference-countertransference that the only way to establish analytic contact with the patient is to formulate them in words, tones, and rhythms, as Meltzer outlined in *Routine and inspired interpretations: their relation to the weaning process in analysis* (1973b) and in *Temperature and distance as technical dimensions of interpretation* (1976). However, the distinction between action and communication is clear and timely because, in action, it would be more a matter of discharge without metabolisation, whereas in communication, it would have undergone sufficient transformations to become symbolic messages carrying meanings suitable for development. This result requires the collaboration of both participants in the clinical relationship, and this primordial collaboration takes the form of *curiosity*. When both contribute their curiosity, uncontaminated by arrogance or intrusiveness, a passionate encounter occurs, such as that between a brave and honest patient who observes their inner self and offers it to the analyst, and an analyst who is able to return a meaning based on communicative projective identification with the patient's infantile states and introjective identification with their own internal objects that inspire them. When dialogue and exchange with these characteristics occur, such an encounter can be called a *loving relationship*, capable of tolerating pain when obstacles to communication make their presence felt. Such a *passionate relationship* necessarily arouses admiration in those who hear about it. It is the same admiration that is felt for those in love. The same admiration experienced for the loved object and for the love of the method that enables the analytic relationship, stimulates introjection, the desire to care, and the development of both. So, when the analyst's loving curiosity meets that of the analysand and both are willing to participate in the creation of understanding, one is faced with a relationship that exudes *passionate kindness*, in Stevenson's (1881, p. 25) felicitous expression: "... the essence of love is kindness; and indeed it may be best defined as passionate kindness". A passionate kindness that is not limited by the sexual characteristics of the protagonists of the relationship. In this sense, the differentiation made in *A Memoir of the Future* (Bion, 1991c, p. 546) is appropriate: "men are similar to women, and women to men. That is the problem stated in terms-correct terms-of biological sex. We try to show people there is more to passionate love than simply the activity-contact-between genitalia". Then, freed from the constraints of language, Bion (1991a, p. 183) asserts that "'passionate love' is the nearest I can get to a verbal transformation which 'represents' the thing-in-itself, the ultimate reality, the 'O', as I have called it, approximating to it.", which in this case names *love*.

The essence of love, or passionate kindness, does not germinate alone. Love claims as much responsibility as that of cultivating a rose, as the old fox used to say, tolerating the process of its gradual discovery and avoiding straying into pure excitement and sensualism.

3.3.2.5 Notes from a Session

As an example of the different emotional states that occur in a session, which show the lack of integration of the mind and the coexistence of different states of mind in the same subject and at the same time, I will give a *summary* of a session with Raúl, the patient mentioned earlier who could not tolerate being separated from the analyst. Raúl's treatment allowed him and me to have experiences of great intensity that could be repeatedly analysed; the language used by Raúl shows the learning process that takes place in every treatment, especially if it is prolonged, as in this case. On this occasion, at the end of the first analytical week after the summer holidays, in which he was able to sustain himself without fear of disintegration and having maintained a certain friendly relationship with a young woman—Amalia— the following happened in the session:

> He began the session sitting on the couch; before lying down, he moved his neck around as if stretching, expressing that it hurt and that he had the sensation of having a slug stuck to his back, level with his shoulder blade, and that this could express his desire to be touched by the analyst, perhaps to be touched as his masseur touches him, rubbing him. Then, fully stretched out, he said that it was more like his grandmother's hugs; but more precisely, he said that his desire would be to play, to also play erotically, with his shirt off, that is to say, with skin-to-skin contact. Then came the memory of Amalia, whom he is beginning to feel he loves, although he still does not know if he is falling in love. He then asked if he could help Amalia with her difficulties in the same way as I am help-ing him. "When I have children, I will take care of them," he said, "as I have been taking care of him". Then he said, "I would like to look at you, to get to know you, to look at your hands, like a child playing with a big boob. Can you imagine how weird it would be to play with a big boob? But I am curious about you, and I also feel tenderness for you. I also think I would like to have sex". Then he said: "This weekend I'm going out to the country with friends. How many different facets I have! A baby who wants to be held in arms, a child who wants to play with a boob and get to know the analyst, a young man who wants to have sex, but I have to be patient with Amalia, whom I am just getting to know. I feel content. I can feel love here, and this allows me to feel love outside. I already feel like leaving. My friends and Amalia are waiting for me".

In this *synthesis* of a session that takes place with a partially hypomanic joy, Raúl was able to express different desires of his corresponding to the different aspects of his personality; from wanting to establish a *fusional, erotised* relationship with me—like the one he had with his mother—to a relationship based on *curiosity* re-garding the other, based on *tenderness*; in this session *sexual desire* appeared—in this case homosexual desire—but encountering their object outside of the analytic relationship, in heterosexuality, in Amalia, whom he is getting to know. Loving feel-ings appear. Sentiments that can extend throughout the world, so typical of lovers who *irradiate* their love. He is living a psychoanalytic experience where all of his desires are contained *without being seen as scandalous.* He is able to feel *a* desire to *care for* others, his children and his partner, in continuance of the task of *reparation.* The *playful* atmosphere in the session meant that there was no pressure or coercion (typical of *propaganda*), which facilitated the development of *passionate kindness,* which is why Raúl said: "I can feel love here, and this allows me to feel love outside. I already feel like leaving. My friends and Amalia are waiting for me".

3.3.2.6 *The Strong Woman Model*

Tolerating the turmoil of the love relationship, promotor of development, requires strength of character, i.e. dependence on the whole internal objects in a good rapport with each other. This assumption can be described and metaphorised by taking the strong woman described in *Proverbs* (pp. 31, 25–27) as a model:

> She is clothed with strength and dignity; she can laugh at the days to come.
> She speaks with wisdom, and faithful instruction is on her tongue.
> She watches over the affairs of her household and does not eat the bread of idleness.

The strength and grace that sustains the analyst in their ability to experience passionate kindness in the analytic relationship depends on the introjective identification with the combined object functioning as a task force (Bion, 1961), thus sustaining hope and not shrinking in the face of the pain and pettiness of relationships. Their tranquillity arises from the inspiration of their internal objects that guide them in moments of turmoil and disorientation, while at the same time helping them not to get overexcited by success and flattery. As they are supported by their inner reality, they emanate kindness and are able to experience passionate virtuousness by accepting, unsurprisingly, the anti-links. From this inner security, they can look and observe their inner house, and think about its inhabitants without exaggerating either the triumphs or the pain, allowing themself to enjoy the original development of its inhabitants who surprise them day after day and, as they are able to work in silence and with perseverance, they feel that they can eat peacefully and rest, because the house is in order, with the oscillations of living beings.

The "strong woman" can be a good model for the psychoanalyst who ventures to live clinical practices with "*passionate kindness*" in *difficult times.*

3.3.3 Placental Model of Intimacy

From the initial fragility and helplessness of human mammals, there is no greater yearning than to find an object who will become a container. While we were protected in the womb,[13] our life was spent entertaining ourselves by satisfying a continuous circuit of gratifications and games with no greater responsibility than respecting the mother's rhythms. Everything changed when it was time to leave the place we had conquered in the last months of pregnancy. Thrown into the world, we never stop wondering about the reason for the eviction, which is not always smooth. Surprise accompanied us during the eviction, but the longing for a return presides over our entire lives; we yearn to find an object that will rescue us from helplessness and loneliness, as Freud had said before (1926, p. 109): "the child's biological situation as a foetus is replaced by a psychological object-relation to its mother", or as Levy (2017) recently said: "In our life, we never cease to seek that comforting warmth of an intimate bond with another human being" (p. 208). An intimate bond that cannot be idealised either in foetal life or at any other time because intimate loneliness is consubstantial to human existence.

Just as we long after intimacy, it is not always achieved, as much because objects suited to being containers were not found, as of fear of establishing a confusing relationship with an object. Intimacy requires daily care, and above all, in the post-modern society where interiority is often devastated by exhibitionism, the unfiltered externalisation of private life, and the degradation of intimacy through social networks... I think that dependence on the object has been disturbed by social networks where it seems that you exist if others look at you, with the inevitable outcome of increasing addiction. The object does not become a transforming container and generator of interiority but instead epidermal support that makes identity superficial. Instead of identity, a "being fashionable" is generated, and in replacement of emotional bonds, excitation. When maternal care fails, or toxicities impossible to symbolise exist, the ego cannot integrate properly, ending up organised like a stained-glass window, which is not always well put together (Tabbia, 2004a). In this sense, Masud Khan (1979), referring to the ego of the perverse subject, compared it to a collage in which resistant and manipulative qualities coexist together with a terrifying vulnerability. Another way to refer to this conjunction is that which Bion (1957) pointed to with the differentiation between psychotic and non-psychotic parts of the personality. This differentiation of aspects of the personality, such as harmonisation and development, is subsidiary to the quality of the encounter between subject and object. In this sense, the dream of a patient[14] who did not find an object that was sufficiently containing is suggestive. Her mother had not taken care of her in infancy and instead gave her to a wet nurse:

> She is looking for a cosier home for herself and her children and is waiting for the estate agent to send her photos of houses. She receives a photo showing an erect penis; in the second photo, there is a sitting sow and a newborn piglet returning to the womb, passing through a large, wide open vagina, as if it were an upside-down delivery, but the movement to return to the womb has something masturbatory, sexually erotic; the head moves as if to stimulate orgasm, a paedophilic thing, filth, just shameful...

In the patient's associations, the penis was missing its testicles; the pig reminded her of the book by Orwell (1945), *Animal Farm*, where the animals carried out a revolution that ended up being even worse than in the world of humans. She said, "It is a defeat I remember with bitterness".

Based on my previous knowledge of this case, I believe that the erotised compulsion in which this patient was trapped at this stage of her life did not prevent her from dreaming and therefore from thinking that on this path, she would not find a containing object capable of sustaining her. She was able to recognise that she was on a path of defeat—a prefigured defeat in her dream because instead of finding a house/container, a penis with no testicles appeared—that is to say, a part object apt for excitation, but lacking the possibility of offering generativity; in this very same fashion, the pig's vagina did not offer access to a placenta capable of feeding her, but rather only sensory excitation. Thus, she was unable to find a welcoming home for her and her children. It was indeed a rebellion, but one that was ruled over by pigs, as in Orwell's novel. The model of relating and the coitus that appeared in the dream were of exhibitionism without contact, masturbation without acceptance, and intercourse without intimacy. In this sense, it would seem to be an example of what Massud Khan (1979, p. 24) calls a "charade of intimacy" where "a heightened maximal body-intimacy of orgastic nature" is created, with which to "avoid total ego collapse and an irreversible regression to psychotic states" (ibid., p. 28). Was the "filth" and the rejection expressed by the patient in the dream a warning of defeat or collapse? Was it a premonition? The fact is that the patient did not come to the next session because she fell down a staircase, losing consciousness.

The patient needed a "cosy" home for her and her children. I believe this is the requirement of all patients who go to see a psychoanalyst. What does this "cosy" task consist of? It consists of offering a *placental attitude* that transforms somatic or hallucinatory discharges into thoughts, that transforms actings-out into continence, excitations into bonds, transforming emotions into experiences.

Comparing the analytical attitude with the placenta enriches the understanding of the clinical task. In order to go deeper into this, it would be useful to point out some essential elements of the origin, structure, and function of the placenta.

The first characteristic to mention is that the fertilised egg creates the placenta for sustenance.

> Albeit commonly thought of as a mutual product, half maternal and half foetal, the placenta is in fact a tissue created by the foetus, differentiated from the endometrium, although deeply embedded in it. Even though it is created by the foetus, it behaves almost independently of it. Even in the womb there is no fusion between mother and foetus, nor is there an empty space between them, but rather a semi-permeable membrane of linkage and separateness.
>
> (Bergstein, 2013, p. 625)

The placenta (newly created object) is differentiated from the endometrium[15] (mother). This semi-permeable membrane is a "large surface for the exchange of different materials through the placental membrane, a very thin barrier between the foetal and maternal circulations" (Rev. Médica Electr., 2017). This membrane separates maternal and foetal blood.

> The main functions of the placenta include the exchange of metabolic and gaseous products between the maternal and foetal circulatory systems, and the production of hormones. It also ensures that there is no immunological rejection of the mother by the foetus.
>
> (ibid.)

This nourishing and monitoring function of the placenta is complemented by the reverse transport of metabolic waste from the foetus into the maternal circulation.

Similar to the foetus/placenta exchange, psychotherapy consists of a two-way movement: splits, confusions, denials, voids, and non-mental products of the patient seek a sensitive membrane in the unconscious of the analyst, who can return detoxified meanings suitable for emotional development. Bion called this function the capacity of reverie.

I want to highlight two characteristics of the placenta: one is that there is no fusion between it and the foetus, the other is that there is no space separating them. They are neither fused nor separated but united by a membrane so thin that it allows the *generative exchange that characterises an intimate relationship*. The placental membrane is equivalent to what Freud first called "synapse" and Bion later called "contact-barrier".[16]

When both members of the analytic dyad are able to create a bond that respects the limits of individuality[17] in the search for a truth that transcends them both, which Bion calls O, there is an emotional experience that can become passionate turbulence that affects both the patient and the analyst. There may also be no such turbulence or emotional experience in the clinical relationship, or worse; there may be a toxic functioning of the placenta by not filtering, or of the analyst by retro-projecting without metabolisation, or by making projective identifications of their own unconscious cores. But, starting from the assumption that the analyst's task is leading towards development, a contribution made by Meltzer (1973b) can be recovered here. He establishes a differentiation with regard to the analyst's engagement in his clinical work. Together with the patient, one can function as an expert who knows the way and leads the patient towards health with an emotional distance, similar to the scientist who knows their trade or the expert tour guide who leads through already explored territories. In contrast to this way of seeing the clinical experience, Meltzer proposes another type of encounter that also becomes an emotional experience for the analyst. This experience occurs when both members find themselves emotionally close to each other in the confines of a metaphorical placental membrane, where they risk getting close and moving each other. The condition is "an atmosphere of adventure in which comradeship develops between the adult part of the patient's personality and the analyst as creative scientist" (Meltzer, 1973b, pp. 300–301); venturing, as the foetus ventures, in full trust of the placenta and the adult in allowing itself to be colonised. It is an adventure with an uncertain end. Returning for a moment to the patient's material, she found a wet nurse who efficiently fulfilled her task, but who gave every sign of not having found a passionate mother. In this sense, not infrequently the psychoanalyst can function as a good wet nurse capable of giving fair interpretations, based on the observation of the material and supported by theory, but detached from passion and personal experience. Perhaps some interruptions and abandonments of treatment can be explained as much by a restricted understanding of analytic asepsis, as by the analyst's incontinence.

This membrane that separates and unites at the same time becomes even thinner when patient and analyst meet in the dream space with the task of analysing dreams. At that moment, the limits of both become blurred to the point of fear of confusion. A fear that can be circumvented when they feel impelled to walk behind that O of their own that hides behind the dream images. Mutual trust is essential. This creates an intimacy that is not restricted to looking at each other but "*looking outward in the same direction*", as the fox said to the Little Prince.

Focusing more on the clinician who metabolises beta elements by giving back alpha elements and who risks betas accumulating inside them if their own psychoanalytic function fails them, like placental insufficiency, I am interested now in referring to the analyst's dream screen or membrane. The dream screen fulfils a function analogous to the placental membrane. The analyst, as object/parent, has the responsibility to take in what the patient/foetus communicates: words, thoughts, images, emotions, and acts. When the patient relates their dreams, they do so by transmitting oneiric images, more or less armed, articulated, with more or less altered sequences, or baroque descriptions... Faced with this production, the analyst listens[18] and creates a dream, *their* dream, on their own dream screen. They assemble it from their *relative* neutrality, contributing their share of contamination that is impossible to discard. In the same way as in the placental membrane, the analyst's own elements enter into the exchange, which can not only be nutrients but also contaminants, despite the placental filter... This shared construction demands the subsequent work of *distinguishing one from the other*. Once the analyst has made this initial discrimination, they will have to allow and tolerate the emergence of evocations from their unconscious. The analysis of the countertransference and the intuitive function allow us to unravel the meaning of a relationship or a dream, which involves and nourishes both. Intuitions are hypotheses that will find their complementarity and meaning in the test of the (inner) reality of the patient's mind. Consequently, we are now working with rapport and empathy to eventually understand the fascinating phenomenon of introjective identification.

Summarising, we could say: "in the beginning", there was the patient's dream image recreated in the dream image of the analyst; one is thus at the first level, the most sensitive, that of the transformation of the unconscious. Later, when the analyst/placenta—tolerating the exchange—transforms it into word and meaning, there is an opportunity to experience companionship, the sincerest comradeship between the two participants becoming a *model of intimacy.* When the couple becomes intimately united, the truths of each one[19] and the truth of the intimate encounter are born.

Just as the placenta functions independently of consciousness and will, the therapist's emotional response is unconscious. In this unprotected and solitary situation, the analyst risks sharing part of their life with a stranger who will slowly become intimate, although *without sharing secrets*. In a certain sense, the intensity reached in the *intimate encounter with a patient* could be likened to the erotic and passionate encounter, where love (L) and hate (H) commanded by the desire to know (K) lead to that experience of intimate solitude. Thus, it is fair "to say that after satisfactory intercourse each partner is alone and is content to be alone. Being able to enjoy being alone along with another person who is so alone is in itself, an experience of *mental health*" (Winnicott, 1958) *and of intimacy with oneself.*

I have taken the turbulent and passionate dream encounter as a model of intimacy. It would be desirable for the clinician to be able to achieve a similar intimacy with those people who act out, who are verbose, or who settle into stubborn silences, etc. I believe that with the products collected from these generally distressing situations, one can try to produce meanings. The task would consist of collecting them and throwing them on the therapist's dream screen until images capable of evoking sensations, emotions, and occurrences can be constructed, in the hope that they can gradually and slowly be transformed into words that can be articulated in a meaningful text.

Only the plasticity of the placenta allows the development of the foetus. In psychoanalytic practice, only an attitude of maximum availability, nothing like that of the sow in the dream, will enable the development of a transforming container. The availability that every patient needs is that based on the fundamental principles of psychoanalytic theory (unconscious, conflicts, deficits, defences) and on the parental functions[20] (Harris and Meltzer , 1976, p. 36) of the container. However, without a little "madness"[21] on the part of the analyst, sustained by love and faith in the method of personality research, it is impossible to risk *intimacy with a stranger*.

The model of intimacy presented in terms of *the exchange between the placenta and the foetus* is also applicable to the *intimacy encountered in all couples* in which both members *find mutual nutrition and disintoxication.*

3.3.4 Intimacy in Analytic Work[22]

No one can deny that the analytic relationship is a "singular relationship" (Etchegoyen, 1986, p. 473), essentially complex and with specific intentionality. The complexity arises from the emotional currents and counter-currents present in every relationship. In that sense, analytic intimacy is not fundamentally different "from the transactions of any intimate relationship" (Meltzer, 1992a, p. 112). It is different, however, in that those emotions seek a thinker. It shares with other intimate relationships a certain constancy of relationship. What is extraordinary about the analytic encounter is its ability to bring together two "human beings who are together, hour after hour, day after day, for years" (Meltzer, 1984a, p. 135) with the intention of understanding, symbolising, and developing thought. It differs from other intimate relationships in that sexual intercourse is excluded, and physical contact is limited.

Although the body is present in all relationships, the transference relationship and the mind-to-mind contact are specific to the analytic relationship. The place of the body in intimate relationships varies according to whether it is, for example, a relationship between lovers or adolescents, or a relationship where the aim is symbolic development. Although physical contact is alien to the psychoanalytic method, this does not prevent it from being used "as a particular means to achieve contact between minds" (ibid., pp. 135/136), or to express itself as in the treatment of children or patients with serious problems with symbolisation. These singularities differentiate analytic intimacy from the intimacy of lovers, parents/children, or enemies.

I would be interested in pointing out some conditions of the development of analytic intimacy as a substratum of the transference relationship and the exploration of the unconscious. For this, we must start from the state of mind of each of the two participants of the analytic encounter, particularly the analyst. The analyst, because the responsibility for the conduct of the emotional experience falls on them.

Whatever the relationship established with the analysand, the analyst is supposed to be in a state of mind capable of participating in the analytic experience. This requires that it be authentic and sincere in order to be at one[23] with the reality of the patient (Bion, 1970, p. 28). The analysand usually comes to this experience with a state of mind that needs, at the very least, rehabilitation. The analyst is supposed to arrive at the analytic encounter in a position to present themself "to the patient as a person full of life" (Meltzer, 1984a, p. 164). What Meltzer would mean by being full of life is beyond the scope of this study, however, it can be assumed that the psychoanalyst will have been able to remove the "obstacles to participation in the psycho-analytic experience" (Bion, 1970, p. 26), i.e. that they have freed themself from the obstacles that impede the perception of the object and that, in addition, they are able to sustain the parental functions.[24] A necessary result of one's own analytic experience would be to have achieved an adult state of mind,[25] characterised by introjective identifications with living objects in good mutual relationships. If an adult state of mind predominates, the analyst will be able to empathise with the patient. Sustaining an adult state, always fluctuating, makes a continuous self-analysis necessary during the encounter. A self-analysis makes it possible to transform personal characteristics and reactions of the analyst into an instrument for research, for example, through the discrimination and analysis of countertransference relationships. The *dual* nature of the analyst's work is manifested in the fact that, on the one hand, they sustain the transference in their capacity as a parental figure for the child parts of the patient and, on the other hand, they are responsible for their own psychic reality. This capacity will allow them to observe the psychic reality from various points of view, both the patient's and their own. The analysand's work is also dual, and at the same time as they observe their inner self, they maintain a dialogue with their analyst. The *bifrontal* and *two-person* character of the analytic experience is manifested and concretised in the psychoanalytic interpretation, understood as an actual event of an evolution of truth, "that is common to analyst and analysand" (Bion, 1970, p. 27). Sincere participation in the analytic relationship also brings with it the stimulus to collaborate in a "common" experience of development that benefits both.[26]

Enabling the evolution of truth demands the analyst's readiness to preside over the analytic process, i.e. to collect and sustain the transference. It also demands an adequate state of mind to access deep layers of the mind in order to observe the constellations of the patient's unconscious phantasies and one's own. Along with the ability to empathise and tolerate the not understanding (*negative capacity*), a certain virtuosity in language use is required to transmit the analytic experience. The proximity of unconscious to unconscious and the analyst's appropriate state of mind are essential ingredients to creating the emotional atmosphere that fosters the *intimacy* necessary for the transference to unfold and for glimpses of truth to be captured.

One is not always willing to tolerate glimpses of O, the glimpses of one's own truth, because they entail turmoil. Nor is intimacy tolerated when one senses a possible transformation. This is the case when intimacy becomes intimidation. The paradox of the situation is that the patient, while willingly attending the analysis, fears growth and development. They prefer to free themself from emotional pain rather than benefit from a sincere relationship, even if it involves pain.[27] It is not always possible to tolerate pain or to transcend its painful sensation. The problem lies in the fact that our most primitive and non-mental dimension makes us repel it. In this sense, Bion (1970, p. 34) said that "resistance to growth is endo-psychic and endo-gregious; it is associated with turmoil in the individual and in the group to which the growing individual belongs". This individual and group resistance to growth and maturation is based on the fact that "the human animal has not ceased to be persecuted by his mind and the thoughts usually associated with it" (ibid., p. 126). This is the unconscious substratum with which those who voluntarily wish to have the analytic experience come to analysis. Then, as soon as turmoil becomes a regular occurrence and the "wish to maintain the *status quo* versus the drive toward integration" (Meltzer, 1967, p. 1) arises, it will be up to the analyst to seek and find "ideas sufficiently accurate and robust to survive the emotional storms they should illuminate" (Bion, 1970, p. 1).

Following, I will refer to three tools (Tabbia, 2013) required to construct the intimate relationship that makes possible both the development and the analysis of the transference.

Meltzer (1967), in *The Psycho-analytical process*, points out that the first task in an analysis is to collect the transference, that is, to collect the various elements of the personality that are dispersed and removed from the analytic relationship. The focus capable of collecting the transference is the analyst's *attention*. I am not referring only to free-floating attention, named by Freud, but to the analyst's readiness to grasp the emotions that manifest themselves in the initial encounters. The degree of sensitivity of the analyst's attention is an essential tool for becoming a container of the analytic encounter. Sensitivity is highly necessary to capture states of mind with little symbolic development. For example, this would be the case of patients who cannot tolerate the restrictions of mental space, are unable to make contact with psychic reality, and cannot construct basic visual images, ideograms capable of being registered. In such a situation, the analyst's ability to collect, articulate, and construct images and myths becomes an essential container for the patient. Therefore, the first link in the chain for transference to unfold is the analyst's capacity for observation (Tabbia, 2004b) and attention (Grotstein,[28] 2007). The analyst must have the "patience" (Bion) to take into account "any one of many facets of the patient's explication" (Bion, 1970, p. 8) until it is named (*selected*).

While every moment of the analytic process could be examined in terms of the close relationship between analyst and patient, I will now focus on the compromising situation that is created when both partners face the challenge of the *dream* hieroglyph. I say challenge because in the dream, the unconscious desire—yearning for access to the dreamer's world—and the fearful dreamer confront each other. In an ambivalent position, the latter tries both to restrain the irruption of the unconscious and to lend it materials so that it can manifest itself without abandoning its mysterious longing. In this sense, dreaming would fulfil the function of the *establishment*[29] of the new ideas expressed by the genius, according to Bion's (1970) proposal in *Attention and Interpretation*. When the dream becomes present in the analytic relation, multiple worlds meet in turn: the worlds of the analysand and the analyst, each with their longings and fears, with their passion for knowledge and their hatred of truth. Mutual and containing collaboration will prevent catastrophe and enable the development of emotions, ideas, and the analytic encounter. This will have the temperature that both participants tolerate. I agree with Meltzer (1987, p. 162) when he states that

> the emotional situation between analyst and patient at the non-transference level (as two adult people working together at a task with knowledge, skill and an agreed-upon format of procedure) at no point reaches such heights of pleasure, intimacy and mutual confidence as in the unique process of dream-analysis.

A double temperature is thus obtained: one that is derived from the encounter of the idea with the dreamer, and the other: that of the dreamer with the analyst. Unnamed but present is the temperature of the analyst when faced with the patient and their dream. All these encounters produce turmoil. The turmoil of dream creation is unobservable, but that of dream analysis lends itself to observation in the immediacy of the analytic session. The patient in dreaming seeks meaning and thoughts. This implies that waking and dream experiences are worked through by the alpha function. The analyst receives and dreams the different communications of the patient in order to understand them. Thus, by using the totality of their personality, the analyst has to observe all parts of the patient's personality to transform the experience into images and thoughts. Faced with this response, the patient finds in the analyst's empathic resonance the possibility of thinking themself. To meet this need, Meltzer (1987) proposed a working technique called *counter-dreaming*, which would consist of the analyst's possibility of thinking or dreaming the emotional experience that the patient cannot dream by themself. Here Meltzer took up Bion's suggestion that "The analyst must 'dream' the analytic session. That is, they must 'dream' the patient's as yet undreamed or incompletely dreamed emotions" (Grotstein, 2007, p. 83). When listening to the patient's account, the analyst observes the image that emerges in the patient's mind, allowing the evocation of a dream in which both the patient's dream work and the analyst's own characteristics converge. The collaboration of both creates a plot to be unravelled. This will require the analyst's expertise to discriminate between the proper and the strange. It is precisely at this point that an intimate rather than private space emerges (Tabbia, 2010b; see Section 3.3.1). There, each participant brings their own inner world into play, creating a kind of *contact barrier* where both states of mind meet while at the same time differentiating identities and creating meanings.

The task of intuiting meanings becomes larger and more complex when patients offer material with a sensory quality far removed from the psychic dream reality, which is the primary material of analytic work. In this sense, it is necessary to acquire sufficient skill to transform anecdotal material into material suitable for developing thoughts. To achieve this transformation, Meltzer (1995, p. 70) suggested listening to anecdotal material as if it were dream material, thus acquiring the habit of listening in two ways:

> It's like having two kinds of dream screens in one's mind. One is the dream screen onto which you can project this anecdotal material; the other would be the dream screen on which you have the flowing quality of the dreams and on which the symbols, the symbolic implication, make their impressions on us. This is exactly what happens when we observe children at play: we observe them with specific toys, we see their particular games, and, at the same time, on the dream screen all this acquires a symbolic implication, in a completely unconscious way.

With this material, and using the notation or mode of reference[30] which describes objects and relationships and which the analyst uses to create meanings, a container is generated in which transference meaning can be explored. In the face of the proposals of the *double dream screen* and the *contact barrier*, it is worth asking whether there can be *a more intimate relationship for exploring transference and creating thoughts than the analytic relationship*. Only a passion for knowledge can bring both participants into such an encounter.

The alpha elements generated in that encounter will be articulated or not, depending on the state of mind of the analyst and the patient. The development and deterioration of the articulation of meanings are ever-present options. When positive transference predominates, it stimulates cooperation between analyst and analysand, and the threads of alpha elements develop. However, if envy or fear of change fight against any kind of bonding, the task becomes more complex, and crises come to the forefront of our attention. When the analytic work stops due to the analyst's deficit and the countertransference[31] is impaired by the analyst's blind spots or unanalysed conflicts, observation, attention, and intuition are altered (Hahn, 2005) to the point of degrading the alpha function and inverting it (Bion, 1962). We would then be facing a critical point because the analyst would be failing as the main person responsible for the analysis.

An indicator of the deterioration or the development of the analytic relationship is the type of language produced in the analytic meeting. In one case, it could be an agglomeration of non-meanings; in another, the construction of an idiosyncratic, intimate language accessible only to the partners.

Once attention has been developed, and the intimacy of dream exploration has been shared, I would like to mention, as a third step in the construction of an analytic relationship, the non-intrusive way of looking into the analysand's private world. I refer to *imagination* that is neither intrusive nor voyeuristic, but rather imagination driven by the desire to know, and sustained by the tolerance of the contradictions of the object. I endorse the way Meltzer (1984a, p. 141) describes imagination as the

> truly free to space out and look inside the mind of others, it is that [imagination] based on the child's ability to look in a friendly way inside the mother, to be able to see and understand the children[32], the thoughts, the inner feelings, everything that is going on without experiencing jealousy. I want to underline how difficult it is to free one's own imagination because this means knowing how to look into the mind and life of others without invading them; it means knowing how to control one's own curiosity so as not to invade that private part of the life of others (such as the sexual life of the parents),

or—in the case of the analyst—the adult sexuality of the patients.

Both the joint creation of meaning and the imaginative and intuitive decipher-ing of a dream generate a climate capable of promoting pro-life changes in each participant. A climate that spontaneously transcends the limits of the encounter itself, extending "to life and relationships in the outside world" (Meltzer, 1984b, p. 46), as happens with lovers or serenely happy people who stimulate coexistence. In analysis, it manifests itself in increased analytic collaboration. Other consequences of this emotional climate are the feelings of gratitude that the analyst experiences when they are in an intimate relationship with themself and with the patient. Feel-ings of gratitude which, as a "countertransference experience, parallels the pa-tient's transference feeling of presenting a gift, a deed of gratitude" (ibid., p. 134). I said that the analytic relationship is complex because the web of mutual love and hatred that nourishes the relationship is complex. Therefore, in the same way that gratitude coexists with distrust of introjection capable of producing change, the intimate analytic relationship coexists with anxiety in countertransference, fear of invasion, confusion, or rejection.

Bion (1991c), in *A Memoir of the Future*, said that whoever does not fear the analytic encounter is not in a position to attempt it. This can be related to Abra-ham's challenge to the sacrifice of his son: who is sure that the dagger will not kill Isaac or that the bull's horn will not pierce the fascinated genius? Meltzer once encouraged me to enter deeply into an analytic relationship and told me that I "had good lungs"; it was not about my thoracic capacity to float in the turbulent ocean but to trust my internal objects to immerse myself in the analytic relationship. It is they, the internal objects, that can sustain the passion for knowledge, the passion necessary to become intimate with an object loved and feared, always unfathom-able and strange.

When the *passion* for knowledge begins to fade, dreams begin to diminish, and boredom and loneliness take the place where intimacy used to be; something is happening in the inner world of both participants of the analytic couple. It is time to pay attention to it.

3.3.5 The Isolated Adolescent[33]

At all ages, involuntary and persistent isolation is a matter for concern. At the end of infancy, it may be worrying, but the isolation that appears in adolescence is frequently a symptom of emotional disturbance and can feel deeply alarming for the family. This conflictive developmental period can be better understood psychoanalytically but remains a common topic in the media which often focuses particularly on the influence of electronic games in causing adolescent isolation.

Following infancy and latency, puberty emerges with a vigour that can surprise the young person, the family, and friends. Particularly unsettling is the imbalance created by the unintegrated movement of the personality, prone to splitting while sustained by obsessional defences. Puberty also seems to destabilise the physical "centre of gravity". This is reminiscent of the physical experience that takes place with ice skaters. The Olympic ice skater Yulia Lipnitskaia won a gold medal at the Olympic Games in Sochi, Russia, in 2014 at the age of 15. One year later, she had to modify her skating technique because her bodily changes had shifted the centre of gravity she had established over many years of training. While her coaches refer to her physical loss of equilibrium, we might also imagine a loss of emotional balance in the face of the changing states of internal objects.

The centre of gravity of the personality starts and develops in the highly complex relationship between baby and mother; with the nipple in its mouth, the baby gazes into its mother's responsive eyes (Meltzer, 1989, p. 133), while its hearing is alert to the mother's voice and words. The baby introjects this experience of the early relationship, gradually internalising a good object which becomes a cornerstone of the budding personality. Hence, the baby's dependence on such an internal object forms the core of its emotional stability. Destabilising factors, such as the increment of intrusive identification, interfere with the potential to promote further introjective identification with live, whole objects.

3.3.5.1 The Shift from Latency to Adolescence

The pathogenic consequences for a child who reaches the end of infancy with an unstable centre in their personality, while going through pathological splittings, are described by Meltzer (1999, p. 145) in "Clinical Dialogues with D. M.: Graciela":

> In general, we think that puberty takes place as a result of physiological and hormonal changes, but we have found evidence that in anorexia, the hormonal system is strongly linked to states of mind and is capable of setting back the physiological developments of puberty: children remain in latency for years and, among other things, do not have menstrual periods and do not develop breasts and pubic hair.
>
> It is also possible to encounter premature puberty when these children were the target of sexual stimulation and abuse, which prematurely awakened their sexuality and interfered with the onset of latency. In this case, we may come

across early menstruation at nine or ten years of age, precocious development of the breasts, and becoming young women at the age of 12.

Puberty and adolescence are states of mind. In addition to having a physiological component, the pubertal state of mind is reached when the obsessionality of latency is relinquished. As a result, there will be a dispersal—a splitting of the ego—that requires a group structure to hold together the parts of the ego to prevent its fragmentation. Progression towards normal adolescence in the presence of this fragmentation will necessarily be conducted under the influence of the core of the personality that was operative in earlier life. At this point, the child may throw themself into the experience of puberty or take refuge in, for instance, isolation.

The experience of puberty often involves multiple dissociations, which are projected into a group. Each group member becomes a provisional container for an aspect of the personality. Fluctuations within the group are common, and it can often feel like an anguished strategy to eliminate psychic pain. While some adolescents can tolerate oscillations, others become terrorised and prefer to withdraw from the group, remaining on the periphery. The group constantly needs to expel pain, and it does this by projection into the weaker members, friends, and family.

It is important to recognise that the paranoid anxiety triggered by disintegration in the genital period luckily finds some containment in the paranoid group, leading Meltzer to believe that puberty was the "maddest" period in human development. It would seem paradoxical that the road to health should include the experience of a paranoid group, but Meltzer thought it was essential for development to have the experience of "belonging" to a group, and that shortcuts were not the best way to prepare for the adult world. Shortcuts are alternative defences, often stimulated by the social intolerance of juvenile conflicts.

Some shortcuts can result in young people remaining as latency members of the family group or—in Identification with the parental model—creating an idealised and infantile couple. Alternatively, they might flee from adolescent turmoil by becoming hard-working students, only to become brilliant, but emotionally fragile executives or, lastly, joining the worrisome community of those who choose isolation.

In pubertal, same-sex groups, individuality is a grave threat to the group mentality and is not tolerated. The same hostility towards powerful people can be found in institutional groups where expression of individuality, leadership, or creativity is not tolerated. Anyone entering the group with a weak "centre of gravity" will have to either submit to the group tyranny or emotionally isolate themself and remain on the periphery.

Within these groups, there are roles and functions. Focusing on the pubertal (Meltzer, 1967, p. 67) and adolescent group, Ríos (1985) has considered the significance of the leader, the best friend, and the marginal member.[34] A healthy adolescent can perform different functions and roles at different times, whereas a disturbed adolescent cannot. In order to gain access to the adolescent community, it is extremely important to have a "best friend". According to Mantykow de Sola

(1991), the best friend's function is to promote sufficient tolerance to bear oedipal turmoil. It is a maturational link that takes place, first with the same sex and then with the opposite sex. The absence of a best friend may indicate a perpetuation of latency and difficulty in moving freely into puberty and adolescence. The best friend may function as a transitional object that allows entry into and exit from adolescence. Having a best friend indicates a capacity to give up isolation, and the adolescent without a best friend suffers terribly.

Within the group, the isolated young person can become a pariah or marginal. They will become a receptacle for the psychotic part of the group and will, in this way, contribute painfully to the creation of the gang. This is the price of belonging to a group into which they can project the healthier and potent parts of themself, in particular into the group leader.

When an individual becomes stuck on the margins, they cannot swap roles freely with other group members; the individual loses the benefit of the group experience and can no longer reduce their dissociations, omnipotence, and paranoid anxieties, nor distance themself from the lure of megalomania. We have here the ingredients of a more disturbed psychopathology. Isolation becomes a dangerous and painful refuge where the benefits to be gained from the adolescent community become unreachable.

What prevents this young person from being part of a group and from being able to socialise their conflicts, as Meltzer (1973a) framed it? One adolescent, 16-year-old Esteban, said, "*If I don't hang out with drug addicts and drop-outs, I would have no company and would be all alone*". Terror of loneliness may prompt the adolescent to "create" an unconditional friend, as in the case of Héctor (discussed below), who adopted a dog whom he named Puma.[35] Héctor, isolated, turned to Puma for companionship, loyalty, and comfort when he became trapped in a narcissistic gang with his parents.

From what does the adolescent isolate themself? *Isolated* means to be separated from other people or things. They are there but not accessible, making the "socialisation of conflicts" impossible. As isolation expresses itself in many ways and responds to different states of mind, it may be useful to make some differentiations, without aiming to cover the whole psychopathological range of isolated adolescents.

First, we must differentiate two types of isolation from the vertex of loss and mourning; an adolescent may suffer from the collapse of their same-sex group, becoming unable to benefit from its group dynamics; they may develop a *depressive illness* when their best friend couples off and may end up isolating themself.

Then there are adolescents who, after the loss of infantile idealisations, withdraw into a narcissistic organisation that may lead to calm but dangerous "megalomania". These adolescents are unable to recognise their dependence upon parental objects and may believe that they have conceived themselves and that they have a mission in life. The manic basis of their personality may express itself in the conviction that they have to educate their parents to become better parents, and to change the state and its institutions. Such arrogance does not disappear with loneliness, nor does the sense of isolation,[36] but rather, it increases with their resentment.

This becomes worse when delusional jealousy leads to the kind of extreme vandalism involving the murder of children or young people.

Beyond the paranoid-depressive and the megalomaniac isolated adolescents, there are other manifestations that deserve scrutiny because of their frequency in psychoanalytic sessions. These are friendless young people who do not belong to a group and usually lock themselves away at home. They leave home only to go to school but have no relationships with other students, making contact only in the atmosphere of social media where there is no physical contact, and some wander the streets. I believe that this could be due to the massive use of narcissistic identifications and the fear of having to forego their narcissistic defences through the loss of their obsessional control. This loss of control at the time when they are immersing themselves in an adolescent community creates the conviction that they will not be able to regroup and reorganise themselves. The ambition to join the group can create the secret urge to run it and become the leader. Alternatively, they might join the group but remain slightly apart, like a fly on the wall, spying and judging the other group members. None of these strategies help such adolescents to participate in the group experience. Indeed, this false link enables them to feel grandiose and even to occupy a prestigious place, despite not feeling included, as the group recognises their partial contact and ends up distrusting them. In that case, the young person is excluded from joining the "human race".

This dynamic can change when the group becomes more depressive and less schizoid-paranoid. At that point, the isolated adolescent may be able to obtain more understanding and containment for their suffering.

I would like to focus now on three omnipotent phantasies that prevent becoming a part of the adolescent community and experiencing its transforming influence. First, I want to refer to those who live in a withdrawn state, followed by those who live in intrusive identification, and, finally, those who become sucked into an object. According to Meltzer (1992b):

At the beginning of psychoanalysis there was much talk about returning to the womb. All this was discarded when the concept of projective identification was formulated. I do think there is a difference. There are the fantasies that exist before birth, and the intrusive phantasies related to states of projective identification. They have a different meaning and also different consequences. In effect, we can identify a return to the womb through which patients retreat inside, isolate themselves and remain in a cocoon. This is where we see states that appear frozen—some with narcolepsy—in which the patient sleeps a lot, some in catatonic states, and they all have a connection with the phantasy of going back in time, to that marvellous situation of being inside the mother before the father turns up.

The conflict created by the father's appearance and other unavoidable frustrations may lead to the joke: "What do we come into the world for? To suffer?; if that's the case, we're going back!"

Even when the idealisation of intrauterine life is debatable, we have to take on board the belief that in the womb, and facing unpleasant experiences, "the foetus gets rid of [these experiences] as soon as it can" (Bion, 1997, p. 50). This fantasy of paradise is always possible when faced with a conflict and finds expression in a dialogue between Somite Thirty and Term, in the third volume of Bion's *A Memoir of the Future*:

SOMITE THIRTY: Get back into the Amniotic Fluid.
TERM: Get out into the sun! Glory! The fields are bathed in light. Moonlight! Don't lie snoozing in bed.
SOMITE THIRTY: Keep warm in bed. Your King and Country want you—you stay in bed. (1991c, p. 443).

This staying in bed, locked in a world without stimulation, is the consequence of relinquishing the external world because it feels too dangerous and frustrating. Meltzer already anticipated (1967) in *The Psycho-analytical process* that possessive jealousy is a motivation for projective identification, observing how it is seen "in the autistic children and in children whose drive to maturity is very low, so that they wish either to remain infantile or to die. This means in their unconscious to return-to-sleep-inside-mother" (1967, p. 15). This omnipotent phantasy is at the core of states of withdrawal and somnolence.

We can differentiate between a wish to sleep inside the mother and a state in which some "parts may be left behind in the womb, producing states of withdrawal quite different in phenomena from those of projective identification" (1992b, p. 127). I think that when there is a predominance of intrusiveness—as in the head/breast compartment of the internal mother—we find states of Oblomovian lassitude, where the subject has no desire to leave the object because they enjoy inactivity. In the case of isolation due to unborn parts of the personality, however, the baby shows an absence of stimulation or incentive to come out into the world and appears drowsy. According to Meltzer, some parts have not been born due to a failure in the aesthetic conflict between baby and mother. He relates this to the possibility that puerperal depression may be more common than is reported; if a baby does not find a passionate containing object, it is not likely to be fully born.

Whether returning to the womb or not wanting to abandon it, there is a universal fantasy that there is no experience of need in the womb because a constant provision makes the notion of lack or desire impossible. Nevertheless, in the womb, it is possible:

to experience unpleasantness, sometimes violence linked to sudden alterations of the biochemistry of the environment as it is also possible to feel comfortable in a stable environment protected from external interference. These differences in intrauterine life will surely influence the growth, strength and vitality of the capacity to take an interest in the objects present in the womb and in the last instance, how they can be prepared for the delivery and life.

(Caccia, 2007, p. 60)

The fantasy of lost paradise, together with the fear of conflicts in the external world, can attract and sustain states of mind characterised by isolation and somnolence. This fear can be observed in adolescents who spend most of their day locked in their rooms, only emerging explosively, as if in a panic, opposing everything that stands in their way.

3.3.5.2 Gerard

Sixteen-year-old Gerard had been a "good kid", adapting well to school and belonging to a latency group. Once he reached puberty, he isolated himself after getting into trouble with the police: he had been caught shop-lifting in supermarkets and touching girls while stealing their mobile telephones. For Gerard, the external world was full of dangers, and he experienced his sessions as approaching the horizon and being about to fall into hell. His parents were confused professionals with a problematic relationship and were very annoyed with their frustrating adolescent. It seemed that his entry into adolescence was not supported by objects capable of containing him; his parents found it unbearable to see him even too isolated to sustain a therapeutic process, and they decided to break off his therapy and have him medicated. The "*case or sheath as an exoskeleton*" (Bion, 1991b, p. 431) that Gerard chose for himself was a caricature of a wild west bandit: his thin arms always looked like they were poised to draw out his pistols. He was so terrorised that he could only find refuge within the four walls of his room.

Certain ways of locking oneself in a room can be as serious as those found in the psychotic states linked to addictions and video games (Rosenfeld, 2001).

Some isolated adolescents with a borderline psychotic psychopathology manage to go through life appearing to be well-adjusted, enjoying successful academic or athletic lives, but nevertheless enduring great difficulties in establishing intimate relationships. Their painful isolation surprises those who know them. Gerard was an educated, studious, and well-adjusted child, and we can assume that he left latency in a pseudo-mature state; while his brothers played football, he studied philosophy and discussed politics. This enabled him to avoid juvenile emotional turmoil and allowed him to look at the world with arrogance, judging his friends, relatives, and neighbours. In some sense, this arrogance is characteristic of adolescents because it is the consequence of confusional states. In the same way, however, just as all adolescents go through confusional states, this can become chronic when one tries to escape the limitations of the ego and an attempt is made to "seize an object's identity by intrusion into it" (Meltzer, 1973a p. 53). But intrusion is not innocuous. To live in intrusive Identification (see Section 3.1.5), the part that lives in an internal compartment remains alienated from the external world. Meltzer doubted if it was useful to speak "in terms of external world or internal world because the patient who lives in projective identification loses a sense of differentiation between inside or outside", as he is dealing with compartments rather than inside and outside (Meltzer with The Psychoanalytic Group of Barcelona, 1995, p. 18).

These compartments form the barrier that prevents true emotional contact with the world, as shown by Jana (see Section 3.1.2.1.).

Elitism and arrogance that stem from intrusive identification with qualities of the object stimulate feelings of superiority and self-sufficiency in these adolescents, but these feelings do not anaesthetise completely the state of isolation that overwhelms and persecutes them. Nor does it mitigate feelings of fraudulence, nor do they feel persecuted by the fear of being found out and belittled. They do not arouse interest in their colleagues, their telephone seldom rings, and their diary is only filled if they take the initiative. They are efficient and appreciated as being cooperative with adults, but their private life is confined to masturbation, pornography, and despair. In relation to people of their own age or younger, they can adopt a protective attitude that can be understood as a desire to look after healthy aspects of themselves projected into them, while at the same time, they can jealously control the younger ones to abuse and exploit them.

3.3.5.3 Alejandro

Another young man, Alejandro, has been living an isolated life for many years. At first, he was the idealised object of his parents' hopes, but this changed when his brothers were born. Each new baby became their idealised love object while, at the same time, they would push the older siblings aside, as if to confirm the infantile fantasy that, "Adults are fascinated when they have babies, but later they drop them, and it all boils down to the fact that what they really like is making babies, simply the product" (Meltzer, 2002, p. 30). Jealousy and resentment stimulated a wish in Alejandro not to be excluded, and he dissociated his world in such a way that, in relation to his mother, he developed a narcissistic identification and became her counsellor and support. With his father, however, he became a dutiful son, and, while he tolerated his father's contempt by placating his brutality, he managed to stay near him and become the manager of the family business without feeling that he had earned it because of his intellect or his managerial skills. He was unable to have a relationship with his sisters and had a sadomasochistic relationship with his older brother. His life took place in the greatest solitude.

During adolescence, he tried to establish friendly relations, but these, somehow, wore off. Internet pornography became his refuge from isolation in which women would get undressed and praise his penis. But, terrified by the prospect of a physical encounter, he never went beyond the internet. Only intrusive identification allowed him to overcome his isolation, but these invaded objects, far from improving his feelings of safety, undermined his personality and made him increasingly distrustful and fearful of meeting other people. Through his lengthy therapy, he has partially been able to restore his internal objects, which he has come to trust. This has allowed him to give up his masturbatory activity and his use of marijuana, diminish his total isolation, and become increasingly more devoted to his children, though more interested in the boys than in the girls. He has, laboriously, managed to create a group of friends from whom he still feels the pain of being excluded from time to time. All this does not mean that he has become able to tolerate emotional pain; when this increases, he flees, preferring to placate his persecuting paternal object rather than rebelling: being left alone is more persecuting to him than being hurt or going out into the external world. As long as the pleasure from the different compartments of the internal mother protect and gratify him, he will continue to avoid the external world in which his parental objects are not very interested in discovering their son's individuality.

In the same way that Alejandro forced his way into his objects through masturbatory intrusiveness and, in doing so, acquired a pseudo-identity, there are situations in which isolated, solitary, and bored adolescents become vulnerable to the intrusiveness of other people. This is the equivalent of being swallowed up by an *aspirated projective identification*, as occurs with the psychopathology of the *folie à deux*, where mixed projective identifications make it difficult to create an emotional link with one member of the collusive couple.[37] For the adolescent girl, this might entail an inseparable, twin-like alliance with her mother, almost sharing an identity. This might revolve around their beauty, expressed by their referring to themselves in terms of "*us, us, us*".[38] These perverse[39] alliances can have different objectives, such as exploiting others with the bait of their beauty, intelligence, or delinquent plotting. In these cases, the family group has become the adolescent gang, for whom transgression offers shared excitement. It becomes very difficult for an adolescent immersed in this delinquent culture to abandon the group and join the real adolescent community; the adolescent may feel that they are betraying their family by rejecting the erotisation of orgiastic family life.

3.3.5.4 Héctor

This is what Héctor believed when he struggled to prevent his bipolar mother from walking around the house wearing only her knickers and feeling free to touch his body, something that his father did nothing to prevent. He was frequently sandwiched naked between his promiscuous parents—three *polymorphous adolescents*—in a state of shared excitement. This did not prevent Héctor from feeling isolated; with his excessive greed and jealousy, he struggled to make friends. Héctor's imprisonment in his family gang only offered temporary relief that could not protect him from urgently seeking any object that would fill a void. It seemed as if Héctor would not have to worry about his future because he would inherit the small business, as well as various family properties. The family pact was "us against the world", but this did not soothe his sense of isolation and helplessness. His compulsive eating, drinking, promiscuity, and the temptation of addiction to cocaine, amphetamines and LSD were not enough to fill his emptiness. For Héctor, other children were not so much rivals as objects for consumption. As the geographical confusion and the symbiosis in the family were dissolved, his anxiety increased, and he expressed a great desire to possess the analyst as a transference object. He said in a session:

> I get annoyed about having to pay €2 for parking even when I have a nice car, I get annoyed about paying €2.5 for a beer in a nice place. I hate humanity. I'd make 50% of them vanish. Everything has to be for me. I would like to eat you up whole so that you become only mine and nobody else's.

Once he recovered from his anaesthetised state, born out of the confusion with his family gang, his needs increased as well as his understanding of his states of mind, and he could recognise his wish that everything should be his for free. There was no hunger attached to the erotised family sandwich, but the moment he separated and had to pay for himself, he became furious. Not so long ago, Héctor dreamed that he *was robbing a bank. When he reached the safe, he noticed it was open and that other thieves were already present. At this point, he lost interest and left because he wanted the loot just for himself. He wanted to monopolise the object.* After much work, Héctor recognises that he cannot relate to anyone or love in that state of mind.

> I feel as if I am in a big container, in the shape of a bowl or a cone, and that everything that falls into it is for me, but I cannot feel love, I feel I have no love for others, or for you.

Héctor is slowly leaving behind the borderline/psychotic gang that isolated him and made him feel that his only friend was his dog, Puma. He is also leaving behind the sad feelings that made him chase people, pay for meals, or offer them lifts, only to receive in exchange their contemptuous and demolishing comments, like being told that he is always running after people, begging.

3.3.5.5 Conclusion

Adolescence is a time when maturational processes are synthesised and when the gates towards adult life open. If the adolescent arrives at this point with a faulty centre of gravity, the way to adulthood will require a restructuring that is likely to have an uncertain outcome.

I believe that many of the disturbances suffered by isolated adolescents fall into the category of borderline psychotic states that are always linked to geographical confusions. In my opinion, overcoming these states of isolation requires going through stages that have been avoided out of fear of emotional turbulence. The itinerary that leads to maturity was clearly described by Meltzer (1967, p. 22) when he wrote:

> the resolution of this configuration of object relations stands as the border between mental illness (psychosis) and mental health, just as the resolution of the obstacles to the dependent introjective relation to the breast traverses the border

between mental instability and mental stability, and as the passing of the Oedipus complex leads from immaturity to maturity.

In order for the isolated adolescent to resolve conflicts at every stage, they must rely on the containing capacity of the analyst, because

if an analyst can bear to persevere when geographical confusions are in the forefront of the transference, he will certainly be rewarded with progress

(ibid., p. 22)

Notes

1   Published in *Docta, Revista de Psicoanálisis*, Asociación Psicoanalítica de Córdoba (Argentina), #6, December 2010, pp. 47–61 and in Italian in *Psicoterapia Psicoanalítica*, Rivista de la Società Italiana di Psicoterapia Psicoanalítica, Rome, Publisher. Borla, 2010, XVII(2), pp. 63–81.
2   During the clinical seminars in the Psychoanalytic Group of Barcelona (1986–2002).
3   When Dr. Hahn (2020) read this text, he offered a comment that adds value.

> *Murciélago* [Bat in Spanish] is a word that contains all the vowels, and the idea of vowels makes one think of the orality or oral greed of Felipe, who lusts after women with the greed he projects onto them and who are quickly reprojected in the form of attacks on his potency and ability to relate. The fact that they stick to his chest suggests he is talking about a maternal transference, to which I would add the problem with the controlling father of the family.

4   Meltzer appreciated the term comradeship, perhaps originating in his military training where soldiers sleep and eat together in a barracks and share activities, jobs, or interests, in close and intimate proximity. But that same comradeship sometimes carries with it a penumbra of association stemming from the existence of an external danger (fight or flight basic assumption).
5   The model constructed by Meltzer (1992), known as *The Claustrum*, refers to the construction of the representation of the maternal object based on the care that the first object offers the baby. From the experience that the baby has in its erogenous zones (mouth, genital, and anus), it constructs the characteristics of the maternal object based on equivalences. This object, in its complexity, acquires different meanings if it is observed from the outside or the inside; in the first case, the representation would arise from the imagination, and in the second case, from intrusion. Both representations are opposites and have different consequences for the development of the subject.
6   This play was analysed in Section 3.1.5.
7   The expression "passionate encounter" carries with it a penumbra of associations that merits some discrimination. "Passionate" means to be dominated by passion. In the case of the young person who throws themself into new affiliations, the libidinal drive in search of objects to unite with would command their actions. In this case, the sensual/sexual dimension takes on its full meaning. But passion can change, for example, into striving for knowledge. Freud (1910) recognised Leonardo's capacity to substitute sexual activity for the tenacious dedication and constant struggle for knowledge. Bion, in reformulating the drive theory by the links of love, hate, and knowledge (L, H and K), articulated the intense and tender emotion: the bonding passion. Bonding that is disallowed when the bonding elements are denied (-L, -H, -K) or when it is experienced with violence.

8   Carlos Ménem: President of Argentina (1989–1999).
9   At the time, suspicion was circulating in Argentina that the plane crash in which Ménem's son died had been instigated by his own father.
10   Published in *Docta. Revista de Psicoanálisis*. Publication of the Asociación Psicoanalítica de Córdoba (Argentina), year 11, N° 9, Nov. 2013, pp. 54–69, and in *Rev. de Psicoanálisis*, Asociación Psicoanalítica de Madrid, 2017, Issue 80, pp. 223–247.
11   Catastrophic anxiety and the anxiety of falling in space is at the basis of the feeling of instability that engenders the conservative character of the child personality; as Bick (1986, p. 299) says, a child demands "sameness, stability and support from the outside world".
12   With this expression, I am referring to the childish phantasy that adults are omnipotent.
13   "ROLAND Why should Truth be so incompatible with ourselves that it comes to us as a threat? P.A. …That is too terrible to grasp after the *protection of the mother's womb; later the womb of our ignorance*." (Bion: A Memoir of the Future, 1991b, p. 283. My italics).
14   I am grateful to the psychotherapist Lidia Compagnino (Genoa) for permission to publish this material.
15   The endometrium is the mucous membrane that lines the inside of the uterus. It is rich in connective tissue and highly vascularised. Its function is to house the zygote or blastocyst after fertilisation, allowing implantation. It is the site where the placenta develops and presents cyclical alterations in its glands and blood vessels during the menstrual cycle in preparation for the implantation of the human embryo.
16   "Freud used this term to describe the neuro-physiological entity subsequently known as a synapse […] This contact-barrier, thus continuously in process of formation, marks the point of contact and separation between conscious and unconscious elements and originates the distinction between them. The nature of the contact-barrier will depend on the nature of the supply of alpha-elements and on the manner of their relationship to each other."
17   For the topic of optimal distance and adequate proximity, see Section 3.3.1.
18   The analyst listens from the availability that Michel de M'Uzan (1976) calls "original psychic activity", annexed to the patient; an activity that he characterises by saying that the patient

> needs above all that which they perceives in the depths of themself […] is elaborated and finds its full figuration thanks to the work of a psychic apparatus that has been annexed. The analyst, for their part, seems to withdraw as an individuality inhabited by passions and possessing a history in order to only leave active functional capacities there.
>
> (p. 192)

These capacities are nourished by the passions (the interplay of positive and negative links) of the analyst themself and are filtered.
19   The analyst's truths are expressed in two areas; one is what they reveal of themself through the discrimination of the countertransference; the other is the truth that is revealed upon becoming an analyst.
20   Parental functions (Harris and Meltzer, 1976): generating love, promoting hope, containing pain, stimulating thinking. But also tolerating and sustaining anti-links, i.e. opposition to love, hate and knowledge.
21   I have put the term madness in quotation marks to express the freedom and spontaneity needed to face complex situations. In the Catalan language there is the word *rauxa*, which refers to the ability to make quick and somewhat capricious decisions without thinking too much. It is not uncommon to refer to the rauxa of poets and creators. Without contact with the psychotic parts, it is difficult to be a creator, but here madness does not refer to psychosis.
22   Presented at the 50th IPA Congres, Buenos Aires, in a panel with Patricia Checa (Perú) and Alberto Hahn (London), 1917. Published in *TEMAS DE PSICOANÁLISIS* # 15 – January 2018, pp. 1–12, Barcelona, www.temasdepsicoanalisis.org

23 To join empathically in the service of the task, admitting that like O, or absolute truth, "it can be known about, its presence can be recognized and felt, but it cannot be known" (Bion, 1970, p. 30).

24 See note 20.

25 States of mind are momentary and depend on: (a) the qualities and relations of internal objects to each other; (b) the world inhabited (external, internal, inside, and outside of objects); (c) the type of functioning based on introjective and/or intrusive identification, generators of mature and pseudo-mature states of mind; (d) the degree of integration and/or dissociation of infantile parts and psychotic nuclei, generators of psychopathology; (e) who governs the consciousness. The concept of the adult state of mind can also be found in Harris and Meltzer (1976, pp. 436–438).

26 "Its growth-promoting quality, for both, is unmistakable" (Meltzer, 1992, p. 111).

27 "It seems reasonable to suggest that between rigidity of avoidance and instability of contact there is possibly a middle zone whose stability consists essentially in the readiness to try again. This readiness must, I would suppose, imply a mutual uncertainty of the reasons of the breakdown in intimacy and a readiness to forgive, both oneself and the other. That, in turn, requires a sophisticated attitude towards pain in which the interest in its meaning exceeds the aversion to its sensual quality, the painfulness of the pain" (Meltzer, 1992, p. 112).

28 Grotstein (2007, p. 83) points to forms of observation: "emotional and objective—that is, intuition and attention".

29 "Establishment", as Bion (1970) thinks of it, has the function of protecting the genius from being crushed by the resistance of the community that feels perturbed by their new ideas, and of protecting the community from being destroyed by the new ideas expressed by the genius.

30 See the preface of *The Psycho-analytical process*.

31 See the original view of negative transference and countertransference that Meltzer presented in his last lecture in Venice (2001), published in 2017 by Karnac, under the title *Meltzer in Venice*.

32 In the Italian translation (Meltzer spoke English) it says: "guardare in modo amichevole dentro la madre, di poter vedere e capire i bambini, i pensieri, i sentimenti interni, tutto quanto vi accade senza provare gelosia". I think what he means here is recognising the existence of the internal babies of the mother without jealousy.

33 Published in *Doing Things Differently. The influence of Donald Meltzer on Psychoanalytic Theory and Practice*, edited by Margaret Cohen & Alberto Hahn,London, Karnac, 2017, pp. 95–107 and in *Psicoanálisis APdeBA*, XXXVIII(1), 2016, pp. 157–174.

34 "Introjections that are linked to the figure of an unconditional friend are of great importance as the basis that is used for the choice of a loved object, and we could almost say that it is the most important identificatory substratum" (Ríos, 1985, p. 508).

35 According to his grandparents, this animal was characterised by cunning and strength.

36 "When a particular infantile part, or organization of them, seizes upon consciousness and dominates a person's behaviour, temporarily, say, the sense- of-identity is bound to be oppressed by the loneliness, however defiant, of the child-in-the-adult-world" (Meltzer, 1971, p. 202).

37 Meltzer (1967, p. 3) explains how difficult it is to establish the transference situation when the mother involves the child in her anxieties:

> I have had [the] experience where it was not the mother who was 'bringing' but rather was the mother who was involved in the *'folie'* which prevented the 'gathering' from sufficiently taking shape to set the process of analysis in motion.

38 See: "Elsa: Temor a la comunidad adolescente" in Meltzer and Harris: *Adolescentes*, Spatia, Buenos Aires, 1998, pp. 215–246.

39 These alliances can be intergenerational or intragenerational, as between children and parents or between siblings: see "Ramón, a hostage in the Claustrum" at Meltzer and Harris: *Adolescentes*, Buenos Aires: Spatia, ed., 1998, 269–294.

Bibliography

Anzieu, D. (1975): *El grupo y el inconsciente*, Madrid, Biblioteca Nueva, 1978.

Bauman, Z. (2003): *Liquid Love: On the Frailty of Human Bonds*, Cambridge, Polity.

Beckett, S. (1957): *Fin de Partie*, Paris, Les Éditions de Minuit. 1993. Translated from the original French by the author, *Endgame*, London-Boston, MA, Faber and Faber Limited, 1988.

Bergstein, A. (2013): "Transcending the caesura: Reverie, dreaming and counter-dreaming", *International Journal of Psycho-Analysis*, 94(4), pp. 621–644.

Bick, E. (1986): "Further considerations on the function of the skin in early object-relation", *British Journal of Psychotherapy*, 2(4), pp. 292–299

Bion, W. R. (1957): "Differentiation of the psychotic from the non-psychotic personalities", in *Second Thoughts*, London, Karnac, 1984, pp. 43–64

Bion, W. R. (1961): *Experiences in Groups and Other Papers*, New York, Tavistock Publications Limited.

Bion, W. R. (1962): *Learning from Experience*, London, Karnac Books, 1984

Bion, W. R. (1970): *Attention and Interpretation*, London, Karnac Books, 1984.

Bion, W. R. (1991a): "The dream", in *A Memoir of the Future*, London, Karnac Books, pp. 1–218.

Bion, W. R. (1991b): "The past presented", in *A Memoir of the Future*, London, Karnac Books, pp. 219–426

Bion, W. R. (1991c): "The dawn of oblivion", in *A Memoir of the Future*, London, Karnac, pp. 427–578. Books.

Bion, W. R. (1997): *Taming Wild Thoughts*, London: Karnac.

Caccia, O. (2007): "La nascita della mente", in *Pensieri prematuri. Uno sguardo alla vita mentale del bambino nato pretermine*, edited by S. Latmiral & C. Lombardo, Roma, Borla, pp. 41–71.

Erikson, E. (1950): *Childhood and Society*, London, Paladin Grafton Books, 1977

Etchegoyen, R. H. (1986): *Los fundamentos de la técnica psicoanalítica*, Buenos Aires, Amorrortu ed.

Fisher, J. (1995): "Identity and intimacy in the couple: Three kinds of identification", *Intrusiveness and Intimacy in the Couple*, edited by S. Ruszczynki & J. Fisher, London, Karnac books, pp. 74–104.

Freud, S. (1910): "Leonardo da Vinci and a memory of his childhood", in The Standard Edition of the Complete Psychological Works of Sigmund Freud, edited by J. Strachey, London, Hogarth Press, 1966, Vol XI, pp. 59–230.

Freud, S. (1921): *Group Psychology and the Analysis of the Ego*, London, The Hogarth Press, 1949.

Freud, S. (1926): *Inhibitions, Symptoms and Anxiety*, London, The Hogarth Press, 1949.

Freud, S. (1930): *Civilization and Its Discontents*, London, Penguin Books, 2004.

García Márquez, G. (1985): *Love In The Time Of Cholera*, translated by Edith Grossman, New York, Alfred A. Knopf, 1988.

Goncharov, I. A. (1858): *Oblomov*, New York, Macmillan, 1915.

Goyena, J. L. (2002): "L´intime et le secret", *Champ Psychosomatique* 27, pp. 33–52.

Grotstein, J. (2007): *A Beam of Intense Darkness*, London, Karnac.

Hahn, A. (2005): "A note on intuition", read at the memorial conference for Donald Meltzer at the Tavistock Clinic (London), 12 November, 2005. Available at www.psa-atelier.org

Hahn, A. (2017): "Concluding thoughts on the nature of psychoanalytic activity", in *Doing Things Differently. The Influence of Donald Meltzer on Psychoanalytic Theory and Practice*, edited by Margaret Cohen & Alberto Hahn, London, Karnac, pp. 233–236.

Hahn, A. (2020): Personal correspondence.

Harris, M. & Meltzer, D. (1976): "A psychoanalytic model of the child-in-the-family-in-the-community", in *Sincerity and Other Works*, edited by Alberto Hahn, London, Karnac, 1994, pp. 387–454.

Joseph, B. (1989): *Psychic Equilibrium and Psychic Change*, London, Routledge.

Khan, M. (1979): "Intimacy, complicity and mutuality", in *Alienation in Perversions*, London, Karnac, 1989, pp. 18-31

Klein, M. (1959): "Our adult world and its roots in infancy", in *Envy and Gratitude and Other Works 1946–1963*, edited by M. Massud R. Khan, New York, The Free Press, A Division of Simon & Schuster, 1975, pp. 247–263

Levy, R. (2017): "Intimidad: lo dramático y lo bello en el encuentro y desencuentro con el otro", *Revista de Psicoanálisis, APM*, 33(82), 2018, pp. 363–391.

Mantykow de Sola, B. (1991): "El amigo íntimo de la adolescencia: su lugar en el proceso psicoanalítico", *Psicoanálisis, APdeBA*, XIII(3), pp. 565–583.

Meltzer, D. (1967): *The Psycho-Analytical Process*, London, William Heinemann Medical Books Limited.

Meltzer, D. (1971): "Sincerity: A study in the atmosphere of human relations", in *Sincerity and Other Works: Collected Papers of Donald Meltzer*, edited by A. Hahn, London, Karnac, 1994, pp. 185–284.

Meltzer, D. (1973): *Sexual States of Mind*, London, Karnac, 2018.

Meltzer, D. (1973a): "Identification and socialization in adolescence", in *Sexual States of Mind*, London, Karnac, 2008, pp. 51–57.

Meltzer, D. (1973b): "Routine and inspired interpretations", in *Sincerity and other Works*, edited by Alberto Hahn, London, Karnac, 1994, pp. 290–306

Meltzer, D. (1976): "Temperature and distance as technical dimensions of interpretation", in *Sincerity and Other Works*, edited by Alberto Hahn, London, Karnac, 1994, pp. 374–386.

Meltzer, D. (1984a): "Sulla immaginazione", in *Quaderni di psicoterapia infantile*, edited by Carlo Brutti and Francesco Scotti, Roma, Borla, 3, pp. 132–169.

Meltzer, D. (1984b): *Dream-Life: A Re-Examination of the Psychoanalytic Theory and Technique*, London, Karnac Books, 2009

Meltzer, D. (1987): "Conflicts of desire and paradoxes of thought", in *Sincerity and Other Works*, edited by Alberto Hahn, London, Karnac, 1994, pp. 557–560.

Meltzer, D. (1989): "Narcisismo y violencia en los adolescentes", in Meltzer, D. & Harris, M. (1998): *Adolescentes*, edited by L. Jachevasky & C. Tabbia, Buenos Aires, ed. Spatia., pp. 197–199.

Meltzer, D. (1990): Conference, Psicoanálisis APdeBA, XII, 1, pp. 123–134.

Meltzer, D. (1991): "Foreword", in *The Chamber of Maiden Thought*, edited by M. Harris Williams and M. Waddell, London, Tavistock/Routledge, pp. IX–XVII.

Meltzer, D. (1992a): *The Claustrum. An Investigation of Claustrophobic Phenomena.* Strath-Clyde, The Clunie Press.

Meltzer, D. (1992b): Supervision in the Psychoanalytic Group of Barcelona: Christian. (Unpublished).

Meltzer, D. (1993): "Implicaciones psicosomáticas en el pensamiento de Bion", *Psicoanálisis, APdeBA*, XV(2), pp. 315–338.

Meltzer, D. (1994): *Sincerity and Other Works*, London, Karnac.

Meltzer, D. (1998a): "Ramón, a hostage in the Claustrum", in Meltzer, D. & Harris, M. (1998): *Adolescentes,* edited by L. Jachevasky & C. Tabbia, Buenos Aires, ed. Spatia., 269–294.

Meltzer, D. (1998b): "Elsa: Fear of the adolescent community", in Meltzer, D. & Harris, M. (1998): *Adolescentes*, edited by L. Jachevasky & C. Tabbia, Buenos Aires, ed. Spatia.

Meltzer, D. (1999): "Clinical dialogues with DM: Graciela", *Psicoanálisis, APdeBA*, XXI(1/2), pp. 119–146.

Meltzer, D. (2004): "A relação da psicoanálise com as ciências e áreas afins", *Revista de Psicoanálise, de la Sociedad Psicoanalítica de Porto Alegre* – Homenagem a Donald Meltzer,11(3), pp. 437–448.

Meltzer, D. (2017): *Meltzer in Venice. Seminars with the Racker Group of Venice*, editado por Petrilli, Márquez y Rossetti, London, Karnac.

Meltzer, D. & Harris, M. (1998): *Adolescentes*, edited by L. Jachevasky & C. Tabbia, Buenos Aires, ed. Spatia.

Meltzer, D. & Harris Williams, M. (1988): *The Apprehension of Beauty: The Role of Aesthetic Conflict in Development, Art, and Violence*, London, Karnac, 2008.

Meltzer, D. with The Psychoanalytic Group of Barcelona (1987): "Clinical seminars in the Psychoanalytic Group of Barcelona: Victor", in *Psychanalytic Work with Children and Adults – Meltzer in Barcelona*, Karnac, 2002.

Meltzer, D. with The Psychoanalytic Group of Barcelona & Mack Smith, C. (1995): *Psychoanalytic Work with Children and Adults: Meltzer in Barcelona*, edited by The Psychoanalytic Group of Barcelona, London, Karnac, 2002.

Meltzer, D. et al. (1986): *Studies in Extended Metapsychology.* Strath-Clyde, Perthshire, Clunie Press.

M'Uzan, M. de (1976): "Contratransferencia y sistema paradójico", in *Del arte a la muerte. Un itinerario psicoanalítico*, Barcelona, ICARIA, 1978, pp. 183–201.

Orwell, G. (1945): *Animal Farm.* London: Collins Classics, 2021.

Pardo, J. L. (1996): *La intimidad*, Valencia, Pre-Textos (S. G. E.), 2004.

Proverbs, in *English Standard Version Bible.* (2001): ESV Online. Available at https://esv.literalword.com/

Rev. Médica Electr. (2017): "La placenta: desarrollo, estructura y función", *Artículos, casos clínicos, imágenes médicas – ISSN 1886–8924*, PortalesMedicos.com, 14 octubre, 2017.

Ríos, C. (1985): "Las identificaciones en la adolescencia", *Psicoanálisis, APdeBA*, VII(3), pp. 499–515.

Rosenfeld, D. (2001): "Psychotic addiction to video games", in *A Language for Psychosis: Psychoanalysis of Psychotic States*, edited by P. Williams, London, Whurr, pp. 149–174.

Saint-Exupery, A. (1943): *The Little Prince*, translated by Katherine Woods, Thorndike, G.K. Hall, 1995

Schaeffer, J. (2006): "100 años después de 'Tres ensayos…' ¿qué queda de los 'Tres escándalos'?", *Psicoanálisis, APdeBA*, XXVIII(1), pp. 139–155.

Stevenson, R. L. (1881): *Virginibus Puerisque and Other Papers*, New York, Charles Scribner's Sons, 1896.

Tabbia, C. (2000a): "La grandiosidad en la identificación narcisista", in *El narcisismo a debate*, Barcelona, GRADIVA, pp. 85–91.

Tabbia, C. (2000b): "Living in intrusive identification", *Exploring the Work of Donald Meltzer. A Festschrift*, London, Karnac Books, pp. 173–187. See Section 3.1.5.

Tabbia, C. (2003): "Los valores en la clínica", *Intercambios. Papeles de psicoanálisis* 10, pp. 53–65.

Tabbia, C. (2004a): "Abordatge de la 'improvisada personalitat' del psicòtic", *Revista Catalana de Psicoanàlisi [SEP– IPA]*, XXI(1–2), pp. 117–123.

Tabbia, C. (2004b): "Observâçao e descrição na gênese do significado", *Revista de Psicoanálise da Sociedade Psicoanalítica de Porto Alegre*, XI(3), pp. 489–518. See Section 3.2.1.

Tabbia, C. (2009): "El concepto de intimidad en el pensamiento de Donald Meltzer". See Section 3.3.1.

Tabbia, C. (2010a): "La intimidad", in *De la angustia y otros afectos,* Barcelona, GRAD-IVA, pp. 109–120.

Tabbia, C. (2010b): "El concepto de intimidad en el pensamiento de D. Meltzer", *Docta, Revista de Psicoanálisis* 6, pp. 47–61, publication of the Asociación Psicoanalítica de Córdoba (Argentina), and in italian in *Psicoterapia Psicoanalítica,* Roma, Rivista de la Società Italiana de Psicoterapia Psicoanalítica, Ed. Borla, XVII(2), pp. 47–61, 63–81. See Section 3.3.1.

Tabbia, C. (2013): "La caja de herramientas del psicoanalista. Un aprendiz en los Talleres de Bion y Meltzer", Revista *Psicoanálisis, APdeBA,* XXXV(2), pp. 283–324, y en *Revista de Psicoterapia Psicoanalítica* (Asoc. Madrileña de Psicoterapia Psicoanalítica), N° 21, febrero 2017, pp. 11–52.

Tabbia, C. (2018): "La intimidad en el trabajo analítico", *Temas de Psicoanálisis* 15, pp. 1–12 See Section 3.3.4.

Winnicott, D. (1958): "The capacity to be alone", *International Journal of Psycho-Analysis,* 39, pp. 416–420.

Chapter 4

The Analyst's Task

To introduce the topic of the psychoanalyst's task, I have chosen to do so accompanied by Freud's (1914) brief and dense work *Remembering, Repeating and Working Through*, from which I will make mention. The first element I want to highlight refers to the fact that the task takes place in the mutual presence (physical or virtual, depending on the situation) of both members of the dyad because this is the condition for emotions and thoughts to be presented and elaborated; this requirement is based on the fact that transformations are impossible before "an enemy who is absent or not within range". The emerging contact and intimacy will have an impact on the emergence of a "more comprehensive" and "present-day" view of the analysand.

The analysand becomes more vital and real when the second element is established: the transference, which is capable of creating "an intermediate region between illness and real life through which the transition from the one to the other is made".

Transition calls for the third element, that is, the task of discovering the transference and the resistances which "is never recognized by the patient" but which the psychoanalyst describes, names, and communicates to the analysand. At this point, the professional would function in a similar way to a midwife who presents the newborn to its parents. This intermediary work is neither simple nor easy, but rather "an arduous task for the subject of the analysis and a trial of patience for the analyst"; as Bion (1991) said: there is nothing that provokes more fear and opposition than growth and development. Although it is a difficult task for both protagonists, it is not less demanding for the psychoanalyst themself, who is called upon to show extra courage and honesty in order to avoid secret pacts (quid pro quo) against the discovery of the truth of the analysand and of themself. A psychoanalytic attitude is required that is capable of encouraging the analysand to "mean it" (Meltzer, 1997), sincerely, freed from defensive traps and the disguises of language: to become oneself, with all the greatness and miseries of one's own truth.

Bibliography

Bion, W. R. (1991): *A Memoir of the Future*, London, Karnac Books.

DOI: 10.4324/9781003347156-12

286 The Analyst's Task

Freud, S. (1914): "Remembering, repeating and working-through", in *The Standard Edition of the Complete Psychological Works of Sigmund Freud*, edited by J. Strachey, London, Hogarth Press, 1966, Vol XII, pp. 145–156.

Meltzer, D. (1997): "Concerning signs and symbols", *British Journal of Psychotherapy* 14, 175–181.

The Analyst Faced with Protomental Functioning[1]

Humour and jokes have the quality of telling lapidary truths while raising smiles and stimulating thought. One such joke refers to the five Jews who have contributed most to changing the way we see the world:

Moses said, "The law is everything."
Jesus said, "Love is everything."
Marx said, "Money is everything."
Freud said, "Sex is everything."
Einstein said, "Everything is relative."

Western civilisation has developed, to a great degree, from these different ways of seeing the world: law, love, unconscious motivations and desires, capital, and finally, relativity, but not relativism. Each new way of seeing the world has shaken and wounded narcissism. The supposed universal truths and values have been and are, time and again, called into question. As always, this questioning provokes unease, surprise, and doubts that can heal precipitously through partially true responses, capable of being transformed into fanatical slogans. Dogmatism and authoritarianism are masks that attempt to conceal ignorance, anaesthetise fear and prevent questions. Fanaticism reveals paranoid-schizoid and confusional anxieties that it aimed to discredit.

When the Berlin Wall fell—organised paranoidly by the western world—all of the divisions and fragmentations arose in Europe that had been frozen behind perverse pacts signed in the name of essences. Pacts do not resolve contradictions; they only freeze them. But just as authoritarianism does not solve problems, neither does the tendency to fragmentation, to divisions, in the manner of adolescents who imagine that they will solve their problems by leaving their parents' house. In reality, neither delusions nor compulsive action are good alternatives to thinking.

The five characters in the joke mentioned above have some elements in common: they were interested in understanding something beyond the immediate. On the one hand, they were mystics, philosophers, scientists, and people who were interested in questioning the depths of issues… and who were capable of formulating ideas and values that have been revised, questioned, denied, anathematised, and

DOI: 10.4324/9781003347156-13

confirmed on many occasions, having largely withstood the test of time and cultures. Today, on the other hand, and in a dangerously schematic contrast, it could be said that disorientation reigns and that values are determined in centres of power such as Hollywood, where fashion is overvalued, or on Wall Street, where money is the supreme value. We are living in a time when lobbies have acquired supranational power, and fashion has become all-pervasive, to the point that it has become "the determining factor in all fields, and it is so", Meltzer said, "because it is connected with money. Only fashions change, but fashion values do not" (Meltzer and Harris, 1998, p. 321). Moreover, the media generate and transmit values. In fact, it could be suggested that the media disseminate the fashions created by the lobbies. The omnipotence of these pressure groups is manifested in that they feel able to propose models of identification in areas as diverse as family organisations, sexual identity, mental health, the way to be happy, to enjoy leisure, or to solve economic crises, even the colours and clothes to wear, and the music we consume, etc. There is almost no area that is free from their influence. The pressure exerted by these groups is so great that it requires great emotional capacity to preserve one's own opinion. Although most people can be conditioned by these groups, I believe that teenagers are the most vulnerable and are seduced by propaganda and the dictates of fashion. This is logical since this age is characterised by confusion, and any proposal that offers a way out will be listened to and welcomed; but, whereas some adolescents will use the fashions and then make their own way with more personal choices, others will remain attached to these slogans. During this turbulent stage, the adolescent needs criteria to guide them through the hazardous journey. This is all the more difficult in a culture that can become confused and blur the lines and the differences because it believes that *everything is relative* and, therefore, *anything goes*. The French psychoanalyst Florence Guignard (2001, p. 394) noted:

> Nowadays, I would say that the lack of differentiation of the stages from the so-called 'latency' period to late adolescence is prolonged by an increasingly important coexistence of promiscuity between young adults and their parents, in the sexual and sentimental avatars of one and the other. This prolongation is far from being solely the outcome of economic factors; the adult generation experiences a certain pleasure, even a great narcissistic complacency in 'rejuvenating' in this way, while favouring in adolescents the avoidance of the recognition of the difference between the sexes and generations, as well as the painful work of solitude that awaits every subject in becoming. [...] The social erasing of the difference between the sexes by the group that surrounds them allows, or even favours, the expression of a certain form of drive excitation in a mostly unisex way, encouraged by the media for commercial reasons.

Guignard even dares to find economic reasons in the exploitation of generational and sexual confusions. I believe that the economic benefits are secondary to the pleasure of manic triumph over the pain of enduring differences and castrations. As with addictions, the denial of differences is intended as an alibi for avoiding mental pain. But there are other variables. Pain in the face of the various castrations acquires more prominence and significance if we add to it the effort required to understand the complex nature of the objects, affects, and relationships with which it has to be negotiated. Complexity requires analysis and synthesis, which is not always within the reach of troubled children and adolescents, which is why mottoes, slogans, and prejudices become a lifeline.

However, if there is something complex, it is the human mind. Given this complexity, there are no simple answers. The history of thinking is a register of humanity's attempt to understand itself and unveil the mysteries of the soul. In this process of becoming, concepts are reformulated within each thinker. Psychoanalysis is another attempt to understand the human mind. Its concepts, models, and formulations have a history. Psychoanalysis, with its complexity and richness, can both excite and overwhelm the scholar because it certainly requires a tolerance for pain to assimilate it. In the face of this effort, responses may arise similar to those given by the adolescent who tries to become an adult by eliminating their parents, as if one could be a psychoanalyst while ignoring metapsychology and the history of concepts. In this case, one is likely to acquire a vehement belief in being able to develop new thoughts, even if, in reality, they are hasty simplifications and superficial thinking. It is also true that what is superficial is highly marketable and fashionable. The epistemophilic impulse pushes towards discovery, and this is a heritage not to be squandered. However, in order to make discoveries, it is necessary to know something about the antecedents without dissolving the complexity with impoverishing historical reasons. Nor should we proceed by getting ourselves hopelessly bogged down in confusion, which may lay beneath the criticism of the concept of asymmetry in the analytical relationship. It would be better not to confuse the difference in functions between subjects with equal rights with a concept more linked to hierarchy, privileges, or authority; I believe such confusion would respond more to an adolescent state of mind or a prejudiced and hasty conclusion than to solid psychoanalytical thinking.

Thinking about the joke at the beginning: not everything is relative (see Section 1.2); it would be harmful if fashion were to destroy the foundations of the psychoanalytic edifice… If this were possible, we would find ourselves with fashion[2] having colluded with the protomental areas to the detriment of symbolic development and autonomous thinking. When there is collusion, two come together to the detriment of a third party. If the slogans of the fashion world encounter a confused state of mind, these slogans might be readily accepted to paralyse a conflict, block a question, or hinder a personal resolution. By using the term protomental, a reference is being made to the division of mental life that Bion (1961) pointed out; he considered the subject to have two areas of functioning; the protomental area as non-symbolic, concrete, quantitative, composed of external facts, and resistant to the process of symbolisation, and the symbolic mental area based on emotions, attentive to the qualitative and aesthetic more so than to the quantitative. The symbolic area is more concerned with finding meanings through introspection than through action. The differentiation between symbolic and non-symbolic areas arrives at a new disparity depending on whether or not mental life derives from contact with objects. Contact permits apprehending the object that can generate a meaning. In contrast, if meanings were established earlier, their effect would be of an individual with their own cosmovision of the closed and ritualised tribal world, as Bion discussed (1961) and Meltzer pointed out (1978). However, everyone's life "...develops not only in the sphere for symbolic functioning, but rather also in the protomental areas. These areas manifest themselves as social behaviour characterised by obedience, routine, and constant hallucinatory experiences that reside outside the emotionally significant area" (Meltzer, 1981, p. 328). Given that the subject operates with these two modes of functioning, the dictates of the fashion world find protomental areas fertile ground to encourage the subject's obedience, the forsaking of thinking, and adherence to the dictates of mass media. Media targets—subtlety and insistently—these non-mental areas of the mind that oppose learning from experience and, by rejecting the pain implicit in all learning processes, assume the seductive propaganda by saying: "Don't worry. If you're not happy, we'll refund your money, because the customer is always right" because "money talks..." This promotes an irresponsible way of functioning based on basic assumptions (Bion), which express the subject's desire to resolve conflicts on the basis of the pleasure principle. In today's society, however, another basic assumption can be set out, along with its function of resistance, as Meltzer does in relation to the family group of a patient, Elsa:

> The basic assumption of this group is money, which is the origin of all good. It is not that having money is the root of all evil, but the other way around. It is the basic capitalist assumption: money is the root of good.
>
> (Meltzer and Harris, 1998, p. 238)

But functioning based on basic assumptions makes it practically impossible to think, and communication ends up being organised around "clichés and slogans" (ibid.) as occurred with this patient. I believe that people trapped in similar ways of functioning to Elsa's could be considered to be like the patients who challenge the analyst's work because they almost lack psychic reality. If people do not think, do not have fantasies, if they are stuck to the concrete world, expressing themselves through slogans and clichés, if they have no other values than those offered by a culture that is seated on money and consumption, etc., the psychoanalyst finds themself with the enormous task of creating a free, thinking subject. This type of patient could be considered to be an exponent of a culture that unreservedly assumes the slogans of "hurry up" because "there's no time to lose", above all to think and much less to mourn and work through grief; a constant push towards pseudo-mature ways of functioning in a culture where *dependence* is not valued, and independence based not so much on responsibility as on oppositionism is demanded, not without cynicism. This evokes the memory of a pubescent who defined the bombs of military planes as "a piece of metal that explodes, making a beautiful visual effect, and that kills just by pure chance". This culture is capable of generating frustration and discouraging young people or stimulating isolation, such as was experienced by that pubescent boy who conserved an intact intelligence but who had not yet been able to enter into contact with the world. However, suffering is not limited to merely that subject. Because when opposition, distrust, an urgency to flee from a situation, and cynicism come together, then the foundation for non-mental functioning is laid that becomes a penchant for searching for and finding scapegoats for one's own failures and for persecution. This conjunction can also motivate the search for messiahs or the idea of salvation that frees us from pain, always caused by another, as occurs—in extreme cases—in juvenile groups and gangs. In the face of such types of functioning, it is worth asking what psychoanalysis can offer. I believe it can only offer the confidence that psychic reality will develop if the psychoanalyst has the tolerance, perseverance, imagination and intuition to transform this specific way of operating, which is typical of immature and infantile functioning. The analysand will likely arrive with a pre-formed transference, i.e. assuming to know what the analysis consists of and what kind of material the analyst will be interested in. It will be the analyst's task to dismantle this preconception in order to create a terrain where a new way of relating can be experienced.

The terrain for this task needs to be prepared, clearing it out and ploughing the ground, and the resource, the instrument, will be none other than to focus exclusively on the interest in the subject, based on observation rather than on information. The patients who come to analysis saturated with information can only be surprised by the analyst's serene availability and non-intrusive curiosity. Gradually, the patient will abandon the social mask that protected their life until this moment. Their armour will turn to rust as the mutual interest of both participants in the analytic relationship develops. However, this process is non-linear and develops by leaps and bounds because the fear of remaining without protection from the other does not immediately dissipate because the one who suffered will need time to trust—maybe for the first time ever. The mask is abandoned when there is sufficient trust in the other, and the patient feels safe in an intimate relationship with the analyst. As I said elsewhere (Tabbia, 2010, p. 118):

> We will consider as intimate that private space in which the participants exchange affects—amorous and hostile—without being able to anticipate an outcome. This will depend on the interplay of drives and the state of the participants' internal objects, and the interplay of introjective and projective identification. Intimacy in the adult state of mind is an experience in which the same experience modifies both participants; in this sense, we can retrieve the Bionian concept of *at-one-ment*, the oneness that names the possibility of participating in the experience of making something unprecedented, intense and unconscious with another person, which generates nostalgia and which is sustained in solitude and in the tolerance of the inexhaustible mystery of the other, which would be one way of defining intimacy. But, like the analytic experience, the experience of intimacy is something that will be understood at its end, and which only the brave can risk.

This intimate context becomes the adequate and necessary container for symbolic development. It is not surprising that groups that are intolerant to thinking and, indeed, defenders of monolithic thinking distrust intimate relationships that they confuse with dangerous ones. In much the same way, they distrust relationships and encounters where thinking develops. Both distrusts have fallen and fall upon psychoanalysis and the work of psychoanalysts. For this reason, I said earlier that only the brave can take the risk. I believe that psychoanalysis is enhanced when it is not assimilated into the comfort of bourgeois groups. In the mollification of those in possession of fame, prestige, and money, psychoanalysis may become a fad suitable for consumers, but it will have lost the subversive character implicit in the process of discovery.

I would not like to finish this communication without first making reference to analysis as an experimental situation in which the analyst and analysand enter into a relationship with the purpose of putting into motion a process of exploration and description more than an explanation. It is a situation in which there are no certainties or predictability and no aims, but in which each session becomes the possibility for an encounter in which both participants will have to mutually discover and transform each other, embracing the hope that God will cure them, as Freud's patient Smiley Blanton put it.

Notes

1 Published in *Intercambios, Papeles de psicoanálisis*, N° 30, June 2013, San Boi, Barcelona, under the title: Función "subversiva" del analista en las sociedades homogenizadoras, 79–83.
2 "I have been compelled to notice that 'fashions' in beliefs, in theories, in varieties of psycho-analysis and in psycho-analysts, are as plentiful as fashions in cosmetics" (Bion, 1991, p. 525).

Bibliography

Bion, W. R. (1961): *Experiences in Groups and Other Papers*, New York, Tavistock Publications Limited.
Bion, W. R. (1991): "The dawn of oblivion", in *A Memoir of the Future*, London, Karnac Books.
Guignard, F. (2001): "El psicoanalista y el adolescente. ¿Existe una especificidad de la formación para el ejercicio psicoanalítico con el adolescente?", *Psicoanálisis APdeBA*, XXIII(2–2001), pp. 389–403.
Meltzer, D. (1978): *The Kleinian Development*, London, Karnac, 2008.
Meltzer, D. (1981): Implicaciones psicosomáticas en el pensamiento de Bion, *Psicoanálisis APdeBA*, XV–W(2–1993), pp. 315–338.
Meltzer, D. & Harris, M. (1998): *Adolescentes*, edited by L. Jachevasky & C. Tabbia, Buenos Aires, Spatia, ed.
Tabbia, C. (2010): "La intimidad", in *De la angustia y otros afectos, VI Jornades d'Intercanvi en psicoanàlisi*, Barcelona, Gradiva, pp. 109–118.
Tabbia, C. (2011): "Grupo familiar (externo/interno) y ética", *Barcelona, Revista de Psicopatología y salud mental del niño y del adolescente*, 17, pp. 83–92.

The Analyst's Mental Availability[1]

One of the manifestations of the analyst's psychic vitality is expressed in their personal availability to connect with their analysands. Being available to become the container of another container is not only an act of generosity, service, and risk, but also a clear manifestation of the drive for life. It cannot be denied that availability will have been enriched and cultivated by resolving the analyst's own personal obstacles, which is why I believe that the analyst's availability, psychic vitality, and mental health are necessarily interrelated. The quality of that conjunction will determine the possibility of connecting with anyone willing to investigate their unfathomable psychic reality. Furthermore, if the conjunction is absent or insufficient, not only will analytic contact be hindered, but it will also expose the analyst to occupational and personal risk.

Exploration of the importance of emotional contact[2] captivated Bion's interest; following his paths and those of other analysts, I will approach the subject, focusing on the conditions of the analyst to make it possible.

In the Tavistock seminars,[3] Bion (2005, p. 35) asked: "When you see today's patient tomorrow, who are you seeing? What are you in contact with?" These two questions refer to the many uncertainties and emotions that present themselves in the analytic encounter and in any new contact, for that matter. In this situation, anxieties awaken that can have similarity with anxieties aroused when presenting a communication in a scientific meeting, where it is often assumed that the other is wiser than oneself... This would be an emotional situation somewhat equivalent to what Bion (1992, p. 24) pointed out when he noted that the soldier was "aware of his own troubles but not of his enemy's". This is not to say that the encounter with a patient is comparable to a battle, but, in any case, it will be necessary to have the "fortitude and high morale" (ibid.) to enter the unknown unconscious world; the "what are you in contact with?" that Bion asked. When Bion uses the term "fortitude", he is not referring to a defensive construction but to the "commonly recognized equipment" (ibid.) that would imply the capacity to withstand problems, adversities, and anxieties always present when one wants to discover unknown territories. I think that in the term *fortitude*, all of the characteristics of mental health, according to Melanie Klein (1960), could be included: emotional maturity, the ability to adapt oneself to the external world without loss of one's own emotions and thinking, to tolerate painful

DOI: 10.4324/9781003347156-14

emotions and be capable of managing them properly, and finally, to have achieved the integration of the different parts of the self. These items—now a part of psycho-analytic criteria—can be complemented or encompassed by another statement by Klein herself, who considered that mental health was incompatible with superficial-ity. Mental health demands mourning; that is to say, mental pain and identification. If the analyst has not achieved introjective identification with the parental functions of their progenitors functioning as a work group (Bion, 1961), they will not have achieved the appropriate fortitude, nor will they have constructed the suitable mental equipment to carry out this transforming task. This transforming function will have to sustain itself on the *trust* towards the internal objects that will support the *faith* to explore O, that inexhaustible world. The *fortitude* of the equipment is not something that remains unaltered, but rather it wears out even with the daily contact with pa-tients. Therefore, the conquest of mental health requires continuous work, "sanity, then, is not something we are born with, but, in varying degrees, painfully acquire" (Money-Kyrle, 1969, p. 437) throughout life.

The analytic relationship, if there is a process, has its turbulent moments, which can be threatening for both participants. One does not know "who we are seeing" (Bion, cf. up supra), nor does it resemble a comfortable *commensal* relationship, taking this term in its original, sociological sense, where nothing new emerges be-cause each is immersed in their own world even though they share a close space. In an avoidant relationship, the "peculiar zone of contact" (Freud, 1912) from uncon-scious to unconscious, which characterises analytic contact, is not created. Without this emotional contact zone, there is no analytic process or symbolic development. Therefore, on the one hand, if there is a serious intolerance to emotional turbulence and psychic change, one can either attempt stubborn isolation or "...manipulate feelings and ideas so that they conform to a principle of perpetuity" [...] so "that nothing should disturb the sense of permanence" (Bion, 1991, p. 170), preventing the development of thinking. On the other hand, if one is open to a relationship in which there is confrontation and where "The thought proliferates, and the thinker develops" (Bion, 1970, p. 118), one requires sufficient availability to allow ideas to develop, "even though the germ of an idea is going to displace him and his theories" (Bion, 2005, p. 49). Such availability will involve tolerating dispersion, misunderstanding and "persecution [...] until a new coherence emerges..." (Bion, 1963, p. 102), which may be different from what was anticipated or longed for. Therefore, a tolerant analytical contact calls for a state of mind available to encoun-ter what is not sought after; it calls for tolerating that knowledge, ideas and intui-tions surprise us, and independently of our occasionally insistent interventions, as a "mental content that was present in some way without being present, that enters as if floating through free-floating attention-association, and will vanish, once again" (Serebriany and Sor, 1987, p. 53) for new coherences, for new experiences on the tracks of the road travelled "without memory or desire". Sometimes Poe's letter looks at us slyly in the face of our obstinacy....

The *dispersion* and *coherence* mentioned above refer to the oscillation between Ps↔D, whether from a minuscule fragmentation to integration, or from analysis to synthesis. If this oscillation is well-tolerated without excessive anxiety and with a predominance of depressive creation or recreation, intimating and empathising with the patient without confusing coming together (*at-one-ment*) with erotisation, nor enactment with collusion, becomes possible. Concerning collusive relationships, I believe it necessary to point out that in every analyst, there are unexplored areas where alien psychotic cores can take refuge; that is why I think it is necessary to differentiate between becoming an accomplice to collusion and tolerating the acting-out for a time until it is symbolised. If becoming an accomplice is to pervert the transference, tolerating acting-out may be part of the technique, especially with borderline patients, in whom acting-out replaces thinking (Cassorla, 2008). Not infrequently, the analyst becomes an involuntary container of primitive aspects of the patient that, by *colonising them*, can alter their function. I believe that in order to tolerate temporary colonisation, the analyst must be able to maintain a stable, intimate, and tolerant relationship with themself; a tolerance that implies assuming without offence that phrase of Shakespeare's, in *Hamlet*, quoted by Freud in letter 71: "…that every man after his desert, and who should 'scape whipping?" (1897). Neither arrogance nor intolerance of emotional contact is the best equipment for exercising the psychoanalytic function and sustaining symbolic development.

The necessary condition[4] for exercising such a function with tolerance is to have *cured* own's own "mental abnormalities or eccentricities" (Meltzer and Harris, 1998, p. 323), which, in the face of uncertainties, could stimulate transformations in -K or facilitate the abandonment of emotional contact. Controlling the pressure of their own conflicts and with improved possibilities to identify with their patient, i.e. empathise, the analyst will be more predisposed towards intuition (Hahn, 2005). This ability, so essential for a psychoanalyst, allows them to go beyond the knowledge obtained through rational discourse and the information received from the senses because thoughts and emotions—as Money-Kyrle used to say—"cannot be sensed—in fact, they do not belong to the physical world at all but to the psychic one" (1977, p. 457). In order to perceive O's emanations initially present in the form of glimpses, more than good cooperation, sufficient availability is needed to perceive the brief manifestations of thoughts barely glimpsed intuitively and to receive the inspiration of the internal objects that provide reference points amid uncertainty. The analyst will also have to be supported by the necessary resources to fortify the most vulnerable part of analytic functioning, whether it be the difficulty in understanding, the problem of misunderstanding, the obstacles coming from the negative counter-transference, or the difficulty to empathise with the infantile parts of the analysand. With these attitudes and resources, the analyst will be able to venture into the unconscious and initiate an investigation of the meaning of what is observed (Tabbia, 2004, 2013), the meaning of the object relations present in the here-and-now, and moving forward to the moment of the interpretation. Moving forward, however, is not without obstacles in our own primitive, psychotic cores that do not want to renounce the conquest of the conscious as the organ capable of governing behaviour. This opposition can infiltrate our minds as new theories that, like the song of the sirens, push against the rocks of superficiality and place distance between the two unconscious minds. This opposition to the discovery of the internal world can manifest itself with changes, like those that Hahn (2017, p. 235) pointed to:

> …unconscious phantasy and the understanding of part-objects have given place to new para-analytic theories; work with the infantile transference has been replaced by a discussion of the intersubjective relation between the patient and the person of the analyst in the here and now, with no reference to meaning or symbolizations; and the interpretation of dreams has fallen away as the 'royal road to the unconscious', to be replaced by a more pragmatic understanding of the dream content with less reference to internal emotional links.

The different formats that the analyst's personal difficulties acquire can transform the analytic relationship into a relationship between conscious minds, the most efficient way to devalue and denaturalise "the importance of rapport" (Bion, 1992, p. 385).

In order to illustrate some of the personal difficulties that can act as an obstacle to the analytic task, I will present a brief clinical vignette.

This material comes from a patient who is a psychoanalytic psychotherapist. His analytic availability is hindered by types of functioning derived from splitting and intrusive identifications. He does not feel free or authorised in his professional task. He suffers because in order to exercise his function, he must withstand a disqualifying internal critique. To exemplify these criticisms, I will mention the following: "you don't have the necessary credentials to be a psychotherapist", "you're a farce", "you're an intruder"… When his despair increases, he can feel empty and inconsistent. Trapped in his own conflicts, he is unable to transcend the manifest material of his patients' narratives and consequently establishes a superficial dialogue with them. In his work, in order to be able to interpret, he needs to dissociate himself and flee from a persecutory object relationship, concretely, a paternal persecutory object. At the same time, his narcissistic defences gratify him, making him feel omniscient. This situation hinders not only the possibility of him learning in general but also the calmness necessary to be able to observe, to be able to give meaning to what he was capable of intuiting, to choose the moment to intervene, and to decide how best to do so. Far from being able to achieve an instrumental dissociation in order to be more available, he finds himself struggling with his psychopathology and functioning as if he were a thief who intervenes the moment he is not being watched. His request for analysis was motivated by his suffering and a certain awareness[5] that a massive identification with a persecutory object could precipitate him into a dogmatic attitude, thus increasing the obstacles to his clinical work.

In his family romance, a competitive and disqualifying engineer father and an affectionate but operatory mother, incapable of thinking, who somatised, both appear. The patient is the youngest of three sons. Rafael—the eldest brother—maintained a jealous relationship of control and beleaguerment over the child, who thought he had seduced the mother because he was "cute". The patient has always suffered from learning disabilities despite his intelligence. Raising him was difficult not only because of his intolerance to frustration but also because the paternal objects, from what I can observe, have not been very capable of containing him. During the analysis, which the analyst economically facilitated,[6] there lurked a suspicion that he was receiving special treatment because the analyst, seduced, wanted to make him his successor or because the old analyst wanted to "suck out" his youth, thus revealing fantasies of substitution rather than aspiring to an enriching identification.

His learning disabilities are diminishing, but a paranoid core still restricts him. At this time, the patient has acceded to the role of team coordinator, while Rafael has just lost his role as director of the hospital where they both work.

In this session, which takes place early in the morning, the patient arrives late and says, on entering: "I completely overslept". Later, he asked me if I was angry with him for arriving late.

I interpreted that he projected into me a persecutory object (brother/father) when, perhaps, it was a way to test out what would happen if he transgressed as if attempting to free himself from the controlling object. Questions came to my mind, however, that I did not give voice to: Why should I be angry? Can I not be without him? Do I represent the mother that had been seduced? Does he do things behind my back, and should I feel jealous or threatened? Does he want to provoke me? To what degree am I the depository of his persecutory part object?

Next, he remembered and narrated the following dream scene:

> We're in my town, and it's a cold and unpleasant day. You're my father, and you were waiting for me to take me to a maths exam; Rafael stood outside of the car looking at us distrustfully, watching what we did, and at times I didn't know if Rafael was in the car or not.

Here we see reflected the transference dissociation between Rafael—in whom the instrusivity is projected—and the father/analyst who awaits and accompanies him. However, the relationship with this father/ally/protector is not sturdy because the possibility of it being invaded by Rafael exists, because at times, he was unsure if Rafael was inside or outside the car. This doubt leads him to occasionally feel that no allies are possible or—worse yet—that he is surrounded by persecutors. His emotional situation, the reintegration of the dissociation made impossible, is characterised by the alternation between persecutory and idealised objects (whether people or places). When either defensively and/or enviously intruding into idealised objects, he acquires the feeling of grandiosity and power that necessarily leads to claustrophobic states. This claustrophobia manifests itself, for example, in dream material, in being trapped inside holes, or hanging over a very high fence without being able to climb to the other side... In this manner, he fails to find peace anywhere, as if he were an intruding inhabitant of an object (Meltzer, 1992).

Taking into account the previous associations, as well as the knowledge that I have of him, I interpreted that his paranoid Rafael part distrusts our relationship because our joint work is rescuing him from the oppression and submission to the tyranny of the internal-Rafael object, while at the same time leading him towards the development of abstract, (mathematical) thinking. At the time, I omitted to tell him that the dissociation between the paternal/capable of thinking object and his competitive Rafael part hinders his development. This is because, at the same time that he can identify with the symbolising function of the paternal/analyst object, allowing him to learn and tolerate an evaluation, his Rafael part that projects jealous rivalry, contaminated with envy, subsists, and prevents him from having some peace to be able to enjoy learning. In this sense, my patient resembles those paranoid, intelligent personalities that have special sensitivity—frequently motivated by the need to control the dissociation—for observation, albeit an observation contaminated by paranoia. This implies only registering a part of reality, and he experiences difficulties in the relationships with his patients.

This patient usually attributes to his brother the intention to dominate him, something that might have occurred during infancy; nevertheless, through dream material and reiterated associations, it was possible to intuit that he had not given up the idea of invading the older-admired-desired brother-object. It usually presents itself in masturbatory fantasies in which he seduces Rafael, thus reinforcing the persecutory cycle. This can also be observed when he tries to provoke or seduce me. He often projects into me fantasies of wanting to penetrate him, thus justifying his fear of the analyst. In his psychic reality, this fantasy hides the intrusive desire to plunder the object. The consequent anxiety leads him to placate Raphael or me. It cannot be ignored that having obtained a better job than his brother has increased not only his persecution but also his triumph. In any case, and for the purpose of understanding how mental health is the basis of analytic availability, in this patient, we find that his receptive/decoding capacity diminishes when he feels oppressed by the internal object-Rafael, who disavows him and accuses him of usurping a function belonging to others, whether it be that of the parents or of Rafael himself. This forces the patient to be inhibited, to function with the overexertion of keeping his paranoia under control or to act stealthily, i.e. without freedom, as he does not know whether Rafael is inside or outside the car, taking complete possession of his internal world. Consequently, at present, in order to be able to work, he has to dissociate himself beyond the necessary instrumental dissociation, with the logical loss of peace of mind that limits his possibility of functioning as a container.

Although his availability for analytic contact is diminished because he has to keep a double, attentive eye on the patient's inner world and his own, to the extent that he can sustain a sympathetic and unprejudiced look at both worlds, and the tension between them, he could benefit from intuiting meanings. But the fatigue caused by his conflicts occasionally stimulates the desire to abandon his work. Summing up this brief clinical presentation, it can be stated that, considering the patient's present state of mind, he still lacks all the *fortitude* necessary to be available and confident for an encounter with his patients' unconscious.

With this patient, as with others, there is the possibility for both participants in the analytic relationship to develop or deteriorate, and so I believe that in order to be psychoanalytically available, "The only 'faith' that is required is an absolute belief in one's feebleness, ignorance, impotence and mortality, to open to view the beauty-of-the-world and passionate feelings" (Meltzer, 1992, p. 115) which will make possible "closer contact with the psychoanalytic experience" (Bion, 1994, p. 385) and which will open the doors to the mysteries of O.

Notes

1 Paper presented in Milan, (Italy) at the International Bion Conference 2016: *Emozioni, Trasformazioni e vitalità psíchica*. Published in the *Revista Psicoanálisis* (Colombia), XXIX(1), 2017, pp. 61–72.
2 "...I am attempting to elaborate on the importance of *rapport*. I feel some unease if it is suggested that I am departing from psychoanalytic technique, not because I have any objection to innovation if it seems to be necessary, but because it is unlikely that the intuitions of experienced psychoanalysts can be lightly laid aside. I do hope, however, that the points I make may help psychoanalysts to think themselves into *closer contact with the psychoanalytic experience*" (Bion, 1992, *Cogitations*, p. 385, my italics). Bion said this after receiving comments on his paper *Notes on memory and desire* (1967).
3 Seminar 5 July 1977.
4 "The analysis that every psycho-analyst is obliged to undergo as part of his training is necessary because it removes obstacles to participation in the psycho-analytic experience" (Bion, 1970, p. 26).
5 Like the soldier aware of "his own troubles".
6 Adjusting my fees to the patient's means.

Bibliography

Bion, W. R. (1961): *Experiences in Groups and Other Papers*, New York, Tavistock Publications Limited.
Bion, W. R. (1963): "Elements of psychoanalysis", in *The Complete Works of W. R. Bion*, edited by Cris Mawson, London, Karnac, 2014, Vol. V, pp. 1–86
Bion, W. R. (1967): "Notes on memory and desire", *Psychoanalytic Forum*, vol. 2, Nº 3. Publicado en la *Rev. de Psicoanálisis*, APA, XXVI, 3, pp. 679–682, Buenos Aires, 1969.
Bion, W. R. (1970): *Attention and Interpretation*, London, Karnac Books.
Bion, W. R. (1991): "The dream", in *A Memoir of the Future, London, Karnac Books*, pp. 1–218.
Bion, W. R. (1992): *Cogitations*, London, Karnac.
Bion, W. R. (2005): *The Tavistock Seminars*, London, Karnac.
Cassorla, R. M. (2008): "The analyst's implicit alpha-function, trauma and enactment in the analysis of borderline patients", *International Journal of Psycho-Analysis*, 89, pp. 161–180.
Freud, S. (1897): "Letter 71 extracts from the Fliess papers", In *The Standard Edition of the Complete Psychological Works of Sigmund Freud*, edited by J. Strachey, London, Hogarth Press, 1966, Vol I, pp. 263–266.
Freud, S. (1912): "Recommendations to physicians practising psycho-analysis", in *The Standard Edition of the Complete Psychological Works of Sigmund Freud*, edited by J. Strachey, London, Hogarth Press, 1966, Vol XII, pp. 109–120.
Hahn, A. (2005): "A note on intuition", read at the *memorial conference for Donald Meltzer at the Tavistock Clinic* (London), 12 Nov. 2005. Available at www.psa-atelier.org

Hahn, A. (2017): "Concluding thoughts on the nature of psychoanalytic activity", in *Doing Things Differently. The influence of Donald Meltzer on Psychoanalytic Theory and Practice*, edited by Margaret Cohen and Alberto Hahn, London, Karnac, pp. 233–236.

Klein, M. (1960): "On mental health", in *Envy and Gratitude and Other Works 1946–1963*, edited by M. Masud R. Khan, New York, The Free Press, A Division of Simon & Schuster, 1975.

Meltzer, D. (1967): *The Psycho-nalytical Process,* London, William Heinemann Medical Books Limited.

Meltzer, D. (1992): *The Claustrum. An Investigation of Claustrophobic Phenomena,* Strath-Clyde, The Clunie Press.

Meltzer, D. & Harris, M. (1998): *Adolescentes,* edited by L. Jachevasky & C. Tabbia, Buenos Aires, Spatia ed.

Money-Kyrle, R. (1969): "On the fear of insanity", in *The Collected Papers of Roger Money-Kyrle*, edited by Donald Meltzer, London, Karnac, pp. 434–441.

Money-Kyrle, R. (1977): "On being a psycho-analyst", in *The Collected Papers of Roger Money-Kyrle*, edited by Donald Meltzer, London, Karnac, pp. 457–465.

Serebriany, R. & Sor, D., (1987): "Atención-Asociación libre-flotante y vínculo analítico", *Psicoanálisis, APdeBA*, IX(2), pp. 47–60.

Tabbia, C. (2004): "Observâçao e descriçâo na gênese do significado", in *Revista de Psicoanálise da Sociedade Psicoanalítica de Porto Alegre*, Brazil, XI(3), pp. 489–518.

Tabbia, C. (2013): "La caja de herramientas del psicoanalista. Un aprendiz en los Talleres de Bion y Meltzer", *Psicoanálisis, APdeBA,* XXXV(2), pp. 283–324.

Psychoanalytic Attitude, Faith, Belief, and Intuition[1]

The psychoanalyst's emotional and mental disposition is built up as much as it is destroyed. Being a fundamental tool to sustain the analytic process, it becomes an instrument that demands to be maintained in the best condition possible. Throughout his work, Bion made valuable contributions to untangle characteristics, elements, potentialities, and the dark spots of emotional experiences in general and to develop and perceive the psychoanalyst's state of mind. The analyst's state of mind determines the psychoanalytic attitude.

The almost unfathomable dimension of psychic reality, both the patient's and the psychoanalyst's, can provoke a fear similar to that experienced by Pascal in the face of infinite spaces. The situation, at least while presiding over the process, demands of the psychoanalyst as much courage and daring as Buber (1942, p. 148) demanded of the anthropologist to discover human nature:

> …the philosophical anthropologist must stake nothing less than his real wholeness, his concrete self […] it is not enough for him to stake his self as an object of knowledge. He can know the wholeness of the person and through it the wholeness of man only when he does not leave his subjectivity out and does not remain an untouched observer. He must enter, completely and in reality, into the act of self-reflection, in order to become aware of human wholeness. In other words, he must carry out this act of entry into that unique dimension as an act of his life, without any prepared philosophical security; that is, he must expose himself to all that can meet you when you are really living. Here you do not attain to knowledge by remaining on the shore and watching the foaming waves, you must make the venture and cast yourself in, you must swim, alert and with all your force, even if a moment comes when you think you are losing consciousness: in this way, and in no other, do you reach anthropological insight.

Thrown, on occasion, into turbulent waters, the psychoanalyst will have to risk entering into the world of emotions and phantasies and reach the other side. Dr. Resnik (1920–2017) liked to tell us that the psychoanalyst could enter a forest and emerge with a metaphor, whereas the psychotic surely would get lost in the forest. In order to orient themselves in the forest of people, it is necessary to develop an

DOI: 10.4324/9781003347156-15

acute sense of observation (Tabbia, 2004) "for upon the accuracy and detail of this observation 'of the emotional experience' [...] growth depends" (Meltzer, 1978, p. 375), as does the richness of mental processes. The essential value of observation for the development of psychoanalysis stimulated Bion (1970) to produce one of his fundamental works, *Attention and Interpretation*, with a title that announces an intention: to pay attention and observe in depth in order to be able to interpret.

So much courage is required, as Buber pointed out, because, although it may seem paradoxical, "of all the hateful possibilities, growth and maturation are feared and detested most frequently" (Bion, 1970, p. 53). Rejected out of fear of change and the birth of an idea, as expressed by the character of *The Past Presented*, "Is there not a danger that someone will give birth to thought?" (Bion, 1991b, p. 352). The fear of the birth of thinking is as intense as that which is felt at the push of new ideas; thinking overwhelms (Bion, 1991a, p. 38) the container that receives it and, if not sufficiently consistent and ductile to receive it, another container will be sought to develop. It is something similar to the overwhelming force of the drive that will lead to a symptom if it does not find a subject with the capacity to symbolise. If the birth of an idea is a challenge and a threat, it is not only for the analysand but also for the psychoanalyst and the community of both. Therefore, a large part of psychoanalytic attitude will consist in denouncing the sirens' songs that are offered as alternatives to these transformative ideas.

4.3.1 Observing with "Faith"?

Not infrequently, Bion states something that provokes disconcertion. An example would be the following: "How, then, are we to 'observe' and 'record' the patient's state of mind? Since I wish to discuss this but do not know the answer, I shall say 'by F'" (Bion, 1970, p. 57). He does not limit himself to going to F when he has no answers, but he also depends on F to observe; he even takes it further. He places F at "the heart of his psychoanalytic technique" (Vermote, 2011a, p. 355).

It is undeniable that F, from Faith, possesses "vague and confusing qualities" (Meltzer, 1978c, p. 369); as enigmatic as the reason for which Bion abandoned the term F after *Attention and Interpretation*, as López Corvo (2002, p. 24) pointed out. In my opinion, the disconcertion increases when he employs *faith* in *Attention and Interpretation*, and almost simultaneously, while writing *A Memoir of the Future*, he has already left off using *faith*, instead opting for *belief*. I wondered if it was another of Bion's variations or if a meaning radically different from both terms existed in the English language. Comparing (Webster, 1996) *faith* with *belief*, it is difficult to find a big difference between these terms because they both refer to a feeling of trust and confidence in something. However, in *faith*, there is a certain emphasis on trust or belief in a person or a thing, which is not based on proof; *faith* also designates a nuance of fidelity to promises. Whereas *belief* places more emphasis on something which is believed, in an opinion or conviction, it also includes trust in the truth even though it may not be immediately proven; in *belief*, what stands out is an unconditional belief—profound and sincere. Based on what I have been able to discern, the term *faith* is not linked to a supernatural or religious senti-ment, although it can be used to refer to religious beliefs. It refers more, however, to a feeling of trust.

At the time, I was confused by a statement made by Sandler (2005, p. 292) that the term Faith had been "borrowed from Lurianic/Christian cabbala" because it referred to Faith in the world of religious cosmovisions. On the one hand, if Faith were framed in the religious world, its model would fall to Abraham, the father of believers, who did not doubt in accepting the proposal to sacrifice his son as a demonstration of his *faith*. On the other hand, Abraham's God was a god without limits but saturated in the meaning as was illustrated by theologist and philoso-pher Nicholas of Cusa (1401–1464)—pioneer of modern thinking—an author who seems to me to be recognisable in some passages of Bion. In order to depict the relationship between faith and saturated knowledge, I will quote some of Nicholas of Cusa's eloquent thoughts (1440, p. 224):

> All our forefathers unanimously maintain that faith is the beginning of under-standing. For in every branch of study certain things are presupposed as first principles. They are grasped by faith alone, and from them is elicited an under-standing of the matters to be treated.[…] But there is no more perfect faith than Truth itself, which is Jesus. Who does not understand that right faith is a most excellent gift of God?

A faith that illuminates the path and knows where it must reach. A faith without mystery. A counter-intuitive faith. Indeed, this is not the faith to which Bion re-ferred nor the observation open to O.

The faith of the religious systems is based on the projection to infinity[2] of the ad-mired qualities of the protective figures, or to the contrary; for that very same reason, gods and demons circulate throughout history from the earliest times of humanity. Lack of protection is not well-tolerated by the human infant born without sufficient resources to survive without the mediation of sustaining objects. On this basis,

> the strength of the endurance of religions (it is thought that in the course of hominisation 100,000 religions were generated) leads us to think that the reli-gious vertex is underpinned by an energetic latent emotional force that remains perennial over time.
>
> (Martínez and Sor, 2004, p. 95)

Is there anything more disturbing than the lack of protection of the infant or the fear of death in adults? But Bion does not turn to F after one of the thousands of religious thoughts but only because he does not possess "the answer" (Bion, 1970, p. 57). With F, a useful concept albeit loaded with associative penumbras, Bion demands a scientific state of mind capable of penetrating into the darkest areas for the psychoanalyst. His proposal follows Freud's suggestion to blind oneself in order to illuminate the darkness. From there, Bion can propose: "Through F one can 'see', 'hear', and 'feel' the mental phenomena of whose reality no practising psycho-analyst has any doubt though he cannot with any accuracy represent them by existing formulations" (ibid., pp. 57–58).

However, it cannot be denied that the method proposed by Freud, as that of Bion, bears some similarities with the mystics' mode of operation. As Vermote (op. cit., p. 355) points out, "Bion used mystical metaphors and techniques in his search to apprehend the psychoanalytic object". However, it cannot be inferred that Bion was a mystic or a "religious writer". I believe as Sandler (2005, p. 294) says, that attributing a religious dimension to him is the consequence of a "superficial" or intentional reading. This is why I find López Corvo's statements (op. cit., p. 23) appropriate when he alerts us of "the danger of connecting F with the supernatural or with undesirable aspects of the mind, and thus saturating it", as well as Caper's evaluation of the Symingtons' *The Clinical Thinking of Wilfred Bion* pertinent. According to Caper (1998), these authors have given a religious view of Bion's work. Insofar as the mystics have come closest to ultimate reality, the psychoanalytic approach should be as close as possible to the mystics. It is one thing, though, to approach these search models and another to saturate the answer, which is why Caper's conclusion (op. cit., p. 420) seems to me to be correct when he says:

> If one wishes to take the term 'mystic' literally, then Bion is providing a model of mysticism abstracted from his psychoanalytic experience of the interplay of interpretation, projection, containment and resistance. But this is a psychoanalytic model of mysticism, not a mystical model of psychoanalysis.

I think it is appropriate at this point to recall Bion's own words when he says: "An 'act of faith' is peculiar to scientific procedure and must be distinguished from the religious meaning with which it is invested in conversational usage" (Bion, 1970, pp. 34–35). It is important to differentiate faith from other objects. There have been many attempts to give Faith a place in the personality as a whole, for example, the attempts of Hume, who wanted to humanise religion and naturalise faith (Pérez Andreo, 2009). One way of giving it a place involves recognising its difference from *knowledge*. This implies the presence of a non-thing. In knowledge, thought, the name is in the place of the absent object-thing, whereas Faith refers to an expectation that knowing something is possible. The faith of the analyst lies in the expectation of the emergence of a *selected fact* that evokes a name. *Faith means that thought will be possible* and that O is on its horizon, very different from the Ω of the early Christians. Here it is worth mentioning Bion's answer to Caper (1998, op. cit., p. 420) concerning the concept of infinity, so closely linked to that unknowable and unattainable O:

> He once told me that his concept of the infinite was the extent of what he didn't know. It is unknowable not because it is ineffable, but because there is not enough time in one life to know everything, or even enough time to know all there is to know about any one thing.

What has been said so far does not exclude a respectful and even reverential attitude towards the unknown and unfathomable (Vermote, 2011b), but without idealising the terms and without losing sight of what Bion himself (1967b, p. 3) said:

> Since I don't know what that reality is, and since I want to talk about it, I have tried to deal with this position by simply giving it a symbol 'O' and just calling it 'O', ultimate reality, the absolute truth.

Each person's ultimate truth is frightening, not only because of the emotional turbulence it creates but also because of the implicit possibility of change and the uncertainty of its direction. Being oneself is not usually a tempting project. Amongst other reasons because, as the poet said: "... there is no path, the path is made by walking" (Machado, 1912).

Another meaning of the term *faith* refers to the obligation of *loyalty or fidelity* to a person, promise, commitment, etc. In this sense, I believe that one of the meanings of *faith* is linked to the possibility of glimpsing the truth and being faithful to it. Thus in *A Memoir of the Future* (Bion, 1991b, p. 340), a relationship between truth and science is presented, and the kind of association that sustains it:

> P.A. ... A 'scientific view' only means one which claims loyalty to truth.
> PRIEST Similarly, loyalty to God should be indistinguishable from loyalty to truth.

The theme of the truth is fundamental for all thinking. Here, I would like to digress with respect to the article that precedes the term "truth"; I am referring to "the truth" as if only one existed. I believe that the pretension of there being only one sole truth originates from the intolerance of multiple truths existing at different times of life. When I hear reference made to "the" truth, it sounds like intolerance to polytheism, from which monotheism arose, despite having been so incapable of maintaining the unity of the monotheistic peoples that still fight in the name of "the" truth that they all believe they possess. O is caged when the transformations *in* O are not tolerated.

Although I do not intend to repeat Pontius Pilate's question, I might wonder what is being named. In this sense, the mention that E.T. de Bianchedi makes (2016, p. 22) of "truth":

> ...the definition that Freud explicitly accepts is that of the correspondence of a formulation of reality, to the real, external world (Freud, 1933). Faced with the reality of the psychic world [...] truth will also be the correspondence of the formulation with the facts. Nevertheless, the truth intuited in the psychoanalytic relationship and formulated in a hypothesis (interpretation) that plausibly conveys what has been discovered can neither be corroborated nor refuted with the

scientific method. The analyst can only take for granted the truth that this is his interpretation of the facts, his hypothesis constructed at that moment about what is happening in the emotional contact.

The Faith that the analyst has in their ability to establish a correspondence between facts and their formulations sustains their enunciation of the truth. Loyalty to the relationship between observed-intuited and what is interpreted characterises the psychoanalytic attitude and true psychoanalytic contact. This, by the way, is not achieved by running behind facts as if to hunt down truths, but rather the contrary, since it is truth that hunts us because

> ...the achievement of truth is more passive, requiring submission to the operation of container and contained, the mechanism of Ps↔D under the vertex of L, K and, if possible F, where the value is placed on creating rather than destroying.
> (Meltzer, 1978, p. 377)

It is not trite to refer here to the fact that the search for truth accentuates creation, not destruction, because not only is it about constructing truths but also preserving (Cf. Meltzer, 1967) the receivers of the same. To this end, it is necessary to have Faith that the destructive and envious parts dissociated from the very same analyst will not destroy their psychic reality. Neither can one ignore that the psychotic and non-mental parts of patients empower those of the analyst, for instance, making them believe that they know the truth. For truth is as nourishing to the mind as falsehood, lies and unperceived inoculations are toxic. At the same time, the readiness to encounter truth, which presents itself in the midst of turbulence backwaters, invites trust that truth will be conceived, and if tolerated, it will appear as a light that shines through the mist and darkness alike.

When the analyst has grasped the emotional reality of the patient, they can even have the certainty, the Faith, that they will be able to identify it; that is why both Sandler (2005, p. 294) and López Corvo (2002, p. 22) say that the analyst is in that state in which they can no longer doubt. Nevertheless, just as Faith does not admit doubt, doubt can nestle in the heart of belief. I think that *belief* entails a possibility of doubt before reaching *faith*, the certainty that authorises us to name and communicate that truth in interpretation.

4.3.2 Beliefs

The theme of faith and belief has given rise to multiple disputes in the history of thought.

Ferrater Mora (1965), on the one hand, has pointed out that belief has been identified with faith and has opposed knowledge; on the other hand, it has been said that all knowledge and, in general, all statements have, at their base, a belief. Now we must distinguish faith from belief. I dismiss "fanatical belief" as a resource for knowledge because of its radical opposition to knowledge.

In the following text from *A Memoir of the Future* (Bion, 1991b, pp. 319–320), one can observe the confusing interplay of the terms "knowledge", "fanaticism", "belief", "faith", and "arrogance":

PRIEST The king paid with his life for the bigotry of the doctor.
P.A. Was it his bigotry or his religion?
PRIEST He believed in his medicine; it was almost his god. He worshipped his king and queen—this side of what you would call idolatry. They told me he thought the king was dying—
P.A. —and you and your like told people he would survive, and if they went into the pit with his body and were buried they would go to Heaven.
PRIEST Heaven? Nonsense! That idea has only grown up during the last few thousand years.

(Rosemary fades in)

ROSEMARY (luxuriously, admiring her well-shod foot) This is my idea of Heaven. I would hardly have dared to believe that I would live to call my mistress and hear her say 'Ma'am' to me when I gave her orders.

In this text, there are different types of objects in which one believes: medicine, religion, the inversion of social classes, and erotised part objects (the feet); but what is common is that beliefs lead to us burying ourselves in death, superstitious thinking, or eroticised superficiality. Any object can be idealised. It is an ancient and typical aspect of human frailty to create gods or heavens as "*during the last few thousand years*", but it is undeniable that in every belief, there is some knowledge and, therefore, some truth, a point of support from which a representation, a thought, is constructed. Compared to symptoms such as delusions, however far removed from reality as they may be, there is always something to stand on. Nevertheless, just as the delusional construction is based on certainty, "Belief rests on probability" (Britton, 1998, p. 8), leaving a margin for doubt (ibid. p. 13), surprise, or limits. When belief becomes certainty, it does not lead to heaven….

It is important to differentiate *belief* from *thought*. Plato already raised this issue. He linked belief to the sensitive or physical world, whereas knowledge referred to an intelligible reality or abstract ideas. Plato differentiated *doxa* from *episteme*. By *doxa*, he meant an opinion, a knowledge that did not offer certainty, but a reasonable belief, an apparent knowledge of sensitive reality characterised by constant flux. On the one hand, this changeable character is what made it difficult to understand. *Episteme*, on the other hand, referred to knowledge of true reality, an abstract, intelligible, and immutable reality. Its ideal was eternal truths. Although the suggestive differentiation between *doxa* and *episteme* has not been maintained since the development of historicist analysis and the contributions of quantum physics, it cannot be denied that both express both the starting point of knowledge and the desire to transcend the data obtained up to that point. *Episteme* was as utopian an ideal as Bion's O. Although unattainable, it functions as a beacon of curiosity.

The polarisation between *doxa* and *episteme* marks the limits of a vast territory where different levels of belief are registered by the interference of the experimenter and by the limits of the methods of knowledge.

Insofar as beliefs carry an intense emotional commitment because they become a guide for our actions, they can become ideologies based on religious or dogmatic faith. Their "calm" and "satisfying" emotional component that offers stable representations (Wittgenstein, 1992)—like the longed-for *episteme*—enhances the fascination that beliefs and fanaticism generate, although with different degrees of truth between them. The defensive function of beliefs had already been formulated, for example, by Peirce (1877), when he said that we resort to them to free ourselves from unsatisfactory and unsettling doubt. Popular wisdom expresses this by saying, "better the devil you know than the devil you don't".

Given that there are different points of support, it is convenient to differentiate truths that correlate with realities (sensitive or mental) in order to separate them from those based on pre-judgements, scotomisations, or intolerant perceptions founded on divisions. That is why I also agree with Gustavo Bueno (2002) when he affirmed the need to criticise beliefs not so much in order to "annihilate them (which is impossible) as to distinguish their constitutive (ontological) components from their unpremeditated or superstitious components". The hygienic task that Bueno proposes for the beliefs of social groups requires another, more specific, step for unconscious beliefs. To this end, it is necessary to have made it "conscious and recognised to be a belief" [and in this way] "it can be tested against perception, memory, known facts and other existing beliefs" (Britton, op. cit., p. 9). But the condition for making the transition from *doxa*-belief to *episteme*-knowledge is tolerance of doubt and reality-testing. In any case, it has to be admitted that this desired *episteme* can never be reached no matter how much evidence one has, not only because of the interference exerted by the observer ("uncertainty principle") but also because of the fact that "there is not enough time in one life to know everything, or even enough time to know all there is to know about any one thing" (cited ut supra). This is why I agree in turn with Saab (2013) when she states that one can only have degrees of belief depending on the available evidence.

Both observer interference and the limitations of methods mean that access to knowledge of the nature of psychic phenomena or physical causes in the natural sciences is limited. Rigorous observation of the underpinnings of beliefs and ideologies becomes essential in order to discriminate truths from falsehoods. This is the task of the scientist and the psychoanalyst. The psychoanalyst's task is to identify the points of support of certain representations that function as guiding beliefs, often engendered or intoxicated by superstitions or misunderstandings (Money-Kyrle). To this end, Bion's task, drawing on the thinking of Wittgenstein, among others, consisted of creating resources to disentangle falsehoods from truths because "There can be no genuine outcome that is based on falsity" (Bion, 1970, p. 28). This task demands, among others, that the psychoanalyst really be so, because this condition will allow him to "… be at one with the reality of the patient" (ibid.). To be a true psychoanalyst implies, therefore, the courageous attitude of recognising one's own mistakes and wrongdoings in order to repent and make reparation. In this sense, it is enlightening to suggest that the concept "to be at one" refers to that important Jewish holiday, *Yom Kippur* or *Day of Atonement*, the day of forgiveness from which Bion would have extracted the *at-one-ment*, i.e. the ability to re-integrate and be oneself as a condition for empathising-being at one with the patient.[3] This is becoming a psychoanalyst.

If we consider Faith as *the expectation that the transit towards O is possible* and belief-doxa as *an occasionally confused but always revisable step towards that goal*, it remains to us only to mention the *reality-testing* that allows belief to evolve towards knowing; knowledge that does not stubbornly hold back on *transformations of O*, but is available to express *transformations in O*. In this transition, I find *intuition* because it is capable of transcending the data of the external and internal world; an intuition like analytic intuition. The analyst receives and modifies the data from the external and internal worlds in such a way that they create a transformation of and for the patient, a transformation that comes from the approach to a believable, interesting, and convincing truth.

4.3.3 A Beam of Tremulous Light...

When beliefs find support in reasons, experiences, and intuitions, the subject feels closer to having a true experience. It is implicit that truth lies beyond immediate data, such as those derived from the senses. In this sense, Fuentes Benot's (1961, p. 10) introduction to Nicholas of Cusa's *La docta ignorancia* is suggestive:

> ...absolute truth always eludes finite knowledge, consisting in a gradual and endless approximation [...] If wisdom is total knowledge of realities, man must conform with ignorance, but not with ignorance that comes from an absence of knowledge, but rather from ignorance that results from the knowledge of the limitations of human understanding. This is learned ignorance, which does not lead to scepticism, because it knows that it does not know, and knows it with complete certainty.

This "learned ignorance" echoes throughout Bion's thought, and behind its inspiration, one has to search "in an obscuring mist, knowing that within this mist" (N. de Cusa, 1961, p. 246), one will intuit what lies behind the data joined to immediate experience, and captured by the external and proprioceptive systems; without scepticism, despair, urgency, or omniscience. That is why we can say in a clinical situation: "I am confident" as Bion (1970, p. 39) said, at the same time as we recognise that "we intuit rather than observe the emotional atmosphere in the consulting room as it changes from moment to moment", as Meltzer (1984b, p. 90) said. We observe from "learned ignorance" but with enough *faith* to catapult ourselves, with the courage claimed by Buber, into the progressive *approximations to truths*. For this journey, we must include the privileged instrument proposed by Bion in our saddlebags, to keep ourselves "*without memory, without desire and without understanding...* to make possible and favour the intuition... of psychic reality'" (de Bianchedi, 2016, p. 18). This psychoanalyst considered Bion's pro-posal "disturbing and cryptic", just as Meltzer considered F "disconcerting", not to mention the disparate reactions to Bion's (1967a) stimulating short work: *"Notes on Memory and Desire"*. Stimulating "Notes" from the "Freudian innovator" as Parthenope Bion (1997) called her father. Nevertheless, it is questionable whether intuition will be powerful enough to illuminate "in an obscuring mist".

When it comes to projecting light onto an object, we have two terms—intuition and insight—which designate the direct and immediate vision of a reality. Just as the latter term has become a fundamental element of psychoanalytic technique, the former encompasses a larger universe, both internal and external, with the par-ticularity that intuition leads to insight. Therefore, it is appropriate to illuminate intuition to enrich ourselves with its potentialities. For this, we begin with the con-tributions of Descartes (1628, p. 14), who, in *Rules for the Direction of the Mind*, devotes Rule III to intuition and deduction. He states the Rule thus:

> By 'intuition', I do not mean the fluctuating testimony of the senses or the de-ceptive judgement of the imagination as it botches things together, but the con-ception of a clear and attentive mind, which is so easy and distinct that there can be no room for doubt about what we are understanding.

In this concise formulation, universal characteristics attributable to intuition and intuitive knowledge are pointed out: it does not depend on the senses, nor does it trust them, nor does it depend on a misleading judgement derived from an imagi-nation not based on serious observations, it is discerned through intelligence and leaves no room for doubt. Here we have, in synthesised form, the characteristics common to the different conceptions of intuition, as later presented by Ferrater Mora (1965, T. 1, p. 990):

> ...that of being direct (in intuition there are no detours of any kind); that of being immediate (in intuition there is no mediating element, no reasoning, no inference, etc.); that of being complete (not every intuition apprehends entirely the object it intends to intuit, but every intuition apprehends entirely what is intuited [...] The generality of these characteristics is shown in that they cor-respond equally not only to the intuition of realities (sensible or not) but also to the intuition of concepts and propositions.

In these characterisations of intuition, the immediate character of understanding is emphasised as if it were the work of a single channel of light or a single bolt of lightning. However, it is more likely that observation (including the psychoana-lyst's observation and intuition) is a convergence of perceptions and discernments made simultaneously from several vertices, as happens, for example, *in binocular vision* or *common sense*. Sometimes I think that the difficulties in intuiting de-rive more from defensive hindrances and rational thought, which, in its successive character, is intolerant of simultaneity. That is why I believe that babies and certain borderline personalities are capable of intuitively grasping the emotional state of others, although they are not usually capable of grasping their own, because they lack *adult* control. In this sense, intuition could be compared to the collection of data from *multiple vertices* that converge in a *selected fact* that evokes a name, thus becoming the *proof of reality* that was required before. It would be something equivalent to the action of a beam of not-too-excessive light[4] that creates a new order in the darkness, and the multiple photons of the beam allow us to discover what was hidden, at the same time as it leaves an enigmatic environment in semi-darkness. In this respect, Meltzer (1984a), in his lecture *On the Imagination*, said that observing from as many points of view as possible was necessary. Vertices or points of view can vary, for example, according to the moment chosen by the subject to observe or the senses participating in the observation. As a sample of the great variety of possible vertices, I will name those that Grinberg, Sor, and Tabak de Bianchedi (1991, p. 110) list in their work: "*social, political, educational, financial, scientific, philosophical, moral, religious, sexual, superego, paternal, false, true, psychoanalytical, etc.*". In the conference above, Meltzer (1984a, p. 147) suggested that a clinical situation could be looked at from imagination, adaptation, and point of view of learning. This was not the end of the possible points of view, for later, in the same conference, he cited others and said that

> From Bion's point of view, in analysis, richness is more important than care, precision or systematic approach; from Klein's point of view, the most important thing is the process, the systematics of the process; in the Freudian view, probably, it is the reconstruction of the patient's history. But analysis brings together all these possibilities: there is reconstruction, there is process, there is also a very rich experience that arises precisely from examining things from all possible points of view, from our imagination and from that of the patient.

But the possible vertices to observe did not end there, because at another time, in the clinical seminars in Barcelona (1996), he proposed other means by which to capture the patient's inner world: the *structure of the personality*, the ability to establish *intimate relationships*, and the capacity to *think*. I believe that all these vertices work as different and optional beams of light that converge in intuition, enhancing it.

But where is the light to be directed? Faced with the "formless infinite" (Bion, 1970, p. 31) of the patient's inner world, one does not know what to look at. One can feel as bewildered/astonished as before Leonardo's drawings of hair and water, as before a verbose exposition or a tenacious silence, or before a harmonious and communicative game... all behaviours pose questions. Finding out what the patient wants to say is an objective, never an offering, no matter how much positive transference is manifested in the consulting room. Just as Leonardo's drawings stimulate and evoke thoughts, Bion (1991a, p. 213) asked, "I wonder what I do while attempting to draw an analysand's attention to a pattern to which my attention has been drawn by his contributions to a session by the fleeting activity of interpretations?" Patient and analyst draw each other's attention. When the material comes[5] like a trickle of water or as a mysterious desert, can the psychoanalyst's toolbox come to the aid of the troubled analyst? But what is ephemeral: the activity or the interpretations? Moreover, with what intention do we intervene? These are some of the many questions that haunt the analyst's mind when they contact their patient.

I certainly chose the image of water to make Meltzer's (1984a, pp. 137/138) metaphor of the oil more visible when he said:

> One of the most important changes that Bion introduced into analytic technique is that of no longer asking what the material brought by the patient means, but what the patient means. This implies that what is not clear is not the material, but the patient. In the first place, it is not clear if we do not know what meaning the patient attributes to the words they are pronouncing. Once we have clarified with them the meaning of the words they have used, the second step will be to try to understand what they meant by those words (it is necessary to do this even if it seems that it has already been understood). Having clarified what the patient meant by the question asked, or by the verbalised fantasy, one can move on to Bion's method of breaking down the question into a multiplicity of other questions: thus new material emerges from the initial question in the same way that when oil is broken down, various by-products emerge.

Although in agreement with the transcript, it is obvious that language analysis is not enough to unravel the "oil" of the patient's inner world. Something more is needed. I am by no means attributing to Meltzer a rational cognitivist approach. It is enough to refer to his proposal for exploring dreams in *Dream-life* (1984b). But returning to the subject of the object of enquiry, the following text from *A Memoir of the Future* (1991a, p. 206) is illustrative: it speaks of grasping something of the other, understanding it, perhaps sensing it. The text begins with MAN's invitation to ROSEMARY for coffee; in this situation, another couple (ALICE and ROLAND) engage in dialogue:

ALICE I can't see what she sees in him.
ROLAND Nor can I.
ALICE You seemed to have seen something in her.
ROLAND So did you.
ALICE Perhaps we both saw something in her and she in both of us.
ROLAND Perhaps; but I doubt it.
ALICE Nevertheless, there must have been something both ways.
ROLAND Something neither of us saw?—but which may nevertheless exist?

In this dialogue, quite typical of some inhabitants of *The Claustrum* (Meltzer, 1992) who devote their lives to watching what others are doing while remaining bored in a life without interiority, there is a hint of curiosity about the couple

(MAN-ROSEMARY) and about ROSEMARY's personality. They recognise that they are interested in the "something" that nestles in each of them; the curiosity that ROSEMARY may feel for them is also mentioned. But it seems that the curiosity does not go beyond "something". Something as dark as the colour of oil? Dark and enigmatic like the bonds that might exist between the characters in this psycho-analytical novel: bonds of love, of hate, of knowledge? Or bonds of less love, less hate, and less knowledge capable of generating excitement and/or boredom and/or fanaticism? Or just interest in the tasty and appetising chocolate bar Man had in his pencil case? Perhaps their curiosities could be satisfied by discovering some recordable data, such as marital status or frequency of sexual acts, but that does not allow us to know the other, as Bion (1970, p. 57) thought when he said:

> While it can be precisely stated that the patient is married and has four children, it is not easily said that his state of mind is that of a married man with four children because there is no such state of mind. Furthermore, such a 'memory', and the remembrancer that such a note would provide, would greatly obscure observation of the patient's state of mind suppose it were to be more nearly what one might expect of a bachelor.

Only the *state of mind* is of interest! This is the territory for the practice of the psychoanalytic function, even if it is watery or desert-like. Therefore, to know the other, to intuit another person's state of mind, one must have the capacity to perceive "something" that transcends the immediate data, similar to what would happen to Mozart when he listened to music. ALICE was curious about Mozart's musical listening "…when he played or heard someone else play, a clavichord would seem to him to be the same sounds that come from a modern concert grand piano played by a present-day master". Answering or supposing, MYSELF says: "I should expect him to feel that the 'tune' was familiar" (Bion, 1991a, p. 211). What would Mozart listen to? To recognise the composition, would it matter much whether it was a particular object (harpsichord or grand piano) or who was playing it? Would he listen to the sounds of the notes or the "tune"? To get closer to a pos-sible answer, I needed to turn to the original text of *A Memoir of the Future*. In the text (op. cit., p. 211), MYSELF replied, "*I should expect him to feel that the 'tune' was familiar*". In the Spanish edition, they have translated "tune" as "melodía", whereas in the Italian edition, conducted under the supervision of Parthenope Bion, it was translated as "armonía". This difference surprised me and raised another question: the difference between "melody" and "harmony". Not being an expert in music theory, I searched and found a difference. Musical harmony studies chords (different and simultaneous notes—sounds—written one on top of the other in the score) in combination, i.e. considering their connecting principles. Harmony, on the one hand, is considered to be the structure of songs and one of the most impor-tant elements in art. Melody, on the other hand, refers to the succession of sounds, and its notes are transcribed one after the other. This slight and even daring digres-sion is to say that intuition, of that "something" mentioned above, has as its object the description and understanding of the elements that are part of the "harmony" (chords, connections, and silences) that structures each state of mind. This implies that the psychoanalyst will grasp what the patient means if, behind the melody of the discourse, they can unravel the chords (composed of internal objects with different degrees of integration/disintegration) and their connections, objects, and links that build structure. This will have the consistency or quality depending on which links (L, H, K and -L, -H, -K) govern the relationship between the objects. Thus, for example, disharmony resulting from attacks on linking is a product of anti-links because of the inability to tolerate the beauty produced by the harmony of a relationship based on love, hate, and knowledge.

This is not the place to expand on the subject of states of mind, to which Bion devoted special attention in *Attention and Interpretation* (1970) and in *The Grid and Caesura* (1975), as did Meltzer in *Sexual States of Mind* (1973a) and with Martha Harris in *A psychoanalytic model of the child-in-the-family-in-the-community* (1976). I did not want to fail to highlight, nevertheless, two characteristics: one is that they are transitory, although they may predominate at certain times or stages of life, and the other is that they condition the perception of reality (Muñoz Vila, 2011). As Bion would say, a patient can be "married" but with a "single" state of mind, just as a child can be an adult, or a pseudo-adult, depending on the type of operatory identification and the type of object constructed in their internal world. That is why the task of the psychoanalyst is to find the truth (and not "The" truth, as I said) of each state of mind, whether adult (preceded by a harmonious partner or combined object functioning as a *work team*) or infantile (in the various forms of rebellion against the dependence on the combined object) (Harris and Meltzer,[6] 1976). The degree of chronification of a *non-adult* state of mind will make the analyst's task more challenging. It will be the psychoanalyst's attitude towards the task (Tabbia 2017, 2018a, 2018b) that will enable their greater or lesser capacity to intuit states of mind. In any case, without intuition they will lack the basic tool to grasp it, modulate pain, and modify anxiety through interpretation (Meltzer, 1976) of the transference. A special type of intuition will be necessary for those patients trapped in primitive personalities in which neither symbolisation nor language has been minimally developed.

New questions arise… from where would Mozart hear the structure of songs? How would he pick up the music? How does a mother perceive her baby's messages? And how does the psychoanalyst perceive the sounds coming from the unconscious? Certainly, that "…cannot be done by the conscious intellect alone, but that any true understanding is based on intuition and not mere decipherment" (Meltzer, 1973b, p. 301). Decoding[7] can be enriching when one wishes to know "about", but this is not the attitude of Mozart, a mother engaged in parenting, or the psychoanalyst who is not afraid of catastrophic change for themselves or their patient. Certainly, one can choose to know *about*, not just because one prefers to live on the surface or because one chooses lies for fear of truths or change. One can also take refuge in a bourgeois *golden mean*, like ALICE and ROLAND, when limits are not tolerated, or the effort necessary to overcome the limitations of the data of sensitivity (cf. N. of Cusa, 1440). That is one option. The other is to intuit, to place oneself before the challenge of "learning from experience" and becoming another.

Now, focusing on our object of study, what is intuition for a psychoanalyst? This was the answer Meltzer gave us: "Intuition is primarily the product of unconscious mental processes that have their origins in emotional experiences, thus counter-transference is the typical manifestation of intuition and unconscious imagination" (Meltzer and Harris, 1998, pp. 325/326). Intuition is a "product of unconscious processes", which "originates in emotional experiences" and which "manifests it-self in countertransference and unconscious imagination". These are dense con-cepts in a few lines. I think that a step towards understanding this definition would be to start from the passionate, emotional experience (L, H, K intertwined with -L, -H, -K) during analytic contact, which can be understood (through an introspective unconscious imagination, like an oxymoron) in the countertransference. Since the patient's O is as unknown as the *absolute being*, or the *thing itself*, it is up to the psychoanalyst, that *finite* being, to explore their inner world, i.e. to analyse their countertransference (during the encounter with the patient, or outside, in their own analysis or in supervision). In this countertransference, they will intuit the emo-tional dynamics or interplay of internal objects and links. The countertransference *"need not be lexical or intelligible"* (Meltzer, 2005, p. 181) or organic[8] but intui-tive. To understand it, the psychoanalyst can identify with their patient and with the tools obtained during their own analysis—insight into the manifestations of their own unconscious—and with the theoretical knowledge of the unconscious, they can observe and intuit the meaning of the patient's behaviour (Money-Kyrle, 1956) and thus grasp what they mean. This task requires the courage and willingness to identify with the patient's inner world. On the one hand, this task calls for an at-titude characterised by and based on a state of vulnerability as if one were diving without the protection of a wetsuit (like an "exoskeleton"), i.e. without too many theories or defences; furthermore, on the other hand, relying only on the introjec-tive identification with the combined object (support of the creative imagination). As Hahn (2017, p. 234) puts it, the analyst "is capable, through his own relations to his internal objects, of gaining access to deeper strata of his mind in order to have a view of the constellations of his own and the patient's unconscious phantasies". From this receptive attitude, they will be able to look at the scene that the patient's inner world registers within them. In that sense, it would be a situation equivalent to the dream scene that spontaneously arises within the psychoanalyst and captures their attention. In the midst of this scene, disturbing because it is unknown, the at-tentive analyst may claim to discover within themselves primitive thoughts or alpha elements that, on closer inspection, form a pattern (Meltzer, 2005, p. 181). These incipient elements will form a pattern when they encounter the transformative qual-ity of the emotional meaning-generating container. This is what the psychoanalyst brings: their readiness and tolerance for the *selected fact* to find an evoked name. That is where the surprise so characteristic of intuition will emerge. Surely it will not have the brilliance of insight because it requires more time for the field to or-ganise itself, but when the name knocks on the analyst's door, the expectation will capture their attention and begin to transform itself into "security". For this process, *negative capacity* is necessary, that is, "…the capacity to suspend action, the possibility of having doubts, the wish to plumb the depths of a problem, to search for truth instead of rushing for solutions or experimental actions" (ibid. p. 180).

The analyst must become pensive starting with the experiencing of the necessary *patience* and *security* (Ps↔D) for the alpha elements to manifest themselves, be perceived through intuition, and be contained. This demands tolerance to mental suffering. It requires recognising the overlapping of the analyst's personal experience with the patient's transference information. All of this work is needed to be able to receive alpha elements.

However, if it is about tolerance to suffering and work, nothing less is required to develop this fundamental tool: intuition. Regarding this same point, another response given by Meltzer is quite eloquent (Meltzer & Harris, 1998, pp. 323/324):

> Generally speaking, people who have nothing to do with analysis, and most people inside analysis, have no idea how difficult it is to become intuitive. And as far as preparation for psychoanalytic work is concerned, the main function of training analysis is to become intuitive. The healing of our mental abnormalities or mental eccentricities is not the function of training analysis but of personal analysis. The function of training analysis is to develop intuition. So when people dismiss this analyst or that analyst because they have this or that symptomatology or abnormality or eccentricity, etc… that is not the issue; the issue is not that analysts are normal in the sense of statistical normality; they can be as crazy as they need to be if they are intuitive and can be honest; therefore to try to disqualify Freud by the revelation of his abnormalities is absolutely irrelevant.

In this reply, intuition is related to honesty: honesty towards the analyst's own psychic reality, and honesty with the patient's internal world. It is only the truth regarding the present state of mind. From this vertex, the psychoanalytic process depends not only on the transference but also on the analyst's state of mind that, as one more element of the setting, will honestly collaborate so that the transference will unfold and be intuited-named-interpreted.

A manifestation of honesty and a requirement for knowing (K) to be attracted to O is to tolerate the freedom and mystery of the object; as Martha Harris put it: "to construct an object with the imagination means to allow it to have a mysterious part" (Meltzer, 1984a, p. 145). In the same way that one tolerates not only the mystery of the object but also its limitations and ambivalences, a psychoanalytic attitude also calls for tolerating those moments when the psychoanalyst loses their capacity for contact or when the analyst's state of mind causes the momentary loss of the capacity to intuit and is moved, occasionally, to make interpretations based only on theoretical knowledge.

Shared and passionate emotional experience (Bion, 1963, p. 31), together with a communicative projective identification, becomes other essential tools to grasp-intuit states of mind. These tools will be most valuable for grasping the interior of an object and for observing how thoughts develop when L and H are spurred on by the epistemophilic drive. It may come as a surprise that I would consider H an implicit element in the act of knowing. Surprise is dependent on the meaning of H. The H of positive links is the emotion that arises in response to the frustration generated by the difficulty in grasping the object. It is a passionate hatred that, sustained by the loving experience, can tolerate the difficulty in intuiting. But it could also generate an alternative to the passionate hatred of positive links and degenerate into an -H, i.e. hypocrisy (Meltzer, 2001) or dis-honesty. But, as Grotstein (2007, p. 312) says,

> Bion often stated that we cannot love without hating and cannot hate without loving. K is more often mentioned by Bion scholars and others, but it is my opinion that there can be no K without L and H, only attempts at pretence of their absence.

Therefore, if approaching the patient's state of mind requires sufficient courage (Buber) to throw oneself into the sea with no other protection than the Faith that the investigation of the inner world is possible, to ride the waves of uncertainty and test the beliefs and the truth of psychic reality, the only tool the psychoanalyst will have is intuition from the attentive observation of the transferential-countertransferential encounter. The particularity of this encounter is that it takes place in two simultaneous and complementary scenarios. One is the unconscious setting "of the patient whence the 'natural history' of the analytic process emanates" (Meltzer, 1976, p. 78). The other is that which unfolds within the psychoanalyst, in their basic and essential collaboration; a contribution that requires honesty, curiosity, and tolerance for that natural history to unfold and be named. To this end, it is essential that *a beam of intense darkness illuminates and allows intuition* so that this *beam of tremulous light approximates truths of psychic reality.*

> …when you have a particularly dark spot, turn onto it a shaft of piercing darkness […] if you want to see a very faint light, the more light you shut out, the better, the bigger the chance of seeing the faint glimmer, if you're not blinded by the 'light' as Freud himself describes it.
>
> (Bion, 1967b, p. 9)

Notes

1 Published in *Temas de psicoanálisis*, # 18, July 2019, Barcelona: www.temasdepsico-analisis.org
2 Nicholas of Cusa describes the most obvious traits of the structure of the Absolute Maximum Being by elevating to infinite finite conditions like the line, the triangle, the circle, and the sphere.
3 I thank Dr. Alberto Hahn for this clarification.
4 "let in a flood of light, and then goodbye to our intuition because the flood of light that we let in blinds us to what is actually going on" (Bion, 1967b, p. 9).

5 Some material is as concrete as that mentioned by Stevenson (1887, p. 147, my italics) in his short story *Olalla*:

> It is true I had before talked with persons of a similar mental constitution; persons who seemed to live (as he did) by the senses, taken and possessed by the visual object of the moment and *unable to discharge their minds of that impression*.

6 Harris and Meltzer (1976) devoted a chapter to the subject of personality organisation in *A Psychoanalytic model of the child-in-the-family-in-the-community*.
7 Decoding is a term with different connotations. It can mean both understanding and clarifying what is obscure and difficult to understand and unravelling an ancient document on the basis of a code [such as the Rosetta Stone]. The differences lie in the commitment of the researcher and the object under investigation, and rational knowledge may be employed more than emotional/intuitive knowledge.
8 The analyst's motor manifestations or sensations while with the patient (especially with primitive states of mind), such as the analyst's involuntary movements, e.g. crossing and uncrossing their legs $_4$.

Bibliography

Bion, P. (1997): "Bion a Freudian innovator", *British Journal of Psychotherapy*, 14 (1), pp. 47–59.

Bion, W. R. (1959): "Attacks on linking", in *Second Thoughts*, London: W. Heinemann, 1967, pp. 110–119.

Bion, W. R. (1963): *Elements of Psychoanalysis*, London, Heinemann.

Bion, W. R. (1967a): "Notes on memory and desire", *Psychoanalytic Forum*, 2(3), Published in *Rev. de Psicoanálisis, APA*, XXVI (3), Buenos Aires, 1969, pp. 679–682.

Bion, W. R. (1967b): "Los Angeles seminars", in *Wilfred Bion: Los Angeles Seminars and Supervision*, edited by Aguayo Joesph & Malin Barnet, London, Karnac Books, 2013.

Bion, W. R. (1970): *Attention and Interpretation*, London, Karnac.

Bion, W. R. (1974): *Bion's Brazilian Lectures*, Rio de Janeiro, Imago Editora Ltda.

Bion, W. R. (1975): *Two Papers: The Grid and Caesura*, London, Karnac Books, 1989.

Bion, W. R. (1991a): "The dream", in *A Memoir of the Future*, London, Karnac Books, pp. 1–218

Bion, W. R. (1991b): "The past presented", in *A Memoir of the Future*, London, Karnac Books, pp. 219–426

Bion, W. R. (1991c): "The dawn of oblivion", in *A Memoir of the Future*, London, Karnac Books, pp. 427–578

Bion, W. R. (1992): *Cogitations*, London, Karnac.

Britton, R. (1998): *Belief and Imagination: Explorations in Psychoanalysis*, London, Routledge.

Buber, M. (1942): *Between Man and Man*, London, Routledge, 1947.

Bueno, G. (2002): "El concepto de creencia y la Idea de creencia", Separata de la Rev. *El Catoblepas*, ISSN 1579–3974, N° 10, diciembre 2002. Available at http://nodulo.org/ec/aut/gbm.htm

Caper, R. (1998): "The clinical thinking of Wilfred Bion. By Joan and Neville Symington", *International Journal of Psycho-Analysis*, 79, pp. 417–420.

de Bianchedi, E. T. (1991): "Cambio psíquico. El devenir de una indagación", *International Journal of Psycho-Analysis*, 72, pp. 6–15. Republicada en Mentalización (abril, 2016): *Revista de psicoanálisis y psicoterapia*, 6, pp. 1–12.

de Cusa, N. (1440): *Nicholas of Cusa on Learned Ignorance. A Translation and an Appraisal of De Docta Ignorantia,* Minneapolis, MN, The Arthur J. Banning Press, 1990.

Descartes, R. (1596–1650): "Rules for direction of the mind", in *The Philosophical Writings of Descartes,* volume 1, Cambridge, Cambridge University Press, 1985, pp. 9–78

Ferrater Mora, J. (1965): *Diccionario de filosofía,* Buenos Aires, Sudamericana.

Fuentes Benot, M. (1961): Introduction to Nicolas de Cusa: *La docta ignorancia,* Buenos Aires, Aguilar, 1961.

Grinberg, L., Sor, D. & de Bianchedi, T. (1991): *Nueva introducción a las ideas de Bion,* Madrid, Tecnipublicaciones, S. A.

Grotstein, J. (2007): *A Beam of Intense Darkness,* London, Karnac.

Hahn, A. (2005): "A note on intuition", in *Read at the Memorial Conference for Donald Meltzer at the Tavistock Clinic* (London), 12 nov. 2005. Available at www.psa-atelier.org

Hahn, A. (2017): "Concluding thoughts on the nature of psychoanalytic activity", in *Doing Things Differently. The influence of Donald Meltzer on Psychoanalytic Theory and Practice,* edited by Margaret Cohen & Alberto Hahn, Londres, Karnac, pp. 233–236.

Harris, M. & Meltzer, D. (1976): "A psychoanalytic model of the child-in-the-family-in-the-community", in *Sincerity and Other Works,* edited by Alberto Hahn, London, Karnac, 1994, pp. 387–454.

López Corvo, R. (2002): *The Dictionary of the Work of W. R. Bion,* London, Karnac books, 2003.

Machado, A. (1912): *Campos de Castilla,* Madrid, Cátedra.

Martinez, M. S., & Sor, D. (2004): *Brechas en el sueño. Fragmentos escogidos de El Sueño de W. R. Bion. Memorias del Futuro,* Buenos Aires, Ed. Polemos.

Meltzer, D. (1967): *The Psycho-Analytical Process,* London, William Heinemann Medical Books Limited.

Meltzer, D. (1973a): *Sexual States of Mind,* London, Karnac Books, 2008.

Meltzer, D. (1973b): "Routine and inspired interpretations", in *Sincerity and Other Works,* London, edited by Alberto Hahn, Karnac, 1994, pp. 290–306.

Meltzer, D. (1978): *The Kleinian Development,* London, Karnac, 2008.

Meltzer, D. (1984a): "Sulla immaginazione", *Quaderni di psicoterapia infantile,* 3, Borla, pp. 132–169.

Meltzer, D. (1984b): *Dream-Life: A Re-Examination of the Psychoanalytic Theory and Technique,* Karnac Books, 2009.

Meltzer, D. (1992): *The Claustrum. An Investigation of Claustrophobic Phenomena.* Strath-Clyde, The Clunie Press.

Meltzer, D. (1996): *Clinical seminars in the Psychoanalytic Group of Barcelona* (unpublished).

Meltzer, D. (2001): "Il transfert negativo", in *Seminari Veneziani (1999–2002), en Transfert, Adolescenza, Disturbi del pensiero. Mutamenti nel método psicoanalítico,* edited by Gruppo di Studio Racker di Venezia, Roma, Armando, 2004, pp. 19–23.

Meltzer, D. (2005): "Creativity and the countertransference", in *The Vale of Soulmaking. The Post-Kleinian Model of the Mind,* edited by Meg Harris Williams, Londres, Karnac, pp. 175–182.

Meltzer, D. & Harris, M. (1998): *Adolescentes,* edited by L. Jachevasky & C. Tabbia, Buenos Aires, Spatia.

Money-Kyrle, R. (1956): "Contratransferencia normal y algunas de sus desviaciones", in *The Collected Papers of Roger Money-Kyrle,* edited by D. Meltzer with Edna O'Shaughnessy, Strathclyde, Clunie, 1978, pp. 330–342.

Muñoz Vila, C. (2011): *Reflexiones Psicoanalíticas,* Bogotá, Ed. Pontificia Universidad Javeriana.

Peirce, Ch. (1877): "La fijación de la creencia", in *El hombre, un signo (El pragmatismo de Peirce),* edited by Charles S. Peirce, J. Vericat (tr., intr. y notas), Barcelona, Crítica, 1988, pp. 175–99. Available at www.unav.es

Pérez Andreo, B. (2009): "La verdadera religión. El intento de Hume de Naturalizar la Fe", in *Publicaciones del Inst. Teológico de Murcia OFM,* Serie Mayor 51, Murcia, Editorial Espigas, 2009, pp. 357–396.

Saab, S. (2013): "La creencia", in *El conocimiento,* edited by Luis Villoro, Consejo Superior de Investigaciones Científicas, Madrid, Editorial Trotta, pp. 63–87.

Sandler, P. C. (2005): *The Language of Bion. A Dictionary of Concepts,* Londres, Karnac.

Stevenson, R. L. (1885): "Olalla*",* in *The Merry Men and Other Tales and Fables,* London, Chatto & Windus, 1905.

Tabbia, C. (2004): "Observação e descrição na gênese do significado", *Revista de Psicanálise da Sociedade Psicanalítica de Porto Alegre* (*Brasil*), XI (3), pp. 489–518.

Tabbia, C. (2017): "La disponibilidad mental del analista", *Revista Psicoanálisis* XXIX(1), pp. 61–72.

Tabbia, C. (2018a): "La intimidad en el trabajo analítico", *Temas de psicoanálisis,* núm. 15-Enero, Barcelona; Available at www.temasdepsicoanalisis.org

Tabbia, C. (2018b): "La receptividad del analista: la contratransferencia y la *revêrie*", in *El trabajo del analista. Diálogos sobre técnica psicoanalítica,* GRADIVA, Asoc. Estudis Psicoanalítics, Barcelona, Xoroi edicions, pp. 269–281.

Vermote, R. (2011a): "Bion's critical approach to psychoanalysis", in *Bion Today,* edited by Chris Mawson, Londres, Routledge, pp. 349–365.

Vermote, R. (2011b): "On the value of "Late Bion" to analytic theory and practice", *International Journal of Psychoanalysis*, 92(5), pp. 1089–1098. In Catalan: *Revista Catalana de Psicoanàlisi*, Vol. XXXV/1, Barcelona, 2018, pp. 41–53.

Webster's (1996): *Encyclopedic Unabridged Dictionary of the English Language*, New York, Random House.

Wittgenstein, L. (1992): *Lecciones y conversaciones sobre estética, psicología y creencia religiosa*, Barcelona, Paidós - I. C. E. de la Univ. A. de Barcelona.

Index

Note: Page numbers followed by "n" denote endnotes.

abstraction 150; absolute/normal 151, 152; abstracting: observe + intuit 150; feeling as a first principle 198; function of the senses 127, 188, 196, 253

adolescent 268, 269; bored 167–175; boredom defences 170–174; confusional adolescent states and drugs 85–88; establishing the analytical situation 183; isolated 268–275; passion of the adolescent 250; pubertal states of mind 235, 269; treatment 182–185

analyst: dream space and shared experience 261; mental health and analytic availability 293, 294, 298; preserve psychic reality from split off aspects 306; really be psychoanalyst to *be at one* with 308; tolerance to intimate relationships 295; tolerance to one's own occasional limitations 295, 316

analytic attitude 183, 301, 314; availability 298; denouncing false alternatives to transformative ideas 302; faith as scientific attitude 303; faith differentiated from belief 306; placental 259; receptive 315; state of vulnerability 315; tolerance to the infinite as magnitude of what is not known 304; trust in one's own psychic reality 73; truth/lies 26, 46, 96–97, 243, 305

anorexia/bulimia 83, 214n44, 268; bulimic functioning 246; and feeling of loneliness 194; hypochondriac

anorexia/symptomatic anorexia 193–194; structure of the anorexic/bulimic part 194

anxieties 253; breakdown 198; catastrophic 278n11; claustrophobic 79, 278; confusional 85, 99, 144; depressive 100, 250; dilution 68; disintegration 198, 206, 207, 269; dispersal 105, 202; nameless dread 200; paranoid/persecutory 26, 80, 144, 269; primitive 68, 198, 206; separation 44, 68, 192

body 185; alterations of the… as warning signal 190; asthma 200; and matricide 201; body thing/body representation 214n41; enuresis 207; fibromyalgia 191–192; impotence 208; psychosomatic reactions 189, 195; soma-psychotic 187; somatisation 207; somnambulism 186; speech 190; thoughts of 188

boredom 167; of the analyst 175, 182; approach to 182; and defensive attitude 179; and lack of contact 168, 181; non-mental generator of 172; and observational deficit 170; projective counteridentification and 178; *vs.* psychic reality 170

Claustrum: and boredom 312; claustrophilia 105, 106; entrance into 78; and feeling of fraudulence 99

clinical, relationship: amorous/passionate relationship in the analytic

relationship 255; communication
    vs. action 29, 254, 255; interest
    180, 183, 214n39, 254, 291;
    negative capacity 11, 41, 96, 131,
    232, 263, 316; perseverance 72, 96,
    214n39, 257; placental attitude and
    function 259; shared curiosity and
    passionate kindness 255
combined object 25, 28, 32, 91, 93, 94, 96,
    101, 247, 257; basis of thinking 52;
    and container, contained 28; and
    denial of differences 30; model of
    intimate relationship 233; part 102;
    as work group 28, 228
conception of the world 93, 104;
    mathematical binary representation
    of the world 93; one's own
    cosmovision of tribal mentality
    290; in perverse fantasies 93–94
confusion: geographical 83, 91, 103, 236;
    identity confusion 75; zonal 73, 77,
    83, 93, 99, 208
container/contained 28, 247; failed
    containers 272; functioning as a
    container 298; and observation 132;
    transformative containers 292, 315
countertransference 133, 261, 266;
    countertransference irritation 68; and
    imagination deficit 180; intuitable
    315; manifestation of intuition and
    unconscious imagination 315; of
    the negative transference 179; and
    vengeance 176

description 133; basis of the interpretation
    133; describe like a geologist 137;
    exactly 84; from the explanation
    to 135, 292; of the language-
    game 134; and name 134; is a
    transformation 136
diagnosis: borderline 82, 193; character,
    disturbance of the 76; conversion
    hysteria and splitting processes
    190–191; fragmentation,
    tendency to 97; multiple
    illnesses 88; obsessive character
    94–97, 121; psychoanalytical 59;
    psychopathology 46; schizophrenia
    47, 55, 88
dimensionality: bidimensional 82,
    150; tridimensionality 149;
    unidimensionality and autistic
    dismantling 149

dreaming 155; aborted dream 163;
    allegorical dream 166; avoid
    sleeping to prevent 159;
    concrete dream 164; condensed
    symbolisation dreaming 165, 166;
    counterdreaming 265; difficulties
    waking up 162; difficulties
    to dream 159; dream screen
    266; elaborative dream 164;
    evacuative dream 197; insomnia
    80; interruption of dreaming 160;
    models for describing difficulties in
    157–167; narrative dream 164–165;
    night terrors or nightmares 160,
    161; non-storable diurnal remains
    198; that repeats waking behaviours
    162; somnambulism 186; symbolic
    dream 162; symbolising function of
    157; traumatic dream 163

emotions 230–232; ambivalence before the
    aesthetic conflict 230; emotional
    experience 260, 226, 227; intimacy,
    meaning 231; intimacy, thought
    231; passionate and intuition 315;
    shared as tool 316; stripped of the
    communicative function 73
emptiness 78, 80, 275; meanings of
    emptiness in the depressive reaction
    78; moral emptiness 18

fanaticism 139, 287; binary organisation
    145; and defence of the identity
    143; dismantling 149, 151; and
    dissociation 144; dogmatism
    140; fanatical demand
    144; fundamentalism 139;
    fundamentalist therapy 143; and
    generalisation 149, 150, 151;
    integrism 139; and intrusive
    curiosity 129; maximal idea 152;
    and "narcissism of the small
    differences" 146; provincialism
    143; sectarianism 145; and thinking
    according to category 148; and
    violence 142
function: alpha 73, 158, 213n26, 265; failure
    of 197; inspirational of internal
    objects 91; internalisation of 154;
    intuitive 261; para-excitatory
    206; parental 127, 155, 253, 262,
    263, 278n20, 294; pedagogic
    of the analyst 70; pedagogic of

psychoanalysis 90; psychoanalytic
155; psychoanalytic of the
personality 100, 200; of reverie 127,
199, 247, 260; reversed alpha 46,
74, 121; reversed beta screen 196;
symbolising function 157, 196
functioning: adhesive 91; analytic fortitude
of the 293; anti-mental 55; fanatical
53; non-mental 52, 290, 291; non-
mental and basic assumptions 54;
non-mental and hallucinations, lies,
confabulations... 54; non-mental
and psychosomatic disorders 55

group 20, 146; basic assumption 24;
containing function of 146, 174,
269; internal 20, 24; internal and
geography of phantasy 23; leader
created by the 147; vs. mental
activity 147; pubertal groups 269;
work 28; hypochondria 191–195;
differentiation hypochondria/
melancholia 193; hypochondriac
anorexia/symptomatic anorexia
193–194; hypochondriac states
191; introjective identification
with a damaged object 191, 193;
structure of the anorexic/bulimic
part 191; hysteria 189, 214n41;
expresses a meaning 195; related
to hypochondria 191; repression of
memories or of objects 190–191

identifications: adhesive 149, 212n22;
aspirated 79, 87, 88–91, 275;
introjective 91, 251, 257, 261,
268, 294; narcissistic 103;
projective 271; projective as
model for thinking 119; projective
communicative 105, 247; projective
communicative as essential
tool 316; projective counter-
identification 178; projective in
external and internal object 44, 99,
106, 113; intrusive 89, 105, 268,
274, 296; intrusive and entrance
to the Claustrum 78; intrusive and
perception of temporality 75, 105,
106, 115n14; living in intrusive
identification 79, 105
identity 153–155; adult bisexual 247;
false 154; flexible/petrified 154;
internalisation of functions 154

imagination 148, 149, 267; boredom
and lack of 180; and difficulty in
observing 148; from the... towards
non-mental 148; obtain data
through the 253
interpretation: analytic mood more than
contents 68; descriptive 68,
137–139; as evolution of the
common truth 263; metapsychology
of a drama 138; in patients with
character disorder 76; reverted
perspective as defence against 77;
variation of Meltzer's technique 138
intimacy 223, 291; adult 202, 236, 244;
and aesthetic reciprocity 225;
analytic 262; analytic and the
place of the body in 262; analytic
differentiated from other types of
intimacy 262; characterised by 234,
260; comradeship 228, 260, 261;
in the couple 262; distance as a
condition of the 226; distance in the
clinical encounter 227; emotions,
thought 231; fear of transference
intimacy 68; geographic contiguity
227; hindrance for the inhabitants
of the Claustrum 230; and history
of psychoanalysis 225; intimate
and family relationships 60; and
intimidation 264; vs. isolation 294;
model of 261; private/intimate
229, 261; pseudo-intimacy 246; in
states of mind adult 236, 247; in
states of mind infantile 234, 245;
in states of mind latency 235; in
states of mind narcissistic 247, 248;
in states of mind perverse 236; in
states of mind pubertal 235; tools
to construct the 264; transgression
of borders and confusion 227, 229–
230; trust 232, 251, 291; trust and
quality of the maternal relationship
233; two counterposing models 239
intuition 301, 309; the analyst's intuitive
ability 295; basic tool 314, 316;
countertransference and 295, 315;
reality testing 311; selected fact
63, 264, 304, 311, 315; signs and
symbols 95, 126; surprise 315; we
intuit more than we observe 309

language 84, 121; darkness of 122;
deceptive 122; language-games

126; names external reality 123, 126; naming 122; normal 187; vagueness of 122

links 29, 102, 243; anti-links 33, 102; anti-links, admiration/envy 87, 88, 98, 106, 297, 306; anti-links countertransference and lack of fantasy and imagination 180; anti-links creators of disharmony 314; anti-links, hypocrisy 33, 180, 245; anti-links, philistinism 33, 180; anti-links, puritanism 33, 180; *vs.* excitation 258, 259; generativity of the 233; hatred of that what links 106; integrated and aesthetic response 230, 243; intimate 258; passion 74, 243, 253, 254, 267; tropism 54, 226

love 26; ability to love 244; adolescent falling in love 250; bestial love 249; biological sex 255; effects of 251–253; *vs.* excitement, boredom or fanaticism 313; generosity 98; genital and introyective identification 43; is passionate kindness 255; it cannot be defined 249; "on love" 248; passionate experience and mystery of 249; "passionate love" names 255; predatory 249; provisional 241; repairs 252

meaning 23, 97, 125–127, 188, 231; difficulty in grasping 95; stripping of 69

mental health 46, 293, 294; absolute 230; and claustrophobia 96; and distrust 78; emptiness and pornographic excitation 80; *folie-à-deux* 90, 236, 275; insanity and distortion of dependence 83; internal object: core of emotional stability 268; loneliness 261; negative stupidity 83

observation 127–133; accurate 132; bifocal 130; binocular vision 310; careful 127; contaminated 298; counter-intuitive faith 303; to develop thinking and recognition of psychic reality 73; from different vertices 150; of the emotional experience 129; with faith? 302–306; "first principle" (Bion) 198; *vs.* generalization 67, 150; with global attention 129, 132; imaginative 150; *vs.* information 291; intuition *vs.* observation 309; like a geologist 137; with loyalty to the truth 305; non-observation of emotional reality 93; poor observers 128; psychoanalysis as a science of the 72; or with reversible perspective 77; thinking about their observations 129; without interpretation 129

personality: arrogance 84, 151; bidimensional 68; borderline 52, 53, 72, 82, 311; grandiosity 79, 82, 84, 195; infantile 188, 245–246; narcissistic organisation 28, 51; paranoid 298; pride 108; primitive 314; psychosomatic 179; psychotic 163; structure of the 60

psychic reality 9, 14, 42, 290, 298; absolute dependence on external objects 67; confidence in one's own 73; dangers of introjection 71; decisive for health and illness 12; deleterious boredom of the 170; denial of the 52, 53, 66–74; impossibility of symbolising: erotisation and acting out 72; impossibility of symbolising: superficiality 73, 296; inaccessible psychic reality 66–68; internal world and generation of meaning 12; irreality, feelings of 81, 82, 89; stable organisation 10, 11; strip experiences of meaning 69, 296; truth of 83

psychosomatics 189, 195, 199; psychosomatic disorder 195; somatic protest 198; and symbolic deficit 195, 198

relationship: analytical 266, 291, 294; generation of meaning 231; generative exchange that characterises the 260; intimate 25, 244–248; intimate differentiated from casual 225; intimate differentiated from collusive 87,

225, 295; intimate differentiated
from commensal 294; intimate
differentiated from complicit 225,
295; intimate differentiated from
contractual 75, 225; longing for
passivity 86; narcissistic 247, 248;
parasitic 102; placental model 257;
symbiotic 102; true analytic contact
306; trustworthy 232–234, 248,
291; trustworthy and quality of
maternal relationship 233

scenes: law 84, 85; oedipal preconception
101; oedipal scene 93; Oedipus
complex 96, 100; part objects
and envy 100; part objects and
non jealousy 81; pre-oedipal
= triangular 100; primary 93;
triangular 66, 67, 81; whole objects
and jealousy 101
sexuality: adult sexual intimacy 236;
biological sex 255; bisexuality
unsymbolised 94; coitus without
intimacy 259; consume 240;
divorced from love 241; freedom
vs. licentiousness 241; impotence
208; masturbation anal 111, 167,
208, 210; masturbation bimanual
101; obsessive genital masturbation
210; papular urticaria and anal
onanism 210; pregenital 79; psychic
maturity and sexual becoming 244;
ritualised masturbation 99; and
rituals 208; scratching/onanism
209; vomiting 112; voyeurism 80;
and zonal confusion 73, 93, 99, 208
skin 202; eczema 164; atopic 202; erotism
of the 210; internal/external limit
202, 210; scratching 202, 209;
speaking 209; subject/object
discrimination and autoerotism 210
splitting 29, 51; adequate 172; and
cognitive logics 188; and denial
of envy, jealousy and competition
81; emotions of aesthetic conflict
and 85; forced splitting 200,
201, 214n44; mind/body 189;
pathological 81, 214n34; primary
214n34; sensation/experience of
satisfaction 29; word/emotion 29
state of mind 41, 42, 50, 104, 279n20,
313, 314; adult 50, 263, 291; of

the analyst 301; anti-mental 55;
available 263, 294, 298; borderline
and neurotic and psychotic
depressive reaction 78; borderline
psychotic 52, 82, 27; characteristics
of the 314; claustrophobic
297; confusional 77, 85, 289;
exoskeleton 25, 45, 47n6, 47n7,
82, 171, 273; false self 44, 45, 79;
grandiose 79, 82, 84, 89, 95, 96,
195, 297; immature 42, 91, 188;
infantile 49, 53, 234; latent 235;
manic depressive 69, 71, 88; mature
42, 43, 209, 276; non mental 52,
55, 290, 291; of orphanhood (in
anorexic/bulimic) 194; perverse
236; primitive 54; protomental 287,
289; pseudomature 45, 75, 79, 85,
88, 92, 290; psychotic 51, 273;
pubertal 53, 269; scientific of the
mind 303; stable based on internal
objects 267; transience of 42

technique: the analyst's emotional
commitment 185; the analyst's tools
264–267, 316; bifrontal character
of analytical work 263; dream
screen as placental membrane 261;
establishing the analytic situation
71, 76, 88, 183; therapeutic alliance
and comradeship 228, 260
thinking, thought 60, 94; vs. acting 295;
from belief to thought: doubt
and reality testing 308; contact
barrier 68, 213n26, 260, 265,
266; contact barrier and alpha-
elements 73, 266, 278n16, 315; vs.
daytime fantasising 68; depends
on the internalisation of 52;
desmentalisation 199; development
of the 127; difficulties dealing with
complexities 34, 122, 129, 148,
267, 289; difficulties thinking in
normopaths, over-adjusted people
and adolescents 199, 198, 288;
difficulty for autonomous thinking
198; disorders of the 127; vs.
emotions 94, 95; vs. fabulation
127; fashion and media obstacles
to autonomous thought 29, 172,
288, 289; vs. generalisations
149, 150; grid (Bion) The 122,

131; mathematics model of 93, 95; moments of interruption of symbolisation 198; negative grid 56n1, 74, 97; *vs.* omniscience 151, 170; operatory 197; *vs.* paraphrase 96, 97; preconceptions 101; quantitative mode of 243; reversible perspective 121; reverted 74; *vs.* ruminations 68, 73; symbolise 173, 198; they are not perceived by the senses 295; transformation in hallucinosis 197

transference 132, 243; acting out in the 76; maternal 80, 96, 99; negative 179; paternal 78, 164; preformed 128, 291

values 15, 16, 287, 288; aesthetic 70; confusion of the 240; cynicism 33, 291; of the depressive position 70; differentiated of goods and price 16, 33; good/bad 18, 25, 27; irresponsible functioning 290; quantity *vs.* quality 32; relativism 288; respect 15, 28, 34, 88, 200, 228; responsibility 18, 26, 104, 253; team respect and responsibility, the 33, 34; value system 15, 18, 71

vertices 120; to grasp the patient's internal world 311; observation from the different 121, 150, 311

For Product Safety Concerns and Information please contact our EU
representative GPSR@taylorandfrancis.com
Taylor & Francis Verlag GmbH, Kaufingerstraße 24, 80331 München, Germany

www.ingramcontent.com/pod-product-compliance
Lightning Source LLC
Chambersburg PA
CBHW050627280326
41932CB00015B/2554